MW01127064

BENJ. FRANKLIN NATUS BOSTON. VA XVII.

MDCCXVI.

WHEN I RECOLLECT, AS I FREQUENTLY DO THE PLEASURE I HAVE
ENJOYED, I SOMETIMES SAY TO MYSELF THAT WERE THE OFFER MADE
TO ME, I WOULD ENGAGE TO RUN AGAIN FROM BEGINNING TO END THE SAME
COURSE OF LIFE.

ERIPUIT COELO
FULMEN
SCEPTRUM QUE
TYRANNIS

HE SNATCHED THE LIGHTNING FROM THE SKY AND THE SCEPTRE FROM
TYRANTS

R. Winthrop 1841 (handwritten)

HISTORY

OF THE

MIDDLE AND WORKING CLASSES;

WITH A

POPULAR EXPOSITION

OF THE

ECONOMICAL AND POLITICAL PRINCIPLES

WHICH HAVE INFLUENCED THE

PAST AND PRESENT CONDITION

OF THE

INDUSTRIOUS ORDERS.

ALSO AN

APPENDIX

OF PRICES, RATES OF WAGES, POPULATION, POOR-RATES, MORTALITY, MARRIAGES, CRIMES, SCHOOLS, EDUCATION, OCCUPATIONS, AND OTHER STATISTICAL INFORMATION, ILLUSTRATIVE OF THE FORMER AND PRESENT STATE OF SOCIETY AND OF THE AGRICULTURAL, COMMERCIAL, AND MANUFACTURING CLASSES.

by John ... le. (handwritten)

" Were the benefits of civilization to be partial, not universal, it would
be only a bitter mockery and cruel injustice."—*Ducddtel.*

LONDON:

PUBLISHED BY EFFINGHAM WILSON,

ROYAL EXCHANGE.

MDCCCXXXIII.

Soc 1372.1

1869, Mar. 12.
Gift of
Hon. Robert C. Winth

of Boston.

(H. C. 1828.)

WRITING, BEAUFORT HOUSE, STRAND.

INTRODUCTION.

To ROGER LEE, ESQ.,

Clapham Common.

MY DEAR SIR,

When travelling on the Continent you cannot have forgotten that we arrived at one general, though, perhaps, partial conclusion, namely, that in the command of the substantial elements of national happiness, in the accumulation of wealth, in the diffusion of intelligence, in moral feeling, and in the enjoyment of civil freedom, our own country might justly claim precedency over any European community. Notwithstanding this, we could not conceal from ourselves the fact, that in many respects England exhibited symptoms of a nation suffering under great internal disorders. To reconcile such apparently contradictory conclusions, formed a subject of perplexing inquiry: it might be that the very advantages we had achieved, were the source of our difficulties, or that they had been neutralized by some accompanying evils not yet discovered, or insufficiently appreciated.

The most remarkable circumstance in our social progress, has been the rapid increase and ascendancy

a 2

of manufacturing wealth and population. This is the distinguishing feature of society, and to it, I doubt not, may be traced much of the good and evil incidental to our condition—the growth of an opulent commercial, and a numerous and intelligent operative class—sudden alternations of prosperity and depression—extremes of wealth and destitution —the increase of crime—the spread of education—political excitement—conflicting claims of capital and industry—divided and independent opinions on every public question, with many other anomalies peculiar to our existing state.

Another result of the transition from agricultural to manufacturing supremacy, has been the creation of not only new interests and new questions of discussion, but also a vast enlargement of the circle of inquirers. Questions of government, of law, of commerce, and industry, are not now agitated and solved by a limited and prescriptive class—the clergy, the educated and learned—but by that powerful and multitudinous body, forming at least nineteen-twentieths of the community, denominated the INDUSTRIOUS ORDERS. No monopoly of intelligence is recognised; the dissemination of opinion, as the vend of commodities, is claimed to be free and unprivileged.

It is to meet in some degree these altered conditions of society, this publication has been designed. My purpose has been, first, to present an outline of the history, and a digest of the chief facts illustrative of the past and present state of the Middle and Working Classes; and, secondly, to give a brief and popular exposition of the social and economical questions which agitate the community in its several relations of governors and governed—capitalists and labourers—employers and employed. A work in a cheap and accessible form, embracing these objects, it appeared to me would fill a chasm in the department of useful literature, and might allay jealousies and animosities, by removing their most fruitful source—*defective information.* That I have been entirely successful in my undertaking, I do not flatter myself, but a long and attentive observance of the political, moral, and industrial state of England, imboldened me to make the attempt.

The work is divided into three Parts, exclusive of the Appendix.

Part I. comprises a History of the Middle and Working Classes, tracing their origin and progress, and indicating the chief circumstances by which their social condition, up to this time, has been determined. To judge of their present and prospective state, it was necessary to revert to the past, and point out the measures by which their existing condition has been attained. This part, therefore, may be considered preliminary to those which follow.

The Second Part is denominated Political Eco-

nomy of the Industrious Orders, but is more particularly intended to be a popular exposition of the principles which influence the relations and conditions
of the agricultural, commercial, and manufacturing
classes.   My object here in particular was to be practical, and avoid, both in matter and language, what
may be termed the metaphysics of economical
science. The chapters, however, on Wages, Population, Capital and the Middle Classes, Money, Trades'
Unions, Poor-laws, Rent of Land, &c., will show
that the elucidation of no important truth has been
omitted nor compromised, but that all the great
maxims on which the wellbeing of the several orders
is mutually dependent, have been unshrinkingly,
and, I hope, intelligibly, though briefly unfolded.

Since the days of Dr. SMITH, political economy
has become in some respects a new science, not so
much from the acquisition of new truths, as by the
new questions forced upon its consideration by the
exigencies of society.   Fluctuations in employments
—over-population—the apportionment of wages and
profits — the instrument of exchange — and the
voluntary and compulsory relief of indigence, form
the engrossing subjects of attention, and on which
we find little to guide us in the *Wealth of Nations.*
The treatment of some of these matters will be
found peculiar to this publication.   The Unions of
Trades form a novel feature in our industrial situation.   Formerly we had to struggle for freedom in

the employment of capital against the ignorance of rulers, and the selfishness of individuals; now, it seems industry aspires to establish its monopolies of labour on the exploded errors of the mercantile system. The ostensible object of the trade associations in the equitable conservation of their own interests is laudable; but one always views with apprehension the exercise of secret and irresponsible powers, and I have endeavoured to ascertain the limits within which their operations may be beneficial or injurious to themselves and the community.

On the important subject of the POOR-LAWS, I have differed from some of the more intrepid, but not, perhaps, best informed of my contemporaries. They always appeared to me an institution of police, no less than of humanity, inseparable from a civilised community. Under their operation, the working classes of England may be advantageously compared with those of any European country, and under an improved administration, they may, I doubt not, be made more conducive to the diminution of indigence, than any system that could be substituted in their place. It is a sad mistake to consider the poor an aggregation of vice and imposture, to consider every man in want a suspected, if not convicted, delinquent; or to think that any considerable proportion of them would not prefer —were they attainable — the independent wages of industry, to parish or charitable allowance. I who have had abundant opportunities for observing the poor, know such conclusions to be erroneous; they are the deductions of selfishness or misanthropy, derived from the exceptions not the rule of life. The origin of some prevalent errors on the poor-laws, as well as their more prominent abuses, I have endeavoured to explain. While I concede the necessity of their institution, I know well they are only an imperfect substitute for individual prudence, but till that *prudence* is formed, we must submit to their provisional establishment, as the least of a choice of evils, and the most effective instrument of its creation.

The Third Part is Political Philosophy—a term, which in its more extensive application, also includes political economy, but in this case is retricted to an exposition of the Principles of Government, Civil Liberty, Laws, Property, Morals, the English Constitution, and Popular Education. These are all important themes, and in the estimation of some, of delicate import; but it appears to me as unwise as impracticable, in times like these, to shun their investigation, and it is much better their real foundation should be stated, than that the crude ideas which are constantly being promulgated, should gain a transient—for it could never be permanent—ascendancy. In lieu of social institutions being endangered, I feel assured they will be improved and strengthened by popular inquiry and reflection.

The above affords, I think, a tolerable outline of the scope and plan of the publication. The design is a popular compendium of useful knowledge, to state principles briefly and clearly on public topics of great interest, illustrate and support them by facts, and keep both relevant and applicable to the existing state and wants of society.

In the APPENDIX will be found valuable statements elucidatory and corroborative of different portions of the work; especially the Tables of Prices, of Rates of Wages in different branches of industry formerly and at present, the Progress of Population and Poor-rates, Returns of Mortality, Diseases, Marriages, Crimes, Schools, Education, Friendly Societies, Occupations, and other documentary evidence, illustrative of the past and present state of society, and of the industrious classes. Also several articles, such as those on the Poor-law Commission, Increase of Crime, Maxims of Conduct, &c., which could not without inconvenient digression be incorporated into the body of the work.

Now, Sir, allow me in conclusion to congratulate you on the favourable aspect of human affairs. The temple of Janus is shut; in the new and in the old world there is peace, with hardly a rumour of war, and what is more, there is the spirit of peace, and an aversion in both people and their rulers, to resort to violence, as the arbiter of national rights. Every state in Europe is advancing in wealth and intelligence, and in mutual goodwill. There is no agitation any where, save that of OPINION, which of itself strongly denotes that the natural wants of man are tolerably satisfied. Amidst all this, it is pleasing to think our own country keeps the foremost place. One of the noblest indications of moral and intellectual worth, is the love of justice and humanity, and of this we are about to afford a splendid example. It has long been the boast of the Christian over the heathen world, that it was the first to establish asylums for indigence and misfortune. The second, and not less brilliant triumph of modern over Greek and Roman civilization, will be the extinction of slavery, by the emancipation of the African race.

I am,

My dear Sir,

Truly yours,

J. WADE.

London, June 12, 1833.

CONTENTS.

PART I.

HISTORY OF THE MIDDLE AND WORKING CLASSES.

CHAP. VI.

CHAP. VII.

PART II.

POLITICAL ECONOMY OF THE INDUSTRIOUS ORDERS.

CHAP. I.

LABOUR.

CHAP. II.

DIVISION OF EMPLOYMENTS.

CHAP. III.

MONEY.

CHAP. IV.

PAPER CURRENCY.

CHAP. V.

CAPITAL AND THE MIDDLE CLASSES.

CHAP. VI.

EQUALITY OF REMUNERATION.

CHAP. VII.

WAGES OF LABOUR.

CHAP. VIII.

CAUSES OF HIGH WAGES.

CHAP. IX.

GENERAL CONCLUSIONS ON WAGES.

CHAP. X.

FLUCTUATIONS IN EMPLOYMENTS.

CHAP. XI.

UNIONS OF TRADES.

CHAP. XII.

EMPLOYMENT FUND-SOCIETIES.

CHAP. XV.

POOR-LAWS.

PART III.
POLITICAL PHILOSOPHY.

CHAP. I.

INTRODUCTION.

CHAP. II.

APPENDIX.

PART I.

HISTORY

OF THE

MIDDLE AND WORKING CLASSES.

CHAP. I.

STATE OF SOCIETY UNDER THE ANGLO-SAXONS.

THE Conquest forms the historical horizon which
marks the boundaries of authentic, and, at most, dubious history. All records antecedent to William I.
comprise so much of the marvellous and improbable,
that doubt is thrown over the entire narrative of the
Saxon chroniclers. The most singular trait of this
remote period is the slow march of improvement.
The interval, from the invasion of the Romans to
that of the Normans, exceeds considerably the eight
centuries which have elapsed from the latter era to
the present; yet what a contrast of events in the
two historical terms. Science, laws, and institu-

B

tions have been almost created within the last 300 years; while the long nignt of darkness that preceded them presents only fitful gleams of social amelioration through a chaos of bondage and error. It shows how much the progress of nations depends on the uncertain gifts of nature, the appearance of men of genius, some useful discovery, or the ascendancy of enlightened government.

The era of the Anglo-Saxons has been mostly reerred to as the dawn of civilization in this country: but recent inquiries have tended to lower the previous estimate of the attainments of this period of our annals. It is true, we may trace up to the Teutonic invaders the germ of our language, our laws and local divisions; but could we accurately compare the seed with the produce, it is probable the disparity would not be less great than that which subsists between many of the wild fruits and flowers of the wilderness and the perfection to which they are brought by the arts of horticulture.

Untutored man is only a child in habits, the creature of impulse; and philosophy rejects, as illusions sacred to poetry, representations which would endow the savage with virtues inseparable from refinement. Except so far as they had been reclaimed by Christianity, the Anglo-Saxons continued in a state of comparative barbarism. Their institutions discover few signs of superior intelligence, and are only analogous to the attempts of all communities entering on the early stages of civilization. Neither persons nor property were secure from violence; and robbery, from the absence of police, was tolerated as a legitimate vocation. So little delicacy was there in the relations of the sexes, that arreoy societies, for promiscuous intercourse, of the nature of those in the Polynesian islands, were common, and the utility of the marriage institute scarcely recognised. The code of laws ascribed to Alfred has been extolled as an extraordinary instance of legislative aptitude; but it appears to have been little more than a compilation of the decalogue, and the provisions of the Mosaic dispensation.

But what exemplifies most strongly the spirit of the Saxon institutions is, the civil inequality among different classes. Two-thirds of the people were either absolute slaves, or in an intermediate state of bondage to the remaining third. They might be put in bonds and whipped : they might be branded ; and on one occasion are spoken of as if actually yoked : " Let every man know his *team* of men, of horses and oxen." * Cattle and slaves formed in truth the " live money" of the Anglo-Saxons, and were the medium of exchange by which the value of commodities was measured.

The predominant crimes of the age were of an atrocious character. Assassinations, female violations, the plundering of whole towns and districts, and barefaced perjuries, were offences of ordinary occurrence by persons of condition. The punishment of delinquents was either shockingly cruel, or

* Turner's *History of the Anglo-Saxons*, vol. iii. p. 91.

strangely inconsistent with modern notions of penal justice. The horrible torture of burning out the eyes was not only inflicted for delinquency, but sometimes merely to incapacitate a rival. Although theft to the amount of twelvepence was a capital offence, yet the taking away life might be commuted for a pecuniary penalty. This was the *were*, and varied with the rank of the sufferer : for the murder of the king, the penalty was 30,000 thrymsas ;* for a prince, one-half; for an alderman, or earl, and a bishop, 8000 ; for a thane, 2000 ; and for a ceorl (churl; supposed by some writers to have been a slave), 260. If the legal value of human life were made to vary, it is no wonder that personal estimation varied in the same way; thus the oath of a twelve-hyndman was equal to the oath of six ceorls. Besides the *were*, a security was afforded to the peace and safety of the house, called the *mund ;* and this, like the *were*, varied in amount with the rank of the party.

In institutions of this description it is impossible to recognise a high degree of legislative wisdom or social happiness. If it is further borne in mind that science and literature were almost unknown, we shall be constrained to admit that the Anglo-Saxons are

* A thrymsa exceeded sixpence in value, and was equal to three Saxon pence. Five pence were equal to a Saxon shilling. As the Anglo-Saxon pound troy was equivalent to forty-eight shillings, while the same quantity is at present coined into sixty-six; the silver in the more ancient shillings surpasses that in the modern by about one-fourth.

not the fount from which we ought to seek enlightened examples of order and freedom. Over this part of history, therefore, I shall pass, as an unfruitful waste of darkness and Vandalism, and commence at the subsequent era of the Conquest.

CHAP. II.

Classes of Society after the Conquest—Traffic in Slaves—Beneficial Influence of Christianity—Increase of Towns and Progress of Manufactures—Corporate Immunities—Effects of a Pestilence on Condition of Labouring Classes—Statute of Labourers—Absurd Legislation—Vast Possessions of the Nobility—A taste for Luxury and the Arts generated—Villanage nearly extinct—Occupation, Diet, and Wages of Labourers.

For a long time after the Conquest, the Anglo-Saxon subdivisions of society were maintained, and the inhabitants of England were divided into the two great classes of freemen and slaves. Except the baronial proprietors of land and their vassals, the free tenants and socmen, the rest of the nation was depressed in servitude, which, though qualified as to its effects, was uniform in its principle, that none who had been born in, or had fallen into bondage could acquire an absolute right to any species of property.

The condition, however, of the people who were thus debarred from the first of social rights, was not in other respects equally abject and miserable. One class of villains, or villagers, though bound to the most servile offices of rural industry, were permitted to occupy small portions of land to sustain themselves and families. Other ranks of men, equally servile, are noticed in the ancient records, particularly the bordars and cottars, the former in consideration of being allowed a small cottage, were required to provide poultry, eggs, and other articles of diet for the lord's table; and the latter were employed in the trades of smith, carpenter, and other handicraft arts, in which they had been instructed at the charge of their masters. Inferior to these were the thralls, or servi, principally employed in menial services about the mansion. Their lives were professedly protected by law, and with the consent of their owners they were allowed in some cases to purchase their manumission. In other respects they were in the lowest degradation; so much so as to be considered mere chattels and regular articles of commerce. Giraldus relates that the number of them exported to Ireland for sale in the reign of Henry II. was so great that the market was absolutely overstocked; and from William I. to the reign of John, scarcely a cottage in Scotland but possessed an English slave. In the details of the border wars, mention is frequently made of the number of slaves taken prisoners as forming a principal part of the booty.

It is not easy to ascertain from writers the precise immunities of the several classes of bondmen mentioned; the chief differences in their condition arose probably from the relative utility of their occupations; the servi, or serfs, as least valuable, being a more ordinary article of traffic and transfer than the bordars and cottars who had been trained to useful arts or obtained a fixed habitation.*

All, however, alike appear to have been denuded of the substantial attributes of freedom the law recognised in none the uncontrolled right to property or change of place without the consent of their superiors; the lord had the absolute disposal of their persons, they might be attached to the soil or transferred by deed, sale, or conveyance, from one owner to another; in short they were slaves in the strictest sense of the word—men under an obligation of perpetual servitude, which the consent of the master could alone dissolve, and in all probability enjoyed less legal protection from the ill-usage of their oppressors than the humanity of modern legislation has extended to the brute creation.

The population of England, according to Mr. Tur-

* The difficulty of obtaining precise notions of the civil distinctions of society is not confined to English history. Historians are not exactly agreed about the social rank and immunities of the patricians, clients, and plebeians of ancient Rome. Posterity some centuries hence will be greatly at a loss to form correct ideas of the relative condition of the several classes appertaining to the metropolis; of the franchises of the citizens, freemen, liverymen, and parliamentary electors of the city of London, as distinguished from the inhabitants living without the narrow jurisdiction of the city, and not sharing either in the immunities of the general corporation, or of numerous incorporated fraternities.

ner, after the desolation of the northern counties by the Normans, amounted to about 1,700,000. One hundred thousand souls are supposed to have been swept away by the Conqueror in laying waste the country betwixt the Humber and the Tees. Attempts have been made to class the population existing at the close of the Anglo-Saxon period into its several proportions of nobles, freemen, and those of servile condition, but with no great pretension to accuracy. In thirty-four counties the burgesses and citizens are made to amount to 17,105; the villains to 102,704; the bordars to 74,823; the cottars to 5947; the serfs or thralls to 26,552: the remaining population consisted of freemen, ecclesiastics, knights, thanes, and landowners. In the opinion of Sir James Mackintosh (*History of England*, v. i. p. 78), the persons strictly slaves were not above one out of every seven of the higher laborious classes of villains, bordars, and cottars.

Of the domestic comforts enjoyed by this class of people, history affords little information. It may be presumed that from motives of interest the lord would take care of his villain, and supply him in infancy and manhood with the essential necessaries of food, raiment, and lodging. In this consists almost the solitary advantage of slavery over free-labour, it creates in the master the same motives for rearing and preserving his thralls as his cattle—a tie dissolved by the labourer becoming independent, and left to his own prudence to make a provision for the vicissitudes of health and employment.

The mitigation and final extinction of English slavery was a work of gradual and lengthened operation. The first blow the system sustained was in the disuse of the ancient practice of converting prisoners of war into bondmen. The diffusion of Christianity, by teaching mankind that they were equal, early awakened men to the injustice of a practice which made one man the property of another. Frequently, at the intercession of their confessors, the feudal lords were induced to enfranchise their slaves; and from the ignorance of the times, the administration of justice devolving into the hands of the clergy, opportunities occurred of showing particular indulgence to this unfortunate class of society. In the eleventh century the Pope formally issued a bull for the emancipation of slaves; and in 1102 it was declared in the great council of the nation, held at Westminster, unlawful for any man to *sell slaves openly in the market*, which before had been the common custom of the country.

It would, however, be a mistake to infer from this that slavery ceased in the land, or that men did not long after continue a vendible article. In both Magna Charta, and the charters of Henry III., obtained in 1225, a class of men are mentioned, who appear to have been treated as chattel property. The prohibition to guardians from *wasting* the men or cattle on the estates of minors is a clear proof that villains who held by servile tenures were looked upon in the light of negroes on a rice or sugar plantion. Long after this period they were considered a saleable commodity, of which Sir F. Eden cites several instances from ancient authorities. In 1283 a slave and his family were sold by the abbot of Dunstable for 13s. 4d.; in 1333 a lord granted to a chantry several messuages, together with the bodies of eight natives dwelling there, with all their chattels and offspring; and in 1339 is an instance of a gift of a *nief* (female slave), with all her family and all that she possessed or might subsequently acquire. It was not till the reign of Charles II. that slavery was wholly abolished in England by statute; it was attempted in vain to be abolished in 1526. So late even as 1775 the colliers of Scotland were bondmen; and in case they left the ground of the farm to which they belonged, and as pertaining to which their services were bought or sold, they were liable to be brought back by summary procedure before a magistrate. The existence of this sort of slavery being deemed irreconcilable with personal freedom, colliers were declared free and put on the same footing as other servants, by the act 15 Geo. III. cap. 28.

In the reign of Edward I. the condition of the villains was so far ameliorated, that instead of being obliged to perform every mean and servile office that the arbitrary will of the lord demanded, they had acquired a tenure in lands on condition of rendering services which were either certain in their nature, as to reap the lord's corn, or cleanse his fish-pond; or limited in duration, as to harrow two days in the year, or to employ three days in carting

the lord's timber. As early as the year 1257, a servile tenant, if employed before midsummer, received
wages; and he was permitted, instead of working
himself, to provide a labourer for the lord; from
which it is obvious he must have possessed the means
of hiring one; and secondly, that a class of free
labourers, at liberty to barter their services to the
best bidder, had begun to exist.

These were important transitions, indicating the
rise of a middle class and independent race of workmen. By granting to the vassals a right to property,
they received a stimulus to acquire more; and, by
conceding to them a part of the immunities of freemen, they were raised one step in the social scale,
and put in a state to treat and contend with their
oppressors for the remainder. Whatever advances
were subsequently made, may be considered as an
extension and improvement of these first concessions.

While the people were in a state of slavery, it may
be readily conjectured, that their diet would be the
mere offal and refuse of their masters; and no more
of it than was necessary to enable them to support
their daily toil. At this period, the food of labourers
consisted principally of fish, chiefly herrings, and a
small quantity of bread and beer. Mutton and
cheese were considered articles of luxury, which
formed the harvest-home, of so much importance in
ancient times. Wages were a penny a day in harvest, and a halfpenny at other seasons: the average
price of wheat was 6l. 8s. a quarter, which last
clearly shows the small progress made in tillage

husbandry, and how little the present staff of life entered into the general consumption of the community. Their habitations were without chimneys, and their principal furniture consisted of a brass pot, valued from one to three shillings : and a bed valued from three to six shillings.

The variations in the prices of commodities were great and sudden, arising from the absence of commercial middlemen, whose pursuits, though often viewed with prejudice, tend to produce a regular and equable supply of the most essential articles of consumption throughout the year. The trade of a corn-dealer seems to have been unknown ; nor except in the Abbey-Granges do we meet with instances of corn being collected in large quantities.* The natural consequence must have been, that the farmers, without capital, disposed of their crops at moderate prices, soon after the harvest : purchasers who only looked to their immediate wants, having corn cheap, were naturally wasteful and improvident in the consumption : the price, therefore, almost invariably rose as the year advanced, and was frequently at an enormous height just before harvest, when the supply of the preceding season was nearly or entirely exhausted. Stow relates, that in 1317 the harvest was all got in before the 1st of September ; and that wheat which had before been at 4l. the quarter fell to 6s. 8d., a twelfth part of the price. A reference to tables of prices furnish abundant proof of the extreme misery of these

* Sir F. Eden's *State of the Poor*, vol. i. p. 18.

times, in which, the only buyers of corn were the consumers : and no monopolists, as they are termed, interfered, who by the aid of superior capital, purchasing the redundant produce of one year, made a provision for the scarcity of another.

The progress of manufacturing industry and of town population operated favourably on the condition of the labouring classes. The woollen manufacture had been known so early as the Conquest, and for greater security during a barbarous age had been chiefly established in boroughs and cities. As it was at first carried on principally by the Flemings, who were exposed to the jealousy of an unenlightened nation, it is probable that the privileges conferred by the sovereign on weavers, fullers, and clothiers, in allowing them to carry on their occupations in walled towns, and form themselves into guilds and companies, governed by corporate laws, were not more intended for the advancement of their art than to protect their persons from popular outrage and their property from depredation. Such was the want of police during the thirteenth and fourteenth centuries, that robbers formed themselves into bands under the protection of powerful barons, who employed them in acts of violence and plunder, justified their conduct, and partook of their booty. The king's retinue was often beset and pillaged by banditti ; even towns during times of fairs were assaulted and ransacked, and men of rank carried off and confined in the castle of some lawless chieftain till their ransom was paid. In so general a state of insecurity it was impossible the pursuits of industry should thrive without special protection. But by the immunities granted to merchants and manufacturers of making by-laws for their own government, and of raising troops for their own defence, they were enabled to taste the blessings of order and protection, and acquired the means of enriching themselves, while the occupiers of land were languishing in poverty and servitude. The superior comforts enjoyed in towns no doubt inspired the dependents of a manor with ideas of emancipating themselves from a state in which they could scarcely obtain the necessaries, and certainly none of the conveniences of life. If in the hands of a poor cultivator, oppressed with the services of villanage, some little stock should accumulate, he would naturally conceal it with care from his master, by whom it would otherwise have been claimed, and take the first opportunity of escaping to a town. The law too was so indulgent to the inhabitants of towns, and so favourable to diminishing the authority of the lord over those of the country, that if a vassal could conceal himself from the pursuit of his lord for a year he was free for ever.

By this and similar practices, suggested perhaps originally by the hardships of servitude, and promoted by the demand for manufacturing labour, a large portion of villains were converted into the more useful class of free labourers: The number was also no doubt increased during the beginning of Edward the Third's reign from his long wars in

France, which must have obliged him to manumit many of his villains to recruit his exhausted armies. They are for the first time specifically noticed as a distinct class of people by the legislature in 1350, whose regulations, however unjust and impolitic, afford at least the important information, that labourers in husbandry, as well as those employed at the loom, equally worked for hire.

Another cause operated favourably for the labouring classes. In 1349 the earth was visited with a dreadful pestilence, which swept from its surface nearly one-half the inhabitants. After this terrible calamity labour became extremely dear, and labourers demanded unusual wages. To remedy this evil a proclamation was issued to fix the price of labour; this not being attended to, the famous *Statute of Labourers* was enacted to enforce obedience by fines and corporal punishment. The statute states, that since the pestilence no person would serve unless he was paid double the usual wages allowed five years before, to the great detriment of the lords and commons; it then provides that in future carters, ploughmen, plough-drivers, shepherds, and swineherds and other servants, should be content with such liveries and wages as they received in the 20th year of the king's reign and two or three years before; and that in districts where they had been severally paid in wheat, they should receive wheat or money at the rate of tenpence a bushel, at the option of their employers; they were to be hired by the year and other accustomed periods, and not by

the day ; weeders and haymakers were to be paid at
the rate of one penny, mowers fivepence per acre,
or fivepence a day ; reapers during the first week in
August twopence a day, and from that time till the
end of the month threepence a day, without diet or
other perquisite. Labourers of this description were
enjoined to carry their implements of husbandry
openly in their hands to market-towns, and to apply
for hire in a public quarter of the town.

This unjust interference with the freedom of industry was repeatedly confirmed by succeeding parliaments ; and the same erroneous principle of legislation, further extended by the law of 1363, which
regulates the diet and apparel of labourers ; and
that of 1388, which prohibits servants from removing
from one place to another ; and finally, to conclude
those oppressive enactments, justices of peace were
empowered to *fix the price of labour* every Easter
and Michaelmas, by proclamation.

As a specimen of the absurd system of legislation
prevalent at this time, we may mention the minute
regulations of the statute of 1363 ; which directs
that artificers and servants shall be served once a
day with meat and fish, or the waste of other victuals,
as milk and cheese, according to their station ; and
that they should wear cloth of which the whole piece
did not cost more than twelvepence per yard. The
cloth of yeomen and tradesmen was not to cost more
than one shilling and sixpence per yard. Carters,
ploughmen, ox-herds, neat-herds, shepherds, and all
others employed in husbandry, were to use no kind

of cloth but that called black russet, twelvepence per yard. Clothiers were commanded to manufacture the necessary kind of cloth, and tradesmen to have a sufficient stock upon hand at the *established legal* prices.

It would be superfluous enlarging. on a species of law-making so obviously at variance with the feelings and intelligence of the present age. It cannot, however, be denied that these enactments were in good keeping, for it was not more preposterous to fix the rate at which a labourer should work than what he should eat, or wherewithal be clothed, and one is almost surprised the legislators of the day did not descend to regulations still more minute and intrusive. One important fact may be elicited from these provisions, namely, the evidence they afford of the new social elements that had risen into importance. A great portion of the labourers had clearly extricated themselves from the grasp of their feudal masters, who in lieu of the direct power of compulsory servitude, were compelled to resort to acts of parliament, which, though partial, had the semblance of law in place of the arbitrary will of their employers.

Upon the whole it may be safely affirmed that, before the end of the fourteenth century, the benefits attendant on freedom, order and industry, had made considerable progress : there can be little doubt but that in 1400 the great mass of the people were, in comparison with their forefathers at the Conquest, rich, thriving, and independent ; and although his-

c

torians are silent on many points which are intimately
connected with an investigation of this nature, their
general information will still afford us competent
evidence that the sphere of domestic happiness was
greatly extended.   The various immunities granted
to cities and boroughs, the introduction and firm
establishment of the woollen manufacture, the dawn-
ing, however faint, of the polite arts, and the hu-
manizing tendency of Christianity, are causes which
must have powerfully and beneficially operated towards the amelioration of the condition of the community.   It is principally to their effect that we are
to ascribe the important alteration that appears to
have taken place before the time of Richard II.;
not only in the personal dependence, but in the
political opinions of the labouring classes of society.
In the insurrection of Wat Tyler, in the year 1381,
the language of the rebels, who were chiefly villains,
bespeaks men not unacquainted with the essentials
of rational liberty.   They required from the king the
abolition of slavery, freedom of commerce in market-
towns, without tolls or imposts, and a fixed rent on
land instead of services due by villanage.   These
requests (Mr. Hume observes), though extremely
reasonable in themselves, the nation was not sufficiently prepared to receive, and which it were
dangerous to have yielded to intimidation, were
however complied with : charters of manumission
were granted, and although they were revoked after
the rebellion was crushed, and many hundreds of
the insurgents executed as traitors, it is probable that

the general spirit which had now manifested itself among the people prevented masters from imposing, and vassals from again submitting to the harsh and oppressive services of bondage.

While the united operation of various causes was thus gradually converting villains into free labourers, another and not less useful class of subjects, namely, tenantry, had insensibly been formed, and, like the other, seems to have been much indebted for their advancement to manufactures and commerce. At the Conquest, most of the lands in England were parcelled out among the Norman nobility. Earl Moreton acquired no less than 793 manors; and Hugh de Alrincia received from the conqueror the whole palatinate of Chester. The extensive county of Norfolk had only sixty-six proprietors. The owners of such vast possessions resided almost entirely on their estates, and in most instances, kept them in their own hands. The elder Spencer in his petition to parliament in the reign of Edward II., in which he complains of the outrages committed on his lands, reckons among his moveable property 28,000 sheep, 1000 oxen, 1200 cows, 500 cart-horses, 2000 hogs, 600 bacons, 80 carcasses of beef, 600 sheep in the larder (the three last articles were probably salted provisions), 10 tons of cider, and arms for 200 men. In the following reign, in 1367, the stock on the land of the bishop of Winchester appears by inquisition taken at his death to have amounted to 127 draft-horses, 1556 head of black-cattle, 3876 wethers, 4777 ewes, 3451 lambs. It is probable that Spencer's estate, as of the other nobility in those times, was farmed by the landlord himself, managed by his steward or bailiff, and cultivated by his villains. From there being no costly articles of equipage or dress, for which the surplus produce of the land, beyond the lord's immediate wants, could be exchanged, he was naturally led to spend it in riotous and rustic hospitality. Commerce at length offered allurements of a different kind, and induced him, from motives of personal gratification, to lessen the number of his idle retainers and dependants, and to grant a portion of his demesnes to a tenant, on condition of receiving a rent which might enable him to extend his pursuits beyond gorgeous entertainments, field sports, or domestic warfare.

In this way, the progress of manufactures led to a salutary revolution in the manners of the great landowners, and through them to the subordinate ranks of the community. In lieu of squandering immense revenues in the support of numerous followers, they were expended in the purchase of the productions of art. For a pair of diamond buckles, or something as frivolous, Dr. Smith remarks (*Wealth of Nations*, b. iii. ch. iv.), they exchanged the maintenance of a thousand men for a year, and with it, the whole weight and authority which it could give them. It is not, however, to mere personal vanity, but to more rational causes, this change may be ascribed. The desire of bettering our condition, which is the parent of so many social virtues, would alike compel the lord to pre-

fer comfort to barbaric splendour, and the villain to
quit his livery for the independence of trade: and
happily these exchanges produced advantages conducive to general security and happiness.   A man
who, by dismissing half of his useless domestics,
purchased the means of multiplying his enjoyments;
who could thereby clothe himself in woollen and
fine linen instead of coarse canvass and a leathern
jerkin; who could add the wholesome and grateful
productions of horticulture to his table; and could
render a dreary castle more habitable by substituting
warm hangings for bare stone, or at most, white-
washed walls; and that elegant conveniency, glass
for latticed windows, would act conformably to principles which are not more natural to the masters
than to the labouring part of mankind.

From the complaints of the Commons in 1406,
we have evidence of the competition which had commenced between rural and manufacturing industry.
To evade the statutes, passed some years before, for
compelling those who had been brought up to the
plough till they were twelve years of age to continue
in husbandry all their lives; agricultural labourers
had recourse to the expedient of sending their children into cities and boroughs, and binding them
apprentices when they were under that age. In order
to counteract this, it was enacted that no person,
unless possessed of land of a rental of twenty shillings
a year, should bind a child of any age apprentice to
any trade or mystery within a city, but that children
should be brought up in the occupation of their

parents, or other business suited to their conditions ;
they were, however, allowed to be sent to a school
n any part of the kingdom, which is a proof of
growing civilization, and of attention to education,
even by the legislature.

In the reign of Henry VII. the race of villains was
almost extinct, and wages were nearly quadruple the
amount they had been in the preceding century. Civilization and the useful arts had made a wonderful progress.   In the Statute of Labourers of 1496 (11 Henry
VII. c. 22) bricklayers are for the first time mentioned
among artificers.   Tilers are noticed in the statute
of 1350 ; and tiles were used in Suffolk as early as
1358.   Another occupation is likewise mentioned in
1496, namely, that of glaziers.   But Sir F. Eden
very much doubts whether glass, although it had
long been the ornament of churches, was used at this
time in private houses.   In 1567 glass was such a
rarity as not to be usually found in the castles of the
nobility.   It is probable glass windows were not introduced into farmhouses much before the reign of
James I.   In Scotland, however, as late as 1661,
the windows of the ordinary country houses were not
glazed, and only the upper parts even of those of
the king's palaces had glass ; the lower ones having
two wooden shutters, to open at pleasure and admit
the fresh air.   Previously, lattice, horn, or bevil, was
the substitute for the uses to which glass is now
applied.

The diet of labourers had become more wholesome
and plentiful by the introduction of various useful

roots and vegetables. Their dress appears to have been simple and well-contrived, consisting of shoes, hose made of cloth, a jacket and coat, buttoned and fastened round the body by a belt or girdle, and a bonnet of cloth. Hats were not much used till a century after; though mention is made of them in a statute of Richard III., by which the price of a hat is limited to twenty pence. Sumptuary laws were in force, regulating apparel, both as to quantity and quality. In the reign of Henry VIII. it was enacted that no serving man under the degree of a gentleman, should wear a long gown or coat containing more than three broad yards, and without fur, under the penalty of forfeiture; nor any garde hose or cloth above the price of twenty pence. The fashion of wearing peaks to shoes or boots of a length exceeding eleven inches was prohibited to all but gentlemen.

The rate of wages may be collected from the statute of 1496 mentioned above, and were as follows:

AGRICULTURAL SERVANTS, WITH DIET, FOR ONE YEAR.

	l. s. d.		l. s. d.
To a bailiff of husbandry, not more than	1 16 8	—and for clothing	0 5 0
A chief hind or chief shepherd	1 0 0	ditto	0 5 0
A common servant of husbandry	0 16 8	ditto	0 4 0
A woman servant	0 10 0	ditto	0 4 0
A child under 14 years of age	0 6 8	ditto	0 4 0

WAGES APPOINTED FOR ARTIFICERS.

	Between Easter and Michaelmas.	Between Michaelmas and Easter.
A free Mason, Master Carpenter, Rough Mason, Bricklayer, Master Tiler, Plumber, Glazier, Carver, Joiner	with diet 4d., without 6d.	with diet 3d., without 5d.
Other labourers (except in harvest)	with diet 2d., without 4d.	with diet 1½d., without 3d.
In harvest, every Mower, by the day	....	with diet 4d., without 6d.
A reaper, ditto		with diet 3d., without 5d.
A carter, ditto		with diet 3d., without 5d.
A woman, and other labourers ditto	....	with diet 2½d., without 4½d.

If any unemployed person refused to serve at the above wages he might be imprisoned till he found sureties to serve according to the statute. The latter part of this statute regulates the hours of work and meals, by providing that the hours of labour, from March to September, shall be from five o'clock in the morning till seven in the evening; that one hour shall be allowed to breakfast, an hour and half for dinner, and half an hour for *noon-meate:* the hours of labour in winter are from " springing of day" to dark, and only one hour is allowed for dinner, the extra half-hour at the meal being only allowed for sleeping, from the middle of May to the middle of August.

Although provisions advanced considerably in the

succeeding twenty years, it does not appear that wages underwent any material alteration; in 1514 the prices of the different kinds of labour mentioned above were exactly the same. It is impossible to judge correctly of the comfort and relative situation of the working classes at different periods, they depend so much on circumstances with which we are very imperfectly acquainted. The proportion between the rate of wages and the price of provisions is undoubtedly the best criterion; but if we are not also informed of the diet and domestic economy of labourers, we can know very little of their real situation. Labourers in the north of England, similarly situated as to the price of provisions and wages, will have the means of comfortable subsistence, while labourers in the south would perish from wretchedness and privation. From the statement above it appears, that in 1496 the diet was considered equivalent to one-third of the income of an artificer, and one-half the income of a labourer, which indicates a greater degree of independence among the working classes than prevails at present; for the board, both of labourers and artificers, would now be reckoned at a much higher proportion of their wages. The hours for meals and relaxation were more liberal, too, than at this day.

The labouring poor, however, were still a long way behind their successors, in their diet, dress, and habitations; and even so late as the reign of Queen Mary, the dwelling of an English peasant was little superior in comfort and cleanliness to what we observe in the

clay-built hovels of the Irish.   The dwellings of the
common people, according to Erasmus, had not yet
attained the convenience of a chimney to let out the
smoke, and the flooring of their huts was nothing
but the bare ground : their beds consisted of straw,
among which was an ancient accumulation of filth
and refuse, with a hard block of wood for a pillow.
And such in general was the situation of the labouring classes throughout Europe.   Fortescue, who
wrote in the reign of Henry VI., speaking of the
French peasantry, says, " Thay drink water, thay
eate apples, with bread right brown, made of rye ;
thay eate no flesche, but, if it be selden ; a littell
larde, or of the entrails or heds of beasts, sclayne for
the nobles or merchaunts of the lond."

CHAP. III.

Origin of the Poor—Influence of Personal Freedom on Indigence—Vagabondage and Mendicity—Licensing of Beggars
—Treatment of the Poor in the Netherlands—The elapse of
four Centuries not changed the objects of Legislation.

In the last chapter we arrived at the close of the
reign of Henry VII.; previously to which period had
originated that numerous class emphatically denominated the poor, consisting of those personally
free, but without the means of supporting themselves by their industry or capital, unaided by the
gratuitous assistance of their fellow-men.   Indi-

viduals in this unhappy condition are clearly in a state of slavery; those who cannot live independently of the support of others, cannot, in the affairs of life, act the part of freemen : and, in truth, the great mass of English poor is nothing more than the continuation, under a mitigated form, of the race of villains who have exchanged baronial for parochial servitude. How they originated, and became a separate and recognised class of the community, I shall briefly explain.

While the feudal system prevailed, a regular chain of subordination subsisted from the highest to the lowest in the community ; all thought of personal independence was precluded, and each individual, during sickness or infirmity, looked to his next superior for maintenance and protection. From the same motives the lord took care of his cattle, he took care of the tillers of his ground. When this system declined, and men ceased to be the life-apprentices of their employers, then their only dependence in impotence or old age was either upon their own prudence and forethought, or the voluntary charity of others.

We thus see how different the functions of individuals are in a state of bondage and of liberty. In the former, men may be mere brutes—without knowledge, prudence, or economy ; in the latter, these qualities are indispensable. The extension of education and the domestic virtues, therefore, ought always to keep pace with the extension of personal freedom.

Next to the increase of freedom among the people, as a cause of pauperism, may be reckoned the growth of commerce and manufactures. Rousseau properly inquires (*La Nouvelle Héloïse*), "Why it is that in a thriving city the poor are so miserable, while such extreme distress is hardly ever experienced in those countries where there are no instances of immense wealth?" One answer is, that in cities people are more poor because they are more independent than in the country. It is one of the natural consequences of freedom, that those who are left to shift for themselves, must sometimes, either from misconduct or misfortune, be reduced to want. This, however, furnishes no solid argument against the advantages of liberty. A prisoner, under the custody of his keeper, may perhaps be confident of receiving his bread and his water daily; yet there are few who would not, even with the contingent necessity of starving, prefer a precarious chance of subsistence from their own industry to the certainty of regular meals in a gaol. It has been frequently urged, in extenuation of the slave-trade, that the condition of negroes in the West Indies is in general more comfortable than that of many day-labourers in this country. Admitting this position to be true, it proves no more than that those, who in the mass often rise high in the scale of affluence, will sometimes furnish instances of extreme destitution. But in the case of slavery, degradation and misery are the rule; in the case of freedom, they are the exception: in one there are doubtless many pains, but in the other there are no pleasures—nor hardly hope.

Another cause may be assigned for the contrast presented between rural and civic industry, in the different conditions under which labour is exercised. In the country, labourers are often hired for a year, during which term they are guaranteed against all casualties. Then, again, their remuneration does not so exclusively depend on wages ; if unemployed, they have (or shall I say had?) often a pig, or the produce of a plot of ground, on which they can retreat as a temporary resource. Add to which, they are not exposed to those temptations to pleasure and irregular habits which are among the most prominent causes of extreme wretchedness in the inhabitants of towns.

The experience of the period that has elapsed since Sir F. Eden wrote (and from whose work the preceding observations have been mostly abridged), shows that agricultural districts may be subject to as severe visitations of poverty and privation as manufacturing towns. But this by no means impugns the truth of the general principle, that the extension of commerce was one of the causes of the origin of the poor. It is an evil inseparable from commercial pursuits—that it tends rapidly to augment population, without simultaneously providing a permanent source of subsistence to the people. The employment resulting from commerce must always be liable to variations ; depending on a state of peace or war, the invention of machinery, or the ever-varying taste and fashion of the times.   Unless there be some certain provision for the people, independent of these fluctuations, it is evident that they must not only be exposed to great occasional distress, but that even commerce itself cannot be advantageously pursued. Without it, when the demand for labour decreases, numbers must perish from want; and on the other hand, when the demand for labour increases, hands cannot be obtained to meet it.   Therefore, to prevent the evil, and secure the advantage of such vicissitudes, provision must be made, either by the community or the people themselves, for their occasional maintenance, independent of their occupations.

There is one error which it is essential to guard against, before leaving this part of our subject; namely, the inference which might be drawn, that because the poor are not mentioned during the feudal age there was no poverty or distress.   No doubt, in disastrous times, from the lateness of harvest, from the failure of crops or the ravages of warfare, a great landholder was often as much embarrassed to supply the hungry mouths around him with food, as a free labourer was to support himself; and a famine, we may be assured, fell with no less fury on the cottar than the manufacturer : but the poor not having become an object of legislative enactment and provision, we have no record of their sufferings and privations.

Having premised these general remarks, I shall next notice the principal facts in the progress of the poor to the period of the Reformation.

In the year 1376 we have evidence of a strong disposition to vagrancy among labourers, in the complaint of the House of Commons that masters are obliged to give their servants high wages to prevent them running away; that many of the runaways turn beggars and lead idle lives in cities and boroughs, although they have sufficient bodily strength to gain a livelihood, if willing to work; that others become *staff-strikers* (cudgel-players) wandering in parties from village to village, but that the chief part turn out sturdy rogues, infesting the kingdom with frequent robberies. To remedy these evils, the Commons propose that no relief shall be given to those who are able to work within boroughs or the country; that vagrants, beggars, and staff-strikers, shall be imprisoned till they consent to return home to work, and whoever harbours a runaway servant shall be liable to a penalty of ten pounds. This is the first time beggars are mentioned; it shows the earliest opinion of parliament on mendicity; and from the language of the Commons we learn that they were chiefly found in towns, where, owing to commerce and the introduction of manufactures, the principal wealth of the nation had accumulated.

Two years after, by 12 Richard II. c. 7, it is directed that impotent beggars should continue to reside in the places they were at the time of passing this act: in case those places are not able to maintain them, they are to remove to some other place in the hundred, or to the place of their birth. From the tenour of this act, it is evident, that the district where they finally settled, was bound to maintain them ; and the legislature of 1388 proceeded on the same principle of a compulsory assessment as that of the celebrated act of Elizabeth in 1601. It seems, too, from the enactments of this period, that the indigent classes had a legal claim on the revenues of he clergy. In 1391 it is declared that, in all appropriations of tithe for the support of monastic institutions, a certain portion should be set apart for the maintenance of the poor.

In these regulations we see the foundation of our present system of poor-laws ; and instead of referring their origin to the 43d Elizabeth, we ought only to ascribe the concentration and development of an ancient practice that had prevailed for some ages before her time. It is apparent, indeed, from the acts to which I have referred, and from others in the public statutes which might be quoted, that for nearly two centuries prior to the Reformation, the legislature was sedulously struggling against the evil which accompanied the transition from slavery to free labour, and that their policy was directed to objects similar to those which now engage attention, namely, to analyse the mass of vagabondage, imposture, and real destitution, which infests society, to punish the former and relieve the latter. Branding, whipping, imprisonment, and setting in the stocks, were the punishments chiefly employed for the suppression of vagrancy. Scholars were liable to these penalties unless provided with written testimonials from the chancellor of their respective universities. Sailors, soldiers, and travellers were also to be provided with passports, and were required to travel homewards by the straightest road. Artificers and labourers (11 Henry VII. c. 2) were forbidden to play at unlawful games, except during Christmas, and two justices were empowered to restrain the common selling of ale in towns and places where they should think expedient, and to take surety of alehouse keepers for their good behaviour as they might be advised at the time of the sessions. All these enactments, however, evince a great improvement in the condition of the people; while they show that their newly-acquired liberties were accompanied with those excesses and disorders which mostly, for a season, attend their first enjoyment.

. By an act passed in 1530, beggars were divided into two classes; namely, the aged and impotent, and vagabonds and idle persons; and justices were empowered to license persons of the first description to beg within certain precincts. Their names were directed to be registered, and to be certified at the next sessions. Begging without a licence, or without the limits assigned, subjected to imprisonment in the stocks for two days and nights, and to feeding on bread and water. Able-bodied vagabonds found begging, were flogged at the cart's tail, and then sworn to return to their places of birth, or where they last dwelt for the space of three years, and there put themselves to labour.

It is probable, inconveniences arose from begging being authorized by the legislature; for, within five years, several material alterations were made in the laws respecting the impotent poor. In the 27th Hen. VIII. c. 25, we have a near approximation to the principles of the poor-rate; the preamble states that it had not been provided " how poor people and sturdy vagabonds should be ordered at their repaire and coming into their countries, nor how the inhabitants of every hundred should be *charged for their reliefe*, nor yet for the setting and keeping in worke and labour the said valiant beggars at their repaire into every hundred of this realme." From these expressions, the legislature seems to have been convinced of the necessity of a compulsory maintenance; and although a regular tax for that purpose was not immediately imposed, yet it is clear, from the regulations of the statute, that the poor, even at this period, should be maintained by the public.

The act makes it obligatory, under a penalty of twenty shillings a month on the head officer and householder of every parish, to maintain by the collection of voluntary and charitable alms, the poor of their parish in such a way, that " none of them of very necessity be compelled to go openly on begging." The alms to be collected on Sundays, holidays, and festivals. Every minister in their sermons, collations, biddings of the beads, confessions, and at the making of wills, are required to "exhort, move, stir, and provoke people to be liberal in contributions towards the comfort and relief of the poor, impotent, decrepid, indigent, and needy people, and for setting and keeping to work the able poor." Certain of the poor are directed twice or thrice every week to go round and collect from each householder his broken meat and refuse drink, for equal distribution among the indigent; but precautions are taken by fines and penalties, to guard against the embezzlement of the parochial alms and doles by constables and church-wardens.

Similar regulations, originating in similar causes, were about this period adopted on the continent respecting the poor. In 1531 the emperor Charles V. published a long edict in the Netherlands against vagrancy; wherein it was declared, that the trade of begging created idleness and led to bad courses; none, therefore, except mendicant friars and pilgrims, were permitted to beg under pain of imprisonment and whipping. All poor persons who had resided in the provinces a whole year, were directed to remain in the places where they were settled, and were to share in the alms that were ordered them. Collections for this purpose were to be made at poor-houses, brotherhoods, and hospitals; and the magistrates were to collect alms in the churches and private houses once or twice every week. Idlers and rogues were to be compelled to work. Poor women and orphan children were to be provided for, and the latter put to school and taught on Sundays and holidays their paternoster, creed, and ten commandments; and, at a proper age, to be placed out in service or trade.*

Such were the laws enacted for the maintenance of the poor, the regulation of wages, and other matters immediately affecting the labouring classes; although they do not evince much knowledge of political economy in the legislature, they show a spirit of benevolence, and even of justice. The prominent evils which afflicted society after the decline of vassalage, were the vast increase in the number of those who were able, but unwilling, to work, and of those who were real objects of commiseration, and without claim on others, or the means of supporting themselves. Hence, the objects of legislation were twofold—preventive and charitable; to coerce the idle vagrant into habits of industry, and to relieve the infirm, aged, and real unfortunate. The same objects have continued to engage attention from the fourteenth to the nineteenth century: the great object of our vagrant and poor-laws being to punish the idle, and relieve the necessitous; and the chief difference between the two periods is, that in the latter the difficulty is not to subdue reckless vagabondage, but to find productive sources of employment.

* Anderson's *History of Commerce*, vol. ii. p. 55.

CHAP. IV.

Influence of the Reformation on Property, and the Condition of the Labouring Classes—Immense Wealth of the Religious Houses—Mistaken Notions on the Hospitality of the Conventual Bodies—Increase of Mendicity, and severe Laws for its Repression.

THE influence of the Reformation on the condition of the labouring classes has been greatly exaggerated or misunderstood. That great event affected much more the property than the industry of the community ; by causing a transfer of a large portion of the soil of the kingdom from the spiritual corporations into the hands of lay individuals. The effect of this new disposition of ecclesiastical possessions has been variously represented by writers. Discontent is inseparable from the reform of every established practice and institution. Those who profit by abuses, and those who benefit by their removal, must view in different lights and hold forth different representations of measures by which they are oppositely affected. Of the favourable influence of the Reformation on the progress of national wealth no doubt can exist at this day ; since every one is aware that incorporate bodies are little adapted to the successful pursuit of either commerce or agriculture ; and it is evident from the Mortmain Act, passed in the reign of Henry VII., that government had become fully sensible of the hurtful tendency of the vast accumulations of the religious houses. It is not so much the excellence of our political institutions as the Reformation, which, by severing the property of the community from an indolent priesthood, has enabled the people to take the lead of the nations of Europe in the career of wealth and intelligence. Had the vast possessions of the clergy remained tied up in their hands, it must have formed an insuperable obstacle to the development of the productive power of the country, and it would probably have presented no more distinguished spectacle of internal improvement than those states of the continent that continued for centuries later the victims of an impoverishing superstition.

The amount of revenue ingulfed by an insatiable priesthood cannot now be precisely ascertained. Of the annual value of 388 religious houses, we have no estimate ; but computing the value of these in the same proportion, as of the 653 of which we have the returns, the total revenue of the 1041 houses in England and Wales was 273,106*l*., —a prodigious sum in those days if we consider the relative value of money, and the smallness of the national income. Incredible as this revenue is, it was only the reserved rents of manors and demesnes, without including the tithes of appropriations, fines, heriots, renewals, deodands, &c., which would probably have amounted to twice as much. Upon good authority it is stated the clergy were proprietors of seven-tenths of the whole kingdom ; and, out of the three remaining tenths, thus kindly left to king, lords, and commons, were the four numerous orders of mendicants to be maintained, against whom no gate could be shut, to whom no provision could be denied, and from whom no secret could be concealed. Such representations of ecclesiastical cupidity would appear inadmissible, were they not corroborated by more recent instances in the state of church property in Spain, Italy, and France before the revolution, and of Ireland in the nineteenth century.

Although the policy of dissolving the monastic institutions is unquestionable, there may reasonably prevail difference of opinion regarding the appropriation of their confiscated revenues. The wily and self-willed monarch, indeed, who ventured on this great measure may be justly charged with a breach of faith. It is well known that Henry VIII., to obtain the concurrence of the parliament in his project of spoliation, declared that the revenues of the abbeys should not be converted to the king's private use, but applied towards the exigencies of state, and that no demands should in future be made on his subjects for loans, subsidies, and other aids. At the suppression of the monasteries, however, no provision was made to carry the king's promises into effect; and Lord Coke remarks, that the king, in the very year when the great and opulent priory of St. John of Jerusalem was suppressed, demanded subsidies both from the laity and clergy. The parties who ultimately benefited by the disso-

lusion were the aristocracy, who acquired not only
the chief portion of the abbey-lands, but the numerous benefices and tithes appropriated to them.

It has been represented by some, that the Reformation operated unfavourable on the interests of the
working classes, by depriving them of the almsgiving
and hospitality of the conventual bodies. The great
northern rebellion has been ascribed by Mr. Hallam,
to the summary abolition of the religious houses, and
it is apparent, from the language of the popular ballads
of the time, the poor were hostile to their dissolution.
But this dissatisfaction may have originated in the
ignorance of the people, and the power possessed by
the clergy to impress them with mistaken apprehensions of the tendency of the Reformation. While
the people continue unenlightened, they must always
continue subject to their superiors, or those who
possess influence enough to direct or delude them.
A similar union of selfishness and vulgar apprehension opposed the opening of turnpike-roads, and the
introduction of the cow-pox, steam-carriages, and
machinery. With respect to the charitable doles of
the convents, Sir F. Eden, with reason, greatly
doubts, whether the monasteries generally, troubled
themselves with relieving the poor that did not
immediately belong to their own demesnes. The
same sort of charity was usually practised by the
nobility on their estates. The truth is, the abbeys
were more burdened with the *rich* than the *poor*.
Sheriffs and other great men often travelled from
abbey to abbey with great retinues, and besides

regaling themselves at each, extorted considerable presents at their departure. That the charity of the monks was not very lively might be inferred from their conduct in respect of the appropriate livings. By masses and obits, and other sanctimonious pretexts, they had possessed themselves of a large number of the richest benefices in the kingdom; instead of applying the incomes of these to the purposes of religion and charity, they perverted them to the enriching of their own fraternities, and a compulsory act of the legislature (15 R. II. c. 6.) was necessary to compel them to restore to the poor a portion of their rights, and allow a decent maintenance to the parish priest.

The merits of the Reformation, and of the sovereign under whose auspices it was effected, are very different questions. Henry VIII., it is now admitted, was determined in his conduct, more by personal resentments, by low prejudices, and motives of avarice, than just indignation against the abuses of monastic institutions. But the vices of the individual, in this instance, happily tended to the public benefit. How favourable the new disposition of ecclesiastical estates was to the advancement of national wealth has been adverted to, and it may be added that the intellectual and moral advantages were still more indisputable. Knowledge was incompatible with the power of the monks whose influence was founded on the general belief of miracles, the sanctity of relics, and other pious frauds, to which popular enlightenment would have been fatal.

Hence their dispersion became a necessary preliminary to freedom of discussion, and the general diffusion of science and literature. It is difficult to imagine how the religious orders themselves could suffer by the change in their condition. A life of celibacy, seclusion, and the unceasing iteration of religious solemnities is so unnatural, that it could not be favourable either to virtue or happiness. If exempt from the cares of life, they were also unparticipant, without hypocrisy or a violation of religious vows, of its pleasures; it was an unnatural and artificial mode of existence, which could only have originated in the most gloomy and mistaken notions of religious duty.

The great increase of monasteries was the radical inconvenience of the Catholic religion, and every other disadvantage attending that communion was inseparably connected with their institution. Papal usurpations, the tyranny of the inquisition, the multiplication of holidays, all these fetters on liberty and industry, were derived from the regular clergy. They also fostered a vicious dependence among the laity, by supporting a numerous and idle poor, whose sustenance depended upon what was daily distributed as alms at the gates of the religious houses. Upon the total dissolution of these, the inconvenience of thus encouraging habits of indolence and beggary, was quickly felt throughout the kingdom; and abundance of statutes were made, in the reign of Henry VIII., for providing for the poor and impotent, which, as the preambles of some of

them recite, had of late years strangely increased.
This evil no doubt was occasioned by the expulsion
of the religious, as well as the cessation of the
accustomed charitable doles.   By the suppression of
the monasteries, 50,000 monks were converted into
miserable state pensioners ; and, unaccustomed to
the active exertions of industry, were thrown among
the busy crowd, to whose manners and modes of
life a long seclusion from the world had rendered
them indifferent.   The necessary consequence of
forcing so many helpless individuals into society,
was to add to the amount, and still more to aggravate the spectacle of wretchedness and vagabondage,
under which the community had so long suffered
and the legislature vainly essayed to subdue.

The state of the market of labour, for many years
before and after the Reformation, presented a contrast to the present ; the chief difficulty in the former
era not being to find sources of productive employment for the working people, but to bring them
into habits of industry.   To conquer the propensity
to " idleness and vagabondries," most severe laws
were enacted early in the reign of Edward VI.   In
the preambles to the 1st Edw. VI. c. 3, it is declared,
" that the godly acts which had hitherto been framed
on the subject had not had the successe which might
have been wished," and which is partly ascribed to
the " foolish pitie and mercie, of those who should
have seene the same godly laws executed."   It is
then provided, that if any person refuse to labour,
and live idly three days, he shall be branded with a

rod-hot iron on the breast with the letter V, and he
adjudged the *slave* for two years of the person who
informed against the idler.   And the master is directed to feed his slave with bread and water, or
small drink, and such refuse meat as he thinks
proper; and to cause his slave to work by beating
or chaining him.   If the slave absconds for fourteen
days, he is condemned to slavery for life; and *if he*
runs away a second time, he is liable to suffer death
as a felon.   These enactments were too severe even
for the age, and were speedily repealed.   The latter
part of the statute provides that certain of the poor
shall be employed by the town, or by individuals
who would provide them meat and drink for their
work.   This is the mode by which the poor in many
of the parishes in the south of England are maintained.   They are called *roundsmen*, from going
round the town from house to house to solicit employment.

CHAP. V.

Decay of the Nobility—Progress of the Middle Classes—Rise
of Country Gentlemen—Industry fettered by Patents and
Monopolies—Absence of Police, and dreadful Disorders—
Manners and Education—Diet and Dress—Abortive Efforts
to fix Price of Labour—Compulsory Assessment for the Poor
forced on the Legislature after the Failure of other Expedients.

HAVING adverted to the changes consequent on
the introduction of commerce and manufactures,

and to the influence of the Reformation on property and the condition of the labouring classes, it is important to mark the progress of the middle orders about the same period.

In pursuing the various occupations of industry, the people had discovered the means of emancipating themselves from feudal servitude : and the nobility, in judiciously preferring a turn of expense, which promoted the arts, to the coarse enjoyments of baronial splendour, which were the source of idleness and disorder, had necessarily exchanged their personal authority for private luxury and comfort. While their individual influence over their dependents was thus gradually wasting away, their collective preponderance in the scale of government which had often enabled them to resist, even kingly power, with success, was completely overthrown by the destructive wars between the Yorkists and Lancasterians. So many ancient families were annihilated in the contest, and so many noblemen on both sides perished either in the field or on the scaffold, that Henry VII. could only summon twenty-eight peers to his first parliament : nor was the number much increased during his reign ; only thirty-six temporal peers were summoned to the first parliament of Henry VIII. By the dissolution of the monasteries, the ecclesiastical branch of the aristocracy was destroyed ; and many of the obstacles that had opposed the progress of industry being removed, the middling ranks insensibly advanced to wealth and independence ; although it is justly observed by

Hume, that in the interval between the fall of the nobles and the rise of this order, many of our monarchs availed themselves of the times, and assumed an authority almost absolute.

Other causes had materially contributed to lessen the ascendancy of the aristocratic orders. It had been the sage policy of Henry VII. to unfetter the territorial possessions of the great landholders, and thereby promote a more general partition of proprietary influence. The statutes which enabled the nobility to alienate their estates, the seizure and sale of the abbey-lands, and the general effects of increasing opulence must have powerfully operated towards a more equal division of property, than could possibly have taken place in times when the nation was poorer, and the shackles of mortmain and entails more rigidly observed. Under the influence of this policy, a great portion of the estates of the nobility and church passed into the hands of the COUNTRY GENTLEMEN,—an intermediate order of proprietors which was now fast increasing in number and importance, and forming a new and influential section of society. Contemporary with the rise of this class, was the decay, and ultimate extinction of the cottar tenantry, which was a consequence necessarily resulting from the improved state of agriculture. The half-starved proprietor of ten or twenty acres, will often be persuaded to part with his land to a rich neighbour, who farms, with peculiar advantages on a larger scale. These changes, which indicated increasing wealth, caused no little alarm to the legislature; and it was often attempted to "make farms and houses of husbandry of a standard;" a device, which Lord Bacon dignifies with the appellation of "profound and admirable!" The mistaken idea of limiting the size of farms, appears to bear some analogy to the late doctrine of equality in possessions, and would have been alike hostile to improvement, enterprise, and national wealth.

Another change in society may be noticed about this period in the decline of cities and boroughs. In the 3d Henry VIII. c. 8, it is remarked that most cities, boroughs, and towns corporate, had fallen into decay, and were no longer inhabited by merchants and men of substance, but principally by brewers, vintners, fishmongers, and other victuallers, which is the state of many country towns, where the only business carried on is created by the consumption of the inhabitants. Mr. Hume ascribes the decay of provincial towns to the establishment of a more regular police and stricter administration of justice, which, by the greater protection they afforded, encouraged men of property to retire into the country. But the principal cause was doubtless the decline of corporate immunities, which though useful in the early establishment of towns for their security, yet when industry had taken firm root in the kingdom, became not only unnecessary but oppressive, as tradesmen were prevented carrying on their occupations within them unless qualified by patrimony, apprenticeship, or purchase. Manufacturers, no longer requiring the protection of corporations, settled in places enjoying local advantages best adapted to their pursuits, and where they were unfettered by chartered immunities. That such was the case is evinced by the flourishing state of the open towns in the sixteenth century. Birmingham, even in Leland's time, was eminent for its cutlery; and Manchester, so early as 1552, appears to have been a place of considerable importance. An act passed in that year notices its " cottons, rugges, and frizes." In the 33d Henry VIII. c. 15, passed in 1541, it is remarked, that Manchester had a long time been well inhabited; and the inhabitants well set to work in making of cloths as well of linen as of woollen, whereby the inhabitants of the said town have gotten and come unto riches and wealthy livings; and by reason of great occupying, good order, strict and true dealing of the inhabitants of the said town, many strangers as well of Ireland as of other places had resorted thither."

Notwithstanding these evidences of improvement, various causes continued to impede the progress of national industry. One of these was the prerogative of the crown as exercised in purveyance and monopolies. Of the oppressions arising from the former, Lord Bacon has given a long detail, and with regard to monopolies, there was hardly a commodity of importance that was not tied up in the grasp of a patentee. Iron, tin, leather, paper, starch, wool, yarn, salt, sea-coal, and beer, form but a small part of the long list of articles, the exclusive sale of which was vested in individuals, who by virtue of their privileges were enabled to fix on commodities an arbitrary and extortionate price : a member of the House of Commons might well express his surprise that bread was not of the number—an omission, however, which has been subsequently supplied, if not by regal by aristocratic cupidity.

The police of the county was also extremely defective, and shows that the community was far from having attained a general state of order and security. This, however, did not result from a lenient infliction of criminal punishment ; for never were severe laws issued in greater profusion nor executed more vigorously, and never did the unrelenting vengeance of justice prove more ineffectual. Harrison assures us, that Henry VIII. executed his laws with such severity that 72,000 " great and petty thieves were put to death during his reign." He adds, that even in Elizabeth's reign, " rogues were trussed up apace ;" and that there was not "one year commonly wherein 300 or 400 of them were not devoured and eaten up by the gallows in one place and other." In spite of these sanguinary punishments the country continued in a dreadful state of disorder. Every part of the kingdom was infested with robbers and idle vagabonds, who, refusing to labour, lived by plundering the peaceable inhabitants ; and, often strolling about the country in bodies of 300 or 400, they attacked with impunity the sheepfolds and dwellings of the people. The laws and police were totally inadequate to control these ruthless spirits, who, by rendering both property and persons inse-

E

ours, checked the rising prosperity of the country. The cause of these outrages may be partly traced to the changes which had just then taken place in society; the abolition of villanage was undoubtedly both just and beneficial; but the transition of a large body of people, still comparatively barbarous and uninstructed, from bondage to free labour, was naturally attended with transitory outrage and confusion.

Besides the country had not yet attained any thing like a state of refinement as may be learnt from Dr. Henry's description of the defective system of education and manners still prevalent among the better sort. Schools were rare; and before the Reformation young men were educated in monasteries, women in nunneries, where the latter were instructed in writing, drawing, confectionary, and needle-work, and, what were then regarded as female accomplishments, in physic and surgery. The acquisitions of the former were limited to writing, and a tincture probably of barbarous Latin, but ignorance was so common that Fitzherbert recommends to gentlemen, unable to commit notes to writing, the practice of notching a stick to assist their memories. When removed from these seminaries to the houses of their parents, both sexes were treated in a manner that precluded improvement. Domestic manners were severe and formal; a haughty reserve was affected by the old, and an abject deference exacted from the young. Sons when arrived at manhood are represented as standing silent and uncovered in their father's presence; and daughters, though women, were placed like statues at the cupboard, nor permitted to sit and repose themselves otherwise than by kneeling on a cushion till their mother retired. Omissions were punished by stripes and blows, and chastisement was carried to such excess, that the daughters trembled at the sight of their mother, and the sons avoided and hated their father.

The diet of the people does not appear to have greatly differed from the present. In cities meat entered into the general consumption of the inhabitants. But the food of agricultural labourers was of an inferior kind. In Henry the Eighth's reign bacon seems to have constituted a part of the diet of labourers, but this only in inconsiderable quantities, and it is probable they lived in much the same manner as husbandmen in the north of England did in the last century, and the Scotch peasantry do in the present, their food consisting chiefly of oat and rye bread, milk, and pottage. The substantial diet for which the sixteenth century is renowned was limited to the tables of persons of rank. A maid of honour of Elizabeth's court perhaps breakfasted on beef-steaks, but the ploughman was compelled to regale himself on barley or rye bread and water-gruel. Of dress Moryson observes, "husbandmen weare garments of course cloth made at home, and their wives weare gownes of the same cloth, kirtles of some light stuffe with linnen aprons, and cover their heads with a linnen coyfe and a felt hat, and in general their linnen is course and made at home."

I cannot more appropriately conclude the chapter

than by one or two remarks on the general tendency of the system under which the legislature endeavoured to regulate the labouring class prior to the introduction of the great and final act of Elizabeth in 1601. Experience is a valuable instructor, and we derive an important advantage from the history of the poor in the light it throws on the tendency of suggestions often made for bettering their condition. For nearly two centuries the price of labour was fixed by public proclamation. The injurious, if not futile, tendency of this interference, hardly needs demonstration. The price of labour, like that of other commodities, is best determined by the proportion between the supply and demand ; and it cannot with advantage, either to workman or employer, be regulated by any other principle. If the profits of the master are great, his capital will augment, he will be enabled to employ more labourers, and the competition being increased, the rate of wages will rise. If, on the other hand, profits decline, the fund for paying wages will decline also, and the remuneration of the labourer will be abated. But how, in either case, could the legislature advantageously fix either a minimum or maximum of wages? To compel a master to give higher wages than he could afford and would be voluntarily disposed to give, must necessarily tend to his impoverishment and to destroy his branch of trade; and to compel him to give lower under similar circumstances, would, besides unnecessarily depressing the workman, tend to keep back the supply of labour adequate to the demand.

These are the consequences which would ensue, supposing the interference of the legislature efficient. But the fact is, it would be nugatory. Nothing could prevent the master giving, nor the workman taking, whatever rate of wages suited their respective interests, and all coercive provisions to enforce a contrary conduct would be easily evaded.

I shall only notice one more advantage derivable from the history of the poor. It has been sometimes suggested that a modified system of poor-laws should be introduced into Ireland. This might be allowable, by way of familiarizing the inhabitants with the machinery of their administration; but there is little doubt that the entire system would at length become necessary. In England a similar course was tried, and it was only after the failure of more lenient methods the compulsory principle was adopted. At first parishes were only compelled to maintain their poor, and this they were at liberty to do by the aid of alms and voluntary donations obtained by the gentle exhortations of ministers and the charitable persuasions of bishops. But it was soon found that neither sufficient funds could be obtained by this means, nor would the collectors for the poor render faithful accounts of the sums they received. It was in consequence of this double failure that 5 Eliz. c. 3, gives a power to the bishops to commit collectors to gaol till they settle their accounts; and the statute adds, that if the persons who had been exhorted by the bishop, or his ordinary, shall "obstinately refuse to give weekly to the relief of the

poor, according to his ability, the bishop, or his
ordinary, shall bind him by recognizance to appear
at the quarter-sessions : and at the said sessions, the
justices shall gently persuade and move him ; " and
if he will not be persuaded, they are authorized to
tax him a weekly sum, and commit him to prison
till it is paid.   It is thus apparent the compulsory
system was forced on the legislature, after experience of the failure of milder expedients.

CHAP. VI.

Act of the 43d of Elizabeth—Provisions of the English Poor-
laws derived from Scotland—Curious Expedients for Relief
of the Poor—Act against the Erection of Cottages—Alarm
about the Increase of the Metropolis—Excess of Population
—Pestilence—Comparison of the Elizabethan Age with the
present.

WE are now approaching an important era in the
history of the poor, namely, the introduction of that
system of compulsory maintenance which, without
material alteration, has continued for upwards of
two centuries. The long reign of Elizabeth is filled
with statutes for suppressing the deficiencies or correcting the errors of former poor-laws.   In the year
1597 several acts were passed relative to vagrancy
and mendicity, and the provisions of former acts
in some degree moulded into a uniform system.
In one act four overseers are directed to be chosen
in each parish for setting poor children and others

in want of employment to work, and for raising,
weekly or otherwise, a stock of materials for that
purpose. Justices are empowered to levy the rate
by distress : and for the relief of the impotent poor
the churchwardens and overseers are authorized, with
the permission of the lords of manors, to build convenient houses on the waste, at the general charge
of the parish, and to place inmates of more families than one in each cottage. Parents of old,
blind, lame, and other poor persons, are bound to
relieve their children as should be directed at the general quarter-sessions, on penalty of twenty shillings
for every month they failed so to do. And begging,
unless for victuals, in the parish, is entirely prohibited.
Several acts were also passed for the relief of soldiers
and mariners, and every parish charged a certain
sum weekly for their maintenance.

Increasing inconveniences, at length, produced
the memorable 43d of Elizabeth, which concen-
trates in one act the accumulated experience of
previous years, and still forms the groundwork of
our poor-laws. By comparing this statute with the
provisions of that referred to in the last paragraph,
it appears that its most material provisions were not,
as many erroneously suppose, originally framed
in 1601 : on the contrary, the principal clauses of
the 39th of Elizabeth, respecting the appointment of
overseers, levying the rate, setting the able to work,
providing relief for the impotent, and binding out
children apprentices, were copied almost *verbatim*.
From the tenour of the last clause in this great legis-

lative measure, it was evidently intended only to be
experimental.   It was, however, continued by subsequent statutes; and, by the 16th Car. I. c. 4, made
perpetual.

Although Scotland is, for the most part, exempted
from the poor-rate, it is remarkable that a compulsory provision for the poor was established by law
in that kingdom twenty-two years before the passing
of the 43d of Elizabeth.   In James the Sixth's parliament, held at Edinburgh in 1579, an act was
passed in which every branch of the English system,
the punishment of vagabonds—of runaway servants
—the mode of passing soldiers and seamen to their
parishes—the regulation of hospitals for aged and
impotent persons—the settlements of the poor—
their maintenance by the parish—the appointment
of overseers and collectors—the manner of treating
those who refuse to work—and on putting out poor
children apprentices—are more fully detailed than
in any English statute. The assessment for the poor
is very general : " the hail inhabitants within the
parochin" are to be " taxed and stented according
to the estimation of their substance, without exception of persones, to sik oublie (weekly) charge and
contribution, as sall be thocht expedient and sufficient to susteine the saidis pure peopil." *

* Eden's *Hist. Poor, Scottish Acts,* 1682, 1, 1417.   It is
the opinion of Sir F. Eden that many of the provisions of
English parliaments in the reign of Elizabeth, respecting the
poor, were framed in conformity with the policy of their northern
neighbours.

It is, impossible, at this distance of time, to form any accurate idea of the comparative number of the receivers and payers of parochial contributions immediately after the establishment of the poor-rate. Sir F. Eden was of opinion that, at the period he wrote (1797), the pauper class constituted a larger proportion of the community than at the close of the sixteenth and the beginning of the seventeenth centuries. But the fact is, though the act of 1601 empowered parishes to levy a poor-rate, it was not for many years after carried into execution in various parts of the kingdom. The author of a pamphlet published in 1698, entitled " Bread for the Poor," says that, " though parishes were enabled (by the 43d of Elizabeth) to make rates, and the owners of estates obliged to the payment, yet, in many places, no such rates were made in twenty or thirty years after."

It is probable that the dearth of corn and other articles of subsistence which took place towards the close of Elizabeth's reign greatly accelerated the passing of the act for raising a compulsory poor-rate. In 1587 wheat rose to 3*l.* 4*s.* the quarter ; in 1594 it was 2*l.* 16*s.*, and in 1595, 2*l.* 13*s.* 4*d.* the quarter. For several years there had been a succession of bad weather and scanty crops. In the year 1601, however, the season was more favourable ; which, by rendering the condition of the poor more comfortable, concurred to recommend, even beyond its deserts, the new measure of the legislature.

Among the various funds appropriated to the relief of the poor, previous to the act of 1601, may be mentioned pecuniary forfeitures which, for many statutable offences, especially those relative to profaneness and immorality, are now applied in aid of the poor-rate. As early as 1558, churchwardens were empowered to levy twelvepence upon every parishioner who omitted going to church on Sunday. In 1570 a moiety of the forfeitures for detaining goods belonging to a bankrupt's estate was directed to be distributed among the poor of the town in which the bankrupt was resident; and, in the same parliament, half the penalty for not wearing a woollen cap on a Sunday was appropriated to the same purpose. One-third of the fines for saying mass, and other offences against the established worship, were given to the poor; also penalties for swearing, tippling, and disorderly conduct on the Lord's day. It is not improbable these various mulcts for offences against religion and morality were intended as part compensation to the poor for the loss they had sustained by the dissolution of the monasteries and new disposition of ecclesiastical property.

An impression appears to have been entertained, in the sixteenth and beginning of the seventeenth centuries, that population was increasing faster than the funds for its employment, and that it was necessary to discourage its further augmentation by legislative measures. In the 31st year of Elizabeth's reign a curious act passed, entitled *An Act against the Erecting and Maintaining of Cottages*, which, after reciting that " great inconveniences have been found by experience to grow by the erecting and building of great numbers and multitude of cottages, which are daily more and more increased in many parts of this realm," enacts that, for the time to come, no such tenement shall be erected, unless *four acres* of land be attached to it.* With a similar view was the act or proclamation (for in Elizabeth's reign they were nearly synonymous) issued in 1581, forbidding the erection of new buildings within three miles of the city gates, and limiting the number of inmates in a house to one family. In the year 1630 Charles I. issued a similar proclamation against building houses on new foundations in London or Westminster, or within three miles of the city or the king's palaces. The proclamation also forbade the receiving of inmates in houses, which (it was said) would multiply the inhabitants to such an excessive number, that they could neither be governed nor fed ! There are, however, some judicious regulations in this proclamation for the prevention of fires and the preservation of the health of the inhabitants. All new houses are directed to have partywalls and fronts of brick ; and the windows to be higher than wide, both for the admission of air, and for rendering the piers between them more solid than they would otherwise have been. These provisions have been consider-

* In the year 1638 there was a special commission from Charles I. for enforcing this statute.—*Rymer's Fœdera*, 20, 256. The act of Elizabeth is repealed by 15 Geo. III. c. 32.

ably enlarged by subsequent statutes, particularly by the Building Act, the enforcing of which (though imperfect in its provisions) has doubtless greatly contributed towards the health, the safety, and the beauty of the metropolis.

The deterioration in the cirumstances of the people, no less than the public acts, are evidence of the increasing pressure of population. In 1495 a labourer could purchase with his wages 199 pints of wheat; in the year 1593 only 82 pints; in 1610 only 46 pints. So that in the reign of James I., a labourer could obtain only one-fourth part of the necessaries and conveniences which be obtained in the reign of Henry VII.* The increase of indigence was accompanied with its usual calamity, an increase of crime. A magistrate of Somersetshire, writing in 1596, affirms that " forty persons had been executed in that county in a year, for various felonies, thirty-five burnt in the hand, thirty-seven whipped, one hundred and eighty-three discharged; that those who were discharged, were most wicked and desperate persons, who never would come to any good, because they would not work, and none would take them into service: that notwithstanding the great number of indictments, the fifth part of the felonies committed in the county, were not brought to trial; and the greater number escaped censure, either from the superior cunning of the felons, the remissness of the magistrates, or the foolish lenity

* *On the Growing Excess of Population*, 10. By John Barton. London, 1830.

of the people. That the other counties of England were in no better condition than Somersetshire, and some of them in a worse."[*]

The struggle between law and criminality—legislation and a growing population—schemes of charitable relief—and the increasing privations of the people, appear to have terminated in the severe visitations of pestilence in the succeeding century. In the year 1603 no less than 36,000 persons were swept off in London alone; twenty years after, about the same number perished; in 1636 above 10,000 died; and 68,596 persons died in the last great plague of 1665! The conflagration which destroyed the city occurred in 1666; after which, the plague languished, and finally disappeared from the bills of mortality in 1679. The destruction of capital and industry, involved in these terrible disasters, had a sensible influence on the progress of the country during the next hundred years. Population only again began to increase rapidly about the year 1780. From the survey made to meet the Spanish invasion, in 1575, the aggregate population of the kingdom has been estimated at four and a half millions.[†] According to the inquiries of Mr. Rickman, it amounted only to 5,475,000 in 1700; in the next fifty years, it increased only about a million: but, in the fifty years that have elapsed, from 1780 to 1831, it has increased from 7,953,000, to 13,894,574.

In the opinion of Mr. Barton, the present state of

* Eden's State of the Poor, vol i. p. 111.
† Supplement to Encyclopedia Britannica, vol. iv. p. 149.

the country resembles that which marked the close of the reign of Elizabeth. Both periods exhibit symptoms of the population having outgrown the existing means of employment and subsistence. In both there is a diminution in the rate of wages, and of course, in the means of procuring, by the body of the people, a sufficiency of wholesome food; needful clothing, good lodging, and the other necessaries of life. Let us, however, hope, that the catastrophe will be different; and that the foreknowledge of a more enlightened age, will avert the frightful calamities of the former era !

Although the population, on the accession of the Stuarts, was little more than one-third of what it is at present, it appears to have been considered excessive, by the statesmen of that day; and doubtless, was so measured by the productive resources of the country : for the redundancy of the people is not to be estimated by their numerical amount, but by the proportion they bear to the means for their support, accommodation, and employment. We may smile at the fears of Charles the First, that the capital would become so large, that it could neither be " governed nor fed." This, however, might be a reasonable apprehension two centuries ago, when London was, doubtless, a huge and unsightly spectacle—appearing something like modern Constantinople to an European—without police or local conveniences.*   But its means have increased

* The population of the city of London, in the beginning of the last century, was not much less than 140,000, and the an-

with its wants, and our ancestors would have been quite incredulous, had they been told that it would, hereafter, contain one-third as many inhabitants as the whole country in the days of Lord Burleigh; and they would have been still harder of belief, had they been assured, that with this vast assemblage of human beings, it was more orderly, more amply supplied with water and provisions, more salubrious, and less crowded, than when it contained only one-tenth of the number. What would have been a string of paradoxes in the sixteenth century, have become absolute facts in the nineteenth. It shows that mankind are not prophets in any age, and, that great prospective evils, are often balanced and counteracted, by accompanying advantages.

and mortality was as one to twenty of that population. Fortunately for the health of the citizens, space is become more valuable for warehouses than for human habitations, so that the population of the city within the walls is diminished to 55,778, and the rate of mortality to less than one in forty.—*Remarks by John Rickman, prefixed to Population Returns of* 1831. The average deaths in the Metropolis are about one-fifth less than those in Paris; and the average mortality in the former differs only by a small fraction from that of the whole of France. The annual deaths in Vienna average 1 in $22\frac{1}{2}$ of the inhabitants; Amsterdam, 1 in 24; Rome, 1 in 25; Madrid, 1 in 29: nearly equal to the mortality in London 130 years since.

CHAP. VII.

Chronological Digest of Facts relative to the Industrious Orders, from the Introduction of the Poor-laws to the Present Time.

THE condition of the several classes of society, and their relations to each other, have not undergone any material change since the introduction of the celebrated act of Elizabeth; and, so far as the poor are concerned, the great object of the legislature and individuals has been either to improve the administration, or correct the abuses of a system previously established. The measures for these purposes have been almost innumerable; but, as it would both exceed the limits of these pages, and be void of utility to detail them at length, I shall content myself with briefly noticing, in chronological order, the more important acts, suggestions, discoveries, and occurrences which have had any influence on the state of the industrious orders.

A. D. 1604. Under 2 Jac. I., it is enacted that rogues adjudged incorrigible and dangerous shall be "branded on the left shoulder with a hot iron of the breadth of a shilling, having a Roman R upon it, and placed to labour; if, after such punishment, they are found begging and wandering, they shall be adjudged felons and suffer death." The severe penalties of this act continued in force till the 12th Anne, when they were modified; and, at length, a just distinction was made between idle and disorderly persons, and rogues and vagabonds.

Parliament continued to act on the futile expedient of fixing the rate of wages; under the 2d Jac. I. c. 6, the powers of justices in rating are extended to "all labourers, weavers, spinsters, and workmen, or workwomen whatsoever, either working by the day, the week, month, year, or taking work at any person's hands whatsoever to be done in great or otherwise."

From expressions in the 2d Jac. I. c. 9, against tippling, it appears that at this period it was common, even for country labourers, both to eat their meals and to lodge in inns and alehouses; but it is uncertain whether this mode of living was occasioned by the statute of Elizabeth which prohibited the erection of cottages, and the statutes of inmates, which (in the city of London, and probably in other corporate towns) limited the number of inmates in a house to one family; or whether it was an intermediate state in the progress of society from the absolute dependance of the slave on his master for diet and habitation, to the improved condition of the free labourer, who, at present, rarely resides under the same roof with his employer.

Among the useful laws enacted during the reign of James I. may be mentioned the act for securing the subject against antiquated claims of the crown on lands which had been enjoyed 60 years; the act for putting down monopolies, and the act for repeal-

F

ing the absurd laws of Henry VIII. and Elizabeth
for promoting tillage. It is, however, mortifying
to reflect, that while these salutary measures were
adopted by parliament, neither a Coke, nor a Bacon,
should oppose the law suggested by royal superstition for making it felony to " consult, covenant
with, entertain, employ, feed, or reward any evil
and wicked spirit." Even Sir Matthew Hale left a
man for execution who was convicted of witchcraft,
under the 2d Jac. I. c. 12 : and, so recently as the
year 1711, a British jury could be found, at Hereford,
ignorant enough to be persuaded that a woman
could converse with the devil in the shape of a cat.

A. D. 1610. The high price of butcher's meat
in the reign of James I. (the necessary consequence
of agricultural improvement) is a strong proof that
flesh meat constituted an inconsiderable portion of
the diet of labourers at the beginning of the seventeenth century. About the period mentioned in the
margin beef was $3\frac{1}{4}d.$, and mutton $3\frac{3}{8}d.$ the pound.
At this time the wages allowed by justices in a mid-
land county to labourers in husbandry were from
sixpence to tenpence the day without meat; and to
women haymakers fourpence the day without meat.
In these ratings the magistrates calculated that half
the day's earnings were equivalent to diet for one
day, which is a much less proportion than would be
requisite at present. The price of corn was rather
higher than in the middle of the following century.
The average price of middling wheat from 1606 to

1625 was 1*l.* 14*s.* 1*d.* the quarter; whereas the average price for the twenty years, ending in 1745, was 1*l.* 9*s.* 10*d.*

While such wages and prices continued it was impossible the labourers could command an abundance of the necessaries of life. Besides many esculent plants, which are now cultivated in the fields, and in a scarcity of corn are found to be admirable substitutes even for bread, were in the beginning of the sixteenth century either little known, or exclusively confined to the tables of the rich. Potatos at present are a general article of diet; in King James's reign they were considered as a great delicacy. They are noticed among the articles provided for the queen's household: the quantity, however, is small, and the price 2*s.* the pound. In 1619 two cauliflowers cost 2*s.*, and sixteen artichokes 3*s.* 4*d.*— prices which sufficiently prove their rarity. Tea and sugar, which now form regular articles of cottage economy, were still greater rarities. The former article was not imported in any considerable quantities till after the establishment of a new East India company, with liberty to trade to China and Japan, in 1637. No notice is taken of tea in the book of rates, annexed to the act passed in 1660, for granting Charles II. a subsidy of tonnage and poundage upon all merchandise exported and imported; but in a subsequent act passed in the same session, tea, coffee, and chocolate, are subjected to the excise. It is singular, however, that the duty was imposed on the *liquor* prepared from these articles in lieu of the articles themselves; from which it may be inferred none of these beverages were made by private families, but purchased ready prepared from the compounders.

A. D. 1630. In this year certain orders were issued to the magistracy and others by the privy council, directing that justices shall divide themselves, and hold petty sessions monthly within certain districts, for watching over the administration of the poor-laws. That lords of the manor shall take care their tenants and parishioners be relieved by work or at home, and not be suffered to "straggle" and beg in their parishes. That court-leets take cognizance of all offences in buying and selling, of disorderly ale-houses, and of those that "goe in good clothes and fare well, and none knowes whereof they live; those that be night-walkers, *builders of cottages*, and takers in of inmates." That the laws for the apprenticing of poor children be enforced; and that where any money or stock has been, or shall be given to the relief of the poor in any parish, such gift to be no occasion of lessening the rates of the parish. That wandering persons, with women and children, give an account to the constable or justice where they were married, and where their children were christened; "for these people live like salvages, neither marry, nor bury, nor christen; which licentious libertie make so many delight to be rogues and wanderers."

This year is also distinguished by a singular expedient for relieving the poor, which was recommended to the inhabitants of the metropolis, in a royal proclamation issued for preventing a dearth of corn and victual. It was an old custom still observed in the royal household, by the principal nobility and gentry, and in the universities and inns of court, to take no suppers on Fridays or the eves of fast-days, nor Wednesdays and Saturdays in Ember weeks, nor in Lent; the proclamation recommends the more general observance of this custom, and that the *meat* be appropriated to the relief of the poor.

A. D. 1633. The following prices are directed to be observed in London by poulterers, victuallers and woodmongers :

	s.	d.		s.	d.
The best pheasant cock .	6	0	A henne of the best sort	1	2
A pheasant henne	5	0	A rabbit of the best sort	0	
The best turkey cook in			A dozen of wild pigeons	1	2
the market	4	4	Ditto of tame pigeons .	0	6
A heron	2	6	Three eggs	0	1
A bitterne.	2	6	A pound of the best salt		
A duck	0	8	butter	0	3½
A dozen of larks	0	10	A pound of the best fresh		
A snipe	0	4	butter	0	6
A pewit	0	10	A pound of tallow can-		
A dozen of blackbirds,			dles.	0	3½
fieldfares, or thrushes	1	0	A sack containing four		
The best fat goose in the			bushels of the best		
market	2	0	charcoal	1	2
Ditto at a poulterer's shop	2	4	A sack containing four		
A greene goose	1	2	bushels of best largest		
A capon fat & crammed,			and small coals . . .	0	6
of the best sort . . .	2	4	1000 of the best Kentish		
A pullet fat & crammed,			billets at the water-		
of the best sort in the			side.	16	0
market	1	6			

Of the wages of labourers there is little information

that can be depended on. In 1626 the king's master-saddler's daily pay was twelvepence a day for himself, and threepence halfpenny a day for his servant. The master-mason at Windsor Castle also received twelvepence a day.   To these wages were probably added perquisites : so that no conclusion can be drawn from them respecting the ordinary price of labour. In a small tract published in 1636 the diet and maintenance of a drunken vagabond is estimated at threepence a day.   In 1636 seamen in the king's navy were allowed, in harbour, sevenpence halfpenny a day for their provisions ; and, when at sea, eightpence halfpenny.   At this period, the usual bread-corn of the poorer sort of people was barley. Ordinaries were limited to two shillings a head for dinner (wine included), and to eightpence a head for a servant attending his master.*

A. D. 1650.   The author of a tract published this year recommends the fitting out of busses, and ascribes the increase of the poor to the neglect of the herring-fishery.   The same writer complains of the practice of sending undressed cloths abroad, and recommends the dyeing and dressing of them at home.

A. D. 1662.   In this year the important statute (13th and 14th Car. II. c. 12) which is the foundation of the existing law of settlements was enacted, not only for the purpose of determining who should be considered as the poor of each parish, but to pre-

* For a comparative statement of the progress of wages and prices, see Appendix.

vent labourers, before they became actually chargeable, from wandering from their usual places of abode; thereby burdening particular parishes, abounding in large commons for building cottages and extensive woods for fuel, with new comers. The 21st section of the act provides for the division of large parishes, empowering the several townships to choose their own overseers, and set to work, and provide for their own poor.

A. D. 1697. By 12 Anne, c. 18, justices are empowered to grant certificates which protect persons from removal from any parish until actually chargeable.

Sir Josiah Child proposed to establish petty banks, or *lumbards*, for the relief of the poor.

A. D. 1697. The celebrated John Locke, in his capacity of one of the commissioners of the Board of Trade, drew up a report on the state of the poor, in which he expresses an opinion that one-half of those who receive relief from parishes are able to get their livelihood; and divides all those who are allowed a parochial maintenance into three classes : first, those who can do nothing towards their own support; secondly, those who can do something, although they cannot entirely support themselves by their labour; thirdly, such as can maintain themselves by their labour. Mr. Locke then suggests the necessity of enforcing the vagrant laws; next, the establishing of working schools for the employment of those who are able and unwilling to work.

A. D. 1698. Charity-schools, for the instruction

of the most destitute of the people, who could not otherwise enjoy the benefits of education, were this year established.   They originated in the benevolence of a few individuals in London, and speedily became great favourites wit hthe community. Besides instructing poor children in reading, writing, and ciphering, they also clothed them ; the boys apprenticed to handicraft trades, and the girls prepared for service. The trustees of charity-schools formed themselves into a voluntary association in 1700, and framed rules for their better regulation.   The anniversary meeting, in St. Paul's, of the children belonging to the numerous charity-schools of the metropolis, forms one of the most attractive of our spring festivals.

A. D. 1704.   The celebrated author of Robinson Crusoe, Daniel Defoe, this year published an address to parliament, entitled " Giving Alms no Charity," in which he lays down the following heads, as fundamental maxims, which he endeavours to make out by strong facts, and powerful arguments :—1. There is in England more labour than hands to perform it ; and, consequently, a want of people, not of employment.   2. No man of sound limbs and senses can be poor, merely for want of work.   3. All workhouses, corporations, and charities for employing the poor, and setting them to work, are public nuisances which *increase the poor*.   That there is abundance of employment, he proves, by the difficulty of enlisting men for the army.   He considers the improvidence of the poor a principal cause of their wretchedness.   " We are," says this shrewd observer, "the most *lazy diligent* nation in the world : there is nothing more frequent, than for an Englishman to work till he has got his pocket full of money, and then go and be idle, or perhaps, drunk; till it is all gone. I once paid six or seven men together on a Saturday night, the least ten shillings, and some thirty shillings, for work, and have seen them go with it directly to the alehouse, lie there till Monday, spend it every penny, and run in debt to boot, and not give a farthing of it to their families, though all of them had wives and children. From hence comes poverty, parish charges, and beggary. If ever one of these wretches fell sick, all they would ask, was a pass to the parish they lived at, and the wife and children to the door a begging."

Defoe's observations on the tendency of employing the poor in workhouses are unanswerable, and constitute the staple of all the arguments subsequently employed on the same subject. "Suppose now," says he, " a workhouse for the employment of poor children, sets them to spinning of worsted. For every skein of worsted these poor children spin, there must be a skein the less spun by some poor family that spun it before. To set poor people at work on the same thing that other poor people were employed on before, and at the same time, not increasing the consumption, is giving to one what you take away from another ; enriching one poor man to starve another ; putting a vagabond in an honest man's employment, and putting his diligence on the ten-ters, to find out some other work to maintain his family."

The author adds many other interesting observations upon the subject. It is, however, very justly observed by Mr. Ruggles, that, although Defoe pretends, that he could propose a regulation of the poor, which would put a stop to poverty, beggary, parish assessments, and the like; he waves the performance of his promise, for this very inadequate reason; because he will not "presume to lead a body so august, so wise, and so capable, as the honourable House of Commons, to whom his treatise is addressed."

A. D. 1714. Little alteration was made in the poor system by the laws passed during the reign of George the First. The act of Queen Anne, which enjoined woollen manufacturers to pay their workmen in money, was enforced by additional penalties; and, in order effectually to employ the poor in the silk and woollen manufactures, the use of printed calicoes, either in apparel, household stuff, or furniture, was prohibited by an act passed in 1720.

It appears, from the 5th of Geo. I. c. 8, that it was not an uncommon practice for persons of property to abscond, and leave their families chargeable to the parish; to remedy this, the parish officers were empowered to seize the chattels, and receive the rents of such absentees, and appropriate them to the maintenance of their families.

John Bellers republished his *Proposals for em-*

ploying the Poor in a College of Industry. " The poor," says this writer, " without employment, are like rough diamonds : their worth is unknown." The substance of Bellers's proposal, was to raise a fund, and employ the poor in the cultivation of the waste lands of the kingdom.

A. D. 1721. Dr. Leslie, in his *Essay on the Divine Right of Tithes*, after admitting that the poor, before the Reformation, were generally maintained by the clergy, proposed as the most effectual remedy for the growing evil of poor-rates, then estimated at a million a year, to charge all the poor again upon the church lands and tithes.

A. D. 1723. To check the facility with which justices had granted orders for parochial relief, the 9th Geo. I. c. 7, enacts, that no person shall be relieved, till oath be made before a justice, of reasonable cause, and till the applicant has applied to a vestry, or two overseers, and been refused relief, and the justice has summoned the overseers to show cause why such relief was not given. It also provides that the parish officers, with the consent of the major part of the parishioners, may purchase or hire any house in the parish, and contract with persons for the *lodging, employing, and keeping* of poor persons. Many parishes immediately availed themselves of the power to farm out their poor granted by the act.

Immediately after the introduction of the workhouse system, such was the aversion of the poor to the confinement and employment it subjected them to, that the number of claimants for parish aid was, in most places, reduced a half. Besides reducing the number of paupers, the workhouses appear at first to have maintained them at a much lower rate than they could be supported by weekly pensions at their own houses. Before the erection of a workhouse at Hampstead, in the year 1727, the poor received from 2s. 6d. to 3s. 6d. each person in out-pensions; in the house they cost about two shillings a week each person. Of the usual expense of maintaining a pauper in the reign of George the First, an estimate may be formed from the following particulars :

At Hanslope, in Buckinghamshire, in 1724, the average cost of the diet, lodging, and maintenance of each person in the workhouse was 1s. 6d. weekly.

At Westham, in Essex, the average maintenance of each person for a year in the workhouse was five pounds.

The diet in Stroud workhouse cost 1s. 8½d. a week each person.

In St. George's, Hanover Square, in 1730, 154 poor were lodged and dieted four weeks for 55l. 1s. 7d., or nearly 1s. 9½d. weekly for each.

In St. Giles's, Bloomsbury, the diet of a pauper in 1727 cost 1s. 7¾d. a week.

A. D. 1723. Mandeville, the author of the *Fable of the Bees* strongly deprecates the prevailing passion for the establishment of charity-schools for the education of the children of the poor.

A. D. 1732. A plausible society, under the designation of the Charitable Corporation, excited great interest; it had been incorporated by parliament, under the ostensible pretext of lending money to the industrious poor at 5*l.* per cent. interest, on pawns and pledges, to prevent their falling into the hands of pawnbrokers and other rapacious individuals. In addition, however, to the 5*l.* per cent. interest, these benevolent persons took 5*l.* per cent. more for charge of officers, committees, warehouses, &c. After trafficking in this spurious humanity for the space of three years, the corporation contrived to make *a break*, defrauding the shareholders of great sums. The outcry against these nefarious proceedings was so great that parliament interfered in behalf of the sufferers; and three of the managers, members of the House of Commons, were expelled.

It appears from 6 Geo. II. c. 31, that the laws in force were not sufficient to provide for the securing and indemnifying parishes from the charges of bastards; it was therefore provided that single women might *voluntarily* affiliate their children before delivery, but that they should not be *compelled* to do so till one month after.

To check the clandestine and unnecessary imposition of rates by overseers and churchwardens, it was enacted by 17 Geo. II. c. 3, that every new rate should be published in the church, and that the parish officers should permit every inhabitant to inspect the rates under penalty of twenty pounds. Copies of the rates were also directed to be

entered in a book for public perusal, and to be delivered over to succeeding parish officers.

A. D. 1735.   Mr. Hay, a member of the House of
Commons, published his *Remarks on the Poor-
Laws*, containing judicious observations on the Settlement Code.   His principal objection against the
law was the oppressive power vested in overseers to
remove persons merely on the ground they were
liable to become chargeable ; but as this arbitrary
authority no longer exists, it is not necessary to dwell
on his strictures.

A. D. 1744.   An act passed respecting that class
of poor, considered the outcasts of society—idle and
disorderly persons, rogues and vagabonds, and incorrigible rogues.

A. D. 1752.   Mr. Acock proposes a plan, in many
respects similar to the one recommended by Mr.
Hay.   He quotes the Dutch as exemplary managers in providing maintenance for the impotent,
and employment for the vagrant poor ; and thinks
the way they have succeeded has been chiefly by the
establishment of hospitals or workhouses.

A. D. 1753.   A bill brought in by Mr. Potter,
son of the Archbishop of Canterbury, for taking a
census of the people, distinguishing the marriages,
births, and deaths, and also the total number of
persons receiving alms, in every parish.   This bill
was violently opposed by Mr. Thornton, as subversive of the last remains of English liberty, and
merely intended to facilitate the inquiries of the
political arithmetician, and the exactions of the tax-

gatherer. It passed the commons, but was thrown out of the lords on the second reading.

In this year, an able French author observes, that " notwithstanding the plentiful provision for the poor in France, there was a general complaint of the increase of beggars and vagrants," and adds, " that the French political writers, dissatisfied with their own plans, had presented several memorials to the ministry, proposing to adopt the English parochial assessments, as greatly preferable. This (Lord Kames remarks) is a curious fact; for at that very time, people in London, no less dissatisfied with these assessments, were writing pamphlets in favour of the French hospitals."

Mr. Fielding published a pamphlet on the poor, whom he divides into three classes, the most numerous, he thinks, consisting of those who were able, but unwilling to work. He proposed a general plan for establishing houses of industry, on a large scale, in each county.

A. D. 1758. Mr. Massie, in a pamphlet, ascribes the increase of the poor, to monopolizing farms and enclosures of common lands: he also asserts, that the decrease in the number of labourers, and many other evils, have been occasioned by removing multitudes from the steady employment of agriculture, to the fluctuating demands of trade and manufacture.

A. D. 1760. Mr. Smith, in his able Tracts on the corn trade, states that in his time, wheat had become much more generally the food of the common

people than it had been in 1689; but adds, that
notwithstanding this increase, some very intelligent
inquirers were of opinion, that even then, not more
than half the people of England fed on wheat. This,
however, is evidence of a great improvement in
the general diet on the accession of George III.
Harrison mentions, that in the reign of Henry VIII.
the gentry had wheat for their tables, but their
household, and poor neighbours, were usually obliged
to content themselves with rye, barley, and oats.
It appears from the household book of Sir Edward
Coke, that in 1596, rye-bread and oatmeal formed
a considerable part of the diet of servants in great
families in the southern counties. Barley-bread is
stated in the grant of a monopoly by Charles I., in
1626, to be the usual food of the ordinary sort of
people. Down to the year 1800, the writer of this
remembers, that oaten bread was commonly eaten by
the labouring classes of the West Riding of Yorkshire. " Every one knows (Mr. M'Culloch remarks,
Dict. of Commerce), how inapplicable these statements are, to the condition of the people of England
at this present time. Wheat-bread is now universally made use of in towns and villages, and almost
universally in the country. Barley is no longer used,
except in distilleries and in brewing; oats are employed only in the feeding of horses; and the consumption of rye-bread is comparatively inconsiderable. The produce of the wheat crops has been at the
very least *trebled* since 1760. And if, to this immense
increase in the supply of wheat, we add the still

more extraordinary increase in the supply of butcher's meat, the fact of a very signal improvement having taken place in the condition of the population in respect of food, will be obvious." This representation cannot be gainsayed, it is only to be feared of late years, that the people have not been fully able to maintain the " 'vantage ground" they had gained.

Early in the reign of George III., provision was made for the register of all parish poor, under four years of age, within the bills of mortality. Mr. Hanway, whose exertions on this occasion were conspicuous, remarks, that the measure, if it did not at once accomplish all that was necessary to be done, was the surest way of investigating the subject: and it is probably owing to his forcible representation of the mortality among the children in London workhouses, that an act passed in 1767, for obliging all parishes, within the bills of mortality, to send pauper children, under six years of age, within a fortnight after birth, or received in the workhouse, to a distance of at least three miles from the cities of London and Westminster, to be nursed till they are six years of age : the act further directs, that for the maintenance of every such child, not less than 2s. 6d. a week shall be paid for the first six years of their age, and not less than 2s. a week from that time, to the period the child is taken away. As an inducement to good conduct in nurses, a premium of 10s. was to be given to such as had nursed a child for one year to the satisfaction of the parish guardians. Dr. Price remarks, that prior to this statute, almost all parish infants in the metropolis died in the first six years.

Respecting apprentices, the same act, the 7th Geo. III. c. 39, s. 14, remarks, that "it often disturbs the peace of domestic life, *checks marriage*, and discourages industry, to place out boys to the age of twenty-four years; and enacts, that for the future, parish officers shall be at liberty to bind out boys and girls apprentices, for the term of seven years, or till they attain the age of twenty-one years, and no longer."

Dr. Burn, about this time, offered two suggestions for the improvement of the poor-laws : the first was, to prevent common begging : " till this is done," he says, " all other regulations of the wisest legislature upon earth, will be vain and fruitless. The infallible way to restrain beggars and vagrants is, *to give them nothing.* If none were to give, none would beg; and the whole mystery and craft would be at an end in a fortnight." To accomplish this, he proposes, that every one who relieves a common beggar, shall be liable to a penalty. His other suggestion was, to control the irresponsible power of overseers, by placing over them a superintendent, whose jurisdiction should extend over a certain number of parishes.

A. D. 1764. James Watt, a native of Greenock, in Scotland, began his improvements on the steam-engine, whereby the foundation was laid for the prodigious advance in wealth and population which marked the reign of George III. By the aid of

machinery—of which the steam-engine is the chief
moving power—it is considered that an individual
can produce 200 times more goods than he could in
1760.   Although the labours of Watt are unnoticed
in the general history of the period, they have proved
of more importance to man than all the cotemporary
transactions of war and diplomacy in which Europe
was involved.

A. D. 1767.   An ingenious person, James Har-
graves, a carpenter at Blackburn, invents the spinning jenny, the first of a series of mechanical improvements in the cotton manufacture.   The jenny
was applicable only to the spinning of cotton for
weft, being unable to give to the yarn that degree
of fineness and hardness which is required in the
warp : but this deficiency was soon after supplied
by the invention of the spinning-frame, that wonderful piece of machinery which spins a vast number of
threads of any degree of fineness or hardness ; leaving to man merely to feed the machine with cotton,
and to join the threads when they happen to break.
The author of this extraordinary contrivance was
Richard Arkwright, a native of Preston, and by trade
a barber.   Living in a manufacturing district, his
attention was drawn to the operations carrying on
around him ; and hearing from every one complaints
of the deficient supply of cotton yarn, assisted by
the ingenuity of John Kay, a watchmaker, of War-
rington, he set about contriving a plan for changing
the mode of spinning.   The difficulties he encountered were great, both from want of capital and

practical skill in mechanics. At last he obtained pecuniary assistance to enable him to build a factory, but being driven from Lancashire by fear of violence from those who earned their subsistence by the old mode of spinning, he removed to Nottingham. In 1769 he obtained a patent for spinning with rollers; and in 1771 he took out a second patent, for a new system of carding and roving by machinery. In 1786 Mr. Arkwright was knighted, and in the following year he was high sheriff of Derbyshire.

Since the dissolution of Sir Richard Arkwright's patent, in 1785, further improvements have been made in the cotton manufacture. The *mule jenny*, so called from its being a compound of the jenny and spinning-frame, invented by Mr. Crompton, and the power-loom, invented by the Rev. Mr. Cartwright, are machines that have had the most powerful influence on this branch of industry. In consequence of their introduction the price of cotton cloth has been enormously reduced; but as the demand for cottons has been vastly extended by their extreme cheapness, the quantity of goods produced, and the number of persons employed in the manufacture are now greater than at any former period. Mr. M'Culloch (*Dictionary of Commerce*, p. 415) estimates the number of persons directly employed in the cotton manufacture at 833,000; the aggregate amount of their wages at twenty millions a year; and the annual value of the goods produced in Great Britain at thirty-six millions!

A. D. 1768. By the 7th George III. c. 17, it is

enacted, that the hours of working of *tailors*, within the city of London and five miles thereof, shall be from six o'clock in the morning to 7 o'clock in the evening, with an interval of one hour only for refreshment ; and that their wages shall be any sum not *exceeding* 2*s*. 7½*d*. per diem, except during a general mourning, when for a month they shall not exceed 5*s*. 7½*d*. per diem. Masters giving, or journeymen accepting, higher than these statutory wages may be sent to the house of correction.

The wages of silk-weavers were fixed by statute so late as the 13 Geo. III. c. 68.

A. D. 1772. Baron Maseres publishes a *Proposal for establishing Life Annuities for the Benefit of the Poor.*

A. D. 1781. Robert Raikes, a master-printer of Gloucester, establishes the first Sunday-school. The philanthropic aim of this benevolent individual was greatly facilitated by the institution, four years after, of the Sunday-school Society ; the objects of which were to promote by correspondence and pecuniary assistance the establishment of Sunday-schools : to induce the opulent, and those in easy circumstances, to visit and superintend them, and suggest such improvements as might offer to their consideration. Next to charity-schools Sunday-schools may be considered the second step in the progress of popular instruction. Before their establishment education was at a very low ebb, even among the middle orders; as may be seen by the writing and spelling of respectable tradesmen of that period. The improvement in the education of the working classes gave an impulse to the education of the class immediately above them.

A. D. 1782. The workhouse plan, originally adopted above a century ago, received a great extension from an act passed this year, commonly called Gilbert's Act, from the name of the member of parliament by whom it was framed. This act, aiming to combine the advantages of an assemblage of a number of poor on one spot, of a minute division of labour, and a joint management of expenditure, empowered magistrates to consider any large workhouse as a common receptacle for the poor within a diameter of twenty miles. Judicious as this plan apparently was, it has not been successful: proper care has seldom been taken to separate the inmates of the workhouses according to their age or their habits, nor has the division of employment been carried to the necessary length. Their earnings have consequently been insignificant, and the charge to the parish amounts in general to 9*l*., 10*l*., or even 16*l*. each, while half the sum would suffice, if paid to the poor at their own habitations. It has thus been fortunate that the limited extent of workhouses, prior to 1820, hardly admitted above 100,000 inmates (Lowe's *Present State of England*.) This, however, is not decisive of the utility of workhouses: by improving their managment, and by leaving, as has been suggested, to able-bodied claimants only the option of accepting relief in a poor-house, it is probable many would decline burdening the parish rather than submit to their discipline and coarse fare.

Mr. Gilbert also instituted an inquiry into public charities, and was author of various other expedients for improving the poor-laws and bettering the condition of the poor. One suggestion of this gentleman was, to limit the future amount of the poor assessment to the average expenditure of the three years ending in 1785, namely, to 1,943,649*l.*

After the failure of Mr. Gilbert's plan Sir William Young took up the subject of the poor. It is no slight recommendation of this gentleman that many of his suggestions were adopted by the legislature, and now form the least exceptionable part of the poor-laws. Judicious, however, as Sir William Young was in most of his measures, it is important to observe, that it is to him we must ascribe the hurtful practice of paying a portion of the wages of labourers out of the poor-rates. In a bill he introduced, it was provided that, to relieve agricultural labourers during winter, magistrates should be empowered by notice affixed to the church door, to settle a *rate of wages* to be paid to labourers out of employ, from the 30th of November to the 28th of February; and to distribute and send them *round* in rotation to the parishioners, proportionally as they paid to the rates; the labourers to be paid by the person employing them, two-thirds of the wages so settled, and one-third by the parish officers out of the rates. This clause was borrowed from a practice already mentioned, which had long prevailed in Buckinghamshire and the midland counties. During winter labourers out of employ went round from house to house, and were either employed or paid by each parishioner in proportion to his poor assessment: they were called *roundsmen.*

A. D. 1786. Mr. Acland publishes a project to enable the poor to provide for themselves by a *compulsory* subscription of a portion of their earnings to a general fund: a scheme recently revived by the *Quarterly Review.*

A. D. 1790. Justices of the peace are empowered to visit the workhouses within their jurisdiction, to examine the state of the poor, their food, clothing and bedding, and to summon masters of poor-houses to appear at the quarter sessions to answer complaints against them.

A. D. 1793. The first act, the 33d Geo. III. c. 54, introduced by Mr. Rose, for the regulation of Friendly Societies. It is impossible to trace the origin of these associations; from a curious account of them by Sir F. Eden (*State of the Poor*, v. i. p. 590) they appear to have been coeval with guilds and corporations. A new act was passed for their regulation in 1829, the provisions of which were framed on the recommendation of the more intelligent members of the societies themselves, aided by the suggestions of enlightened individuals who felt interested in the permanency of such useful institutions. In 1831 there were 4117 friendly societies in England, and the number of members probably a million and a half: in 1815 the number of members was 925,429. *Parl. Paper*, No. 522, Sess., 1825.

A. D. 1795. Some grievous abuses were this year introduced into the administration of the poor-laws. The price of corn, which for three years preceding had averaged 54s., rose to 74s. a quarter. As wages continued stationary, the distress of the poor was very great, and many able-bodied labourers, who had rarely before applied for parish assistance, became claimants for relief. Instead of meeting this emergency by temporary expedients, and by grants of relief proportioned to the urgency of each individual case, one uniform system was adopted. The magistrates of Berks and some of the southern counties issued tables, showing the wages which they thought every labouring man ought to receive, according to variations in the *price of bread* and the *number of his family ;* and they accompanied these tables with an order, directing the parish officers to make up the difference to the labourer, in the event of the wages paid to him by his employer falling short of the tabular allowance. An act was at the same time passed to allow the justices to administer relief *out* of the workhouses, and also to relieve such poor persons as had property of their own.

This system, as might have been foreseen, did not close with the temporary necessity in which, it originated, and its evils have been threefold. 1. To make wages vary with the *price of bread*, takes away all motive for economising its consumption in *dear years*, and thus throws the entire pressure of a scarcity on the payers of poor-rates, especially the

middle classes, who may themselves be suffering
from the high price of provisions.　2. To proportion
the parish allowance to the number of children, was
granting a bounty on marriages to the positive injury of the single man.　3. To render wages uniform,
by raising them all up to a fixed standard of remuneration, by payments out of the rates, was placing
the idle and dissolute on a level with the orderly and
industrious.　It was a complete system of levelling
as subversive of the rights of industry, as an agrarian
law, in its vulgar acceptation, would be of the rights of
property, destroying all motives to independent exertion, economy, and forethought.

A. D. 1796.　On the 12th of February Mr. Whitbread, on moving in the House of Commons, that a
bill to regulate the wages of labourers in husbandry
be read a second time, made this statement.　He said
that " in most parts of the country the labourers had
long been struggling with increasing misery till the
pressure had become almost too *grievous to be endured ;* while the patience of the sufferers, under their
accumulated distresses, had been conspicuous and exemplary."　This appears a very extraordinary representation when it is considered that the intolerable
load of war taxes had hardly begun to be felt, and as
the Bank of England had not ceased to pay in gold,
it was anterior to the depreciation of the currency.
Yet there were evident symptoms, even at this period,
of an over-supply of labour, and the remedies suggested for this redundancy were of a most singular
description.　Mr. Whitbread recommended the im-

mediate establishment of a *minimum of wages*; a measure as unjust against the employer as a maximum would be against the employed. Mr. Pitt, in reply, admitted that the condition of the poor was *cruel*, and such as could not be wished on any principle of humanity or policy. But he argued against the proposition of Mr. Whitbread as contrary to sound principles, and concluded in these words: " What measures then could be found to supply the defect? Let us," said he, "make relief (by the parish), in cases where there are a number of children, a matter of right and an honour, instead of a ground for opprobrium and contempt. This will make a *large family* a blessing and not a curse; and this will draw a proper line of distinction between those who are able to provide for themselves by their labour, and those who, after having ENRICHED their country with a number of children have a claim upon its assistance for their support."—*Parl. History*, vol. xxxii. p. 710. Mr. Fox did not enter fully into the question, but appeared to acquiesce in the principles laid down; and Mr. Whitbread, in conclusion, complimented Mr. Pitt, and recommended government " to institute a *liberal premium for large families !* "

These doctrines it is apparent inculcate the most objectionable provisions of the poor-laws, and show how completely the real causes of the depression of the labouring classes were misunderstood by the statesmen of 1796. They seem not to have been aware that the supply of labour, like that of any other commodity, may exceed the demand, and that to encourage the production of an article already redundant must tend still further to lower its price. Had there been a glut in the sugar-market it is hardly possible that Mr. Pitt or Mr. Whitbread would have proposed as a remedy a premium to the planters on the growth of that product.

The opinions of politicians on this subject were agreeable to the principles which had long passed current among distinguished writers ; namely, that the wealth of a state consists in the number of its people. Rousseau, in his *Contrat Social*, asks, " What is the most certain sign that the people are maintained and prosper ? It is *their number*, or in other words their populousness. Do not seek for this sign in any other quarter. That government, when without naturalizations, without extrinsic means, without colonies, the citizens multiply and increase to the greatest degree, is without doubt the best." Applying this test to the actual condition of different European countries it would follow, that the canton of Geneva, where, exclusive of immigration, the inhabitants increase only ... annually, must be one of the most wretched spots in Europe ; while the Irish, who have quadrupled their number within a century, must be in a state of enviable blessedness. It is needless to remark that the fact is the reverse in both instances.

Rousseau, however, was not so singular and mistaken in this opinion as in many of his paradoxes. Mirabeau acquired the title of the " Friend of Mankind," by laying down the principle, that " it is *their number* that constitutes the riches and the power of empires;" and Dr. Price treated that proposition as a generally received and incontrovertible axiom: "Every body knows," says he, "that the power of a state consists in the number of its inhabitants, and that in consequence the *encouragement* of its population ought to be one of the first objects of those who administer its affairs." It was doubtless in conformity with this dogma that the English Chancellor of the Exchequer proposed to augment the fiscal means of the country by taxing *bachelors*, and granting premiums on prolific housewives. So prevalent was the feeling, that it found its way into poetry, and Dr. Goldsmith sings—

> Ill fares the state to hastening ills a prey,
> Where wealth accumulates and *men* decay !

After all, the error of these eminent individuals was rather one of degree and of circumstances, than of absolute principle. They were wrong in thinking that the increase of population ever requires encouragement ; it is sufficient for the state to provide subsistence, and the increase of the people will follow as an unfailing consequence. They were right in considering men the riches of a country, the end of all legislation and public policy. But they must surely have intended men that could be *productively employed;* not pensioners of a parish, nor of the state, who consume without yielding services in return. There is truly no commodity—if so disparaging an epithet may be applied to nature's noblest production—so precious as man. Even an untutored Indian from the plains of Africa will fetch a hundred pounds in the slave-markets of America; but how much more valuable were a civilized, instructed, and indefatigable European! Yet see how he is depreciated! We give nothing for an article with which we are already abundantly supplied, not even for air or water, though indispensable to support life. But an Englishman has become less valuable than either element; he is not only *without price* but has actually become what algebraists call a negative quantity, that is, something worth less than nothing, and a premium has positively been offered for his expatriation!

Messrs. Whitbread, Pitt, Rousseau, and Dr. Price, therefore, were wrong in maintaining, without reference to circumstances, that a multitude of people constitute the wealth of nations; men are only valuable when scarce—when they are in demand, not when the supply of them is redundant.

It is worthy of remark, that while vague and unphilosophical notions on population were being countenanced in the English House of Commons, much sounder principles were inculcated by the Constituent Assembly of France. A committee of that enlightened and patriotic body laid down the following doctrine:

" An *excessive* population, without a proportional demand for its labour, and without abundant productions to supply its wants, cannot but be an overwhelming incumbrance to a state: for necessarily this excessive population must *divide* amongst its greater numbers all these advantages which one *less extensive* would have found amply sufficient for its wants. In such a case it must be an inevitable consequence that the *wages of labour must fall* from the competition of workmen; whence a complete state of indigence must result to those persons who cannot find employment at all, and an incomplete subsistence for those who may be fortunate enough to find it."

The tendency of competition to reduce wages and abridge the comforts of the working classes is here clearly and succinctly announced. A much safer criterion of national happiness than an increase of population is laid down in the proposition, that "the true test of the prosperity of a state is the *decrease of its mortality,* as compared with the number of its births."

A. D. 1797. Dr. Bell publishes a pamphlet under the unassuming title of an *Experiment in Education,* explaining the system of teaching he had introduced in 1789 into the charity-school over which he presided at Madras. The Reverend author had frequently observed the advantages attending the mode of teaching by writing in sand practised from time immemorial in all the native schools of Malabar. He thence resolved to adopt the practice, but met with difficulties from the confirmed habits of the teachers, who were grown up men; and on that account had recourse to the plan of teaching by the elder boys, whose habits and prejudices were more easily overcome, and whom he was able with little difficulty to qualify as instructors to the rest. In adopting this expedient he did systematically what had been done more or less before in most European chools. But Dr. Bell had the great merit of overcoming a specific difficulty in education—the prejudices of adults against sand-writing—by substituting boys. The same benevolent individual also introduced the method of reading and pronouncing by syllables instead of the common way : thus teaching the art of spelling with greater ease and correctness.

Dr. Bell's plan was communicated, as already stated in 1797, and in the following year Mr. *Joseph Lancaster* brought into general notoriety the principles of the Madras system. From these individuals arose the National School Society, and the British and Foreign School Society ; the name of the latter being adopted by the supporters of the Lancasterian plan, after separation from its founder. The chief distinction between the Bell and Lancaster schools is, I believe, that in the former the learning of the church catechism and attendance at a place of worship of the Church Establishment are indispensable conditions.

A. D. 1798. The publication of *An Essay on the Principle of Population* by Mr. Malthus, forms an epoch in the progress of economical science. The main propositions of this gentleman are, that there is a tendency in mankind to increase faster than the means of subsistence ; and secondly, that this tendency is checked, either by the misery occasioned by deficiency of food, or by the moral intelligence which controls the full indulgence of the procreative passion when hurtful to happiness.

Of a portion at least of this philosophy, it may be truly said, that it is nearly as old as the creation, and must have been recognised by the earliest of the human race : but the author was the first to show by a masterly inquiry into the past and present state of mankind, the practical application of his principles to the wellbeing of society. In this respect he rendered a service of inestimable price, and gave a new character to morals and legislation. Contrary to previously established maxims it became manifest that the great merit in governments and individuals consists, not in augmenting the number of people, but the means of subsistence; if the latter is provided, the former follows as unfailingly as harvest does the seed-time.

Had this important doctrine been set forth less with an air of novelty and more as admitted and self-evident truth, as it had been done by Wallace, Smith, Franklin, Young, and other anterior writers, it would not perhaps have encountered the severe and lengthened opposition it has experienced.

After all it may be doubted whether Mr. Malthus embraced the whole of his science. He established incontestably the tendency of mankind to multiply to excess, and its deteriorating consequences; but he did not sufficiently appreciate the operation of another principle of our nature. The important truth overlooked by the author of the *Essay on Population*

H

is, that man is a reasoning and self-loving creature, and though there is a natural tendency in him to increase his number, there is also in him a natural tendency to devise expedients for meeting and controlling its hurtful consequences. The doctrine of population, therefore, is not, as its philanthropic expounder assumed, irreconcilable with the doctrine of human improvement; neither does it afford any ground for the paralyzing inference that all projects of social amelioration are vain, save the single one of limiting the multiplication of our species.

A. D. 1802. An act of this year, still in force, the 42 Geo. III. c. 73, provides, that in all *woollen* and *cotton* mills and factories in the United Kingdom, in which three or more apprentices, or twenty or more other persons are employed, apprentices shall have two complete suits of clothing yearly; that the hours of working shall not exceed twelve hours, exclusive of meal-times, for which three hours are allowed; that they shall be instructed every day for the first four years of their apprenticeship, in reading, writing, and arithmetic; that the apartments of male and female shall be kept distinct, and two only sleep in one bed; that the rooms shall be washed with quicklime and water twice a year, and kept well aired; that at Midsummer sessions two visiters shall be appointed, to report the condition of such mills and factories; and that copies of the act shall be fixed up in two conspicuous parts of the building.

The objection to legislative interference with the labour of *adults* does not apply to *infants*, who are not possessed of the same capabilities, nor subject to the same legal responsibility for their actions. As the law properly interferes to protect children from the neglect and cruelty of their parents, it may, with much stronger reason, interfere to protect them from the neglect and cruelty of masters, who are unconnected with them by the same natural ties.

A. D. 1807.   On the 19th of February Mr. Whitbread brought forward his plan in the House of Commons, for encouraging industry and relieving the poor.   He expressed his concurrence in the principles of Mr. Malthus, and his conviction of the tendency of the poor-laws to deteriorate the condition of the labouring classes.   From returns made up in 1803, it appeared that upon a population in England and Wales of 8,870,000 not less than 1,234,000 were partakers of parochial relief; that is nearly one-seventh part of the people was indebted to the other six, wholly or in part, for support.   Mr. Whitbread's undertaking was very extensive.   Its main principle was to exalt the character of the industrious orders ; to give them consequence in their own eyes; to excite them to acquire property by the prospect of tasting its sweets ; to render dependent poverty degrading in their estimation and at all times less desirable than independent industry.   For the attainment of these issues he proposed a system of national education by the establishment of parochial schools; not compulsory on the poor, which would destroy

their object, but voluntary.   The bill fell to the
ground, partly from a change of administration, and
was finally thrown out of the House of Peers, August
11th, on the motion of Lord Hawkesbury.

A. D. 1814.   The act of the 5th of Elizabeth,
which prohibited the exercise of any trade, craft, or
mystery then exercised in the kingdom, unless a
person had previously served to it an apprenticeship
of at least seven years, is repealed by 54 Geo. III.
c. 96, with a saving clause for the customs of municipal corporations and companies lawfully instituted.
The statute of Elizabeth had long been complained
of as an impolitic interference with the freedom of
individuals; and the courts of law, by some singular
interpretations, had lent all the assistance in their
power to evade its provisions.   For example, the
act plainly includes the whole kingdom of England
and Wales, but it was interpreted to refer to *market-
towns* only, and to those trades which were exercised
when the statute was passed, without reference to
such as had been subsequently introduced.   It was
adjudged that a coachmaker could neither himself
make nor employ a journeyman to make coach-
wheels, but must buy them of a master-wheelwright,
the latter trade having been followed in England
before the 5th of Elizabeth.   But a wheelwright,
though he had never served an apprenticeship to a
coachmaker, might either make himself, or employ
journeymen to make *coaches*, the trade of a coachmaker not being within the statute because not
exercised in England at the time when it was passed!

The long toleration of such absurdities shows how difficult it is to get bad laws repealed, when they have become cemented with existing interests.

A. D. 1815. The practice of setting the assize, or of fixing the quality and price of bread publicly sold, which had been customary from the time of Henry III., was this year abolished in the metropolis, by act of parliament. In other places, though the power to set an assize still subsists, it is seldom enforced. The policy of the legislature, in endeavouring to regulate the price of labour and provisions, was the same, namely, to prevent monopoly and imposition; but this task was futile, if not superfluous; as the competition among sellers, in any extensive branch of business, will be a sufficient guarantee against combinations, and the discrimination of buyers, against fraud and adulteration.

A. D. 1817. A parliamentary committee, of which Mr. Stourges Bourne was chairman, makes an elaborate report on the abuses and tendency of the poor-laws, suggesting divers improvements in their administration, which were subsequently incorporated in acts of the legislature, especially 59 Geo. III. c. 12, empowering parishes to establish managing vestries, and assistant overseers, to build and enlarge workhouses, and purchase land for the employment of paupers.

A. D. 1818. An Infant School, established on Brewer's Green, Westminster, by Messrs. Brougham, Mill, I. & B. Smith, Macaulay, Babington, Leake,

Hase, Walker, Wilson, Sir Thomas Baring, Lord Dacre, and the Marquis of Lansdowne. The idea of an infant school was suggested by the asylum provided by Mr. Owen, for the children of the adult population of New Lanark. (Wilderspin on *Infant Education*, p. 67.) That they might not be a hinderance to the labours of their parents, and be preserved from vicious associations in the streets, they were placed under the care of women, whose business it was to provide amusement and instruction adapted to their years. The success of the first attempt of this kind in England, induced Mr. Wilson, in 1820, to establish an infant school at his own expense, in Quaker-street, Spitalfields. In 1824, a meeting was held for the formation of an Infant School Society, at which Lord Lansdowne presided. Since then, infant schools have become general in England, Scotland, and, I believe, Ireland.

The objects sought by these establishments are threefold; first, to preserve young children from the vice and mischief to which they are liable, from the neglect or inability of their parents : secondly, to instruct them in the rudiments of virtue and knowledge ; by which they may be prepared for a more advanced state of education and improvement; and, thirdly, to accomplish both these ends by a more cheerful and natural mode of tuition than heretofore practised in dame schools. The superior discipline of an infant school, will be at once perceived on examination. Adults have not profited more by the introduction of better principles of civil government, than children by a better system of education.

A. D. 1818. The exposure by Mr. Brougham of abuses in public charities, excites intense interest. The indefatigable labours of this gentleman appear to have had two objects in view; first, to introduce a parochial system of popular education ; and, secondly, to provide funds for the undertaking, either by public provision, or by restitution to their original purposes, of the misapplied endowments of charitable foundations. In 1816, and the two following years, a mass of useful information had been laid before parliament, by a committee appointed to " Inquire into the Education of the Lower Orders," at first in London, and afterwards throughout England. The results of this investigation showed, that a large proportion of the population was without the means of instruction :—in the metropolis, the number of children totally uneducated, was computed at 100,000, and in all England, 500,000. By the returns of education in 1818, it appears there were 23,611 endowed, unendowed, and Sunday schools, at which were *daily* taught 644,282 children, and *once* a week 452,817 children: total taught daily and weekly, 1,097,099. As many of the Sunday are also included in the number of day scholars, it was computed that the actual number of children receiving education was about 850,000 : so that more than one-third of all the children were suffered to grow up without instruction.

Another important result of the inquiries of the Education Committee, over which Mr. Brougham presided, was the appointment of a Commission by the Crown, to inquire into the management of charitable endowments. The commissioners are twenty in number, ten of them stipendiary, and are divided into boards, each board, by examinations on the spot, investigating the charities of a parish, district or corporation. The universities and public schools, charities having special visiters or officers appointed by the founders, and charities supported principally by voluntary subscriptions, are exempt from the inquiries of the commissioners. Their labours are annually reported to parliament, and a voluminous mass of details have accumulated: proceedings have been instituted in the Court of Chancery against some of the grosser cases of abuse: but though the revenue appertaining to the poor has been ascertained to be of immense amount, no legislative measure has yet been introduced to improve its future administration. The powers of the commissioners, unless further continued, expire at the end of the next session of parliament.

A. D. 1819. Mr. Robert Owen attracts attention by the zeal with which he endeavours to promote his *Rational System of Society.* The leading idea of this gentleman is, that the character of man is not formed *by him* but *for him*, either by natural organization or the external circumstances to which he has been subjected from birth. Hence, Mr. Owen concludes, that by improving the circumstances, which surround an individual in his early years, the individual himself may be improved, and in place of an inferior may be made a very superior being. In this doctrine there is much truth, and the errors probably of Mr. Owen do not consist so much in its adoption as in the measures he has suggested for reducing it to practice. The influence of early impressions, in other words of education, on the formation of character, has never been denied; men have only differed about the best mode of applying the principle. It has been well observed, "That at least all differences which exist between classes or bodies of men is the effect of education; it is the cause of difference between a Turk and an Englishman, the wildest savage, and an European. Whatever is made of any class of men, we may then be sure is possible to be made of the whole human race. What a field for exertion! what a prize to be won!"—*Sup. Ency. Brit.*, art. *Education*.

A. D. 1820. On the 28th of June, Mr. Brougham, in an elaborate address to the House of Commons, comprising a vast mass of information relative to the state of education in England, unfolds his plan of popular instruction. The leading feature of this project was to render national education a part of, and subordinate to the national ecclesiastical establishment. Parochial schools were to be established, and partly maintained by a school-rate, levied on housekeepers, and partly by a trifling weekly payment by the scholars. The schoolmaster to be a member of the church of England, to be chosen by the school-rate payers, subject to the approval of the parson, who also was to be authorized to enter the school at all times and examine the children. The expense of erecting schools, it was estimated, would amount to half a million, and the annual charge of their maintenance to 150,000*l*. Mr. Brougham's bill was read a first time, July 11th, and not afterwards proceeded in.

A. D. 1823.   A sum of money, voted by parliament, to effect the removal of a number of persons from the south of Ireland to the Cape of Good Hope and to Upper Canada.   It is intended merely as an experiment to try the practicability of emigration as a mean of relief for the unemployed poor.   The emigration to the Cape consisted of artisans and labourers, with their families, to the number of about 350, under the direction of Mr. Ingram.   The emigration to Upper Canada consisted of 586 persons, under the direction of Mr. Robinson.   The emigrants to America were conveyed to the Bathurst district, in Canada, where portions of uncleared land were allotted to the heads of families, implements of husbandry and building furnished, and supplies of provisions allowed, until they could raise subsistence from the soil.   The success of the first experiment led to a second grant from parliament in 1825, and 2024 of the destitute Irish were conveyed to the Newcastle district in Upper Canada.   Subsequent accounts, received from Messrs. Robinson,

Richards, and Captain Basil Hall, spoke favourably of the success of these attempts at colonization.

A. D. 1823. The London Mechanics' Institution established under the auspices of Dr. Birkbeck and others, principally for the diffusion, by lectures, the formation of a library and reading-rooms of those branches of science most appropriate to the avocations of the industrious classes. Institutions on similar principles had previously existed at Birmingham and in Scotland, but the example of the metropolis led to their establishment in all the chief towns of the kingdom.

A. D. 1824. This and the following year formed an important period of legislation with respect to the working classes; all the old statutes, from the 33d Edward I., amounting to upwards of thirty, relative to combinations of workmen, were repealed, so far as they relate to combinations to fix the rate of wages, or hours of work, or the mode of conducting any business or manufacture. The repeal of these acts has swept out of the statute-book nearly the last remnants of interference with the rights of operative industry. The injustice had long been glaring of allowing masters to fix, in concert, the price of their commodities, and interdicting to workmen an equal liberty in fixing the price of their labour. But the liberty guaranteed by the law must be exercised without abridging the liberty of others. Workmen may *voluntarily* unite to set what price they think fit on their labour, and frame what regulations they please for their own observance; but they are

liable, by 6 Geo. IV. c. 129, to punishment, if by
violence, threats, molesting, or *obstruction,* they endeavour to force any workman to leave his employer or to prevent him from being employed ; or to
belong to any club, or to contribute to any fund ; or
to alter the mode of carrying on any manufacture ;
or to limit the number of apprentices.

The laws were also repealed by 4 Geo. IV. c. 97,
which impose penalties on persons who *seduce*
artificers engaged in the cotton, linen, woollen, and
other manufactures, to settle in foreign countries.
These enactments were framed with the view of preventing the communication of our inventions and
discoveries to other nations. Experience proved
that such precautions were futile or pernicious.

A. D. 1827. A Society established for the Diffusion of Useful Knowledge, consisting chiefly of
public characters of eminence, and individuals distinguished by their literary and scientific attainments. The proceedings of the society were
ushered in by *A Discourse of the Objects, Advantages, and Pleasures of Science,* ascribed to Mr.
Brougham. In the announcement of the society it
is stated, that the object of the association is strictly
limited to " the imparting useful information to all
classes of the community, particularly to such as are
unable to avail themselves of experienced teachers,
or may prefer learning by themselves." The plan
proposed for the attainment of this end is, the periodical publication, under the sanction of a superintending committee, of treatises on science, meta-

physics, ethics, and political philosophy; to which histories of science, of nations, and individuals, are to be added. The treatises, hitherto published, have been principally on subjects of physical science; probably from the difficulty of fixing the precise standard of utility in the dissemination of the truths of moral and political philosophy. The example of the Society's almanac led to considerable improvements in that class of publications; and the *Penny Magazine* of the Society evinces great tact in the getting up of a popular miscellany of amusing matter for the general reader.

A. D. 1827. The inquiries of the Emigration Committee of the House of Commons indicate a great deterioration in the circumstances of the people of the united kingdom, more particularly in agricultural districts, where wages have been so depressed by competition for employment, that the labourer is compelled to live chiefly on bread and potatoes, seldom tasting meat and beer. Symptoms of an approaching servile war are clearly discernible, which can only be averted by measures tending to relieve the overstocked market of labour. From the evidence laid before the Emigration Committee, it felt justified in reporting,—

" That there are extensive districts in England and Scotland where the population is at the present moment redundant: in other words, where there exists a considerable proportion of *able-bodied* and active labourers beyond the number to which any existing demand for labour can afford employment.

That the effect of this redundancy is not only to reduce a part of this population to a great degree of destitution and misery, but also to *deteriorate the general condition* of the labouring classes. That by its producing a supply of labour in excess, as compared with the demand, the wages of labour are necessarily reduced to a minimum, which is utterly insufficient to supply that population with those means of support and subsistence, which are necessary to secure a healthy and satisfactory condition of the community.

" That in England this redundant population has been in part supported by a parochial rate, which, according to the reports of former committees, threatens, in its extreme tendency, to absorb the entire rental of the country. And that in Ireland, where no such parochial rate exists in law, and where the redundancy is found in a still greater degree, a considerable part of the population is dependant for the means of support on the precarious source of charity, or is compelled to resort to habits of plunder and spoliation for the actual means of support."

As a remedy for this state of misery and peril, the Committee proposed a *national system of colonization* in the British settlements of North America, the Cape of Good Hope, New South Wales, and Van Diemen's Land—countries, it is alleged, abounding in extensive tracts of unappropriated territory, of the most fertile quality, and capable of receiving and subsisting in health and independence any portion of the redundant population of the empire.

Between emigration in the ordinary sense, and the plan of colonization projected by the Committee, is a material distinction.   The former has been in progress for years, at the instance of individuals, and might be encouraged by the state, on the same principle, were the object merely to get *rid of the people ;* but the plan of the Committee not only embraces the mere transport of a redundant population, but their full location and establishment in secure and independent circumstances in the country of their adoption.

The funds for this undertaking it is proposed to raise either by an advance out of the public taxes, to be hereafter *repaid* by the emigrants, or by raising a sum on security of the poor-rates, to be paid in discharge of all future claims for parochial relief.

In the opinion of Sir Wilmot Horton, who evinced great zeal and ability in maturing this plan of emigration, the annual expenditure of 240,000*l.* would have been sufficient to carry off the yearly accumulating surplus of labour that had been mainly instrumental in the depression of the labouring classes.

A. D. 1828.   Mr. Brougham, in the steady pursuit of the great object of universal education, which he began in 1816 (see p. 103), in the spring of the year, resumed his inquiries by addressing a circular to the ministers of parishes of each county in England (excepting Middlesex), and received answers in the highest degree satisfactory.   An impulse had evidently been given to the great social obligation of popular instruction.   The number of unendowed schools in the whole kingdom was computed to have increased from 14,000 in 1818, to 32,000 in 1828. The number of scholars had not increased in quite so great a proportion as the number of schools; but it was computed that the number of scholars had increased from 478,000, in 1818, to 1,003,800. The number of Sunday scholars, it was thought, had augmented in a similar ratio, namely, from 452,817 to 905,634. This gives a total of 1,909,434 of Sunday and day scholars; but as many children attend both Sunday and day schools, a deduction from the total number ought to be made, leaving, it is conjectured, about a *million and a half* as the total number of children of the humbler classes in England receiving the benefits of education. As the children of both sexes, between the ages of five and twelve, amount to two millions, when the number of those taught in the higher schools is deducted, it is concluded that no large portion of the children of the working population are now entirely without instruction.

In Ireland the number of schools in 1827 was 11,823; of teachers 12,530; of scholars 568,904.

A. D. 1831. The waste and mismanagement of select vestries originates an act (1 and 2 Wm. IV. c. 60) for improving their constitution, and appointing auditors of parish accounts. The act is not *compulsory*, but may be adopted by a majority of the ratepayers in any parish in England and Wales, where the number of rate-payers exceeds 800; and it may be adopted where the number of rate-payers is *less*

than 800, provided such parishes are within or part
of a city or town.   A salutary clause in the act requires the vestry to make out, at least once a year,
a list, open to the inspection of rate-payers, of all
charity estates and bequests under the control of the
parish; specifying where the estate is situate, its
rental, and the security on which any bequest is invested, its appropriation, and the names of trustees.
The provisions of this statute were chiefly directed
against the abuses of self-elected vestries, deriving
their powers from ancient usage or local acts, not
against those established under Mr. Stourges
Bourne's act, the 59th Geo. III. c. 12.

During the same session an effort was made by
1 and 2 Wm. IV. c. 37, to put an end to what
are termed *tommy shops*, and the practice so general
in various counties of paying wages in *goods*, in lieu
of coin and bank-notes; employers entering into
contracts, or paying wages otherwise than in money,
are made liable to penalties, varying from 5*l*. to 100*l*.;
and wages paid in goods are void, and may be reco-
vered a second time by workmen.

The shocking barbarities perpetrated in manufacturing districts gave rise to a new act for the regulation of factories; and, by 1 and 2 Wm. IV.
c. 39, it is provided, that in no *cotton* mill, where
steam or water power is used to work machinery,
shall any person under *twenty-one years of age* be
allowed to work at night; that is, between the hours
of half-past eight in the evening and half-past five
in the morning; and that no person under *eighteen*

I

years of age shall work more, in any description of employment whatever, than twelve hours in one day, nor more than nine hours on a *Saturday;* and that every such person be allowed, in the course of one day, one hour and a half for meals.

The utility of this act is much impaired by its provisions extending only to apprentices and children employed in *cotton* factories, and not also to those in other employments, especially to the woollen, linen, and silk manufactories. The disgusting atrocities revealed by a parliamentary committee of last session, show that sharp legislation is indispensable to restrain the cupidity of mill-owners, whose cruelties in the pursuit of gain have hardly been exceeded by those perpetrated by the Spaniards on the conquest of America, in the pursuit of gold!

A. D. 1832.   The 21st annual report of the National School Society shows that education, on the principles of the church establishment, is rapidly extending.   In 1826 the number of schools was computed to amount to 8399, and the number of scholars to 550,424.   In 1832 the schools are computed to have increased to 12,973, and the scholars to 900,025.

PART II.

POLITICAL ECONOMY

OF THE

INDUSTRIOUS ORDERS.

CHAPTER I.

LABOUR.

Subject Defined—Different kinds and Progress of Industry—Labour the only source of Wealth.

LABOUR is the exertion of power for the production of utility.

It is of three kinds: if applied to the appropriating or raising of the produce of the earth, it is agricultural; if to the conversion of that produce into articles of use, it is manufacturing; if to the conveyance of that produce, either in its raw or wrought state, from one place or country to another, it is commercial.

There is a fourth species, called intellectual labour, without the co-operation of which physical power is not exerted ; and it is the exertion of this intellectual labour that constitutes the science and art of the agriculturist, manufacturer, and merchant.

Besides the labour occupied in the production of commodities, there is another sort not less valuable, namely, that of legislators and magistrates, men of science, literature, and the arts, the medical classes, and domestic servants : all these are occupied in the production of utility, and contribute, like the husbandman and operative, to increase and multiply the comforts, enjoyments, and conveniences of social life.

Without the application of labour, the earth is a " steril promontory." It offers no spontaneous gifts ; the mineral treasures contained in its bosom, the seas and rivers by which it is watered, and the animals, fruits, and vegetables, that cover its surface, are not directly useful till they have been subdued, gathered, and combined by human industry. The coals that warm us, the candle that lights us, our clothes, our food, our habitation ; in short, every thing we eat, drink, see, or rest upon, afford evidence of the all-conquering power of industry.]

As the comforts of man augment, his labours multiply. The savage, whose occupation is limited to the gathering of fruits or the picking up of shellfish, is placed on the verge of social existence. To increase his enjoyments, he must increase his dangers and exertions. The first step in his progress is to hunt wild animals, to feed himself with their flesh, and clothe himself with their skins. But the proceeds of the chase are uncertain, and, in lieu of depending on such a toilsome and precarious source of subsistence, he tries to domesticate animals ; from a hunter he becomes a shepherd and herdsman—a transition that softens the rudeness of his nature, as well as guarantees him a more unfailing supply of food. His next advance in civilization is to *agriculture*. Flesh alone forms an unsatisfactory repast, and to obtain a supply of vegetable he must till the ground. With flocks and herds, and the produce of the soil, his hunger may be appeased : but this is only one of his wants ; he requires variety of diet, of clothing, and lodging. To attain these he must become a *manufacturer*. He has now reached the last stage of improvement ; he has triumphed over the evils that surrounded him, and acquired a power to minister to his desires, however varied and multiplied, that is only limited by his industry and intelligence.

An interest is felt in tracing the progress of society, analogous to that felt in reverting to the days of childhood. It is the season of hope, of trial, and enterprise. Whether mankind have really advanced in the order I have indicated, can only be matter of conjecture. Nations that grow up in the *natural* way can, no more than individuals, describe the first stages of existence. One writer (Torrens's *Essay on the Production of Wealth*, p. 83) thinks, that manufacturing preceded agricultural industry ; as neither the chase, pasturage, nor husbandry could begin, without the previous contrivance of some implement adapted to the pursuit. It is, however, an inquiry more suited to poetry than science. History shows, that new communities have been mostly propagated by slips or grafts from parent states, and started on their course with all the social advantages of the mother country from which they had emigrated. In this manner, the ancient Greek colonies spread over Italy and Asia Minor, and the republics of North and South America have been founded. To return to our subject.

Although labour is the great architect of our enjoyments and conveniences in diet, dress, and habitation, it is not a creator of them; like a skilful chemist or artist, it only separates, fashions, and combines, and does not add a particle to the matter of the world previously existing. Nature is the great capitalist, that, from the beginning of time, has furnished the raw material on which industry has been exercised.

The culture of the human mind keeps pace with the culture of the material products, by which it is surrounded. When the earth has been reclaimed by industry, it ceases to be an appropriate domain for savage life; it requires an occupant whose passions have been softened down, and reason cultivated. Man uncivilized, and the earth uncultivated, are in their infancy; what labour effects for one, education accomplishes for the other.

So omnipotent is labour, that it is considered by political economists, to be the only source of *wealth*; or of those riches which, apart from the spontaneous and unappropriated products of the earth, alone possess value in exchange. Nature has been lavish in her bounties, but man alone has given them exchangeable value. What I cannot appropriate, and of which every one has enough to satisfy his wants, may be extremely useful, but has no value—will fetch *no price*. The sunbeams that warm us, the air that supports life, and the water that slakes thirst, are all abundantly useful; but, as they are the produce of no man's labour, and no man can appropriate them to himself, they are of no value in the market.

" Labour was the first price, the original purchase-money that was paid for all things." When all things lay in common, alike the gift of nature to all men, who would have the best right to say, *This is mine*? The man who first set his mark upon it by his industry, and thereby gave it a value that could not be severed from it. It was thus, that labour originated appropriation, and appropriation exchangeable value.

As the power of creating exchangeable value is man's peculiar distinction, so there is no other order of the creation that practises *barter*, or the direct exchange of one commodity for another. Man is the only animal who contracts. " Two greyhounds, in running down the same hare, have sometimes the appearance," says Dr. Smith, " of acting in some sort of concert. Each turns her towards his companion, or endeavours to intercept her, when his companion turns her towards himself. This, however,

is not the effect of contract, but of the accidental
concurrence of their passions in the same object
at that particular time.   Nobody ever saw a dog
make a fair and deliberate exchange of one bone for
another with another dog.   Nobody ever saw one
animal by its gestures and natural cries, signify to
another, this is mine, that yours; I am willing to
give you this for that."   When an animal wants to
obtain something either of man or another animal,
it does not exert its labour to produce another commodity of equivalent value, and thereby effect an
exchange; its only resources are force or finesse;
if stronger, it overpowers the possessor, if weaker,
it seeks to overcome it by stratagem. A lion ravages
its prey; a puppy fawns upon its dam, and a spa-
niel endeavours by a thousand attractions to engage
the attention of his master at dinner, when it wants
to be fed by him : but, civilization has made man
superior; the title which he claims for himself to the
produce of his industry, he recognises in another:
what another possesses, and he wants, he seeks fairly
to purchase by an equivalent amount of labour:
thus are the interests of both promoted, and the necessity of fraud and violence superseded.

In the opinion of Mr. M'Culloch, Locke was the
first writer, who clearly apprehended, and fully developed, the creative power of labour.   In his *Essay
on Civil Government*, published in 1689, he says,
" Let any one consider what the difference is between
an acre of land planted with tobacco or sugar, sown
with wheat or barley, and an acre of the same land

lying in common, without any husbandry upon it, and he will find the improvement of labour makes the far greater part of the value.   I think it will be but a very modest computation to say, that of the products of the earth useful to the life of man, nine-tenths are the effects of labour ; nay, if we will rightly consider things as they come to our use, and cast up the several expenses about them, what in them is purely owing to nature, and what to labour, we shall find that in most of them, ninety-nine hundredths are wholly to be put on the account of labour.

" There cannot be a clearer demonstration of any thing than several nations of the Americans are of this, who are rich in land and poor in all the comforts of life, whom nature having furnished as rich as any other people with the materials of plenty, that is, a fruitful soil, apt to produce in abundance what might serve for food, raiment, and delight; yet for want of improving it by labour, have not one-hundredth part of the conveniences we enjoy ; and the king of a large and fruitful territory there feeds, lodges, and is clad worse than a day-labourer in England."

It would have formed a still more triumphant climax to this philosopher could he have foreseen how industry alone would transform the western waste into the site of a mighty empire, rivalling the first states of Europe, in power, wealth, and all the enjoyments of social life.

CHAP. II.

DIVISION OF EMPLOYMENTS.

Division of Labour—It saves Time—Improves Skill and Dexterity—Suggests the Contrivance of Tools and Machinery—Lessens the Cost of Production—Applicable chiefly to Mechanical Employments—Limited by Extent of the Market.

LABOUR being the source of wealth, and wealth of enjoyment, an important inquiry is, how it can be made most efficient in its production.

Prior to the invention of tools and implements, it is likely that a division of employments would be the first expedient devised. All men could not be occupied on the same object, some must cut wood, some fetch water, some fodder the cattle; and the diversity in the taste and talent of each would naturally determine the nature of his trade. He who excelled in making bows and arrows would probably confine his industry to that occupation. Another would be dexterous in the chase, and limit himself to hunting. A third would be skilful in hut-building, and form a sort of house-carpenter. And another would be ready in the cutting and dressing of hides for clothing, and thus be the germ of a tailor or tanner. The practice of barter or exchange would necessarily grow out of this separation of pursuits. The armourer who made bows and arrows would have more than needful for his own use, and would seek to exchange the surplus for the venison of the hunter, or the hides of the tanner; or he would purchase with his implements the services of the hut-builder to erect and improve his dwelling. A corresponding division would arise in civil and military duties. The bravest and most enterprising would be the leader in war; the best spokesman the orator, and diplomatist of the tribe; and those more subtle and observing, would probably devote themselves to legislation, law, and the mysteries of religion.

Whether this is precisely the mode in which trades and professions originated, it is not, perhaps, essential to ascertain. A more important inquiry than into the origin of occupations will consist in showing how much more efficient industry becomes by being concentrated on a single process or operation.

First, the division of employment *saves time.* A man carrying on different occupations, in passing from one to another, must change either his position, his place, his tools, or the direction of his mind, and in any case time is lost in the transition. Lawyers experience something of this in passing from one brief to another, or one court to another, to plead the cause of their clients. The General Post-office has been cited by Dr. Whately as an apt illustration of the division of labour. If each individual had his own letters to carry, the time lost and expense incurred would be enormous; or even if the Post-office had not introduced various subdivisions of employment in its establishment—such as a separate post for each main road, and a district of adjacent streets for each postman, its affairs could not be managed so cheaply and expeditiously as they are at present.

In moving to a new employment a listlessness and sauntering intervene; neither the mind nor muscles readily apply to the new work, and this repugnance can only be overcome after a certain period of resolute application. Practice not only gives greater aptitude and flexibility to particular parts, but strength, and enables them to execute more work with greater ease than could be otherwise effected. A novelist or poet, for instance, will not master an abstruse subject with the same facility as a mathematician, whose mind is habituated to deep and continuous investigation. The physical effects are of a similar nature. The grasp of a blacksmith's hand is well known to be like his own vice, and a porter or coal-heaver acquires an amplitude of shoulder by his employment, which is rarely found in those accustomed only to sketch the tendon Achilles in Hyde-park or the Quadrant.*

* The observations in this paragraph require qualification. They apply, I apprehend, chiefly to mechanical labour, or to labour that must be executed within certain hours, or in a certain place. Both body and mind are relieved by change of pursuit, and business, by the alternation of employment, may be made to answer all the purposes of recreation. In this way a Charlemagne, a Napoleon, a Brougham, and other public characters, have been enabled to accomplish such prodigies of labour. It is refreshing to pass from the stillness and monotony of a bureau to the bustle and variety of a review, an audience, or court of law. A London merchant will spend the morning at desk, midday on 'Change, then dine, and return in the evening with unabated vigour to posting his books, answering

By dividing, and thereby simplifying occupations, less time is requisite to acquire a knowledge of them. A lad will much sooner learn to head a pin or point a needle than to make either of these tools entire. Long apprenticeships were intended to indemnify masters for the time lost in teaching boys successive and complicated processes; but, in an advanced state of society, when employments have been simplified by division, there is not the same reason for the protracted term of seven or five years' servitude.

2. Greater dexterity and skill are acquired by the constant repetition of one single process or operation.

This is only affirming the old saying that " practice makes perfect ;" or that "a Jack of all trades is master of none." A workman in the daily practice of one simple business, acquires a dexterity and despatch which would not be possible were he more variously occupied. Not only is the play of the muscles improved, but each sense and faculty, by concentration of object. A banker's clerk will count over a bun-

correspondents, or concocting a new bargain or speculation. Could a mechanic labour so many hours without bringing on the *disease of his trade*, occasioned by the constant application of one set of muscles or faculty of the mind ? If the object sought be to render an operative a machine, whereby the greatest quantity of work in a given occupation may be extracted from him, no way so effective as division of labour. This is, in fact, the only point assumed to be investigated in the text. Political economy does not embrace moral but physical results. And after all, an employment reduced to its minimum of simplicity must leave the mind at leisure for reflection and conversation ; and these are the effects known to be produced in many manufactories.

dle of notes with ten times the rapidity of another person not used to the employment. Mr. Babbage mentions a clerk of the Bank of England who, upon an emergency, signed his name, consisting of eleven letters, to 5300 notes, during eleven working-hours, and he also arranged the notes he had signed in parcels of fifty each. This affords some idea how the power of execution is increased by the practice of an employment, and its effects on production, especially in piece-work, must be very great. In nail-making, Adam Smith states, a boy brought up to the trade will make upwards of 2300 nails in a day, whilst a common smith, who, though accustomed to handle the hammer, has never been used to make nails, would not be able to make above two or three hundred in a day, and " these, too, very bad ones."

3. The division of employment suggests the contrivance of tools, machinery, and processes for abridging and saving labour.

An operative, whose attention is limited to one simple process, is more likely to hit upon a contrivance for facilitating the execution of it than if he were distracted by a greater variety of circumstances. The simplicity of his employment leaving the mind disengaged, a new tool, or better mode of using an old one, is more likely to occur to him than if he were more intensely occupied. His object, however, would be chiefly to save his own labour, as in the case mentioned by Smith. In the first steam-engines, a lad was constantly employed to open and shut alternately the communication between the boiler and cylinder, according as the piston ascended or descended. One of the boys so employed observed, that by tying a string from the handle of the valve which opened the communication to another part of the machine, the valve would open and shut of itself, leaving him at liberty to play with his companions. Similar causes have probably originated many of our great mechanical combinations. The workman finds out a tool for saving his labour; while minds of greater leisure and grasp step in and combine these tools into a machine impelled by one moving power, and thus effect those miracles of ingenuity and force that are exhibited in our mills and factories.

4. The series of operations necessary to the production of an article do not require a uniform amount of skill and force; by the division of employments, the master is enabled to apply exactly that degree of skill and force to each operation which is necessary to its execution, whereby the cost of production is lessened.

This advantage of the division of labour appears to have been first communicated to the English public in the *Economy of Machinery and Manufactures;* though Mr. Babbage admits the same principle had been distinctly stated by Gioja, an Italian, author of an economical work, published at Milan, in 1815. Its tendency to economise labour might be shown in almost every branch of industry; and Mr. Babbage has elucidated it with great minuteness in explaining the several processes used in the making of pins.

As the Professor's interesting publication is in general circulation it is unnecessary to repeat his description of the successive operations in this curious art; it will be sufficient to recapitulate the results.

To make 5546 pins, weighing one pound, occupies four men, four women, and two children, rather more than seven hours and a half of time, and the total expense of their labour, each being paid according to his skill and the time he is employed, amounts to nearly 1s. 1d. The ratio of the wages earned per day by the persons so employed, varies from 4½d., the sum paid to the boy who assists in twisting and cutting the heads, to 6s., the sum paid to the man who finishes the most difficult part of the art. Of the seven hours and a half consumed, four are taken up by a woman in heading; rather more than two hours by another woman in preparing, and the remaining hour and a half is spent by the other eight persons in drawing the wire, straightening the wire, pointing and tinning. Now it is obvious that if only one person was employed to make a pin, from the beginning to the end, he must not only have the skill and the strength necessary to execute the more easy and simple processes, but those more difficult and laborious. It follows that one half of his time would be spent in putting on the heads—a part of the work only worth 1s. 3d. a day; while his skill, if better employed, would in the same time produce five times as much. Pins in consequence would be nearly four times the current price ; and the reason of their cheapness is a skilful division of labour, an apportionment of the several processes in the trade among men, women, and children, according to the force and ability requisite to the performance of each.

The same principle is in operation in the cotton, flax, and woollen manufactures, in the employment of adult and infant labour. It is the same in agricultural industry. The ploughman and thatcher do not usually lose their time in gathering stones and weeding the corn—labour more appropriately left to women and children.

In intellectual pursuits there is a corresponding gradation of occupation, and according to the diversities of taste and ability men devote themselves to the cultivation of poetry, mathematics, natural philosophy, and jurisprudence. As society advances the divisions of employment become more minute. Chemistry becomes a distinct science from natural philosophy; the physical astronomer separates himself from the astronomical observer; the political economist from the politician, and the legislator from both. Like subdivisions have been introduced in the legal and medical professions: the vocation of a barrister is distinct from that of the conveyancer, equity draftsman, attorney, and solicitor; as that of a physician is from a surgeon, apothecary or druggist. Each confining himself to his peculiar branch of science or business, attains to a proficiency and expertness therein which would be hardly possible were his time consumed and attention distracted by greater variety of pursuits. It follows that the example of a Bacon or Crichton can be emulated

K

with difficulty; when knowledge was less perfect, and not so divided, men might more easily aspire to the honour of universal science or scholarship; but the standard of excellence in any one department is now fixed so high, that to reach it is usually deemed sufficient to occupy the ordinary term of existence.

The degree of refinement a community has attained may be measured by the extent to which the division of employments has been carried. In a rude state of society every man endeavours to supply by his own industry his own occasional wants as they occur. " When he is hungry, he goes to the forest to hunt; when his coat is worn out, he clothes himself with the skin of the first large animal he kills; and when his hut begins to go to ruin, he repairs it as well as he can with the trees and the turf that are nearest it. As each tries only to satisfy his individual wants, no one has a surplus to barter with his neighbour." This state of society, however, must have been of short duration, as the variety in men's natural dispositions and talents would soon suggest the utility of each devoting himself to the occupation for which he was most competent; and, as the produce of his industry would exceed his necessities, he would have a surplus to exchange for the surplus of another differently employed. A general system of barter would thus be introduced; a demand would exist for commodities, and, of course, every expedient that facilitated their production, whether division of labour, or the invention of tools and machines, would be encouraged.

It is the demand for the products of industry that has promoted these minute subdivisions of labour that distinguish rich and civilized communities. The divisions of employment in the making of pins, for instance, could not be carried on as at present, were there not a great consumption of this useful implement. The ten persons now employed in executing the different processes in the art would make probably fifty thousand pins per day. If the demand for pins did not equal this amount, the ten persons could not be employed, and the several branches of the trade could not be distributed so as to be executed in the least expensive and most efficient manner.

Watchmaking is another striking illustration of the principle that the division of labour is limited by the extent of the market, or, in other words, the demand for its products. From the inquiries of a parliamentary committee, it appears there are one hundred and two distinct branches in this trade, each having its separate class of workmen; and that, with the exception of the watch-finishers, whose business is to put together the several parts of a watch, not one of the classes can work at any other than his own particular employment. Now it is plain, if the demand for watches were not at least sufficient to occupy one hundred and two persons, this minute division of occupation could not be supported, and watches would neither be so cheap nor so well executed. The same cause is in operation in almost every department of trade and business: they are all consolidated or divided according as the market is more or less extensive. In a village or small town, for instance, it is common to find the business of a draper, grocer, cheesemonger, and poulterer, all carried on in one establishment, the demand not being extensive enough to maintain a shopkeeper in each line of business. Again, there are some sorts of industry that can be carried on nowhere but in a great city. A porter, shoeblack, or hackney-coach-man, can find employment and subsistence in no other place. A village, or ordinary market-town, would be too narrow a sphere to afford them constant occupation. It is impossible there should be such a trade as a nailer in a small place: such a workman, at the rate of a thousand nails a day, and three hundred working days in the year, will make three hundred thousand nails per annum. But, perhaps in a twelvemonth he would not sell more than one thousand, leaving the market of nails greatly overstocked, and, of course, the price of them ruinously low.

CHAP. III.

MONEY.

Origin of Money—Inconveniences of Barter—Advantages of Gold and Silver as Instruments of Exchange—Effects of an Increase or Diminution in the Supply of the Precious Metals —Forcible Alteration of the Standard of Value.

AFTER each man had begun to occupy himself with a separate trade, the produce of his labour would exceed his consumption. Of the commodity he made he would have more than enough, while of the commodities made by others he would be deficient. As every individual would be similarly situated, the utility of a mutual exchange of surpluses would soon be apparent. Those who pursued the chase might be overstocked with venison, which they would be glad to exchange for a supply of fish; or the maker of bows and arrows might be willing to make an exchange with the maker of some domestic utensil, a wooden bowl, an earthen pot, or stone-hatchet. Barter would become the general fashion of the tribe; from a community of producers, they would, by the introduction of divisions of employment, become a community of exchangers, entering on the first stage of commercial prosperity.

Barter alone, however, would soon be found to be accompanied with two inconveniences: first, it might not be always easy to find a person who had the commodity you wanted, and who was willing to exchange it for your commodity; or, secondly, the commodities might be of unequal value, one having been produced by greater labour than the other. In either case you would be at a stand, no business could be transacted. But the nature of your difficulties will appear more striking by a practical example.

You are, we will suppose, a maker of wooden spoons, and wish to exchange them for animal food. You go to the butcher; but unluckily he is not in want of spoons, he wants bread : there is the baker, however, in want of spoons, but you do not want bread. How inconvenient ! what a miserable state of society, in which every one has too much of one thing and too little of another, and no means of neutralizing your respective necessities !

Let us suppose that matters are not quite so untoward, and you find a butcher in want of spoons; but this may not be enough : he may be a carcass-butcher, and will only exchange his ox or his sheep entire, whereas you are only in want of a joint at most, or perhaps, if a bachelor, a couple of chops or a steak. What is to be done ? This is a second disadvantage of a state of barter. Each individual of the community has applied himself to his calling; but the difficulties attending the exchange of the surplus of his industry, for the precise articles he wants, and the precise quantity of each, are almost insurmountable.

To obviate these impediments to exchange, let us suppose a certain material is discovered, that is divisible into parts, portable and durable; it is not necessary this new article should be consumable either as meat, drink, or clothes, but simply that it shall be prized alike by every member of the society, and every one be willing to exchange his labour or its produce, for the possession of a portion of it. This discovery removes all the obstacles previously existing to exchanges. A medium has been found universally current, that passes with every person, and in every place, and the altered circumstances of the spoon-maker, in consequence, may be easily made apparent. First, it is not necessary he should exchange his stock of spoons directly with the butcher or baker, any other person will answer equally well, provided he can obtain in return what he deems an equitable portion of the new material. Having done this, he has choice of three modes of procedure: first, as the new material is not perishable, it may be stored up for future occasions; or secondly, as it is portable, in lieu of being exchanged in the neighbourhood, it may be conveyed to a more distant part, where better bargains may be obtained ; or thirdly, as it is divisible, it may, in lieu of being all exchanged for one article, meat for example, a part of it may be exchanged for meat, a part for bread, and a part for beer.

It is almost unnecessary to remark, that the material which affords so many conveniences to the spoon-maker, and to every other producer, is MONEY, that universal instrument of exchange, which every civilized community has adopted for measuring the value of labour, and all its productions.

. The introduction of money had two important consequences: first, it gave rise to *prices*, or the fixing the quantity or worth of every commodity in the new standard of value; and secondly, it promoted the formation of a new class in society, called *merchants*, who were not the producers, but the buyers of commodities, to resell in places where they were in the greatest demand, or in quantities suited to the wants of the consumers.

These changes made no alteration in the principle of barter previously existing, it only facilitated the operation, by the introduction of a new agent. The object of barter was to equalise the possession of commodities, according to the wants of each; and the object of buying and selling by the invention of money, is precisely the same: in both cases consumption is promoted, and value for value, in the estimate of the parties, exchanged; only in barter, as just explained, the commodity can neither be so readily obtained, nor in the exact quantity suited to individual wants.

The instrument first used as money was not so perfect, as it subsequently became, and consisted probably of that commodity which constituted the staple wealth of the community. Thus in the early ages, cattle are frequently mentioned as the measure of value. Homer says the armour of Diomed cost only nine oxen; but that of Glaucus 100 oxen.

When mankind became agricultural, corn was substituted for cattle; remains of corn-money are still to be found in old college leases and agreements, that stipulate the payment of rents and wages in that commodity. The English kings even of the Tudor race, under the privilege of purveyance, claimed a large portion of the royal income in kind; that is, in victuals and provisions of all sorts. Salt is said to be a common medium of exchange in Abyssinia; a species of shells in some parts of India; hides or dressed leather in some other countries; and Adam Smith relates, that in his time it was not uncommon in a village of Scotland for workmen to carry nails instead of money to the baker's shop or alehouse. The primitive money of the Spartans was of iron; of the Romans, copper; but gold and silver have been adopted as the common instrument of commerce, among all rich and civilized communities.

Gold and silver being more valuable than the other metals, are better adapted to the uses of money. Iron and copper, like cattle or corn, are too bulky representatives of value; they are deficient in the essential quality of portability: whereas a smaller portion of the precious metals measuring the price of commodities, may be more easily carried about the person, or from place to place. At first they seem to have been used in the mass, in bars or ingots, without stamp or coinage. The party having agreed about the quantity to be given, that quantity was then weighed off. Abraham weighs to Ephron the 400 shekels of silver, which he had agreed to pay for the field of Machpelah.

The use of the metals in this state would be attended with two inconveniences; besides the trouble, mistakes and disputes would occur in the weighing of them; and secondly, there would be the assaying, or testing their fineness. Submitting them to both processes would render a market, or even a single sale, or payment, a lengthy and troublesome business. Undoubtedly the latter point, or the ascertaining the degree of purity of the metals, would require the greatest sketch of science. Fortunately means were discovered for superseding the necessity of both weighing and assaying. According to Goguet, the fabrication of COINS, or the impressing pieces of metal with a stamp, indicating their weight and fineness, belongs to the remotest period of history; and when this was done under the authority of the state, not only were commercial dealings vastly facilitated, but the most effective guarantee introduced against fraud and contention.

By the invention of coins, the precious metals attained the greatest improvement, of which they appear susceptible as the general instrument of exchange. The qualities most essential to money have been already partly indicated, and are, 1. that it should be divisible into portions of greater or less value; without this it would be a convenience for the rich and none for the poor; 2. that it should admit of being *kept* or *hoarded*, without depreciating in value, otherwise no one would exchange com-

modities for money unless he expected to be speedily
able to re-exchange it for something else ; 3. that it
should, by possessing great value in small bulk, be
easily portable from place to place ; 4. that it
should be of uniform denomination ; in other words,
that a piece of coin, a sovereign, or shilling for instance, should represent the same quantity of metal
in weight and fineness : without this quality the intrinsic value of different sovereigns and shillings
could not be known without scales and tests ; 5. that
it should possess *stability* of value : as money is the
standard or measure by which the worth of all other
commodities is estimated, it is as essential that its
own value should be invariable, as that a yard
measure or a pound weight should be invariable ;
without this most essential requisite, it in fact ceases to
be money, and introduces the greatest derangement
in the value of property and mercantile transactions.

With the exception of the last, the precious metals
possess the other qualities desirable in money in
great perfection ; and they possess the last in greater
perfection, perhaps, than any other material that
could be substituted in their place.   Money is itself
a commodity, possessing intrinsic value, and its
price is influenced by the greater or less quantity in
circulation.   Fluctuations in value from this cause
have operated slowly and at distant intervals, and
much less so on gold and silver than on any other
articles of use and consumption.   The greatest
change in their value was caused by the discovery
of the American mines in the sixteenth century,

when the price of silver in Europe fell at least two-thirds. Plate in consequence became much cheaper, and a service might be purchased for one-third of the coin or labour it before demanded. So far it was a social convenience, but as an instrument of exchange the precious metals became less valuable. It became necessary to load the person with a greater weight of them, and carry three shillings in the pocket to make a purchase, where one would have before sufficed. It follows that the speculative avidity evinced in 1824-5 for opening new and improving the working of old mines in South America, was not a passion in which the public was deeply interested. Individuals might have profited by such adventures had they been successful, but they would have been of slight utility to mankind. Capital, flowing into agriculture or manufacture, or applied to internal improvements, augments produce and facilitates the operation of industry. But if the supply of bullion from the mines had been quadrupled, the value of the metallic currency would, in the same proportion have been depreciated. As an instrument of commerce it would have been rendered less convenient; it would have been reduced nearer to a level with copper, and that portability, which forms one of its chief recommendations, would have been impaired.

Causes, however, of an opposite description are considered by many to have been in gradual operation, and that the tendency of gold and silver has been to *rise in value.* That such a rise is in pro-

gress, has been inferred from the following considerations: 1. The unsettled state of South America,
during the last twenty years, and consequent interruption to the working of the gold and silver mines.
2. The increased consumption of bullion in plate and
other articles of luxury, from the increase of wealth.
3. The increased demand for the precious metals as
a measure of value, owing to the increase of population, commerce, and commodities. 4. The general
substitution of a metallic for a paper currency in
England, America, and the continental states. All
these causes, by increasing the demand, must have
increased the value of bullion ; unless its tendency to
rise has been counteracted by the cotemporary effect
of other causes, especially the increased productiveness of the Russian mines, and the less disposition
to hoard treasure, formerly so prevalent in Europe,
and rendered necessary by the insecurity of property, and the non-establishment of banks of deposit.

The rise of bullion in value, if any, has been too
gradual to have had any material share in the
ruinous fluctuations in prices that have been experienced within the last forty years. Greater mischiefs
than the almost imperceptible variation in the value
of the precious metals, have been produced by
suddenly altering the *standard of the coinage ;* that
is, by suddenly introducing into circulation, coins
of the same denomination, but less weight and fineness than those previously issued. This was a favourite device, for cheating their subjects, of Frederic
the Great of Prussia, and of some of the Bourbon

kings: it has been even revived in this country, under the specious pretext of an "equitable adjustment" with the national creditor. But it is impossible schemes of this complexion can be countenanced by a just and enlightened community; they are such barefaced frauds, and disgust more than open robbery. A forcible alteration in the measure of value, is a forcible alteration in all pecuniary engagements—debts, leases, agreements, bonds, and contracts of every kind; and as this alteration is made only perhaps for the benefit, as by the consent of one party, it is a forcible violation of the most sacred rights of property.

CHAP. IV.

PAPER CURRENCY.

Origin of Paper Money—Commercial Paper, and its Uses—Distinction between Paper and Coin—Absence of intrinsic Value in Paper, cause of its over-issue—Proper Functions of Bankers, and Defects in our Monetary System—Money ought only to be issued under the Control and Guarantee of the State—Profit on the issue of Money belongs to the Public, not Individuals—Distinction between a Depreciated and Excessive issue of Paper—Proportions of Bills of Exchange and Bank-notes in circulation—Causes of the Mercantile Crisis of 1824-5—Advantages of a Sovereign over a Bank-note—Stagnation in Trade caused by a want of Credit, not of Bank Paper.

THE advantages of a coinage of gold and silver are so great, that a long time elapsed before mankind discovered a more perfect instrument of exchange. Paper money is comparatively a modern invention, and had its origin principally in the increased number and magnitude of commercial transactions. Although the precious metals possess great value in small bulk, they are not so easily transported as bank-notes. A million of specie could only be sent from London to York in waggons well guarded; but a remittance to the same amount in paper, might be done by post, travelling at the rate of ten miles an hour, and in no danger from brigands. As respects secure and rapid conveyance, paper then is better than gold, and this in a trading community, where the transfer of payments is incessant and multiplied, is a valuable recommendation.

The main purpose of money is to facilitate the exchange of commodities, and as the expense of maintaining this pecuniary machinery is borne by the community, it is desirable that it should be done in the most economical manner. But a currency of the precious metals is the *dearest*, as that of paper is the *cheapest*, that could be issued. Mr. Jacob, in his *Inquiry into the Production and Consumption of the Precious Metals*, has entered into some curious calculations to elucidate this subject. The abrasion, or loss of coins from wear, he estimates at one six-hundreth part a year for gold, and one two-hundreth part for silver coins. The loss from other causes, as by fires, shipwrecks, and accidents, must be considerable. Altogether, Mr. M'Culloch estimates the annual diminution at one per cent.

(*Commercial Dicty*. p. 871.)   So that to repair the wear and tear of a metallic currency of one hundred millions would cost annually a million a year, exclusive of the expense of an annual recoinage to supply the place of the coins that had become unfit, or disappeared from circulation.

The fabrication of so cheap a substitute for coin as bank-notes, might be considered to carry the art of manufacturing money to perfection ; but such has been the ingenuity, stimulated by the wants of commerce, that these constitute only one among many kindred contrivances of mercantile men.   Paper currency is not restricted to the promissory notes of bankers, nor bills of exchange ; but may be defined, after the Abbé Morellet, to consist of every negotiable security, every acknowledgment of debt or pecuniary obligation, every stipulation by writing between a debtor and creditor, which obliges the former to pay, and authorizes the latter to exact a value ; and which security, acknowledgment, and writing, being transferable, are the means of transferring values without the actual transport of the commodities they represent or attest the ownership.

The quantity of money of all kinds necessary to a country depends on the amount of its wealth, and extent of its commerce.   A poor country, with little trade, does not require much money, either to represent its riches, or to facilitate the exchange of its commodities.   England, it is well known, is the most rich and commercial nation in the world, and to represent its wealth, and carry on its vast and varied exchanges, coin, aided even by bank paper, would form a totally inadequate medium. How, for instance, could the value be represented, or the payments be made, involved in the transfer of the hundreds of millions of property that change hands every year, by the intervention of notes and coins? The mere counting of one, or the weighing of the other, would be an incredible labour. Then mark the ingenuity —the delicate and curious machinery that has been introduced to supersede the necessity of either. By the use of bills of exchange, bills of lading, checks, scrip-notes, clearing houses, and a variety of other contrivances, aided by a vast fabric of credit taken and given in open account, money, in its common acceptation hardly ever enters into mercantile affairs; it is indeed the substance really meant and shadowed forth; but it never, as one may say, bodily passes from merchant to merchant; and is only used as petty cash for paying wages and settling balances of insignificant amount: all the great transactions of commerce, all the great masses of property—the roads and canals—the mines of gold, and silver, and iron—the cargoes of sugar, cotton and indigo, that are constantly being transferred from one possessor to another, on the Royal Exchange, or from London to Liverpool, Manchester, and Glasgow—all this is done by the intervention of the credit and commercial paper mentioned; the business of the mercantile classes being reduced, by a wonderful system of balancing payments, to little

L

more than a game at chess, or the working in their counting-houses an algebraic equation, consisting of the debit and credit side of each account, and communicating the result to their agents, customers and correspondents in every part of the globe.

It would be unsuited to the limits of this publication to describe, in detail, the commercial machinery I have indicated : but in speaking of paper money, it is impossible to help glancing at such an extraordinary fabric as our monetary system ; nor think without astonishment of the successive steps of its progress from the state of barter to the use of the raw metal—then to coin—then to bills, bankers' notes and checks—and finally to the winding up and balancing of all commercial dealings in England, Europe, Asia, and America, in that great focus and centre of circulation, the British metropolis !

Paper money has been as powerful a commercial instrument in facilitating the exchange of commodities, as the steam-engine in the production of them. Yet, in one respect, it is inferior to coin. It possesses only *conventional*, not *intrinsic* value. Coin not only measures the value of commodities in exchange, it is a real equivalent for them ; it is the veritable substance, of which paper currency is only the representative. Whether paper money is worth any thing or nothing, depends on the guarantee under which it is issued ; but coined money depends on no such contingency—it is its own guarantee— the universal medium of commerce, and in every

market of the world will be accepted as an equivalent for merchandise, in proportion to its weight and
purity.

This property of coin arises from the material of
which it is made being a regular article of commerce : a coinage of the precious metals could not
be easily maintained in circulation if its equivalent
were not nearly on a par with its representative
value.   To make this appear, it is only necessary to
consider the effect of an issue of gold or silver
tokens, the representative value of which, as money,
greatly exceeded, or fell short of their real value as
bullion.   In one case, a profit might be realized by
converting the tokens into bullion ; and in the other,
by converting bullion into tokens : and either alternative, if the temptation were considerable, would
be sufficient to destroy a circulation so unwisely
constituted.

Coin possessing intrinsic value is an advantage,
inasmuch as it renders it a *safe* instrument of exchange ; it is a disadvantage, inasmuch as it renders
it a *dear* one.

Such conditions do not attach to a currency of
paper. A parcel of bank-notes, if they are not valuable as money, are valuable as nothing. No one
can make a profit by converting them into any thing
else.   If the bank become worthless that has issued
them, they become worthless too, and they cannot
be transmuted into any thing of value. It is different with a sovereign : if it cannot be returned to
the mint, it can be taken to the goldsmith or dealer

in bullion, where it can be exchanged for coin of another sort, or for some article of use or ornament.

The absence of intrinsic value in paper money has formed a principal cause of those disastrous vicissitudes in our monetary system, which have distinguished the last thirty years of our commercial history. Fabricated almost without expense, it executed all the functions of money, and the same advantages were derived from its employment. More of it advanced in loans, and greater the interest realized; more of it employed in trades, and greater the profit. The temptations to issue it to excess were too great to be resisted. Advances were made to individuals without adequate security; a spirit of over-speculation was encouraged in every branch of national industry; prices, rents, tithes, mortgages, every thing, in short, the value of which is measured by money, was forced up to an unnatural height; and then, when the artificial impulse could no longer be supported, came a mercantile reaction—a subsidence of the pecuniary deluge, leaving the land, not enriched, like Egypt, by the overflowings of the Nile, but covered with the debris of aërial castle-building!

It is the readiness with which paper-currency ministers to the avidity of mercantile speculation, that forms the strongest objection to its being issued under the same principle of competition and absence from legislative interference, which ought to govern the supply of commodities. Like the atmosphere we breathe, it forms a medium susceptible of a too sudden power of expansion and condensation : possessing this elastic property, the management of it requires to be subjected to more comprehensive views of the principles and wants of the general circulation, than are likely to be entertained by unconnected individuals, acting under the impulse of their own real or supposed commercial interests.

On the first opening of new marts of commerce, or on the occurrence of a probable deficiency of any article of consumption, it is invariably found that the extent of the demand, of the profits to be realized, or of the deficiency to be supplied, is vastly exaggerated. Subsequent examination and loss correct these errors ; but the eagerness of gain, and the race of competition, leave no time for preliminary inquiry and reflection. On this rock all great speculations have foundered, from the memorable South Sea year to the present time ; and it is because paper money and the credit it facilitates and establishes, is too ready an instrument of over-trading and mercantile precipitancy, that it becomes so hazardous a medium : for it has been productive of the twofold calamities of creating with too much facility the resources for embarking to excess in new undertakings, and of aggravating the evils of the subsequent change in the employment of capital and industry, by the suddenness with which it may be withdrawn from circulation.

A reference to our commercial history for the last seventy years would show that the more frequent and extensive mercantile reactions which have happened during this period, have been mainly occasioned by the power to issue paper money being conjoined with the proper functions of banking. It is difficult to account for the long toleration of a monetary system fraught with so many calamities, so inimical to the steady growth of national opulence ; especially after reiterated experiences in 1793, 1811, 1815, 1818, and 1825, of its infallibly disastrous issues. The all-absorbing interest of the war may be assigned as one reason ; a reluctance on the part of Government to interfere in what appeared a commercial question, involving the principles of free trade and individual prudence, may have been another : but the most potent reason appears to have been an imperfect knowledge of the subject, both on the part of economical writers and statesmen.

Until within these few years *banking* and *money-making* have been most improperly confounded. No two business, however, can be more distinct ; one may be safely left to individual competition ; the other can only safely be confided to the state. The chief business of a banking establishment is to expedite the making of payments, to discount bills, to make advances by loan, and to form a secure deposit for cash. The object of money-making is very different; it is to establish an invariable standard of value for the general convenience of the community ; and this is a duty it is as incumbent on the Government to discharge, as it is for it to establish a standard-weight or a standard-measure of length

and capacity. What confusion and mischief would
ensue if these were left to the caprice of individuals;
more especially if they had an interest in gradually
elongating the imperial yard, or enlarging the imperial bushel; and then again, without notice or
responsibility, restoring them to their former di-
mensions! The consequences have been precisely
similar, in leaving bankers to issue money, or its
representative, without check, security, or responsibility.

The most essential requisite in money is *stability
of value.* Where the power to issue is vested, is
vested the power to alter its value, to alter the rate
of wages, the prices of commodities, and the terms
of contracts. Can a power so universal in its operation, touching every one, from the richest to the
poorest, be safely wielded by any other authority
less than that of the state, whose interests, it may
be supposed, are not partial, but identified with
those of the whole community? In the management of our monetary system there has been singular inconsistency. The guarantee of the value of
the coinage is the purity and weight of the bullion
it contains, and the *public stamp* impressed upon it
authenticates both. But a banker's note, which re-
presents the coin, executes all its functions, and on
which a profit is realized, has been suffered to circulate without any other guarantee than *a promise,*
that might be valid or illusive, according to the folly
or knavery, good or ill fortune of the issuer. It is
true, such a mockery of what money ought to

be was not generally a legal tender in payment; still as government failed to provide a better currency, the people had hardly an option to take it or not: even the working classes were compelled to receive for wages this depreciated representative of value; and not unfrequently shared in the losses of the speculative capitalist, though excluded, if successful, from his gains. This was a sad hiatus in the domestic government of the country, especially so commercial a one as England, and the chasm has only yet been partially filled up.

It must not be inferred that the vulgar error is here committed of attaching an importance to the material of which money is made, whether gold, paper, or cobwebs: provided the requisites before enumerated (page 138) as essential to the instrument of commerce can be obtained, the cheaper it can be produced the better. But the point to be ascertained is, can these requisites be guaranteed without placing the common currency of the country under the watchfulness and control of the state? It might be issued by one or more banking associations, and they might give security in real or funded property to the extent of their issues; but this scheme would not be exempt from difficulty and objection. First, the exacting of securities would require the establishment of a delicate and rather complicated machinery: the amount of the securities would have to vary with the ever varying amount of the issues of each banking firm, and the security after all, as in analogous cases, might ultimately prove fraudulent or inadequate.

Stepping, however, over this difficulty in order to come at another; could the circulation be adjusted under a competitive system, so as neither to exceed nor fall short of the wants of the community; there is no test for estimating precisely the quantity of money necessary to pay wages and expedite the exchange of commodities, depending as it does on the value of money itself; on the amount of population; on expedients for economizing the use of it; on the state of credit; and on the number, magnitude, and rapidity of mercantile transactions. As, however, the gain of the bankers would depend on the bales of paper they issued, it is highly probable the public would have enough of it, and that the spirit of enterprise, which has repeatedly blazed forth of old—though it always proved an *ignis fatuus* in the end—would not expire for want of fuel!

In Scotland there might not be equal danger of an excessive issue of paper; but Scotland is not a case in point: a small number of banking firms, conducted on a few general and concerted principles, may be adequate to the management of her circulation, and be altogether unsuited to the greater trade, wealth, enterprise, and population of England.

Another important consideration connected with this subject is the appropriation of the PROFIT arising from the issue of the national currency. The money of the community need not be made of so expensive a material as the precious metals; it may consist wholly or chiefly of paper, and be issued under such check and control as to be effectually secured against depreciation, fluctuation in value, or any other casualty to which it has been heretofore liable. But if made of so cheap a substance as the last, and the quantity of it required for circulation amounts, say to one hundred millions, why then the loan of this sum to the people for trading purposes, would yield a revenue of four or five millions after defraying all charges. Now is there any reason the bankers of England, or Scotland, or Ireland should share the whole or any portion of this revenue among them, any more than the shipowners, manufacturers, merchants, agriculturists, West India planters, or any other class of capitalists in the kingdom? Most assuredly not: it is not a *commercial profit* arising from the risk and trouble of buying and selling commodities; it is a perquisite appertaining to the people in their national capacity. The privilege of making and issuing money is one of the oldest prerogatives of state; it may be delegated, but can never be safely alienated; and forms a legitimate source of public income, not of individual emolument.

Why so unexceptionable a source of public revenue as the national currency should have been so long overlooked, or been suffered to be appropriated by private associations, will be hereafter a subject of surprise. The government, by resuming its ancient prerogative of issuing money, might easily raise a considerable fund for reducing the public debt, and thereby relieving public burdens. The saving it might effect by substituting a cheap in place of a dear instrument of commerce would be greater than could be effected by any banking firm, however respectable. Even the Bank of England considers it prudent to keep on hand a stock of coin and bullion equal to *one-third* of all her liabilities, including both deposits and issues. This is meant as a precaution against any sudden run on the establishment. But a public currency issued under the guarantee of the state, and the quantity of which could neither be increased nor diminished without the approval of the legislature, would require no expensive preparation against the occurrence of panic or other emergency. It need not be made payable on demand *in coin* to preserve its standard value from depreciation and adapt it to the wants of foreign commerce; it would be sufficient, as the late Mr. Ricardo suggested, to make it exchangeable for bullion only when presented in quantities exceeding a fixed amount, and the store of bullion necessary to keep in reserve for this purpose need not, I believe, be very great.[*]

[*] It may be useful here to guard the reader against an error frequently committed, of not distinguishing between a *depreciated* and *excessive issue* of paper money. The position of the Bullionists that paper could never be depreciated while convertible into coin on demand is correct; but this condition is no security against a redundant issue. Redundancy, however, is quite as great an evil as depreciation, and against this the public can have no protection, save the prudential forbearance of bankers in restricting their issues, or their being compelled to give security to their amount. The inadequacy of the former

Even under this system of a secure and economical currency, it might not be advisable to withdraw our present beautiful gold coinage. For the payment of wages and all the little shopping and retail business of life, the precious metals are more convenient than paper. A sovereign is more portable—more readily passed from one to another—less apt to be lost than a bank-note, and though it may be counterfeited, this is not so profitable and easy a piece of roguery as was formerly the forgery of one-pound notes. Moreover a sovereign cannot be torn, and is proof against the two elements of fire and water. All money, however, above the value of five pounds, might consist of paper, and the public, not the banker, have the profit arising from its issue.

The expense of a metallic currency so limited would be inconsiderable. The great bulk of our currency consists of five-pound notes and upwards ; the small notes in circulation for which sovereigns were substituted, and the withdrawal of which has

---

security has been repeatedly experienced. The paper of the banking firms that failed in 1824, was always payable on demand in *coin* or Bank of England notes ; it was never depreciated prior to their actual stoppage ; yet it was *issued to excess ;* that is, beyond the legitimate wants of trade, and on inconvertible securities for mere speculative adventures. This is the difference I wish to explain between a depreciated and excessive issue of paper. Paper is not *value*, it is only the representative of value ; if that value does not exist in a secure and available shape, then it is a fiction—a deception : it is in excess, according to the only standard by which excess can be measured or the term properly understood.

been so sorely lamented, never exceeded five or six millions, or about one-eighth part of the total issues of paper by the country banks and bank of England.*

The great mass of commercial currency, that by which all the great transactions of trade have been carried on, consists of bills of exchange, and the proportion of these in circulation to bank paper, cannot be very precisely ascertained. Mr. Lloyd stated, in his examination before the committee of the House of Lords, on the resumption of cash payments in 1819, that the proportion between the circulation of bank-notes and bills of exchange was as one to ten. (*Minutes of Evidence*, p. 82.) Admitting this proportion to be correct, and that the bank paper of all denominations in circulation amounts to forty millions, then the total amount of paper currency of all descriptions in England is about four hundred millions.

From this analysis it is apparent how important an element bills of exchange are in the general circulation. Fluctuations in the amount of them afloat have contributed more to the alternations of

---

* Bank-notes are supposed to wear out in three years; so that a banker must annually issue new notes to the amount of one-third of his issues to keep out the same quantity of paper. The issues of the Bank of England, yearly, and even weekly, are known from returns to parliament; but no such returns were ever required from the country bankers, and the amount of paper they had in circulation could only be estimated on the principle mentioned—namely, that it was treble the amount of their annual issues.

commercial prosperity and depression than fluctuations in the issues of the banks. The extension of credit by bills and open account was, in truth, the main cause of the great mercantile crisis of 1824-5. Credit is not capital, no more than a bank-note is coin : but so long as it is current, it is equivalent to capital for all the purposes of trade and speculation. The Bank of England and the provincial bankers, by enlarging their issues in discounts, gave the first impulse to the extension of credit at the period mentioned ; but their increased issue of notes formed only the pedestal of the vast superstructure of commercial paper that was erected upon them. It was the last that afforded the stimulant for overtrading in cotton, hemp, silk, and indigo ; for negotiating foreign loans; for mining adventures ; for canals and railroads ; and for the thousand other schemes, frantic and knavish, which were set on foot. When the banks began to contract their issues, the Bank of England first, and the country banks after ; or, to resume our metaphor, when the foundation began to shrink the upper fabric began to totter, and then followed that catastrophe of ruin and disappointment, of which it is unnecessary to revive the melancholy remembrance by description.

These deductions might all be established by reference to documents laid before parliament, showing the increase in the issues of the banks, and the contemporary increase in bills of exchange ; but this would draw us into a lengthened detail of figures

unsuited to our publication. Let it suffice to remark, that the increase in the issues of the metropolitan and private banks during the three years
preceding the reaction of 1825, amounted to less
than ten millions; whereas it appears from the
returns of stamps issued for bills of exchange, that
the simultaneous increase in that description of
commercial paper alone, amounted to between ninety
and one hundred millions!

The fall in prices and a deficiency in the circulation for the purposes of trade and industry have
been ascribed to the withdrawal of the small-note
currency. But this cause is quite inadequate to
the production of the effect assigned. The place
of the one-pound note was supplied by an issue of
specie, so that no diminution of currency could
ensue from this transition. The mercantile depression, experienced since the crisis of 1825, has resulted, I apprehend, more from the contraction of
credit by bill and open account than the contraction
of bank paper, and this, for the best of all reasons,
the salutary warnings of experience. The check on
commercial activity and enterprise will disappear
with the progress of consumption, and such improvements in our mercantile system as shall afford
more safe and profitable channels for the employment of capital: it will be then seen that the stagnation of trade originated in a want of remunerative returns, not of commercial currency, which
last mercantile men have a ready way of producing

among themselves when not deterred by the aspect of the times.

I shall conclude with remarking, that it appears to me, from long and attentive consideration of the subject, that the national currency can never attain the stability it ought to possess, till the trade of banking is confined to its old and legitimate functions, and the state resumes its ancient prerogative of guaranteeing and issuing both the real and representative money of the kingdom.

CHAP. IV.

CAPITAL AND THE MIDDLE CLASSES.

Capital and its productive Power—How it tends to economize, abridge, and augment the Efficiency of Industry—Conflicting Claims of Capital and Labour—Utility of the Middle Classes, of Bankers, Merchants, Wholesale Dealers, and Retailers—Advantages of Middlemen in equalizing Prices and the Supply of Commodities—Claims of Labour to share in the Profits of Capital—Classification of Society into Productive and Unproductive Consumers—Luxuries stimulate Industry—Utility of Authors, Actors, and Domestic Servants—All classes co-operate for the general good—Recapitulation.

CAPITAL is that portion of the wealth, property, or money of the community, which is productively employed.

Labour is the agency by which capital is made productive of wages, profit, or revenue.

Labour is the parent of capital, and capital cannot be made productive without the co-operation of labour; but labour may be productive without the aid of capital; and this is the only superiority the former possesses over the latter; though it is probable this superiority never practically existed in the world: since it is impossible to conceive mankind in that rude state in which labour is exerted unaccompanied with capital. The implement used by a savage in hunting or fishing, and the food he consumes while so occupied, are his capital, and it is only when the bare hands or teeth have been employed that labour has been unassociated with capital.

It may then be premised at the outset, that it would be a futile inquiry to institute any comparison on the relative claims of capital and industry; as much so as on the relative claims of the ploughshare and ploughman in husbandry. They are alike valuable and indispensable in ministering to human subsistence and enjoyment.

Without capital labour could not be efficiently exerted. The Indian would with difficulty procure the means of subsistence unaided by his hunting-spear and fishing-hook. The power of money, which is capital, need not be insisted upon; it is felt by every one in every pursuit and undertaking to be all but omnipotent: it reclaims the waste, digs the canal, constructs the road, puts ships in motion; it is the sinew of war, and the spring of improvement in peace; it is at once the seed and fruit of national opulence; the soul of commercial and manufacturing enterprise: and without its agency even the bounties of nature would be stagnant and unproductive.

Capital has been called a "giant labourer;" it has certainly long arms and powerful tendons, which connect the ends of the earth, fill up valleys, and level mountains.

A grown-up person, capable of useful exertion, is considered by political economists a portion of accumulated capital: all the sums expended in his maintenance, nurture, and instruction, may be repaid by future labour, and the capital expended in infancy replaced in maturity. Thus capital is *stored up industry*, provided to develop itself in new and equivalent forms; it is collective force, which, like the momentum in bodies, is exhausted by reproducing itself in others.

Capital operates like the application of machinery in economizing, abridging and augmenting the efficiency of industry.

This it does, *first*, by facilitating the division of labour. Before labour can be divided, a stock of goods must be previously accumulated sufficient to maintain the labourer, and to supply him with materials and tools. A workman could not devote himself to his business unless provided beforehand with the means of support till his work is completed, either by himself or employer. A farmer, possessed of capital to pay wages and maintain his servants, may employ them in tilling the ground, in the several occupations for which they are best qualified, till the harvest is reaped.

Secondly, capital saves labour in the production of commodities, and thus by rendering them cheaper, brings them within the reach of a greater number of consumers. This it does chiefly by the intervention of machinery. There could be obviously no machines made without a previous store of money to defray the cost of their erection, of the material of which they are composed, and of the maintenance of those employed in inventing and perfecting them. The advantages derived from this source are so universally diffused, and have been so frequently set forth, that it is unnecessary to dwell upon them. Every thing is now a machine, from a spinning-jenny to a toothpick, and the comforts and luxuries derived from mechanical invention are felt by every individual in his habitation, food, clothing, and mental culture.

Thirdly, it enables work to be executed better as well as cheaper. This is strikingly exemplified in printing. Compare the clearness, precision and intelligibility of a printed volume with the like qualities in the best-written manuscript, and we at once see the superiority of typography to penmanship. The same truth is exemplified in the cotton manufacture. A single pound of raw cotton may be drawn into an even thread 132 miles long—a wonder which the human hand alone could never have accomplished.

In the slicing of logs of mahogany for sideboards
and tables; in the flattening of iron plates; in the
coining of money; in the making the finer sorts of
pins and needles; in the printing of calicoes; in the
staining of paper; in the propelling of steam-carriages and steam-boats, we have examples familiar
to every one, of the better workmanship of machinery, and of the effects produced by the capital
invested in its construction.

Lastly, it enables works to be executed, and
commodities to be produced, which could not be
done without it.

For proof of this we may exclaim in the words of
the epitaph of Sir Christopher Wren— *Circumspice*
—Look around; for all we behold is the production
of capital! What could man have done by his
hands alone, unaided by a previous fund of money?
Could he have built the Pyramids, St. Paul's, Westminster Abbey, New London Bridge, or constructed
the Manchester railway? Could he have drained
the fens of Lincolnshire, made the Breakwater, or
erected Eddystone Lighthouse? All our manufactories, warehouses, harbours, and wharfs; all our
houses, churches, and public buildings—all are the
produce of capital. Without it our lands could not
be tilled from Michaelmas to Midsummer; nor our
merchants bring to our shores the varied products of
the globe. It is as indispensable a preliminary to
production as a charge of gunpowder is to the
expulsion of a bullet from a gun. It is only another
name for civilization. A savage is no capitalist;

and what a miserable and impotent creature ! It is
the chief distinction between man and the brute creation ; for, with the exception of the bee and the
beaver, and one or two others, animals are not capitalists. An absence of it is a primary cause of the
misery and degradation of Ireland, and the possession of it was the chief point of superiority England
possessed over Scotland sixty years since.

But why dwell on such commonplace topics ?
It is really burning candles in daylight, and is only
a theme fit for a nursery, or at most a juvenile aca-
demy. The excuse offered to the reader is, that
recently very strange ideas have been propagated on
the subject even by adult persons. It has been attempted to depreciate the utility of capital, and consider the profits derived from its employment as a
spoliation or tithe-gathering by which capitalists appropriate the reward that justly belongs to industry.
This, it must be confessed, is a singular doctrine,
and the attempts that have been made to stir up
industry into a sort of rebellion against capital re-
minds one of a story related by an ancient Greek
author :

" It happened formerly," says Plutarch, " that the
several members of the body rose in rebellion against
the belly. They thought it hard they should do all
the work and receive so little of the reward : the
legs carried it from place to place with the easy
swing of a sedan-chair ; the hands fed it with dainty
morsels; the ears cheered it with delicious music ;
and the eyes, the palate, and the touch, like so

many sentinels guarded it from all internal and external injuries. For all these services the belly made no return: nay worse; it consumed every thing: all the hands could catch, or the feet could reach, all passed into its devouring exchequer. This was not to be borne, it was intolerable; there was no equality; it was downright aristocracy, or monarchy, or worse. Discontent spread rapidly from one member of the community to another, till, at last, the whole commonwealth became violently agitated: murmuring and petitioning were not enough; remonstrance followed remonstrance in quick succession, some of them of the most seditious and inflammatory character, till, at length, the malcontents broke out into open acts of tumult and rebellion. The legs refused to do their office; the eyes put up their shutters; and the arms were suspended in the air; a terrible crisis was evidently at hand, society was on the eve of dissolution, and every thing fast verging to a state of nature !"

The reader will naturally be desirous to learn (if he has not learnt before) the issue of this civic strife. The fact is it was soon found to be mutually destructive of all parties and all interests. The belly itself was not exempt from suffering, and grumbled internally; but the arms, legs, and other members of the body politic became totally powerless for both good and evil. Friends interfered: a parley ensued, and terms of peace were agreed upon. It was discovered they had no separate interests, that they were bound by reciprocal ties, that there could be no production without consumption ; and that the legs, arms, and eyes, were really as much benefited as the stomach itself by the produce it received and distributed through the different channels and conduits of the social state.

A similar issue, it is probable, will result from the existing dispute between capital and industry. It can only arise from misapprehension of their respective functions ; and when that is removed, they will assuredly act harmoniously together. To hasten so desirable a consummation, I shall shortly notice the relations of utility that connect capitalists and the working orders, including under the former the middle classes, consisting chiefly of bankers, merchants, manufacturers, and retailers.

It has been already shown how efficient an agent capital is in the production of commodities; and this efficiency is greatly augmented, first, by the *territorial divisions* in its application, and, secondly, by the several classes of capitalists devoting themselves to specific branches of employment.

The territorial divisions in the employment of capital arise from diversity of soil, or climate, or from the peculiar taste and abilities of the inhabitants, that render it most advantageous to pursue particular branches of industry.   Thus, Portugal and France are better wine-producing countries than Great Britain and the Netherlands, which find a greater profit in the cultivation of manufactures. Upon the variations in the natural capabilities of kingdoms the great principle of FREE TRADE is

founded : for it is obviously as much the interest of
nations that they should mutually exchange and
cultivate those products for which they are best
adapted by physical situation, as it is for the interest
of individuals to choose a calling in which they are
most likely to excel by peculiar talent and disposition.

Not only do countries vary in the facilities they
afford for the employment of capital, but also different districts in the same country. " A district,"
Mr. M'Culloch observes, " where coal is abundant,
which has an easy access to the ocean, and a considerable command of internal navigation, is the
natural seat of manufactures. Wheat, and other
species of grain, are the proper products of rich
arable soils; and cattle, after being reared in
mountainous districts, are most advantageously
fattened in meadows and low grounds. It is clearly
as little for the advantage of the inhabitants of different districts, as it would be for that of an individual, to engage in every possible employment.
Who can doubt that vastly more manufactured
goods, corn, cattle, and fish, are produced by the
people of Lancashire confining their principal attention to manufactures, those of Kent to agriculture,
those of Argyleshire to the raising of cattle, and
those of the Shetland Isles to the catching of fish,
than if each had endeavoured directly to supply
themselves with these or similar productions without
the intervention of an exchange ?"

Secondly, the productive power of capital is augmenced by the several classes of capitalists following specific employments. This brings us to the utility of different occupations ; and it will be easy to show that there is really no class of middlemen who live, as it has been alleged, at the expense of the working orders, but that they are all alike useful, and give either money or money's worth for every thing they receive. As a general proposition, it may be affirmed, that as all classes have originated in the wants of society, no class would continue to be supported without experience of its utility. But as this is treating the matter too abstractedly, I shall shortly describe the functions of the several classes of capitalists.

First, of Bankers. These appear, at first sight, the least useful of capitalists ; but if we consider their office more attentively, we shall find them indispensable in a manufacturing and trading community. Besides their function of *makers* of money, or its representative, they are also its *carriers* and *retailers*. In the former capacity, we could no more do without them than without Pickford's van or the mail-coach. For instance, a person wishes to remit a sum of money from Leeds to London ; how is it to be done ? He might, in the first place, send it by a friend, but his friend might prove false to him ; or in the second place, he might find a person in London indebted to a person in Leeds, and through this medium negotiate the payment in the metropolis. But look at the disadvantages of both these means of transmission : in the first place, there is insecurity; in the second, trouble and loss of time in finding out the parties necessary to complete the transaction. How much better is the existing practice, to take your cash to Beckett's or Brown's bank, receive an order for payment in London, and thus be saved from all risk of accident or miscarriage, at an expense hardly worth mentioning.

As *retailers* in money, bankers are not less useful and necessary. They receive large deposits from some persons, and afterwards divide, transmit, and circulate them among a much greater number. Every one almost has experienced their utility in this branch of service. A merchant receives a heavy remittance from abroad; he has no immediate occasion for it, so deposits it in safety with a banker, till he finds out a profitable channel for its employment. A manufacturer is constantly receiving bills in payment for his goods; he lodges them with his banker, and draws cash for them as he wants it, either for the purchase of the raw material of his manufacture, or to pay the wages of his workpeople. The shopkeeper is benefited in a similar manner; he sends in his cash as he receives it, for which in some banks he is paid interest; he draws it out in proportion to the wants of his trade, and if of good character and fair prospects, he is accommodated with loans beyond the amount of his deposits.

In their higher functions, as promoters of mercantile credit, they are of great social utility. This is strikingly exemplified in newly-settled countries, abounding in natural resources, which, for want of real capital or its representative, remain stagnant and unproductive. The bankers commence operations; they issue paper-money, they collect small sums into greater, like streams flowing into a reservoir; they borrow from those who have too much, and lend to those who have too little; they collect funds from idle and inactive capitalists, and advance them to those who are more speculative and enterprising: in a short time society assumes a new aspect, all is bustle, invention, and enterprise; agriculture, commerce, and manufactures, are inspired with new life; and the country which had before been parched and bound up, is loosened and refreshed by the pecuniary irrigation that animates every department of industry. The effects of such operations have been witnessed in England, and more especially in Scotland within the last century; and they will also be experienced in Ireland, when internal tranquillity affords scope for their operation.

The numerous class of capitalists under the denominations of Importers, Merchants, Brokers, Shipowners, and Wholesale Dealers, is not less useful and necessary in the pursuits of commerce and industry. Th eabilities and acquirements essential to some of these are so varied and elevated, that they may justly aspire to the rank and dignity of professional life. An acquaintance with foreign languages, laws, manners, and usages, weights and measures, monies and exchanges, are indispensable. They ought to be conversant also in those delicate public questions tend-

ing to disturb the intercourse of nations; to understand the products of different countries, and the
causes influencing their qualities and prices, as well
as the abstruser parts of political economy, explaining the circumstances which determine the supply
and demand, the production and consumption, of
commodities.

The direct utility of the mercantile classes to the
great body of consumers may be easily made apparent.   Their first and principal business tends to
produce *equality of prices*.   Their object being to
buy cheap and sell dear, they are constantly occupied in conveying commodities from low to high-
priced places, and thus making up the deficiency of
one market by the redundancy of another.   Hence,
between two places having a free intercourse, there
can never, for any length of time, be an excess at
one and a scarcity at the other.   The advantage of
this to society is very great.   Some commodities are
of a perishable nature; they can only be kept fit for
use from one season to the next; without the intervention of the merchant they would be alike valueless to producer and consumer; but by his aid they
are promptly transported to wherever they are in
demand, and made nearly as plentiful and cheap at
places hundreds and thousands of miles distant as
at the place of production.

Besides equalizing prices, mercantile transactions
tend to equalize the supply of commodities, and
moderate the evil of a glut or overstocked market.
In this respect they operate like the fly-wheel of the

steam-engine, and the greater is their command of capital, and greater is their power to benefit the community.   To illustrate this I may refer to the different state of the country in the thirteenth and fourteenth centuries, when there were no such middlemen as merchants and wholesale dealers.   It then sometimes happened that there was abundance at one end of the kingdom and famine at the other : this cannot now occur ; if corn be plentiful and cheap in Kent, the interest of merchants will prevent it being scarce and dear in the Lothians.   This is an advantage which may partly be ascribed to improved modes of communication as well as the accumulation of capital ; but suppose another case, in which better roads, canals, and steam conveyance, do not participate.   Suppose the harvest is abundant throughout this island, or even throughout Europe— what does the capitalist do ?   Why he *speculates ;* he considers that though the crop this year may be above an average, it may next fall below it ; upon this contingency he goes into the market, purchases largely, storing up corn in his granaries, and the benefits of this operation are twofold.   First, in the year of redundancy, it prevents agricultural produce falling so extremely low, as to be ruinous to the producer ; and, secondly, in the next, if it be a year of scarcity, the merchant, by bringing his stock into the market, prevents the price rising so high as to starve the consumer.

In manufacturing industry the intervention of the

capitalist is not less salutary in averting extreme
prices.   By the occurrence of war, or the overstock-
ing of the market, the demand for manufactures is
liable to be interrupted; the manufacturer, finding
the demand for his goods slacken, and his remit-
tances along with it, soon deems it expedient to
stop the working of a part of his machinery, and
shorten the hours or discharge a portion of his workpeople.   Here the capital of the merchant steps in
to moderate, if not to avert, the pressure of the evil.
The stagnation of trade has caused a fall in prices;
the merchant, considering that the depression may
be temporary, avails himself of the favourable moment to buy on advantageous terms a part of the
accumulating stock of the manufacturer.   Both
parties are benefited by his interference; the force
of the reaction is abated, the depression in prices is
not so great as it otherwise would be, the manufacturer is not obliged suddenly to reduce to the same
extent either the number of his workpeople or the
working of his machinery, and thus the evils which
are in some degree inseparable from fluctuations in
manufacturing employments, are mitigated if not
averted.

Retailers have sometimes been considered a useless class in society, and it has been hastily concluded, that as the merchant and wholesale dealer
buy in large quantities, and at the cheapest markets, it would be most saving to purchase directly
of them without the intervention of the shopkeeper.

But this is a mistake, and the practice would as ill accord with the interest of the merchant as consumer.

The business of the numerous class of shopkeepers and small dealers is to keep assortments of such goods as are wanted in the places where they reside, serving them out to their customers in such quantities and at such times as may best suit their convenience.   A merchant could with just as little advantage bestow his attention on this branch of trade as a butcher could cook the meat as well as kill and divide it for his customers.   For a wholesale dealer to be also a retailer, would require shops almost without number scattered in different parts of the town and surrounding villages; as he could not be every where himself, he would be compelled to support an agent at each, the risk and expense attending which would be enormous.   In order to cover himself, to pay the rents of his numerous establishments, the interest of the extra capital employed, the salaries of servants, and the losses he incurred by their dishonesty and negligence, he would be compelled to charge a higher price for his commodities than the regular shopkeeper, and that would not remunerate him like sticking to his mercantile pursuits : for between the gain of the merchant and the gain of the shopkeeper there is this important distinction ; one consists chiefly of profit from the employment of capital, the other is little more than the fair wages of labour received for the trouble of standing behind the counter, and for weighing, dividing, and measuring out commodities in quantities suited to the buyer. In the metropolis the experiment has been often tried upon which I am remarking; greedy and speculative men, by establishing numerous branch shops in all parts of the town, have sought to grasp the profits of both the wholesale and retail dealer; they have almost uniformly failed, either from fraud and mismanagement of servants, or the attention of the principal being distracted by his multifarious engagements.

If we test the same principle by its operation on the consumer, we shall have additional reason for admiring the utility of subdivisions of employment in civil life. A merchant imports a cargo of sugar from Jamaica, or of salt pork from Ireland. No person, not a dealer in such commodities, would like to purchase the whole at once, or even a hogshead of each. He does not wish to convert his dwelling into a warehouse, neither perhaps would it suit his income, which may be received weekly or monthly, to lay out so much in two articles. How greatly then he is accommodated by the shopkeeper, who purchases the sugar and pork of the importer and retails them to him in quantities adapted to his means and consumption. Were there no such trade as butcher, every man would be obliged to purchase a whole ox or whole sheep at a time. This would be generally inconvenient to the rich, and much more so to the poor. If a workman was obliged to purchase a month's or six months' provisions at once, it would be necessary for him to have as much money beforehand as would perhaps furnish his house or buy the tools of his trade. Nothing then can be more convenient to him than to be able to buy from day to day, or week to week, his meat, his bread, and his beer, as he wants them.

People sometimes remark that there are too many shopkeepers and retailers; but this is an evil, if it exist, which may be safely left to cure itself. As Adam Smith has long since observed, though they may occasionally be so numerous as by underselling to injure each other, they can never, by their mutual competition, injure either the producer of their goods or the consumer.

Enough has been now said, I apprehend, to establish the utility of a Middle Class, or of a class of capitalists in the business of life. But this does not settle all the conflicting claims between capital and industry. A dispute has been recently started about the appropriation of the profits of capital; it having been contended that the workman, in addition to his wages, has also a right to share in the profits of his employer. Upon what principle this pretension is founded it is difficult to conceive. Wages are nothing more than the market price of labour, and when the labourer has received them, he has received the full value of the commodity he has disposed of. Beyond this he can have no claim. To admit him to share in the profits of his master would constitute him a partner of a very anomalous kind; in which, without risking any thing himself, he would be entitled to participate in the gains, and be exempt from

N

the losses, of trade—a principle of partnership that neither law nor reason recognises.

It is unnecessary to dwell longer on a conceit of this kind. A great deal of misapprehension on the relative claims of different classes has arisen from Adam Smith's inapt classification of society into Productive and Unproductive consumers. The labours of the former, as of an operative or husband-man, he considered to be realized in some vendible commodity of agriculture or manufactures ; while the labours of the latter, as of men of science and of professions, left no visible type of previous exertion. Such distinction is without any just foundation. The inventors of the power-loom and spinning-frame were unquestionably great productive labourers, though they had never actually produced a yard of calico in their lives. Many who are not productively employed themselves are the cause of production in others. A physician, whose exertions in preserving health enable others to produce more than they would do without his assistance, is, indirectly at least, a productive labourer. Legislators, magistrates, judges, and peace-officers, are the same. They are, it is true, not directly employed in producing commodities, but they enable others to do so more effectually by framing laws for the convenience of the community, by adjudicating the disputes of individuals, by preserving the peace, and by protecting persons and property from violence and depredation.

Those employed in mere arts of luxury and amusement are indirectly productive labourers. A jeweller employed in chasing a ring for the finger, or silver shoe-buckle, may be a cause of increased industry in the manufacturer and agriculturist, by the desire he excites in them to possess these articles. " A watch," Dr. Paley observes, " may be a very unnecessary appendage to the dress of a peasant ; yet, if the peasant will till the ground to obtain a watch, the true design of commerce is answered ; and the watchmaker, while he polishes the case, and files the wheels of his ingenious machine, is contributing to the production of corn as effectually, though not so directly, as if he handled the plough or the spade. The use of tobacco is an acknowledged superfluity ; but if the fisherman will ply his nets, and the mariner fetch rice from foreign countries, in order to procure to himself the indulgence, the market is supplied with two important articles of provision by the instrumentality of a merchandise which has no other apparent use than the gratification of a vitiated palate."

Men can only be induced to labour by something they prize, whether it be a necessary, a luxury, or mere fancy. A taste for the drama and opera has the same effect on the production of national wealth as a taste for tobacco or tokay. We wish to be present at these representations, and to get admittance must pay the price, which can only be obtained by an effort of industry. Hence Mr. Mc Culloch observes, " that the amusements afforded by players, singers, dancers, and mimics, how trifling soever

they may appear in the eyes of cynics and soi-disan
moralists, create new wants, and by so doing, necessarily stimulate our industry to gratify them."

Dr. Johnson was a severe moralist, and often a
prejudiced observer of men and things, but he recognised the utility of the same doctrine. " Many
things," he remarks, " which are false, are trans-
mitted from book to book, and gain credit in the
world. One of these is the cry against *luxury*. Now
the truth is, that luxury produces much good. Take
the luxury of the buildings in London : does it not
produce real advantage in the conveniency and ele-
gance of accommodation, and this all from the
exertion of industry? People will tell you, with a
melancholy face, how many builders are in gaol. It
is plain they are in gaol, not for building, for rents
have not fallen. A man gives half a guinea for a dish
of green peas. How much gardening does this occasion? how many labourers must the competition
to have such things in the market keep in employment? You will hear it said very gravely—' Why
was the half-guinea thus spent not given to the
poor?' Alas! has it not gone to the *industrious*
poor, whom it is better to support than the *idle* poor?
You are much surer that you are doing good when
you pay money to those that work, than when you
give money merely in charity."—There is no harm
in luxury when people can afford it, and the indulgence therein is not at the expense of the more
serious duties we owe to ourselves, our family, and
the community.

In this age of mechanical inventions, the power to produce commodities by physical agency, would form a very inaccurate standard of the relative utility of different classes. The application of steam enables us to create force to any amount, but we cannot create intelligence. Where all are useful, it is idle to institute comparisons which is most so; but if any scale of social utility be set up, it certainly ought to be founded on the tendency of different pursuits to augment human enjoyments. All occupations, however apparently unproductive and trifling, are valuable, if they increase our pleasures, our comforts, and wellbeing. In this view we recognise the great utility of literary men, whether their labours are directed to the imagination or understanding. If by their productions, they make our leisure hours more agreeable, if by their sentiments they improve the heart; and, by their maxims instruct us in the better conduct of life, they are the benefactors of their species.

Even the avocations of menial servants ought not to be despised. True, their labour does not produce cloth or hardware, like that of the operative. But cloth and hardware are only valuable because they are useful; they add to our comforts and conveniences; and does not the employment of the domestic do the same? The operative is not a producer of matter, but of utility only. And is it not obvious, the servant is also a producer of utility. As justly observed, the labour of the husbandman who raises

corn, beef, and other provisions, is undoubtedly
productive ; but it is not more useful than that
of the butcher, baker, or cook who prepares these
articles, and fits them for use.   To produce a fire,
it is quite as indispensable the coals should be carried from the cellar to the grate, as that they should
be carried from the mine to the surface of the earth,
and the servant who makes the fire is quite as necessary as the miner, to effect the product of their
joint labour.

It is unnecessary to pursue further the illustration
of so plain a subject.   All classifications of society,
into productive and unproductive consumers, into
capitalists, and the industrious, have manifestly no
just foundation.   It is making a distinction where
there is none, and where it is not in the nature of
things there can be.   The end of all human exertion
is the same—to increase the comforts and conveniences of life, and the diversities in the occupations
of men, arise from diversities in the wants of society ;
and whether their pursuits are commercial or operative, intellectual or physical, professional or mechanical, often depends on circumstances over which
they have as little control, and form as little ground
of pre-eminence as their stature or complexions.
They all co-operate for the common good, and that
jealousy between the several classes of the community, which some persons have very inconsider-
ately endeavoured to excite, would be quite as
senseless as jealousy between the several members

of the body, or faculties of the mind, and would most fitly exemplify the folly of the old fable mentioned at the beginning of this chapter.

I shall conclude with recapitulating the chief points I have sought to establish:

1. Capital is an accumulation of anterior industry, and the profits derived from its employment, form as equitable a source of income as the wages of labour.

2. Capital, by stimulating industry, and economizing and abridging labour, tends to lower the prices of commodities to all classes of consumers.

3. It forms the chief distinction, and is the chief source of superiority of civilized over savage life.

4. Its efficiency is augmented by diversities in its application by different countries, and different districts of the same country.

5. The utility of a class of capitalists has been demonstrated, by showing the advantages derived in society from the avocations of the middle ranks, consisting of bankers, merchants, importers, wholesale dealers, and retailers.

Lastly, it has been shown that the different classes of the social state all co-operate for the common good, and that any assumption of superiority, established on diversities in their pursuits and occupations, is founded on no principle of justice or utility.

CHAP. V.

EQUALITY OF REMUNERATION.

Similarity of Wages and Profits—Circumstances influencing
Remuneration of Employments—Agreeableness or Disagreeableness of Trades—Trades requiring long Apprenticeships
or high Premiums—High Profits of Chemists and Apotheca-
ries, more properly Wages—Profits of Country Shopkeepers
—Effects of Inconstancy of Employment—Trust reposed in
Physicians and Attorneys—Wages vary with chance of Success
in Employments—Gains of Literary and Professional Men—
Inadequate Pay of Soldiers and Sailors—Motives to a Naval
and Military Life—Effects of Long Apprenticeships, the
Poor-laws, and Immunities of Corporations on Freedom of
Industry—Combinations of Trades, like Monopolies.

THE payment of wages, being the direct exchange,
without the intervention of a third instrument, of
money for labour, assimilates to the ancient practice
of barter.

Commodities are the joint produce of capital and
labour, and the profit of the capitalist and the wages
of the labourer are the respective rewards of their
co-operative agency, the only difference being, that
wages are the recompence of present, and profit of
anterior industry.

As the labourer does not live upon money, but
on the necessaries money will buy, it follows, that
wages are high or low, not according to their nominal or money amount, but according to the amount

of provisions they will purchase; in other words, according to the command they give the labourer over the food, clothing, and lodging, conducive to his comfort and maintenance.

The different rates of wages, as well as of profits in employments, are more apparent than real : for it will mostly be found where industry is free and not subject to artificial regulation, that if a high remuneration is derived from any trade or profession, it results from the greater ability it requires, or from the greater risk or other countervailing incident which accompanies its exercise. This necessarily results from the desire of all men to obtain the best and easiest reward for their exertions. Were there any occupation where the gains were disproportionate, and not balanced by any disadvantage, persons would crowd into that channel of employment, so as by their competition to reduce it to the common level of emolument.

The circumstances which cause the recompence of employments to rise above or fall below the common level are stated by Adam Smith to be the five following : 1. The agreeableness and disagreeableness of the employments themselves. 2. The easiness or cheapness, or the difficulty and expense of learning them. 3. The constancy or inconstancy of the employments. 4. The small or great trust which must be reposed in those who follow them. 5. The probability or improbability of succeeding in them.

1. The agreeableness of an employment may arise from the lightness of the labour, its healthiness,

cleanliness, or the estimation in which it is held; and its disagreeableness from circumstances of an opposite character. Wages being equal, persons would obviously be determined in the choice of an occupation by its other advantages. The labour of a ploughman is more severe than that of a shepherd, and is uniformly better rewarded. A compositor employed on a daily newspaper, often working in the night, is better paid than one employed in book-printing. Miners, gilders, type-founders, smiths, distillers, and all who carry on unhealthy and dangerous trades, obtain higher wages than those who are equal in skill, but engaged in more desirable employments. The trades of a butcher, brickmaker, coalheaver, and sugar-boiler, are disagreeable, and accordingly compensated with higher wages. The employment of public executioner is detestable, and in consequence better paid than any other, in proportion to the work done. Agreeableness and the popular estimation of many pursuits constitute a considerable part of their remuneration. Thus hunting and fishing are to many a pastime, and, therefore, make very unprofitable trades. The emoluments of private secretaries and public librarians are seldom considerable, they are chiefly paid in the respectability and pleasantness of their occupation. Smuggling and poaching have singular fascinations to some minds, and the opportunities they afford for the indulgence of an adventurous spirit form their chief recompence : for those who pursue those illicit callings are proverbially poor. The

cheerfulness and healthiness of the employments,
rather than the lightness of the labour, or the little
skill they require, seem to be the principal cause of
the redundant numbers, and consequent low wages,
of common farm-servants, and generally of all
workmen employed in ordinary field-labour.   The
emoluments of ministers of religion, professors of the
sciences, schoolmasters, tutors, and officers in the
army and navy are not proportioned to the expense
of their education ; and they are chiefly rewarded
by the popularity and honourableness of their engagements.

   Disagreeableness and discredit affect the profits of
capital in the same manner as the wages of labour.
The keeper of a small inn, alehouse, or spirit-shop,
who can hardly be said to be master of his own
house, and exposed to the intrusion of every drunkard, exercises neither a very agreeable nor creditable
business; but there is scarce any common trade
in which a small stock yields so great a profit.

   2. Arts and trades that are difficult to learn, and a
knowledge of which can only be attained by serving
long apprenticeships, or the payment of high premiums, are usually well remunerated.

   Wages are a compensation paid to the labourer,
or artisan, for the exertion of his physical powers,
or of his skill or ingenuity.   They necessarily, therefore, vary with the severity of the labour or
the ability required.   A jeweller, or engraver, for
example, must be paid higher wages than a common
servant, or scavenger : a long course of training is

requisite to instruct a man in the business of jewel-
ling and engraving; and were he not indemnified
for the cost of the training by higher wages, he
would, instead of learning so difficult an art, addict
himself to such employments as hardly require any
instruction.   It is the same with other pursuits and
professions; the cost of acquirement must be repaid
by future practice therein, otherwise the parties
would be out of pocket, like a person setting up a
new machine, the saving and gain of which do not
repay the outlay in its erection.   The pecuniary
recompence of physicians, lawyers, sculptors, and
painters, is not so exorbitant as is sometimes
imagined : a fortune is almost spent in acquiring
the knowledge necessary to their occupations, which
ought in fairness to be made up to them by the
liberality of their fees and emoluments.

   The profits of capital in certain employments are
liable to similar misapprehension as wages in the
higher branches of industry. The profits of chemists,
druggists, and apothecaries, are mostly considered
extravagant.   Their gains, however, are frequently
only a just remuneration for skill and labour. They
are almost invariably the medical advisers of the
poor, and not unfrequently of the rich.   Their
rewards, therefore, ought to be proportioned to their
services, and these arise generally from the prices at
which they sell their commodities : but the prime
cost of all the commodities retailed by a well-
employed chemist, or apothecary, in the course of
a year, may not exceed fifty pounds.   Though he

were to sell them, therefore, at four hundred or a thousand per cent profit, this may frequently be no more than reasonable wages of his industry, charged in the only way he can charge them, upon the prices of his preparations. The greater part of his apparent profit is real wages disguised in the garb of profit.

Grocers, and other shopkeepers, are necessary in the smaller towns and villages for the convenience of the inhabitants; but, to enable them to live by their business, and compensate them for their diminutive returns, they are compelled to realize a larger profit on the commodities they sell than dealers in places of greater population. It is thus that most articles of general consumption are cheaper in London than in the country. The quickness of the return, and the greater amount of capital employed by a metropolitan tradesman, enables him to support himself at a rate of profit that would absolutely starve a provincial shopkeeper. The great apparent profit charged on their goods by keepers of chandler-shops, and those in what is called a general line of business, is more properly the wages of labour necessary to compensate them for trouble and loss of time in weighing and measuring out their articles in the small quantities required by their customers.

3. Wages vary with the constancy or inconstancy of employment.

Many trades can only be carried on in particular states of the weather and seasons of the year; and if the workmen cannot turn to other employments, their wages must be proportionately high. Watch-

makers, weavers, shoemakers, and tailors, may usually reckon on constant employment ; but masons,
bricklayers, paviers, gardeners, and in general all
those who work in the open air, are liable to perpetual interruptions.   As every one, however, ought to
live by his trade, their wages ought not only to suffice for their maintenance while they are employed,
but also during the time they are necessarily idle.
" This principle," Mr. M'Culloch observes, " shows
the fallacy of the notions commonly entertained of
the great earnings of porters, hackney-coachmen,
watermen, and generally of all workmen employed
only for short periods, and on casual occasions. Such
persons frequently make as much in an hour as a
regularly employed workman makes in a day; but
their greater hire during the time they are employed
is found to be only a bare compensation for the labour they perform, and the time lost in waiting for
the next job : instead of making money, such persons
are almost universally poorer than those engaged in
more constant occupation."

4. Wages vary with the greater or less trust reposed in workmen.

This is a very natural ground of distinction.
Greater the trust, and greater the probity and ability required.   An overseer, superintendent, or
steward, is always better remunerated than a mere
journeyman or servant. The wages of goldsmiths and
jewellers are superior to those of many other workmen not only of equal but superior ingenuity, on
account of the precious materials with which they

are interested. " We trust our health," says Smith,
" to the physician, our fortune, and sometimes our
life and reputation to the lawyer and attorney. Such
confidence could not safely be reposed in people of a
very mean or low condition. Their reward, therefore, must be such as may give them that rank in
society which so important a trust requires. The
long time and the great expense which must be laid
out in their education, when combined with those
circumstances, necessarily enhance still further the
price of their labour."

5. Wages vary with the chance of success in different employments.

A young man of ordinary ability may hope to succeed as a tailor or shoemaker, but as a lawyer or
artist success is much more dubious. But in professions where many fail for one who succeeds, the
fortunate one ought not only to gain such wages as
will indemnify him for the expenses incurred in his
education, but also for all that has been expended in
the education of his unsuccessful competitors. It is
certain, however, that the aggregate wages of profes-
sionals and artists never amount to so large a sum.
The law, for instance, has great prizes, but the blanks
predominate. It is at the bar, as in the church—a
few fortunate aspirants amass wealth, but if the revenue of the entire body of legalists were shared
equally among them, they would not probably yield
a greater average income than the revenues of the
clergy, or of many classes of operatives. Nevertheless the profession is crowded with candidates, and

for this reason, that mere money forms only one element in their remuneration, the remainder being
made up by the chances of judicial honours, political power, and the reputation of superior talent.

Similar observations will apply to that " unpros-
perous race of men," as Adam Smith terms them,
" called men of letters," who are in the same predicament as lawyers, physicians, and other practisers
of the liberal arts. A few authors realize large sums
from their productions ; but the aggregate earnings
of the entire class are inconsiderable. The injustice,
however, of this, is more apparent than real. Letters
are not cultivated as a *trade*, nor even profession :
they are never deliberately entered upon as a source of
profit ; no one ever thinks of apprenticing a child to
such a pursuit, or training him up with a view of making him an author : for in literature natural fitness is
every thing, and choice nothing. Literary men
mostly become such, not with a view to gain, or even
fame, but to gratify their own thirst for knowledge,
and this in truth constitutes their best and greatest
reward. Their works are often beyond all price ; but
mankind are not greatly their debtors. Like their
fellow men they are occupied in seeking their own
happiness their own way, not in conferring disinterested services on their species. It is not any virtuous self-devotion or forethought which has made them
authors—it has been their destiny—they could not
help it. We cannot help feeling grateful for the
services they render society ; but in truth such feeling is hardly more rational than if entertained to-

wards the fire that warms us, the bird that delights with its note, or flower with its perfume.

It has been alleged that the rewards of authors are not fairly apportioned. He can hardly be a genuine *littérateur* who thinks much of pecuniary gain in a pursuit so entirely intellectual. But let us see how this matter stands.

A mere abridgment, which has been executed in a few months, will sometimes yield a greater profit than an original production that has been the labour of years. But the rewards in these cases differ more in kind than quantity. A compiler, however successful, can never compete in celebrity with a man of genius. The Truslers, and Mavors, and Dyches, get money, perhaps, but that is all. An author of a work of science, comprising new discoveries, which influence public legislation and open new sources of wealth to the community, is rewarded by the distinction conferred by his researches; and is not that enough without being superadded thereto the more humble tribute of lucre? The editor of a newspaper fills a toilsome and influential situation, he derives little distinction from his employment, but he is often compensated with a liberal salary. In truth there is not so much injustice in these things as in the cupidity which would grasp both fame and profit when it is hardly in nature they should go together. Sir Christopher Wren received only 300*l.* a year for superintending the building of St. Paul's, which was probably a less annual emolument than that of his head mason or carpenter, but all the fame of erect-

o

ing that noble pile descended to the architect, while those who merely put together the stone and mortar have been forgotten.

Works of poetry and imagination are usually considered more profitable than works of science and philosophy. This is not universally true. Milton's "ten pound epic" was not profitable to the poet, while our Locke, Hume, Brewster, Herschel, and Arnott, have had no reason to complain of want of encouragement. If a writer of science chooses to indulge in novel, and perhaps dubious speculation, he may expect to be slowly appreciated, but the propagation of established truths, in a more popular form, as it is more extensively useful, so is it more liberally rewarded. Plays, novels, and romances, are not generally productive speculations; for one successful adventure there are many failures. Scott and Byron amused, if they did not instruct, a large circle of readers. Their productions were those of genius, which mere art and industry can never hope to equal, and the public were content to pay for them as they are for the diamond, because of its rarity; or as they are content to pay for the representations of a Kean, Kemble, Paganini, or others endowed with the superior gifts of nature.

I conclude, therefore, that the circumstances which influence the wages of science and literature do not materially differ from other employments. Misapprehension on the subject has chiefly arisen from not duly considering the *mixed coin* in which they are remunerated. Like the pursuits of professional men and artists, to which they are nearest allied, in addition to pecuniary emolument, they are rewarded by incidental, and in the opinion of some, perhaps, shadowy advantages. It is only the booksellers, not authors, who seek profit alone. Besides mere gain, a distinguished writer on political economy, or even politics, may justly aspire to the honours and rewards of public life; an author, eminent as a moral or natural philosopher, is not only celebrated among the learned of his own country, but throughout Europe and America; or if eminent as a poet or novelist, not only a shower of gold awaits him, but the smiles of the fashionable, the rich, and luxurious.

The rewards in the Army and Navy are of the same varied character as those in literature and professions, being partly pecuniary, and partly honorary and contingent. It is, however, the officers who chiefly reap the latter advantages, while the common soldier or sailor receives little compensation beyond his pay and prize-money. These are so inadequate a return for the toils and dangers he undergoes, that political economists have found some difficulty in bringing his occupation under the influence of the five circumstances that tend to equalize the advantages of different employments. To reconcile the anomaly, Mr. M'Culloch observes, that "except when actually engaged in warlike operations, a soldier is comparatively idle; while his free, dissipated, and generally adventurous life, the splendour of his uniform, the imposing spectacle of military

parades and evolutions, and the martial music by
which they are accompanied, exert a most seductive
influence over the young and inconsiderate. The
dangers and privations of campaigns are under-
valued, while the chances of advancement are proportionally exaggerated in their sanguine and heated
imaginations." The excess of confidence so common to most men in their own good fortune and
superior abilities, flatter each aspirant to military
glory with hopes of greater success than others who
have preceded him in the same hazardous career.
" Without regarding the danger," says Dr. Smith,
" soldiers are never obtained so early as at the beginning of a new war ; and though they have scarcely
any chance of preferment, they figure to themselves
in their youthful fancies a thousand occasions of acquiring honour and distinction, which never occur.
These romantic hopes make the whole price of their
blood. Their pay is less than that of common
labourers, and in actual service their fatigues are
much greater."

The lottery of the sea is considered by Dr. Smith
not so disadvantageous as that of the army. " The
son of a creditable labourer or artificer may frequently go to sea with his father's consent ; but if
he enlists as a soldier, it is always without it. Other
people see some chance of his making something by
the one trade ; nobody but himself sees any of his
making any thing by the other." But the temptations to enlist in the army are more enticing to
young men than those to enter the navy. The ac-

companiments of a sailor's life are less dazzling to the imagination ; no regular uniform—no soul-stirring drum ; his employment dirty, and often laborious, while it is a sort of living entombment from the world. In consequence, his wages exceed the pay of a soldier, and the navy, at the breaking out of a war, is manned with greater difficulty than the army is recruited. The compulsory practice of impressment tends also to augment the distaste felt for this branch of the service.*

A moral reason, overlooked by economical writers, may be assigned for the inadequate pay of common soldiers. The army is mostly filled from the same causes which fill the gaols and houses of correction : it is not choice, but necessity which compels many to enlist therein ; having lost their character, or contracted habits of idleness and improvidence, which exclude them from the better paid walks of civic industry, they are constrained to devote themselves to the hardships and perils of military life.

---

* The Americans raise their public navy by voluntary enlistments only ; and it is a singular fact, that by this means they obtain seamen at comparatively lower wages than in England ; while the wages of labourers and artisans are relatively higher here than in the United States. This, as Mr. M'Culloch observes, is decisive of the impolicy of impressment. Above 16,000 British sailors are calculated to have been aboard American ships at the close of the last war, yet the wages of seamen, which in time of peace, rarely exceed 40s. or 50s. a month, had risen to 100s. and 150s. So high had we to bribe, and so difficult was it to render that palatable which force made additionally odious !

A similar explanation will apply to scavengers, navigators, breakers of stones on the highway, and most of the lowest class of labourers, whose wages, unaccompanied with other advantages, are disproportionate to the risk and unpleasantness of the labour. Muscular strength, and not characters exempt from moral turpitude, is required. Hence the low rate of wages, because, in addition to those forced into such employments, either by defect of education or neglect of parents, they are also depressed by the competition of the outcasts of all other branches of social industry.

Enough, however, has been said to establish the main point of inquiry; namely, the general equality of advantages in the employments of civil life. If wages are unequal, if they rise above or fall below the common level of remuneration, it will mostly be found that they are influenced by the agreeableness or disagreeableness of the occupation—its difficulty of acquirement—the uncertainty of success—the distinction or discredit accompanying the pursuit, or some other of the five circumstances which have been shown to influence the price of labour. In order, however, that the equality of advantages may take place, even when freedom of industry exists, three things are requisite: first, the employments must have been long established; secondly, they must be in their ordinary or natural state; and thirdly, they must be the sole or principal employment of those who follow them.

Wages are generally higher in new than in old

trades. The profits derived from the establishment
of a new manufacture, the opening of a new channel of commerce, or from the introduction of some
new invention, are seldom proportioned to those of
old trades. If the novelty succeeds, they are, for a
time at least, very high; but when the trade or
practice becomes thoroughly established, competition
reduces them to the level of other pursuits. Secondly, wages are temporarily influenced by the fluctuations of fashion, the seasons of the year, and a state
of peace or war. The introduction of a new pattern,
or article of dress, will stimulate demand in that line
of business; the demand for rural labour is greater
during harvest, and wages rise with it; the intervention of hostilities would cause a sudden rise in the
wages of seamen; and the same circumstance would
exercise an influence on the wages of those classes
from which the army and navy are chiefly recruited,
as well as on the prosperity of various branches of
manufactures. Lastly, the equality of advantages
may be affected in employments which do not constitute the sole occupation of persons engaged therein. Clerks, and many out-of-door workmen, not fully
occupied by the duties of their situations, are often
found willing to keep accounts, and perform little
jobs at a lower rate of remuneration than they would
if such formed their sole dependence. The various
domestic manufactures carried on prior to the general
introduction of machinery had these advantages,
that they could be carried on at all times and in all
sorts of weather, and were a constant resource for

filling up every leisure moment. A husbandman, who could plough by day and spin and card wool with his family at night, might have continued up to this day to contend in cheapness of production with the regular manufacturer, had not the latter been aided by the prodigies of power created by the union of capital and mechanical inventions.

· In addition to these causes tending to disturb the equilibrium of advantages in employments, others arise, partly from the institutions of society, and partly from the institutions and regulations subsisting among the workmen themselves. The obstructions to the freedom of industry of the former description have been mostly removed by the wisdom of modern legislation, and it will be unnecessary to dwell on them longer than to show their tendency and character. The first I shall notice is the practice of *apprenticeships.*

By the common law of England, every man has a right to employ himself at pleasure in every lawful trade. But this sound principle was almost subverted by an act passed in the reign of Elizabeth, providing that no person should for the future exercise any trade, unless he had previously served to it an apprenticeship of seven years at least; so that what had before been a by-law of a few corporate bodies, became the general and statute law of the kingdom. This impolitic enactment, as before mentioned, remained in force till the year 1814, and the repeal in that year did not interfere with the existing privileges and by-laws of corporations in respect of apprenticeships. But where these do not interpose the term of apprenticeship may now be adjusted by the parties themselves.

Apprenticeships unnecessarily protracted are injurious to both masters and workmen. As the price of labour is influenced by the time and money spent in the learning of a business, it follows, if seven years are wasted in acquiring a trade, when two or three would have been sufficient, employers will have to indemnify their workmen for their previous sacrifices, by paying them proportionally higher wages. Secondly, they are injurious to workmen. An apprentice has not the same motives to industry and exertion as when he becomes a journeyman: he feels himself in a state of bondage, which, if protracted beyond the needful period, tends to generate in him habits of idleness and improvidence that render him less fit for the enjoyment of future freedom.

The impediments to the free circulation of labour arising out of the poor-laws are not so great as formerly. Under the old law, a stranger coming to reside in a place might be forcibly removed by the overseers, on the mere pretext that he was *liable* to become chargeable to the parish, and this arbitrary authority was at first only mitigated by the introduction of certificates: a certificate of residence being necessary from a parish where a person was legally settled, to enable him to live undisturbed in any other parish to which he might consider it advantageous to remove. As parish officers had

power to grant or refuse certificates, they might, if
they thought fit, imprison a person, as it were,
during his lifetime, in the parish to which he belonged, and withhold from him every benefit he
might propose to himself by living elsewhere. This
oppressive power of interference with individual
freedom is now abolished; no certificate is necessary
to check the workman's liberty of locomotion; nor
can any person be forcibly removed to his settlement
parish, unless he become *actually* chargeable to the
poor-rate of some other place.

Still the existing poor-laws operate as a drag on
the free circulation of industry, and must so continue
till both masters and workmen cease to have personal
interests in the local settlement of paupers; in other
words, till the present complexity of rights, on which
the claim to parish relief is established, be reduced
to the simple condition of residence, or other uniform principle. As it is, a workman will not be
altogether determined in his place of abode, by the
demand for his labour, but partly by his reluctance
to exchange the parish settlement to which he is now
entitled, for some other to which he has an aversion.
The employer of a labourer may also be influenced
in his conduct by a desire not to increase the amount
of his poor assessment. This is known to be the
case, especially in the agricultural districts, where
the salutary practice of hiring for a year is not so
frequent as formerly; farmers engaging their servants for shorter period of service, whereby they not
only evade the obligation to maintain their labourers

during the slack as well as busy season of rural industry, but also prevent them obtaining settlement in their parishes.

A third obstacle to the freedom of industry originates in the charters, privileges, and by-laws of corporations. These are of two kinds—municipal and guilds, or fraternities; the former consisting of the incorporation of cities and boroughs, and the latter of the several trades, crafts, or mysteries exercised therein, and are found in London, Bristol, Norwich, Preston, and other old towns of the kingdom. The immunities of these ancient associations were probably defensible at the early period they were granted, tending to promote the divisions of employment, and to perfect and protect in their infancy the arts of industry: but the times have changed, and the remnants of their privileges only operate to the occasional annoyance of individuals, and the disadvantage of the community. The exclusive privileges of an incorporated trade necessarily restrain competition to those who are free of the fraternity. The exclusive privileges of a municipal corporation restrain competition within the limits of its local jurisdiction. In the former case, the free circulation of labour from one employment to another in the same place is impeded; in the latter, its free circulation from one place to another even in the same employment. Both these impediments are often experienced by individuals in the city of London, whose civic institutions, in other respects, are mostly su-

perior to those of corporations in the country. A
resident housekeeper, for example, could not commence the business of a bookseller within the limits
of the city's jurisdiction, unless he were free, first of
one of the city companies, and secondly, of the general corporation of London, and if his admission in
both corporate bodies were to buy, it would cost him
nearly 100*l.* before he could exercise his business.

This example may suffice of the tendency of corporate immunities. I shall next speak of the obstruction to the freedom of industry, from trade-so-
cieties and regulations subsisting among workmen
themselves, and which are unconnected with the
laws and institutions of the country.

Combinations among workmen, intended solely to
keep up the rate of wages, are of precisely the same
nature as combinations among masters, to keep up
the rate of profits. They are both confederacies
against the public, liable to the same objections as
monopolies, in which the interest of individuals is
sought to be supported at the expense of the interests
of the community. One is an interference with the
freedom of industry, the other, with the free employment of capital. Competition is in both cases
restrained; in one, the supply of labour, and in the
other, the supply of capital is kept less then it
would be in a state of freedom.

The nature and objects of Trade Unions I shall
explain more particularly hereafter, in a chapter devoted to their consideration. My present purpose

---

has been to establish the equality of advantages in the several employments, pursuits, and professions of civil life; and, secondly, to show that this equilibrium of remuneration is never permanently disturbed, except either by the artificial institutions of society, or by rules and regulations subsisting among the industrious themselves.

CHAP. VI.

WAGES OF LABOUR.

Reduction of Wages increases Supply of Labour—Effects of Speculation on Wages—Legitimate and Illusive Speculations—Agricultural Speculation during the War, and Mercantile Speculation of 1825—Rate of Wages determined by the Unemployed, not Employed Workman—Consequence of a trifling Excess of Labour—High Wages depend solely on the Conduct of the Working Classes—Futility of various popular Expedients exposed—Government impotent, as respects Condition of Labouring Classes—Cannot relieve an Overstocked Labour-Market—France in 1830—Taxation—Lavish Public Expenditure indefensible—Home Colonization.

WAGES are usually considered under the two heads of the market, or actual rate of wages, and the necessary rate, or that rate indispensable to the subsistence of the labourer, and without which he could not obtain a sufficiency of food to support and continue his race.

It is not easy to perceive the utility of this division; the necessary rate of wages is a quantity that cannot be assigned, the food that would be equal to the support of one man, might be a starvation allowance to another; it varies with the human constitution, and the habits of nations. The important consideration, therefore, is the actual rate of wages, and this is a subject more interesting than any in the whole science of political economy, since those who live by wages so greatly exceed in number those who live by profits, rents, and all other sources of revenue.

The price of labour, like the prices of commodities, is governed by the proportion between the supply and demand; and as this proportion will be equally influenced, either by vicissitudes in the supply or demand for labour, our subject may be appropriately considered under these two heads,— First, the circumstance tending to augment or diminish the supply of labour; and, Secondly, the circumstances tending to augment or diminish the funds, or capital, for the employment of labour. Variations in either of these sets of circumstances, will obviously produce similar results, and tend to advance or lower wages.

To begin with the first, I shall show the effect of a reduction of wages on the labour-market.

A reduction of wages compels a workman either to reduce his expenditure, or by increased exertion make up the diminution in his income. But as the reduction in the price of labour has probably arisen from slackness in the demand for its products, it follows that lengthening the hours of work or similar expedient, only aggravates the evil of scarcity of employment, and thereby accelerates the downward tendency of wages. This must generally be the case where workmen have not any provision on which they can fall back during periods of stagnation of trade; by doing most work when it is least needed, they contend against their own interests.

For want of this resource, the natural effect of a rise in the price of provisions is also counteracted. When provisions rise, wages ought to rise too, to prevent the condition of the labourer being depreciated. Such, however, is not uniformly the case; instead of the prices of labour and provisions varying in the same way, it is often found that wages are lowest when the price of corn is highest.*

In dear years, an increased number of females, and of such poor children of both sexes as are fit to work, are obliged to quit their homes or to engage in some species of employment, while those labourers who work by the piece, endeavour, by increasing the quantity of their work, to obtain the means of purchasing their accustomed quantity of food. These causes will continue to operate to the disadvantage of the working classes, till increased mortality, occasioned by harder living or other circumstance, intervene to lessen competition for employment.

Mercantile speculation increases the demand for

* M'Culloch's *Political Economy*, 2d edit., p. 396.

labour, but whether this will be beneficial or injurious
to the working classes depends on the legitimacy or
illusiveness of the speculation.   A legitimate speculation is mostly founded on the probable scarcity
of an article of consumption; for instance, a deficient harvest, or failure in the crop of cotton,
may be just ground for speculation in either corn or
cotton.   A merchant, under these circumstances,
goes into the market and lays in a stock at a low
price, in order to sell it hereafter at a high price.
His motives are selfish; nevertheless his transactions
tend to the benefit of the community.   By purchasing largely, prices begin to rise; and people,
finding corn or cotton dearer than heretofore, they
are less wasteful in the consumption; the whole
community being thus put on short allowance,
like a ship's company, with a scanty supply of
water, the deficient crop lasts till a more abundant
season returns, and the evils of scarcity are mitigated.

Illusive speculations are nothing more than gambling, or fraudulent devices got up to entrap the un-
wary.   They are not founded upon any calculation of
future scarcity, but too often merely on public gul-
libility.   They are mostly started and endeavoured
to be passed off when the mind of the community
has been excited by the success of the more wholesome and salutary enterprises of capitalists.   One is
the genuine, the other the counterfeit spirit of mercantile adventure.   Speculations for opening new
roads or canals for the convenience of traffic; for

establishing a new branch of commerce, or dealing in a new article of manufacture; for applying a new mechanical invention, by which labour is abridged; or for reclaiming waste and unproductive lands—all these are legitimate undertakings, and the fruitful sources of national opulence. If judiciously planned and executed, they scarcely come under the description of contingent adventures, their results being as susceptible of calculation as experiments in physical science. A master-mariner knows, by sailing a number of days on given points of the compass, he shall reach Madras or Bombay; a chemist, by mixing two ingredients, knows he shall obtain a compound with ascertained properties: their conclusions are not more certain than those of the skilful speculator, who estimates the results that will arise from the outlay of a certain amount of labour and capital. But the spurious adventurer proceeds without or on insufficient data; his schemes are addressed to the passions, not the reason of mankind, and his object is to avail himself of a transitory thirst for inordinate gain.

The spirit of speculation is often epidemic, and no country affords so many examples of its existence as England. It will be sufficient to notice two, merely to show their operation on national industry. The elapse of a quarter of a century has been insufficient to obliterate the effects of the great agricultural movement which originated in the war, and the high prices occasioned by a depreciated currency. Its tendency was to convert pasture into arable

P

land, to cause a rapid increase of agricultural population, and to generate habits of living and divisions
of employment unsuited to the successful pursuit
of rural industry.   The return of peace, and the
old standard of value destroyed the artificial stimuli
previously in operation.   Lands, brought under the
plough, were again laid down to grass ; capital has
been lost in the transition, and a vast body of unemployed labourers accumulated.

Movements in agriculture are more slow than in
commerce and manufactures, and capital can neither
be invested nor withdrawn with the same facility.
Farmers are fettered by leases ; they are not prompt
to change, and are mostly unenterprising in character.   They cannot without difficulty and much deliberation alter the established course of husbandry ;
if, for instance, they have been tempted by the high
price of corn to break the turf and convert pasture
into arable land, it requires years to restore it to its
former state, should a revulsion in prices render it
necessary.   Hundreds of thousands of acres in England have been thus made unprofitable for years to
come under the impulse of the paper-money prices.
Such considerations account for the difficulty with
which agriculture has adjusted itself to the altered
circumstances of the country, and also suggest the
dangers which must result from any interference
which disturbs the regularity of its progress.   Another peculiarity distinguishes this branch of national
industry in the general operation of the causes by
which it is acted upon ; it cannot, for example, be

prosperous from the influence of high prices in Kent and Surrey, and be depressed by low prices in Lancashire and Northumberland. The causes by which it is influenced will be felt throughout the kingdom, and all classes connected with it as a source of income or employment, will be proportionately affected. It is materially different with manufacturing industry, in which one branch may be prosperous while another is depressed ; the iron trade may stagnate in Staffordshire, while the woollen and cotton trades are in full activity.

As changes in agriculture are more slow than in commerce, reactions in it are not so frequent. The commercial cycle is ordinarily completed in five or seven years, within which terms it will be found, by reference to our commercial history during the last seventy years, alternate periods of prosperity and depression have been experienced. The last memorable crisis of 1824-5 was the more disastrous, as it chiefly originated in illusive speculations. Capital and industry were diverted from their regular channels of employment into ruinous and deceptive adventures. An entire decomposition of commercial elements was effected. A vast fabric of fictitious property erected on a baseless system of credit was thrown down, and masses of real wealth transferred and distributed into new channels. Had these been the only results the operation might have been deemed beneficial rather than injurious. Unfortunately the nation sustained an immense loss from the destruction of property occasioned by the fluctuation in prices, and the sudden derangement of all works of utility, of trade and industry. A check was thus given to the progress of national wealth and internal improvements; and in consequence of the blow inflicted on mercantile character and confidence, the legitimate movements of commerce were for a long time fettered and impeded. It is the nature of great and precipitate changes to involve the innocent with the guilty; and this was one of the most fatal results of the late reaction : it not only swept away the delusive projects of the unprincipled adventurer, but paralyzed the operations of real business and commendable enterprise.

All speculative movements in agriculture, commerce, and manufactures, are at first favourable to the industrious orders, by tending to enhance wages and profits. But unless such enterprises are of the legitimate kind, before explained, the advantages they produce will be transitory, while the evils they entail will be more enduring. Revulsions in the great branches of national industry are like the precipitate retreat of an army, they discourage and disorganize; and inflict permanent evils, which far outweigh the ephemeral benefits of the preceding activity and enterprise. It is not by such spurts of prosperity as these the condition of the industrious can be improved ; a sudden rise of wages, to be followed by their speedy depression to as low or lower rate, only tends to derange their domestic economy ; while it gives them no lasting command over increased comforts and enjoyments. This, however, is the great end to be attained, and it can only be attained by that progressive increase in the demand for labour over the supply, which results from capital increasing faster than population. To the consideration of this I shall now direct attention; it is far more important than any of the circumstances yet mentioned as influencing the market of labour.

It is essential to repeat, that the price of labour, like the prices of commodities, is determined by the proportion betwixt the supply and demand. The effect of a plentiful or deficient harvest, in raising or reducing the price of bread, is familiar to every one. If it be rumoured that Mark-lane is scantily supplied with corn, we know, from experience, it is a certain prelude of a rise in the price of wheat. Should the supply of timber, tallow, or hemp from the Baltic be interrupted, or less than usual, an immediate advance takes place in the prices of these articles. This is a fact of such common knowledge and occurrence, that it need not be enforced : but the great effect on prices of a *trifling excess* or deficiency in the supply is not so apparent. Yet every practical man, whether agricultural, commercial, or manufacturing, is well aware that the excess of the supply of a commodity brought to market, will depress that commodity in price, not merely in the ratio of that excess, but in a much higher ratio ; and that conversely the supply being less than the demand, enhances the price in a similar disproportionate manner.

Now this results from a very obvious principle,

namely, that quality and every other incident being alike, there cannot be *two prices* for the same article. Suppose the supply is abundant, and that some of the sellers have more than their usual quantity to dispose of; finding that their stock on hand rather exceeds the usual amount, they naturally feel impatient to begin selling; they therefore try to *force* the market; to tempt the buyers, they offer their goods at something less than the accustomed prices. The stone having once begun to move, it rolls to the bottom of the hill; one man cannot sell dearer than his neighbour; if he attempt it, no one will deal with him; in self-defence he also reduces his price; the example rapidly spreads among all the sellers, and thus, from the circumstance of one or two persons having rather more to sell than usual, the price of the whole commodity in the market is reduced. If in place of a redundancy, there is a *scarcity*, the operation is analogous; in that case, the sellers will hold back, and the increased competition will be among the buyers, each of the latter being apprehensive, from the aspect of the market, he will not be able to lay in his usual stock, will be stimulated to offer a higher price than usual; and the example being once given, it will be followed by all in the same predicament.

Precisely the same principle governs the market of labour. Suppose, in a body of 1000 workmen there are fifty equally good with the rest, who cannot find employment; in this instance, the rate of wages will not be determined by the 950 employed, but by the fifty unemployed. As a matter of course, masters will employ those whom they can hire at the lowest wages; if the fifty unemployed offer to work for 20s. in lieu of 25s., they will discharge that number of their present workmen to make room for them. But the surplus of labour continuing undiminished, and the workmen discharged, urged probably by the same necessities as their unemployed predecessors, they, too, will be compelled to offer themselves at 20s. a week, and thereby supplant fifty more of their employed fellow-workmen. In this manner the reduction of wages will extend through the entire trade ; the trifling redundancy of fifty workmen, like a trifling excess of commodities in the market, reducing the wages of the entire body of operatives.

But this principle operates more imperatively on workmen or dealers in labour, than on dealers in commodities. If the market is overstocked with commodities, the owners may withdraw them—keep them in bond, or store them in warehouses, till the demand increases : but the workman too often has no such alternative ; he cannot withhold his labour from the market—he must forthwith either work or starve, and is thus compelled to take the wages he can get, however inadequate to his wants.

We have thus arrived at two truths of great importance : first, that wages depend on the greater or less competition for employment; and secondly, that it is not the employed, but the unemployed workmen, who fix the price of labour. The connexion of these two propositions with the increase of population, may be easily demonstrated.

If population increase without a corresponding increase of employment, the rate of wages will be depressed. If employment increases, masters compete against each other, and offer higher wages; if workmen increase, wages are lowered by their increased competition. During harvest, work is more abundant than workmen, and farmers give labourers 2s. or 3s. per day; during winter the case is reversed, and they pay them only half these sums. The operation of the same principle renders labour dearer in America than in England, in England than in Ireland: in one, the competition is among masters for workmen; in the other, the competition is among workmen for employers. It follows, that the working classes are the arbiters of their own destiny; their fate is in their own hands. Whether they will be well fed, clothed, and lodged; whether they will command the means which alleviate the pains, and augment the pleasures of life; and whether their children shall enjoy the same advantages, depends on themselves—on the amount of their wages, and their wages depend on the proportion between their numbers and the funds for their employment. But they have no command over the last; they are not capitalists; it belongs not to them to open new channels of commerce, to establish and extend manufactures, or reclaim the waste lands of the earth; they have no power to increase the quantity of labour; but though they cannot increase the demand for labour, they can do what tends not less effectually to increase wages—they can lessen the supply.

This brings us to an important point—the power of the working classes to regulate their numbers by restraints on marriage, by emigration, and other expedients, by which the market of labour may be kept understocked: these are matters of such vital interest to the community, especially to the industrious portion of it, that I must reserve their consideration to a separate and subsequent chapter, expressly devoted to the question of population.

Next in utility to establishing the true and all-important principles on which the welfare of the working classes depends, is showing the delusiveness of expedients which have been suggested for bettering their condition. It would be endless to dwell on all these; I must be content with noticing a few of the principal that have excited the most interest, and commanded the greatest share of attention.

It has been urged that rendering the public institutions of the country more popular, would operate favourably on the condition of the industrious orders. Government is a means to an end, and that end is the happiness of the people. It ought not to imbody partial interests, the interests of monopolists, castes, and classes, but the general interests of the community. Its great functions are to protect persons and property; to frame just laws, and administer them cheaply, promptly, and impartially.

It levies a public revenue for public services, and these services ought to be performed in the best manner and at the least expense. Beyond this, government mingles little in the affairs of individuals, and the various relations subsisting among them. It is not a merchant, nor a manufacturer; neither ought it to be an agriculturist, or landowner; it is not a capitalist, and has nothing to do with the conflicting questions involved in wages and profits. If it meddle with these by futile endeavours to regulate wages, or profits, to fix a maximum or minimum of either, or by vain efforts to control employments by bounties and drawbacks, centuries of experience show that it attempts an office for which it is unfit, injures itself, and inflicts loss on the community. Its proper functions are limited to giving protection and freedom to all, freedom to industry, freedom to capital, and guaranteeing both in the enjoyment of the gains which fair and unrestricted competition awards.

But if government cannot usefully interfere with wages, it cannot interfere with the pabulum on which the wellbeing of the industrious orders depends. This is true. It cannot alter the proportion between the supply and demand for labour ; the former depending on the working classes themselves, and the latter on the extent of the field for the productive application of capital. Government is a destroyer rather than creator of capital; by its imposts it abstracts from, rather than adds to, the funds for the employment of the people.

The impotence of mere forms of government in

determining the condition of the working classes may be easily illustrated. Englishmen certainly enjoy a greater share of political freedom than any other nation of Europe, yet the bitter privations undergone by vast bodies of them of late years have never been exceeded. It would be absurd to allege that government has been directly instrumental of this, that it has been guilty of the suicidal folly of nourishing political discontent by producing national misery. Had our institutions been ten times more democratic than they are, they could not have averted the consequences of increasing population, of the application of machinery, and of the fluctuations inseparable from commercial and manufacturing pursuits. When a million of men are suddenly thrown out of work, government cannot find them employment; neither has it funds to maintain them in idleness. Ireland is subject nearly to the same laws and institutions as England, but how much greater is her moral and physical degradation! All forms of rule, or rather misrule, have swept over Italy within the last four centuries; yet the condition of her labouring classes has not been altered an iota. France, after her glorious revolution of 1830, was plunged in the deepest misery, of which her new government could only be a helpless spectator. The springs of industry were paralyzed, and it had no electric power to reanimate them. When the market of labour is depressed, it is beyond the power of the state, it requires the wants, the increasing consumption of a whole community, to raise it.

These remarks are not meant to extenuate the evils of bad, or to depreciate the blessings of good institutions, but to elucidate the *real causes* of social misery. The power of government over public happiness is rather negative than positive, consisting chiefly, as before hinted, in affording freedom and security, in not being a stumblingblock in the way of national industry, and, above all, in opposing no obstacle to the people themselves, by discussion and inquiry, obtaining a knowledge of the principles on which their welfare depends.

The intolerable pressure of taxation has justly formed of late years a popular theme of animadversion ; but no repeal of taxes, however extensive, even the extinction of the great debt itself, and the abolition of all imposts, would materially affect the condition of the working man. His wellbeing depends on his command over the enjoyments and necessaries of life, on his power to purchase a sufficiency of meat, and bread, and beer; on his ability to clothe himself comfortably, and procure a dwelling adapted to his wants and furnished with the requisite domestic conveniences. Oppressive as our excise and custom duties, and assessed taxes are, how do any of these affect him ? Scarcely at all. Taxation only averages about two pounds per head on the entire population of the United Kingdom. But the poor do not contribute equally with the rich, and certainly a labourer in husbandry does not contribute (see Appendix) 10s. per annum (which, by the by, is just that sum too much, for he ought not to contribute a farthing) on his whole yearly expenditure in food, clothes, and habitation, to the exigencies of the state.

If, however, he contributed ten times ten shillings in tax, and the whole amount was at once repealed, it would not better his lot, provided his labour was redundant in the market. The truth of this *is* incontestable. It results from the principle before explained, namely, that wages are not determined by the employed, but the competition of the unemployed, who, rather than starve, will accept any wages on which they can barely subsist. While the labour-market is overstocked, if a tax on any article of consumption be repealed, the remission is speedily followed by an equivalent reduction in wages, because the remission has left a surplus beyond the means of that bare subsistence for which the unemployed labourer will submit to work, so long as his industry is redundant : his wages in consequence become minus the tax repealed.

Such elucidations, I trust, will be received as they are intended, as the truth, not as apologies for a lavish public expenditure. The legitimate end of taxation is to defray the necessary expenses of government. Any thing abstracted beyond this is unjust—it is robbery ; inasmuch as money is *forcibly* levied on the industrious without a return of equivalent benefits in exchange. Extravagant salaries, sinecures, and unmerited pensions, are all robberies ; they dissever services from their appropriate rewards ; and those who luxuriate on such plunder

are less defensible than the pickpocket or high-
wayman.   The business of government is a branch
of social labour, essential to the wellbeing of the community, but it is quite as proper that this labour
should be executed in the best and most economical
mode, as it is that all the resources of machinery and
science should be brought to our aid to economize
and abridge the operations of the artisan and manufacturer.

Leaving the government, I shall advert to other
projects of popular amelioration.   The operation of
tithe on capital and industry may be passed over;
its impolicy, as a compulsory mode of ecclesiastical
maintenance, is now generally admitted, and there
is every prospect of the country being speedily relieved from this long-standing and grievous oppression.

A project, which has met a favourable reception
with many philanthropists for benefiting the working classes, is " Home Colonization," or the locating
the unemployed labourers and artisans on the waste
lands of the country.   A doubt may be expressed
whether there exists in England at least any extensive tracts of land of this description which could be
advantageously brought into cultivation.   A principal cause of the difficulties in which agriculture
has been involved of late years, has been the *forcing*
system of farming, carried on during the war, under
the stimulus of paper-money prices; and the consequent loss entailed on the landed interest by the
abandonment of the inferior soils that at peace

prices did not yield a remunerative profit. It ought also to be considered that the wastes in their existing state are not entirely unproductive; they yield manure, fuel, and are often available to the uses of the cottager.

Granting, however, that there are tracts of land on which the experiment of home colonization may be tried, the question is, as Dr. Chalmers properly inquires, " Why are they at present unoccupied." Enclosure acts may always be obtained, and no doubt in such a country of law and security, and enterprise as our own, they would have been obtained, could they have been enclosed and cultivated without loss. This is a speculation which may be safely left to the guidance of self-interest in a community abounding in so many individuals, possessed both of the means and inclination to embark in any adventure that holds out a prospect of advantage. Capital is promptly poured out for every undertaking of profit, and the reason more is not employed in the cultivation of new, or the better cultivation of old lands, is an apprehension either on the part of farmers, or money lenders, that the gain, at the current price of farm produce, would be inadequate or none at all. And if individuals would find it a losing speculation, there is no reason to believe that *parish corporations*, still less the largest corporation of all—the government, would find it a safe one.

As an undertaking, then, for realizing the ordinary profit of capital and wages of labour, home colo-

nization must be abandoned ; but the scheme has
been defended on grounds not quite so untenable.
"Half a loaf," the proverb says, "is better than
no bread ;" and it has been contended, that it is
better an unemployed labourer should be made partially productive than live in total idleness. If by
spade husbandry, or digging on the waste, he can
raise half a subsistence, it is better than burdening
the parish for the whole of it.

This resolves the question into the consideration
of the least expensive mode of getting rid of, or
maintaining the surplus population of the country.

The great end of all projects of popular improvement ought to be to render the working man self-
dependent ; to bring the market of labour into such
a state that he may always command, by the exchange of his industry, a sufficiency of the necessaries of life without parish control or assistance.
But a "consummation so devoutly to be wished,"
would not be achieved by the scheme we are considering. The home colonist would not be on a
footing with the independent labourer, earning respectable wages, but on the footing rather of a West
India slave, or vassal of a vestry, toiling on the
parish domain. Here then we should have a new
caste of population, encouraged, and virtually called
into being, who are constrained by their lot to live
as a sort of bondmen beneath the par of human
liberty and enjoyment, and whose very presence in the
land would operate as a depressing incubus on the
condition of the working people. They would form

a body of *reserve*, from whom masters might indefinitely draw in every question of wages between themselves and their men, and by means of whom, therefore, they could, as in a market overstocked with labour, bring down indefinitely its price.

The scheme of the Dutch mendicity colony of Fredericks Oord, upon which the project of home colonization is founded, does not tend, permanently, to relieve the market of its redundancy, or better the condition of the labouring classes, but simply to create a new grade of paupers; whereas, the object of every enlightened well-wisher to the industrious classes, is to have no paupers at all. Emigration, it is probable, would be less expensive to parishes, and far more favourable to the condition of the unemployed labourer. In lieu of wasting his energies on an exhausted, or unfruitful soil, he might remove to climes, where not only his industry would be amply repaid—his personal rights undiminished—but, a future field of prosperity and happiness opened for his posterity.

Q

CHAP. VII.

CAUSES OF HIGH WAGES.

Effect on Wages of an Increase in the Incomes of Individuals—Wages increase with the increase of national Capital—State of Society most favourable to the Working Classes—Population increased faster than Capital in Ireland—Demand for Labour increased by Security of Property—Necessity of Freedom in the Employment of Capital and Industry—Effects of War and civil Commotions on the Condition of the Industrious Orders.

In the preceding chapter, I endeavoured to show the effects produced on the market of labour, by a reduction of wages—by mercantile and agricultural speculation—and by the increase of population: I also adverted to the influence of civil liberty, of government, and taxation on the condition of the working classes, and the tendency of home colonization, and other expedients for bettering their situation: my next object will be to elucidate the circumstances tending to augment the demand for labour, in other words, the funds or active capital for its employment.

The demand for the services of those who live by wages—mechanics, operatives, and labourers of every kind, can only increase in proportion to the increase of the funds destined to the payment of wages.

When a landlord, annuitant, or other private

person, living on an income of any kind, has a greater revenue than necessary to the maintenance of his family, he employs either the whole, or part of the surplus, in the maintenance of one or more servants. Increase the surplus, and he will naturally increase the number of his servants, whereby he is enabled to make a nicer division of employments in his household. In lieu of restricting himself to a single domestic of all work, he will divide the duties between a cook and housemaid; if his income continues progressively to augment, he will, perhaps, add an upper housemaid to his establishment, then, perhaps, a footman, groom, coachman, butler, valet, and gardener; till, at length, he has about him that numerous train of dependants, usually found on the establishments of persons of large fortune.

In this progress two incidents may be remarked, namely, that not only is the demand for servants increased by the increase in the incomes of individuals, but also the duties of each become less onerous, and the number of the more agreeable and lucrative situations is multiplied. If the highest incomes would only allow the possessors to keep one or two domestics, such occupations as those of valet and lady's maid would not be heard of in society.

The increase in the number of those employed in agriculture, trades, and manufactures, keeps pace with the increase in the amount of capital that can be devoted to these employments. A farmer possessed of only a small capital, can only rent a small number of acres; he has neither funds to pay the wages of a large number of labourers, nor to purchase stock and implements of husbandry: if his capital increase, he may increase the size of his farm, and the amount of his outgoings.   The business of the manufacturer, is in like manner circumscribed by the amount of his capital, in proportion to which only can he lay in a stock of the raw material of his manufacture, set up machinery, erect mills and factories, and employ workpeople.   The operations of the merchant—the extent of his dealings—whether he is a home or foreign trader—whether he buys for money or on credit—and the length of credit he allows to his customers, will necessarily be regulated by the quantity of money he can command: if his capital be considerable, he will aim at realizing the higher profits of speculation, by laying in commodities at low, with the view of selling them at high prices. The truth of the principle is so obvious, that it hardly requires further illustration.   Every petty tradesman, shopkeeper, and retailer; in short, every employer of workmen, servants, or apprentices, is sensible that the extent of the business he can carry on, is limited by the capital he can raise.   Why is not every journeyman a master?   Simply for this reason—he has no capital; in other words, he has no money to commence business, to buy materials, and hire the services of other journeymen.

The demand for those who live by wages, therefore, necessarily increases with the increase of capital and individual incomes.   The increase of income and capital is the increase of national wealth. The demand for those who live by wages, therefore, increases with the increase of national wealth, and cannot possibly increase without it.

It is not the actual greatness of national wealth, but its progressive augmentation, which occasions a rise in the price of labour. It is not, accordingly, in the richest countries, but in the most *thriving*, or in those which are growing rich the fastest, that wages are highest. England is certainly a richer country than any part of the United States ; wages, however, are higher in North America than in England : the reason is, that though the United States are not so rich as England, they are advancing more rapidly in the career of wealth ; the demand for labour is greater, and consequently wages are higher. In England, the channels for the employment of capital are filled almost to overflowing; in America, the natural capabilities of the country have not been so far exhausted, and the capitalist is tempted, by the high rate of profit, to increase his demand for labour.

Both capital, therefore, and objects on which it can be profitably employed are essential to the maintenance of high wages. The natural resources of a country alone afford an imperfect criterion of its ability to support and employ labourers. England, in the twelfth century, possessed the same advantages of situation, of climate, of soil, and extent of territory, when it was not able to maintain one-sixth of its present amount of population. These advantages, doubtless, have hastened its progress in wealth and civilization, but that has been all. Before the richest soil can be cultivated, capital, or the produce of anterior industry, must be provided for the support of the labourers employed upon it; as it must be provided for those engaged in manufactures, or any other department of industry.

If the wealth of a country has been long stationary, we must not expect to find the wages of labour very high in it; for, while the funds for the payment of wages have continued the same, the number of hands seeking employment may have increased. In this case, there would be a constant scarcity of work, and labourers would bid against each other to get it. If wages had ever been more than sufficient to maintain the labourer, the competition for employment and the interest of masters would soon reduce them to the lowest rate compatible with the lowest subsistence. China appears to be in this predicament. It is one of the richest and most populous countries in the world; but its wealth has been long stationary, and wages consequently depressed to the point of starvation. By digging the ground a whole day a labourer cannot get more than will purchase a small quantity of rice in the evening. Even artificers are continually running about the streets with the tools of their respective trades, offering their services, and, as it were, begging employment. In the neighbourhood of Canton many families have no habitation on the land, but live constantly in fishing-boats on the rivers and canals. The subsistence

which they find there is so scanty, that they are eager
to fish up the nastiest garbage thrown overboard
from any European ship. Any carrion, the carcass
of a dead dog or cat, for example, though half
putrid and stinking, is as welcome to them as the
most wholesome food to the people of other countries.
It is not, therefore, the stationary, still less the declining state of national wealth which is most favourable to the industrious classes. The progressive
state of society, that in which it is advancing to the
further acquisition, rather than when it has acquired
its full complement of riches, is most favourable
to the happiness and comfort of the great body of
the people. " The progressive state," Dr. Smith
observes, " is in reality the cheerful and hearty
state to all the different orders of society; the stationary is dull; the declining melancholy."

The improving, stationary, or declining condition
of the working classes, therefore, especially depends
on the increasing, stationary, or declining amount
of the national capital which is to feed and employ
them. If they increase faster than capital, their
wages will be reduced; and if they increase slower,
they will be augmented. " In fact," says Mr.
M'Culloch, " there are no means whatever by which
the command of the labouring classes over the necessaries and conveniences of life can be enlarged,
other than by accelerating the increase of capital as
compared with population, or by retarding the increase of population as compared with capital; and
every scheme for improving the condition of the

labourer which is not bottomed on this principle, or which has not an increase of the ratio of capital for its object, must be completely nugatory and in-effectual."—*Principles of Political Economy,* second edition, p. 379.

Ireland is a striking instance of a country in which the population has increased faster than the funds for its employment.   No doubt capital has increased greatly in Ireland during the last hundred years, but not so fast as population.   The cause of this disparity has been ascribed to the introduction of the potato, in 1610; which, placing easily within the reach of the people a low and degrading means of subsistence, enabled them to vegetate, for they cannot be said to live, in " rags and wretchedness," without a desire to obtain a higher and more com-fortable state of existence.   Whatever has been the cause, the consequences of the number of labourers outgrowing the demand for them have been most deplorable.   All inquiries respecting Ireland concur in representing the number of the people excessive, and their condition as wretched in the extreme. Their miserable cabins are utterly unprovided with any thing that can be called furniture; in many families there are no such things as bedclothes; the children, in the extensive districts of Munster and the other provinces, have not a single rag to cover their nakedness; and whenever the potato-crop becomes even in a slight degree deficient, the scourge of famine and disease is felt in every part of the country.   The competition for employment and the competition for land have rendered both wages and profits little more than nominal, and both peasant and farmer are engaged in a constant struggle for the bare necessaries of life, without ever tasting its comforts.

The miseries of Ireland need not be dwelt upon; they are full to overflowing, and are seen every where. They, however, unanswerably demonstrate the evils of redundant population—of a people increasing faster than the means for their employment. Had the labouring classes increased less rapidly than they have done, there would have been fewer soliciting employment, and consequently wages would have been higher, and the condition of the people so far improved. The remedy for this unfortunate state of things is more easily suggested than brought into practical operation. It is obviously essential either that the people should increase in a slower, or the capital of the community in a faster ratio; but the former requires a national change of habits and moral culture, which a lengthened period could alone effect, and the latter would hardly be less tardy in its operation; demanding the persevering exertions of a firm and enlightened government, that would remove every obstacle to domestic industry— give security to persons and property, and guarantee to all internal order and peace. Every step, however, in the march of improvement would help to that which succeeded; and with the triumphant example Scotland has afforded of the co-operative

power of capital and popular education, there can
be no just ground of despair for Ireland.

The next circumstance that I shall notice, as tending to augment the demand for labour, is the *security of property*.   Most men have an aversion to
labour, that can only be overcome by the temptation
of enjoying its rewards, either in future ease or present enjoyments.   The merchant, manufacturer, and
shopkeeper, submit to the toils and anxieties of business in the hope of reaping and enjoying hereafter
the fruits of their exertions.   The rights of property
may not only be infringed by direct and forcible
violation, but by any measures that interfere with its
free use and most beneficial employment.   Every one
ought to be at liberty to employ his capital and industry on such objects as he deems most advantageous to himself, provided the exercise of this liberty
does not abridge the enjoyment of the same right by
others.   A landlord ought to be free to cultivate his
land as he pleases, a capitalist to fix his own rate of
interest, and a labourer to choose his employment,
and accept or not a fixed rate of wages.   On this
principle, commercial monopolies, the antiquated immunities of corporations, and combinations of workmen, are a violation of the rights of property and industry.   Individuals are best able to select the occupations most adapted to their means and natural
capacities; but the freedom of choice is abridged by
the members of these associations enjoying advantages from which those who are excluded are denied.

Capital and industry do not flow into the most profitable channels; and as the demand for labour and its remuneration depends on this circumstance, the interests of the working classes are compromised by such arbitrary interferences with the general freedom.

A state of peace and uninterrupted intercourse with other countries, are the last circumstances I shall notice as favourable to the demand for labour. Foreign war usually tends to disturb the operations of industry, either by preventing the supply of the raw material of some established manufacture, or intercepting the market for our commodities. Hostilities, it is true, give rise to new, and revive dormant employments; but this does not compensate for the loss of capital occasioned by its transfer to other branches of industry, and the stagnation and derangement produced in the pursuits of commerce and manufacture. War is a consumer, and not a creator of national wealth; and from this cause, as already explained, it must tend to lessen the demand for employment. The existence or apprehension of civil commotion has a similar tendency. A general feeling of insecurity and uncertainty, as to the future, is generated; and the mind and energies of the community are diverted from the pursuits of wealth and industry to the consideration of national affairs.

CHAP. VIII.

GENERAL CONCLUSIONS ON WAGES.

Wages can only be settled by Competition of Workmen—Wages of Farm Servants and in Factories—Distinction between Skilled and Unskilled Labour—Standard of Living—High Wages not a source of Idleness and Vice—Necessity of Relaxation—Effects of Arts, Trades, and Professions, on Health —Danger of low Diet and degrading Habits—Contrast of a Potato and Wheat-fed Population—Opinions of M'Culloch and Adam Smith—Government not less than Society interested in the wellbeing of the Working Classes.

IN the two preceding chapters I have endeavoured to explain the circumstances that principally determine the rate of wages ; namely, those that affect the supply of labour, and those that affect the demand or funds for its employment.   Before leaving this important subject, it will be useful to recapitulate the chief conclusions at which we have arrived, and fix attention more explicitly than has yet been done on those points that essentially influence the condition of the industrious orders.

Labour, it is clear, is a commodity of sale, differing from other commodities chiefly in its more perishable nature, in the greater difficulty and expense of storing up a surplus quantity of it beyond the current demand, and in the circumstance that the supply of it cannot be augmented or diminished with the same facility as the supply of a merely physical product.   All the principles of trade, therefore, which are applicable to buyers and sellers, are alike applicable to workmen and their employers.   Wages, like prices, must be determined by the free competition of the market ; there must be no arbitrary interferences either on the part of the state or of individuals ; any compulsory attempt to fix the market price of labour would be as indefensible as an attempt to fix the market price of bread or butcher's meat.

Labour is the property of the working man, and merits the same protection as other property ; but no more.   The trade in it ought to be free, neither protected by immunities, nor restricted by penalties.

As competition, and not any arbitrary regulations ought to determine the price of labour, it follows that high wages are only compatible with an understocked market ; in other words, high wages, can only be obtained when employers compete for workmen, not workmen for employers.   It is upon the ability of the working classes to maintain the market in this state that their wellbeing entirely depends. If their numbers are excessive, if they *bid* against each other for employment, then the market is oversupplied with the commodity in which they deal, and its price, like the price of any other redundant article, will be depreciated.

Should an excess in the supply of labour continue to lower its price, there is no depth of misery and degradation to which the working classes may not be compelled to submit. The low wages, which of late years have been paid to weavers in Lancashire and Scotland, to framework-knitters in Leicestershire, and to farm-servants in the southern and midland counties, incontestably establish the veracity of this principle. The disgusting atrocities practised in mills and factories are another corroborative circumstance. The proprietors of these abodes of wailing and anguish, and vice, are many of them enlightened men—Christian men—men, who, in all other relations of life are swayed by intelligence and humanity, but who in this are callous to every motive, save that of gain—who know no law save that of supply and demand—and who feel justified in running against each other a race of competition in buying the greatest quantity of human toil at the lowest price an overstocked market may compel the owners to accept.

The same principle governs rural industry. Humanity suggests that labourers in husbandry should be paid higher wages in winter than in summer; they require more food, fire, and warmer clothing; but humanity does not regulate wages, they are regulated by competition for employment. In summer, especially during harvest, farmers bid against each other for servants, and thereby raise wages; in winter work is not so plentiful, and servants bid against each other for employment and lower wages. Thus, by the operation of the unavoidable principle of competition, which neither can nor ought to be interfered with in the case of adult persons, the lowest wages are received when the highest are needed to meet the greater inclemency of the season.

The circumstances which influence the action of the competitive principle on the price of labour are different among the several classes of workpeople. All, for example, are eligible to the employments of domestic servants whose *personal characters* are unexceptionable. Among mechanics and artisans *skill* in their occupations is the chief condition; but among the common sort of labourers neither character nor skill are much sought after, it is sufficient if they possess *muscular strength.* As strength is the main qualification requisite in a labourer, he is liable to be competed against by all the able-bodied persons in the community in want of employment; hence the lowness of his wages. A domestic servant can only be competed against by persons with a character; while an operative or skilled labourer has a kind of monopoly in his trade; he can only be bid against by those who, like himself, have paid a premium, served an apprenticeship, or complied with some other established condition, essential to obtain a knowledge of his business. An increase of population therefore, or an immigration of Irish does not affect a skilled labourer as it affects the unskilled labourer, who may be bid against by all capable of work. The wages of a skilled labourer are a compensation for the exertion of both strength and skill; the wages of an unskilled labourer are a compensation for the exertion of strength only. Com-

petition regulates the wages of both; but all the
the able-bodied in society are eligible to compete
against the unskilled labourer; whereas it is only
those who have paid the price, either in money or
money's worth, to obtain a knowledge of the business of the skilled labourer that can compete against
him for employment. The limit, however, to the
employment of both the operative and labourer is
the same; namely, the possibility of the employer
realizing a *profit* on the produce of their industry.
If the rate of wages is such as to reduce the master's
gains below the average profit of capital, he will
cease to employ them, or he will only employ them
on condition of submission to a reduction of wages.

Whether wages are high or low does not depend,
as before remarked, on their *money amount*, but on
their relation to the prices of provisions, and the
command they give the labourer over all articles of
ordinary use and consumption. They have also
reference to the customs, habits, physical wants, and
circumstances of the working people Wages, for
example, which might be considered adequate to
satisfy the wants of a labourer living in a warm
climate, where clothing, a well-built cottage, and
fire, are of secondary importance, might be quite
insufficient in a cold country. The food too, necessary to subsistence, varies in different countries.
In England the ordinary diet of labourers is, or ought
to be, wheaten bread, meat, and beer; in Ireland,
potatoes; in China and Hindostan, rice. In many
provinces of France and Spain an allowance of wine

is considered indispensable to subsistence; in England the labouring class entertain nearly the same opinion with respect to malt liquor; whereas the drink of the Chinese and Hindoos consists of nothing but water. There is similar diversity in habitations. In Ireland the cottars live in miserable cabins, without either windows or chimneys; while in England the cottages of the labouring classes are all glazed, furnished, and are as much distinguished for their neatness and comfort as those of the Irish for their filth and misery. In consequence of this difference in habits the standard of wages varies; so much so, that while 2s. a day is not more than enough for a labourer in England, 5d. is deemed sufficient in Ireland, and 3d. in Hindostan.

The standard of wages has also reference to the hours of labour and periods of relaxation. It has been the policy of masters of late years to encroach on operatives in this respect, by cutting off or abridging holidays, and meal-times, and gradually extending the working hours; knowing that an increase of one-fourth in the time of labour is equivalent to a reduction in the same proportion in the amount of wages. Workmen should be constantly on the alert against such insidious contrivances, and watch them with the same jealousy that they would watch the stopping up of an ancient footpath on which they had been accustomed to amuse and recreate themselves. Leisure is indispensable to all classes, and any abridgment of it not only lessens the just reward of previous exertion, but takes away part of

R

the time essential to intellectual culture and enjoyment.

It has been represented, by superficial observers, that *high wages* tend to generate habits of idleness and dissipation in workpeople. Nothing can be more incorrect, more completely opposed to both principle and experience. Wages are the encouragement of industry, which, like every other human quality, increases in proportion to the encouragement it receives. Where wages are high, accordingly we always find the workmen more active, diligent, and persevering, than where they are low; in England, Holland, and America, than in Ireland, Poland, and Hindostan. Even an Irishman is an example of the stimulating influence of good wages; in his own country he is notoriously lazy and negligent in the extreme; after crossing the channel he becomes a model of laboriousness and enterprise. Some workmen, indeed, when they earn in four days what will maintain them through the week, will be idle the other three : but this is the exception, not the rule. Among the working classes, as among every other class of society, there are some who do not make the best use of their advantages ; they are improvident, intent on present enjoyment, and regardless of the future ; but the greater portion will be actuated by the motives common to our species, of increasing their comforts, and bettering their condition. Why, then, should the weakness and folly of a few be made a pretext for injuring and depressing, by low wages, the greater number ?

The faults of well-paid workmen are not deficient industry, but excessive, or, at least, irregular exertion. When liberally paid by the piece, they are tempted to overwork themselves, and to ruin their health and constitution in a few years. This is the case of porters, coalheavers, and many common labourers in London. A carpenter is not supposed to last in his utmost vigour above eight years. The double wages paid to country labourers during harvest, or to tailors during a general mourning, are frequent sources of permanent injury, from the inducement they offer to over-exertion. Almost every class of artificers are subject to some peculiar diseases, occasioned by excessive application to their peculiar species of work. Ramuzzini, an Italian physician, and Thackray, an English surgeon, have written treatises concerning such diseases. Excessive application during one part of the week is frequently the cause of the idleness complained of during the remainder. " Great labour," Dr. Smith remarks, " either of mind or body, continued for several days together, is in most men naturally followed by a great desire for relaxation, which, if not restrained by force or some strong necessity, is almost irresistible. It is the call of nature, which requires to be relieved by some indulgence," or change of occupation. Relaxation does not always imply idleness, but, as Locke expresses it, " easing the wearied part," by exchange of employment. If not complied with, the consequences are often dangerous, and sometimes fatal; and such as almost always bring on, sooner or later, the infirmity of the trade.   If masters would be more humane, and journeymen more reasonable, both would see the utility of temperate exertions of industry.   The man who works so moderately as to be able to work constantly, not only preserves his health the longest, but in the course of the year executes the greatest quantity of work. Labour, without reasonable intervals of rest for meals and relaxation, exhausts the energies of both body and mind, and is of the two more hurtful than low wages, which abridge diet and physical comforts.

Mr. Thackray, to whom I have just alluded, from his residence in Leeds—which is literally one great manufactory, subdivided into various departments of industry—places of refreshment—abodes varying in their comforts, according as the occupiers are masters, overseers, or workmen—has had favourable opportunities for observing, not only the effect of different occupations on the human constitution, but also of different degrees of exertion.   Some of this gentleman's conclusions in his work on *The Effects of Arts, Trades, and Professions,* are contrary to what might have been anticipated.   For instance, wet, vapour, and changes in the humidity of the local atmosphere, appear not so detrimental to health as is generally supposed; in *temperate* persons these agents produce little injury.   Sudden transitions from heat to cold, as experienced by smiths, iron-founders, and glassmen, are not productive of acute disorders. The exhalations from *vegetable matter* are not found uniformly injurious : but on this point the writer declines giving a decided opinion. The natural odours of *manufactured vegetables*, with the exception of coffee, are little noxious. Tobacco-workers do not sensibly suffer from the fumes of their material; and the crushers of rape and mustard benefit by the odours which these seeds exhale. Members of parliament and persons of fashion will be gratified to learn that the influence of *change in the hours of sleep*, is less than might be expected: millers, watchmen, and coachmen, are not sensibly affected by night-work. Horses, however, suffer from nocturnal labour; and men, too, I apprehend, unless the change, by perseverance, has been made habitual.

Some agents or circumstances connected with employments are favourable to health. Such are the *animal exhalations* to which slaughtermen, butchers, poulterers, fishmongers, gluemakers, buckram-stiffeners, tanners, tallowchandlers, curriers, and grooms, are exposed. *Oil*, or *grease*, applied to the skin, is preservative; as experienced in slubbing, carding, and piecening, in the woollen manufacture.

The chief agents included under the denomination of deleterious, or unfavourable to health and longevity, are excess or deficiency of food, bent-sitting posture, long standing, great muscular efforts in lifting weights, steam, artificial heat, impure air, dust and gaseous impurity of the atmosphere, anxiety and mental application, long sitting, and delay of micturition, compression of the chest, bending of the head for long periods, close application to minute objects, as in watchmakers, engravers, tambour-workers, and dressmakers; poisonous substances acting through the skin, as lead, printers' type, and mercury; or on the eyes, or ears, as scarlet-colour, lime-dust, and the noise of machinery.

Before the whole of Mr. Thackray's conclusions can be safely adopted as *rules of life*, it may perhaps be desirable he should test some of them by a more lengthened experience and wider field of observation. With the exception of this gentleman and Mr. Kay, of Manchester, hardly any medical person has applied himself to the investigation of a subject so important to humanity. One satisfactory result may, I think, be safely deduced from the inquiries of Mr. Thackray; namely, that there is hardly any employment which is not compatible with the enjoyment of tolerable health, when exercised subject to the three following conditions : 1. Moderate hours of labour, according to the greater or less exhausting nature of the employment. 2. Temperate, wholesome, and regular living. 3. Reasonable meal-times, and holidays occasionally, for purer air and exercise. For sake of the last, I hope Mr. Slaney will persevere in his object of obtaining for the people, by legislative provision, public grounds for recreation, botanical gardens, and libraries.

Next to keeping up the price of labour and the preservation of health, a cardinal point with the working classes is to establish and maintain a high standard of comfort and enjoyment in their habitations, clothing, and food; to eschew whatever brings them to the verge of existence, to their last resources in diet, dress, and lodging: and as casualties of health and fluctuations in employment are inseparable from every occupation, a provision should always be made, if possible, for periods of slackness, sickness, old age, and infirmity.

It is a disadvantage to the industrious orders that they cannot more easily adjust the supply of labour to the demand. When wages are depressed by competition for work, they are compelled to submit to coarser and scantier fare; and the danger is, that a mode of life at first repugnant to their feelings, and forced on them by necessity, may become habitual. Should this be the case, it is not likely they will make an effort to check the over-supply of labour which has caused their degradation; and as a lower rate of wages is found sufficient for their maintenance, an evil that might have been temporary is made permanent. This appears to be the condition of the Irish; their wages are under sixpence a day, which their masters, doubtless, think enough for men content to live in mud-cabins and feed on potatoes.*

The potato diet of the Irish is a principal reason that

---

* Not only wages, but gifts are often proportioned to a man's style of living. When James I. heard that Ben Jonson was living in great poverty in an obscure place in London, he sent him 10l. to relieve his necessities. Some of the courtiers remarking on the smallness of the dole, the king said it was enough for "a man who lived in an *alley*."

famines are so frequent and dreadful among them.
The national subsistence depends on a single root, and
if the crop of that fails, there is no other substitute to
which they can resort. A wheat-fed population may,
in the event of scarcity, obtain supplies of corn from
other countries; but a potato-fed population, with
wages to correspond, could not purchase the aid of
foreigners, and if potatoes could be obtained, they
are too bulky a commodity to be imported on an
emergency. How different the state of a people,
when bread and meat, and beer form the chief food
of the labourer. Here, there is scope for retrench-
ment in a period of scarcity. From wheat, the working man may temporarily resort to cheaper food—to
barley, oats, rice, and vegetables. He has room to
fall; but he who is habitually kept on the cheapest
food, is without a substitute, when deprived of it.
Labourers so placed, are absolutely cut off from every
resource. You may take from an Englishman, but
you cannot take from an Irishman—no more than
from a man already naked. The latter is already in
the lowest deep, and he can sink no lower: his
wages being regulated by potatoes, the staple article
of his subsistence, will not buy him wheat, or barley,
or oats; and whenever, therefore, the supply of potatoes fails, he has no escape from absolute famine—
unless he help himself (as is said to have been the
case in the dearth of 1821) to nettles, sea-weed, and
sour sorrel, the last of which was found in the stomach of one poor creature, who perished of hunger!

I conclude then, that the great, the all-important

principle bearing on the condition of the industrious classes, is keeping population in the rear of the funds for its employment. If the market of labour be overstocked, wages will be lowered by competition for work, and an inferior standard of comfort and enjoyment forced upon them : and, should habit reconcile them to an inferior style of living, a long farewell may be bid to their future improvement.

Labour, like gold and silver, can be made valuable by its *scarcity* only, and no other contrivance. All the acts of legislation, all the combinations and devices among workmen themselves, must fail in raising to a high price, that which is redundant, which every where abounds, and which may be indefinitely, and by any one, produced : we might as well seek to give a value to water, or the atmosphere that surrounds us. A scarcity of the employed, and abundance of employers ; a population that follows, and not precedes, the augmentation of national wealth, is the great secret of popular amelioration Without this, the advantages of increasing opulence, civilization, and commerce, can never be participated in by the working classes ; social improvements, in every shape, may advance over the land, but it will never touch the low and stagnant pool in which they are immersed.

As the high price of labour produced by scarcity of workmen, is the fortress that protects all their comforts and conveniences, they ought never to yield an inch of the ' vantage ground,' without dire necessity. The remarks of Mr. M'Culloch on this

point, are dictated by sense and humanity, and
well worthy of attention. "The example," says he,
" of such individuals, or bodies of individuals, as
submit quietly to have their wages reduced, and
who are content if they get only the mere necessaries
of life, ought never to be held up for public imitation.
On the contrary, every thing should be done to make
such apathy esteemed disgraceful. The best interests
of society require, that the rate of wages should be
elevated as high as possible—that a taste for the
comforts, luxuries, and enjoyments of human life,
should be widely diffused, and, if possible, inter-
woven with national habits and prejudices. Very
low wages, by rendering it impossible for any increased exertions to obtain any considerable increase
of comforts and enjoyments, effectually hinders them
from being made, and is, of all others, the most
powerful cause of that idleness and apathy, that
contents itself with what can barely continue animal
existence."—*Principles of Political Economy*, second edition, p. 394.

The father of economical science had inculcated the
same philanthropic doctrine. " Is this improvement,"
asks Smith, " in the circumstances of the lower ranks
of the people to be regarded as an advantage, or as
an inconveniency to society? The answer seems
at first abundantly plain. Servants, labourers, and
workmen of different kinds, make up the far greater
part of every great political society. But what improves the circumstances of the greater part, can
never be regarded as any inconveniency to the whole.

No society can surely be flourishing and happy, of which the far greater part of the members are *poor and miserable*. It is but equity besides, that they who feed, clothe, and lodge the whole body of the people, should have such a *share of the produce* of their own labour, as to be themselves tolerably well fed, clothed, and lodged."—*Wealth of Nations,* b. i. ch. 8.

Government is interested not less than the people, in the diffusion of such sentiments. It can never be the pride of authority to rule over an ignorant, ill-fed, and degraded population. The diffusion of political power has assimilated society to the nature of a joint-stock association, in which the rulers and ruled have a common interest. Government cannot be rich, while the body of the community is indigent; it cannot be safe, while that on which it mainly rests, cannot be depended on for support. It is not the opulent who demand legislative attention; they are exempt from want, and as they assume to be educated, they ought to be exempt from crime; they form that part of the social waste, which has been reclaimed and cultivated: but the poor, if not still in the wilderness, are only on its verge, and require to be brought forward by the application of those practical truths I have endeavoured to explain and enforce.

CHAP. IX.

FLUCTUATIONS IN EMPLOYMENTS.

Variations in Rural Labour—Fluctuations in Manufacturing
Employments—the Commercial Cycle—Changes of Fashion
and the Site of Manufactories—Effects of Machinery—Not
lessened aggregate Employment of Society, but displaced
particular Branches of Industry—Shearmen, Flax-dressers,
and Hand-loom Weavers—Enormous Increase of the Manufacturing, compared with the Agricultural Population—Specific Advantages of Machinery stated—Suggestions for
Mitigating the Effects of Fluctuations of Employment—
Tailors, Brushmakers, and Carpet-manufacturers—Methods
adopted by Masters to meet temporary Stagnation of Trade
—Novelty and Importance of the Subject to Statesmen and
Economical Writers.

THE quantity of employment is not uniform in any
branch of industry. It may be affected by changes
of seasons, the alterations of fashion, or the vicissitudes of commerce. The demand for manufactured products is different at different periods of
the year. In agriculture the demand for labour
is greater during spring and harvest, than in
winter. These are periodic variations in rural industry, which may be foreseen and provided for;
but others are of a more irregular and inappreciable
character. Agriculture, like other pursuits, may
either be in a progressive or declining state; it may
be extending from the natural causes, arising from
the increase of capital or of population, or from
artificial encouragement, which excludes foreign

competition in the home market. The absence of
any of these stimulants, will render agriculture
stationary, if not retrograde; in the latter case there
will be a permanent and increasing redundancy of
labour, entailing calamities of a more serious description, than those resulting from revolutions of
the seasons.

Although rural employment is not exempt from
fluctuation, it is less liable thereto than commercial
and manufacturing industry. In the latter is a
greater expensive power than the former, it is capable of more sudden development or contraction.
A fortunate discovery in mechanics may at once
quadruple the productive power of machinery; or a
manufacturer, when he finds it expedient from
slackness of trade, may at once dismiss his workmen,
and stop the working of his mills and factories. A
farmer has not equal power in husbandry. New
lands cannot be suddenly reclaimed nor abandoned;
neither can capital laid out in the improved culture
of old lands, be hastily withdrawn. It follows
the demand for labour increases or diminishes more
gradually in agriculture than in manufactures. Add
to which, the products of the former chiefly belong
to the class of necessaries, of the latter to luxuries,
the consumption of which may be dispensed with,
or varies with the changing circumstances of the
buyer, or the fluctuations of taste and fashion.

More powerful machinery, an increase of the
hours of working, or the number of workpeople,
always enables the manufacturer to proportion the

supply of his commodities to the demand. This is
one of the most general causes of fluctuation of
employment, and of the alternate periods of depression and prosperity, inseparable from mercantile
pursuits.   Spring is not a more sure harbinger of
summer, than great commercial activity of depression,
or stagnation of trade of its subsequent revival.   It
arises from the opposite influence of high and low
prices on consumption.   A cessation of demand
causes prices to fall, but consumption is promoted
by *cheapness*, as it is lessened by *dearness*.   As
consumption increases, prices increase also; and the
temptation of higher prices tends to increase the
quantity of industry applied to production.   But
a rise in prices operates on consumption like the
power which retards the ascent of bodies on an inclined plane; as prices advance, consumption proportionally diminishes, till at length the additional
employment created by the temptation of high
prices, becomes redundant, and then follows what is
significantly denominated in the commercial world,
a reaction.

Such are the general principles which influence
commercial depression and prosperity. They depend
on the influence of high and low prices on consumption.   Banking and the introduction of paper currency, may have increased their intensity, and
caused them to alternate in shorter periods, but they
would have occurred independently of these machinery.   Mercantile reactions were of frequent
occurrence before the general establishment of

banks; as those of 1763, 1772, and 1793. They have occurred more frequently since the extension of private credit by bills and bankers' notes, and within the last twenty-two years we have had no fewer than four mercantile revulsions; namely, those of 1811, 1816, 1818, and 1825-6. They may be likened to the plague and pestilence which formerly desolated the earth, and return nearly with as much periodic regularity. As improvements in medical science, and the art of preserving the public health, have taught us to avert or mitigate the former, we may hope that a more intimate acquaintance with the principles of trade, will teach similar power of prevention in respect of the latter.

In addition to the general principles which govern the commercial cycle, there are minor causes of fluctuations in manufacturing employments. Some of these are local, others general; without entering into elaborate or minute inquiries, these may be principally classed under the following heads: 1. Foreign rivalry, regulations, and prohibitions; 2. Changes of fashion or of place; 3. Improvements in machinery.

The effect of *foreign duties* and regulations is frequently injurious, and a source of fluctuation in manufacturing employment. Of this we had an example in the American tariff, which was severely felt by the workmen of Kidderminster, Wolverhampton, and other places. The pertinacity with which the French adhere to the restrictions of the mercantile system, is not only a source of fluctuation, by narrowing the commercial circle, but inflicts permanent injury on the workmen of both countries, by lessening the demand for employment.

The alterations of employment from *change of fashion*, are of such constant occurrence, that it is hardly necessary to particularize them by examples. About seventy years ago it was the fashion of all ranks to wear wigs; in 1765 many persons began to wear their own hair, which occasioned great distress among the peruke-makers, for want of employment; they petitioned the king for relief, upon which occasion many of them who attended, gave such offence by inconsistency in wearing their own hair, that they had it cut off by the crowd. The practice of wearing shoe-buckles and metal buttons, has almost entirely disappeared. In wearing-apparel one fabric has been substituted for another. Thus cottons have taken place of woollens and linens, in many articles of dress; and cottons are in their turn in some measure being supplanted by silks. In various other branches of manufacture, similar alterations are almost continual.

The migration, or *change of place* of any manufacture, has sometimes arisen from improvements of machinery, not applicable to the spot where such manufacture was carried on; as appears to have been the case with the woollen manufacture, which has in great measure migrated from Essex, Suffolk, Kent, and other southern counties, to the northern districts, where coal for the use of the steam-engine is much cheaper. The silk manufacture appears also to be taking a northerly direction, and taking root at Manchester and Macclesfield. In some instances these transitions have been caused by the conduct of the workmen in refusing a reduction of wages, or opposing the introduction of some kind of improved machinery or process; so that, pending the dispute, another spot has in great measure supplied their place in the market. Any unreasonable combination for the purpose, or violence used against the property of their employers, is almost sure to be injurious to the workmen.

Improvements in machinery have the effect of diminishing the demand for manual labour, by doing the same work at a cheaper rate than by hand. This diminution of employment is, however, *generally* of a temporary nature, as experience shows, that from the cheaper rates at which the product can be thus afforded, its use is more widely extended; and thus the workmen are again brought into work, though perhaps their employment may be different from what it was before. It is chiefly by successive improvements in machinery, great capital, and many facilities for the conveyance of goods, that our merchants are enabled to keep up a successful competition with foreigners in our staple manufactures.

That the application of machinery has not lessened the *aggregate* amount of employment in society may be satisfactorily established by the progress of our manufacturing population. The number of persons employed in trade and manufactures,

s

in proportion to those employed in agriculture, is greater perhaps in this country than in any other European state. In Italy the proportion of agriculturists to non-agriculturists is as one hundred to thirty-one; in France, as one hundred to fifty; in England, as one hundred to two hundred.[*] But the most remarkable fact as respects this country is the change that has taken place in the employment of the people since the commencement of the present century. In 1801 the number of persons engaged in trade and manufactures in England, as compared with those occupied in agricultural pursuits, was as six to five; in 1821 it had increased to eight to five; in 1830 to two to one.[†] In Scotland the change has been still greater, having risen from five to six in 1801, to nine to five in 1821, and is now estimated at nearly two to one, as in England. During the whole period of thirty years, the general population of the country has increased nearly fifty-one per cent.; which exceeds the proportionate increase in the agricultural districts, but is less than the proportionate increase in the manufacturing districts. In four rural districts the increase of population, during the last thirty years, has been only thirty per cent.; in London fifty-eight per cent.; in ten large manufacturing towns eighty per cent.; and in three of the largest manufacturing towns no less than one hundred per cent., or exactly double.

* *Economy of Machinery and Manufactures,* p. 5.
† *Report on Manufacturers' Employment,* Parl. Pap. 590. Sess. 1830.

In 1774 the *parish* of Manchester is estimated to have contained 41,032 inhabitants—a number which was more than quadrupled in the subsequent fifty-seven years. The population of Preston is said, in 1780,* not to have exceeded 6000, whereas it amounts at present to 33,112. In 1780 the city of Glasgow contained only 42,832 inhabitants; in 1831 it contained 202,426. The growth of Paisley, inclusive of the abbey parish, has been in a similar ratio during the last half-century.

From these statements two important facts may be deduced; *first*, that within the last thirty years trade and manufactures, in place of agriculture, have become the predominating occupation of the people; *secondly*, that as the manufacturing population has increased much more rapidly than the agricultural, or even the general population of the country, it shows that the application of machinery to manufactures has not had the effect of lessening the aggregate amount of employment of the working classes. The latter fact will be made more evident by recapitulating the rapid progress of population in those towns where machinery has been most extensively introduced. The first three towns, as is well known, are the great emporiums of the cotton manufacture; Birmingham of hardware; Leeds of woollen and linen; Nottingham of stockings.

* McCulloch's *Dictionary of Commerce*, p. 416.

s 2

	1801.	Increase per cent.	1811.	Increase per cent.	1821.	Increase per cent.	1831.
Manchester	94,876	22	115,874	40	161,635	47	237,832
Glasgow . . .	77,385	30	100,749	46	147,043	38	202,426
Paisley . . .	31,179	18	36,722	28	47,003	22	57,466
Birmingham	73,670	16	85,753	24	106,721	33	142,251
Leeds	53,162	18	62,534	34	83,796	47	123,393
Nottingham	28,861	19	34,253	18	40,415	25	50,680

Although it is clear, from this decennary statement of the progress of population, that the aggregate quantity of employment has increased with the increase of machinery, yet it would be sacrificing the truth, for the maintenance of a principle, to allege that a specific class of workmen on the first substitution of a machine for their manual labour does not suffer by its introduction.

The first effect of the substitution of machinery is to reduce the price of labour or cost of production of the commodity on which it is employed. Unless this end can be attained, the machinery will not be adopted. A new competitor is introduced in the form of wood and iron, which either forces the workman from his trade or compels him to accept a lower rate of wages. It is true consumption will be stimulated by the cheaper rate at which commodities can be produced, but this has its limits; for, however cheap cottons, woollens, and hosiery may be manufactured, the supply may ultimately exceed the demand even at the price of the raw material. Increased consumption may cause the labour of the workman to be absorbed in some other occupation not greatly different from that in which he was originally employed; but the value of his labour will be depreciated; he will not receive the same wages he received in the employment from which he has been ejected by the substitution of machinery.

Some branches of industry, within the last thirty years, have been wholly, others partially, superseded by the application of machinery; as those of shearmen in the woollen, and of flax-dressers in the linen manufacture. The introduction of the power-loom is a striking example of loss of employment from mechanical invention. Every power-loom can do at least as much work as three hand-looms; and it appears that the number of the latter in 1830 were about the same as in 1820, namely, 24,000;* whereas the former, which in 1820 amounted to about 14,000, had increased to above 55,000, showing an increase in the amount of work done by power-looms equal to the work afforded by 123,000 hand-looms. Hitherto the use of the power-loom has been confined chiefly to the cotton manufacture; should it ever be found practicable to make use of it extensively in the fabrics of woollen and silk, it is probable its effects would not be less important.

While the use of the power-loom has been extending, it is almost unnecessary to observe that the wages and employment of the hand-loom weavers have been fluctuating. It is better to concede thus much than, as has been usual, to disguise the

* *Parliamentary Paper*, No. 590. Sess. 1830.

question, and suffer erroneous notions to be propagated of the tendency of mechanical improvements. The direct tendency of them is to substitute *cheap* for *dear* labour; and by it being known that this is not a temporary but permanent change, the workman is apprized of his altered circumstances and the best means of providing against them. In pursuing this course the evil is not aggravated, since the policy of giving full scope to the application of machinery is no longer contested. Master and workman are alike entitled to freedom, and in the maintenance of this principle the interests of society are best consulted. If commodities can be produced cheaper by machinery than manual labour, the plainest understanding revolts at the idea of compelling the whole community to *buy dear* merely that a single class of workmen may be guaranteed in the monopoly of high wages: they had better be pensioned off by the public. There would be no limit to interference with machinery; it extends through every operation of life, and if we once began to control its application, we could "never stop, till we came," as significantly expressed by a Glasgow weaver, to a committee of the House of Commons, "to our teeth and nails."

The three most important advantages which result from the application of machinery are the following:

1. It tends to benefit the whole community by facilitating the production of commodities, and thereby rendering them cheaper and more accessible to all classes of consumers. 2. It tends to lessen

fluctuations in employment; for a manufacturer, with a large capital invested in machinery, would sustain a double loss by its standing idle : a loss of profit on the capital so invested, and a loss by the damage his machinery would sustain by being inactive. In consequence, his interest consists in keeping it in constant action; and this he can only do by regulating its productive power agreeably with the average demand of a long series of years rather than a particular season. The third is an advantage I have not before seen noticed; it consists in the change the introduction of machinery must ultimately effect in the relative proportions or composition of society : the working classes are usually considered the least favourably situated for the enjoyment of independence and happiness : if so, the aggregate happiness of communities must be augmented, since the effect of machinery is finally to lessen the proportion of individuals dependent on labour for support.

The general conclusions from the inquiries of this chapter are that all employments, whether agricultural or manufacturing, are liable to fluctuation, and that, therefore, it is expedient to make provision for such alternations of prosperity and adversity.

Employments in agriculture appear less subject to vicissitude than in manufactures; in the former they are periodic, arising chiefly from changes of the seasons and the different demands for labour in winter and summer. As these variations are of annual occurrence, the evils resulting from them would be averted by any arrangement between the labourer and em-

ployer which provided for the maintenance of the
former throughout the year.   The practice of *hiring*
for a twelvemonth is an arrangement of this nature,
and was formerly the general usage in husbandry.

The causes which influence manufacturing employments are more various and complicated, depending not only on the season of the year, on
fluctuations of fashion, and fertility of mechanical
inventions, but also on the stimulus of high and
low prices on the production of commodities.
Some of the former causes cannot be subjected to
calculation; but the latter, though not returning
annually, or at any fixed intervals, yet return with so
much certainty and almost regularity as to be entitled
to be considered periodic.   It is for fluctuations of
this description, at least, that the workman ought to
be prepared; he ought to be prepared to encounter a
scarcity of employment after a previous redundancy,
and the intensity and duration of this scarcity will
mostly be proportioned to the preceding excess.

It never happens that all branches of industry are
simultaneously depressed, and one method of meeting
the varying demands for labour in different trades
would be for a workman not to depend on any single
occupation for support. He ought to be so instructed,
it has been suggested (*Westminster Review*, No. 36,
Jan. 1833), as to be able to shift his position with
the shifting requirements of the market.   But this is
an expedient more easily suggested than practised.
It might suit particular individuals; but to learn
one trade and become expert therein is sufficient

for the generality of mankind.　There could be no obstacle, however, to the several members of a family learning different trades ; so that they may not be all out of work together.

To provide for changes in employment occasioned by periodic alternations of prosperity and depression two suggestions may be offered.　First, the workman, by saving out of his high wages during years of brisk demand for labour, might lay by a fund for a period of stagnation of trade ; or, secondly, he might enter into an agreement with his master to serve at an average rate of wages for such a term of years as would embrace the ordinary commercial cycle of depression and prosperity.　Various other expedients might be suggested ; but it appears superfluous, as they must be either generally obvious, or are already partly acted upon.　The object sought is to make the *good* years cover the *bad* ones, and *vice versâ.*　That this is partly possible there does not appear any doubt ; since it appears, from the inquiries made into the rate of wages in the principal trades and manufactures (see Appendix), that the earnings of workmen are sufficient, on an average of years (if the earnings could by any means be spread over the whole period), to maintain their families in comfort and independence.

In some of the trades of London (particularly the tailors) all the journeymen are in organized clubs for mutual support during want of work ; and out of the general fund, to which they all contribute when in work, each man out of employment has a right to a weekly allowance. Such a society is, doubtless, highly beneficial, especially in a trade where the demand for labour is much greater at one period of the year than another. It has one drawback, in operating as a combination to regulate and keep up wages; and so far has this been successful, that no reduction in the wages of tailors appears to have taken place since 1815, notwithstanding the change in prices of almost every article of life. As respects a class of journeymen employed entirely on articles of home consumption, this may not be esteemed a disadvantage; but it is evident that if the same combination existed among workmen manufacturing articles of export which had to compete with the fabrics of other countries, such a system might be ruinous both to masters and men.

The journeymen brushmakers, amounting to not more than one thousand in number throughout the kingdom, support a union for mutual aid in scarcity of employment. The carpet-manufacturers, and other trades, are united for a similar purpose. Few of these, however, have any fund beforehand, but draw the support from increased contributions by the men who remain at work.

Some workmen of superior character make a provision for periods of temporary stagnation of trade, by accumulating a small fund in a savings-bank; but the great majority have no resource when out of work but to live much worse, to exhaust their credit, pawn their clothes and furniture, and finally apply to the parish, where their spirit is broken and independent feeling lost.

The master-manufacturers resort to two expedients of a very different character for meeting temporary stagnations of trade. In the one case, on the demand for goods becoming slack, the quantity made is diminished; a less amount of work being given out and the workmen paid (by the piece) nearly as much as before. Having, however, but three or four days work per week they are obliged either to economize their expenses or resort for support during the other days to whatever fund their forethought may have provided; thereby, the quantity of goods made being reduced nearly to the real demand, no glut is formed in the market, and on the revival of trade the men again resume full work without great loss. This is the case with several trades having a fund to fall back upon, and is beneficial to all parties.

In the other case, where there is no fund or provision for support during temporary stagnations of demand, the reduction takes place by *lowering the wages* of workmen on the same amount of work done; the consequence of which is, that they endeavour to make up the difference by lengthening the hours of labour and redoubling their exertions: hereby, at the time when the actual demand for their manufacture is the least, raising the supply to the highest point. By this means a great accumulation of the goods made take place; and even when an

increased demand again commences it takes a long
time to work off the stores in the hands of capitalists, which have been supplied at a rate of wages
ruinously low to the working classes.   In many
important trades this is more or less the case; it has
been exemplified in the iron trade at Wolverhampton and elsewhere: and a very intelligent master-
manufacturer of Manchester informed a parliamentary committee that in the cotton trade "the worst
years are almost always accompanied by the greatest
quantity of work done."

I shall conclude with remarking that the subject
of this chapter has not before been brought specifically under public notice; but in the existing state
of society it is of vast importance, well meriting the
attention of both statesmen and economical writers.
Fluctuations in employment are the great bane of
communities.   A nation had better be stationary in
riches than be carried transiently forward by a sudden impulse of prosperity to be followed by equal or
deeper depression.   The high price of farm produce,
occasioned in different degrees by the war, by paper
currency and corn-laws has been a primary cause of
the redundancy of labour, and consequent low wages,
privation, pauperism, and insubordination recently
experienced in the agricultural districts.   Were our
vast superstructure of commercial and manufacturing industry to sustain a corresponding reaction,
the effects would be far more tremendous in the
densely-peopled midland and northern counties.

CHAP. X.

UNIONS OF TRADES.

Classes of the Industrious confederated either for an increase of Profit or Wages—Origin and Downfal of the Trading Guilds and Fraternities—First notice of Combinations of Workmen—National Association for the Protection of Labour —Principles and Constitution of Trades' Unions—How far they are defensible—Examples of Combinations hurtful to Operatives—Better Wages should be high than Profits— Comparative Treatment of Factory Children now and Thirty Years ago—Proof that Wages are not always regulated by Profit, and that Industry sometimes needs legislative Protection—Foreign Trade not injured by Unions but Competition of Manufacturers—Effect of extreme Low Prices on Masters and Workmen.

SIMILARITY of pursuit offers so many motives to association it may be safely assumed, that the unions of trades are hardly less ancient than the origin of the trades themselves. The builder of a hut or canoe would naturally seek the society of other builders, either for help or improvement. Inducements of a like kind have consolidated into castes other classes of society—the learned for the advancement of science; merchants for the promotion of commerce, and the wealthy and aristocratic orders for the pursuits of pleasure and ambition. So constant and universal has been the operation of this principle that I can hardly find a single division of labour which is not associated; the shipowners, coalowners, West

India planters, bakers, brewers, gas-light companies, and booksellers ; as well as the woollen-manufacturers, coopers, cotton-spinners, coachmakers, brushmakers, tailors, and printers, are all in direct or tacit combination, the object of which is their separate conservation and advantage.   Anciently the trades united for personal security as well as improvement in their respective crafts ; these purposes have been superseded by the progress of industry, science, police, and government, and the great ends now sought to be attained by mercantile and operative unions are the maintenance by the former of a high rate of profit, of the latter a high rate of wages.

It cannot be uninteresting shortly to advert to the progress of Trades' Unions in order to prepare the way for a few observations on the principles on which they have been established.   The only portion of the industrious classes which has not resolved into associations of this nature are those employed in agriculture, and which may be ascribed to their scattered location, and not enjoying the same facilities as those employed in manufactures for acquiring information.

The most ancient examples of the unions of workmen are the trading guilds or fraternities, remains of which still subsist in many of the principal towns of England, and on the continent.   Traces of these societies may be found under the Roman emperors ; and during the times of the Anglo-Saxons, when they formed a separate and favoured portion of the

community possessing exclusive grants and immunities. Combinations, in the modern sense, of workmen against their employers, could have no place
in these associations; each constituted a distinct incorporation of all those engaged in the same mystery
or occupation; they were governed by by-laws, which
regulated the taking of apprentices, the admission of
new members, the prices of their manufactures, &c. :
in short, they performed all those functions in common, that are now performed separately by masters
and journeymen, and the only combination that existed was that formed by the union of both against
the community. The monopoly thus established
against the public was the cause of their downfal,
and at an early period made them an object of legislative enactment. In the 1st stat. 9 Edw. III., it is
declared that the franchises of guilds are " preju-
dicial to the king, prelates, and great men, and oppressive to the commons." By the gradual abridgment of their privileges, they lost their municipal
government; stranger workmen were introduced into
the trades, who did not acknowledge the authority
of masters and wardens; and, finally, the fraternities resolved into the two great and independent
divisions of masters and journeymen—the former
finding the capital, the latter the labour for their co-
operative industry. From this transition may be
derived the first origin of trade unions, for the express purpose of keeping up the rate of wages, the
operatives forming a distinct class, with interests
occasionally opposed to those of their employers, and

against whom they are frequently compelled to act in concert, to prevent their social degradation.

The decline of the guilds, it is evident, like that of most other oppressions, resulted from an endeavour to exercise a power incompatible with the general welfare. Their object was to promote the interests of their own monopolies, by the sacrifice of the interests of the community. This was conspicuous in the selfish and contracted policy with which they opposed the admission of apprentices, against which several statutes, in the reigns of Henry VII. and VIII., were specially directed. The admitted mechanics, however, were not wholly satisfied with their masters; for, by an act passed in 1465, the *truck system* was made illegal : and in 1482 the fullers and thickeners of hats, bonnets, and caps, were gratified with the laying aside, for two years, of a piece of machinery which *abbreviated their work*. The Shrewsbury case (8 Eliz. c. 7, and 14 Eliz. c. 12) is strikingly illustrative of the mistaken course of the chartered societies against the freedom of industry, as quoted by the author of the valuable work on the *Combinations of Trades*. The mechanics connected with the mystery of drapers, incorporated in the town of Shrewsbury, complain that artificers, neither belonging to their company nor brought up to their trade, " have, of late, with great disorder, upon a mere covetous desire and mind, intromitted with and occupied the said trade, having no knowledge, skill, or experience of the same; and do buy, commonly and daily, such Welsh clothe and flannels as is defective, and not truly made, to the impeachment and hindrance of 600 people of the art or science of sheermen or frizers, within the said town; whereby, as well they as their poor wives and families, are wholly maintained." The legislature listened to this representation, and expelled the rival artisans. Six years after the act was repealed, with an avowal, that " it is now likely to be the very greatest cause of the *impoverishing* and *undoing* of the poor artificers and others, at *whose suit the said act was procured*, for that there be now sithence the passing of the said act much fewer persons to set them to work than before." This is a very striking illustration of the tendency of that sort of legislation which some persons would have tried four centuries later; the complaint of the Derby dressers was precisely that made against machinery and knobsticks in 1831-2, and there is little doubt that a repetition of the policy of the former period would produce similar results, involving the destruction of industry, and sacrifice of all parties.

The history of our chief manufacturing towns shows how essential freedom is to the successful pursuit of industry. The great seats of our manufactures are Manchester, Birmingham, Sheffield, and Leeds; to these places the most expert operatives and enterprising tradesmen resorted, to escape the arbitrary jurisdiction of incorporate guilds, and the no less vexatious statutes dictated by religious intolerance; and these unprivileged and obscure hamlets, enriched by their presence, speedily left behind the

T

ancient cities and boroughs, with all their immunities.

The trading guilds were doubtless useful in their origin, and only at a subsequent period became hurtful to the public interests. Their institution tended to foster and advance the manufacturing arts, which, without the co-operation of capital and skill they afforded, might have perished in infancy, or made a slow and almost imperceptible progress. In this respect they may be considered the germ of our commercial wealth and prosperity. But though valuable as the nursery of national industry, they became an obstacle to its development after it had taken root; their exclusive privileges impeded its growth, through the power they afforded to punish intruders, to suppress competition, and keep the practice of their mysteries within the narrow paling of their own corporate interests.

In another point of view, the constitution of the guilds may be deemed advantageous. One of the most desirable ends to attain in the condition of the industrious is, that they should be secured from want and dependence. Now, this appears to have been tolerably well attained in the economy of the ancient associations, each society being a brotherhood, the members of which had mutual claims for support in all the vicissitudes of life : hence the purposes of a benefit society were answered, and the necessity for a poor-rate superseded. Mutual assurance against want was further guaranteed by the power of the fraternities to limit their number, by which any tendency to a redundancy of workpeople that might depreciate the value of their industry, was checked. This is one of the objects sought to be attained by trade unions, to the institutions of which I shall now advert.

The first notice of combinations of workmen is in the year 1548 ; the 2d & 3d Edward VI. c. 15 of that year premises that " artificers, handicraftsmen, and labourers, have made confederacies and promises, and have sworn mutual oaths, not only that they should not meddle with one another's work, and perform and finish that another hath begun, but also to constitute and appoint how much *work they shall do in a day, and what hours and times* they shall work, contrary to the laws and statutes of this realm, and to the great hurt and impoverishment of his Majesty's subjects." In this is no allusion to wages, but as the unions had been entered into to fix the quantity of work and regulate the hours of working, the objects were of an analogous nature, and directed to the control of the market of labour. Subsequently, acts were passed expressly to restrain combinations for raising wages ; the frequent occurrence of statutes of this nature only serve to show their futility ; for combinations multiplied, and union and secrecy were forced upon them, by their illegal character. In 1824 the entire system was abandoned by the legislature ; it was discovered that laws to prevent the combinations of workmen, and not their employers, were partial and unjust ; that, if successful, they could only tend to depress one class of the community, at the expense of another; but what was much more important, it was ascertained, that all such efforts, whether politic or not, were abortive; since it was beyond the power of legislation to prevent the open or covert union of workmen.

The act of 1824 (5 George IV. c. 96) repeals all laws, previously made, against combinations of workmen, to advance or fix the rate of wages, to alter the hours of working, to decrease the quantity of work, to induce others to quit, or to return to work, &c., provided no violence is used. In the following year this act was amended, in conformity with its fundamental principle, of leaving workmen individually and collectively free in the disposal of their labour. With this view provision was made for protecting workmen, who did not choose to be members of any association, by which they were enabled, independent of any combination, to engage their industry on whatever terms, or to whatever master, they may choose, in perfect security against molestation, insult, or personal danger.

From 1825 to the present period, the law of combinations has been left untouched. In some places these societies have been formed, and have since almost disappeared, as at Bristol; in others, as Manchester, they have not only rapidly extended; but at no period, during the last seven years, has the district been without the confusion and excitement of turnouts, caused by these associations. (*On Combinations of Trades*, p. 28.) The evidence taken by a Committee of the House of Commons, in

1824, shows that each trade in London had at that time some organization, and the accounts there given of the unions of spinners at Glasgow, Bolton, and Manchester, several of which had long been rich and powerful—of hatters—of the Liverpool shipwrights—of tailors, and others, differ in no respect from the societies now in existence.

Besides the separate unions of trades, attempts have been made to organize a National Association; for the protection of labour, composed of an aggregation of trades' unions, and having for its sole object, the prevention of a *reduction of wages*. On the 28th of June, 1830, a meeting was held at Manchester, of the various delegates from branches of the General Trades Association, in order to elect officers ; the number of twenty trades having joined the union. No trade can be admitted members of this association, that is not regularly organized and united in itself. It was arranged that so soon as the funds of the society permit, an office is to be taken, and a printing-press and types purchased, for the establishment of a newspaper, and other purposes of the association. The contribution of each member is limited to one penny per week. Supposing, out of the millions of workmen in the United Kingdom, only one million become subscribers to the Union, their subscriptions, in one week, would amount to 4166*l.*; in a year, to 216,666*l.*; and in five years, to the sum of 1,083,333*l.*

These calculations will remind the reader of the various projects which have been submitted for the liquidation of the national debt; they are arithmetical problems, easily solved on paper, but in practice prove wholly illusive. The General Trades Association, as might have been foreseen, has failed to realize the expectations of its projectors, and though more magnificent in its pretensions, is not likely to rival in utility the subordinate societies. Let us now attend to the specific objects embraced by the Trade Societies, as I find them set forth in the publication on the *Combinations of Trades*, and in the *Leeds Mercury* of November and December, 1832.

The first duty of a trade union is to oppose a reduction of wages, and maintain, according to a scale fixed by themselves, a fair remuneration for labour. Secondly, the increase of the money prices of labour is to be occasionally attempted. Thirdly, the associated workmen endeavour to sustain the value of their particular industry, by laying down strict regulations respecting the admission and time of servitude of apprentices. The fourth duty of a union is connected with the preceding, and consists of the prevention of the employment of any but regularly *associated* workmen. Fifthly, wages are to be regulated by the *profit* the employer may derive from improvements in machinery. Lastly, the union is bound to prevent the insidious reduction of wages, by an extension of the hours of labour, or otherwise, without a corresponding increase of remuneration.

The affairs of the union are managed by a committee, president, and secretaries, supported by a common fund, the produce of a weekly subscription of each associated workman. In case an employer attempts to controvene any of the rules of the society, by a reduction of wages, or otherwise, the mode adopted for making him conform thereto, is, first, for his workmen to demand an abandoment of the obnoxious proceeding ; in case of refusal the men *turn out*, they are placed on the books of the union, and supported out of its funds, until either the refractory employer gives way, or a compromise is effected.

From the preceding representation it is apparent that the several purposes of a union may be all resolved into one, namely, that of keeping up the *price of labour*, and this object must be deemed laudable, so long as it is sought to be attained by unobjectionable means. But no class of workmen is justifiable in the adoption of measures for the advancement of its interests, which involve an invasion of the rights of others. In this view some of the objects of union appear of questionable utility ; or at least it is not conceivable in what way they can be enforced in practice without violating the freedom of industry. For example, how is the employment of *non-associated* workmen to be prevented ? Refusing to work with them, is as great a power of coercion as a union ought to exercise, and greater, I apprehend, than would be found legal, provided such refusal could be proved a *concerted* act of resistance. Waving this, there can be no doubt if they resort to violence—if they intimidate, or, as is sometimes the case in the north, personally maltreat a *knobstick*,

as a recusant workman is termed, then they are
guilty of an injustice punishable by law, and indefensible in reason : for every individual ought to be
protected in the uncontrolled disposal of his labour,
independent of the dictation of any club or society.
Again, the proposition for regulating wages by the
profit the employer may derive from improvements
in machinery, is hardly tenable. Is no allowance to
be made for the loss and interruption masters sustain
by the introduction of mechanical improvements? It
would be quite as reasonable to assume for the standard of wages, the master's skill, capital, industry,
or enterprise. The principle is not less objectionable
than that of the tithe system, under which those
reap who have not sown—participate in the gains
but not the losses of industry.

Another proposition is, that workmen may frame
regulations respecting the admission and servitude of
apprentices; this they may do, but they are not justifiable in compulsorily enforcing them, further than
by refusing to work. In short, the legitimate powers
of unions are strictly passive ; they may unite for
any object beneficial to themselves, provided they seek
to attain it by peaceable means, and without injury
to or abridgment of the freedom of others, either
masters or fellow-workmen. Any degree of coercion
beyond this—any attempt to intrude in their collective capacity as a third party in disputes between
employers and their workpeople—to prescribe the
rate of wages, or the mode of conducting work—
would form a species of foreign intervention wholly

incompatible with the successful pursuit of trades and manufactures, and quite as mischievous as the immunities of corporations or any oppressive monopoly.

Wishing well to many objects embraced by the trade unions, and believing that like friendly societies, they might be made subservient to salutary purposes, I should regret to witness their failure by the assumption of functions neither just nor useful. The intelligent among them, and they are not few in number, will not fail to profit by the fate of the guilds, as already described. The existing power of unions is great, but it would be speedily abased, should it be unwisely perverted into an engine of general annoyance and oppression. A union of masters, aided by the law and the authority of the state would, in six months, dissolve all the unions of men in the kingdom. But I trust there will be no need of any such hostile combination, and it is with a sincere desire to avert a catastrophe of this kind, that I shall take the liberty to submit two or three points for the consideration of the members of the trades' associations.

The *first* is, that workmen cannot, by any combination, force wages beyond a certain limit, without producing injury to themselves. If wages are raised so high, that the gains of the master on the sale of his commodities are reduced below the average profit of capital, he will either withdraw his money from so unproductive an employment, or remove his business to another place, where it can be carried on under more favourable circumstances.   In either case, the occupation of workmen is gone, and grasping at too much they lose all.

The practical examples which I could cite, of detriment to operatives from unreasonable or unjust pretensions, are numerous.   A considerable number of lace-frames were removed from Nottinghamshire to the western counties, in consequence of the combinations of workmen. In the fourth Parliamentary Report respecting Artisans and Machinery it is related, that one of the partners of an extensive cotton factory at Glasgow, fettered and annoyed by the constant interference of his workpeople, removed to the state of New York, where he re-established his machinery, and thus afforded to a rival community at once, a pattern of our best machinery, and an example of the best mode of using it.   The croppers of the West Riding of Yorkshire, and the hecklers or flax-dressers, can unfold a " tale of woe," on this very subject.   Their earnings exceeded those of most mechanics, but the frequency of " strikes" among them, and the irregularities in their hours and times of working, compelled masters to substitute machinery for their manual labour.   Their trades, in consequence, were in great part superseded.   The manufacturers, at first, saved little or nothing by the substitution of machinery, but it formed a more peaceable and unfailing agent. If I understood the Marquis of Londonderry correctly, the colliers and keelmen of the Tyne and Wear have been reduced to greater humiliation than heretofore, by the discomfiture of their combinations to raise wages. But of this fact I am not sure; I am not sure, in this instance, whether the men or the masters were at fault: but this I do know, that the noble Marquis, my Lord Durham, and other great coal-mine owners, form a most detestable confederacy against the inhabitants of the metropolis, in the supply of coals, and which confederacy, I trust, will be speedily destroyed.

Secondly, it appears to me an impracticable attempt on the part of the unions, to fix either the hours of working, or the rate of wages, by one uniform and invariable scale. They may have a general rule or usage on these matters, but it ought to be one with many exceptions.

The natural tendency of wages is to vary with the prices of commodities, but as the unionists cannot prospectively fix the prices of commodities, they cannot prospectively fix the price of their own labour. If they had power to enable their employers *to sell* the produce of their industry at a fixed price, they might have some right to compel them *to buy* it at a fixed price. To attempt to maintain wages at an invariable standard, by the mandate of a committee or association, is nothing less, than journeymen, in the nineteenth century, repeating the follies of the masters in the fourteenth, when the price of labour was fixed by royal proclamation, or act of parliament. The injustice and futility of this, has been repeatedly shown in the foregoing History of the Middle and Working Classes.

The operatives of the Leeds Union affirm, that

their design is, to " protect the *upright* manufacturer against the unfair competition of the avaricious
one, and to secure a fair remuneration for labour."
Let them stick to this—let their association be directed solely against the under-selling, grinding employer, and their confederacy will be viewed with as
much favour by many of the masters, as it is by the
journeymen themselves.

. The *last* point I beg to submit, is the interference
of the committees of unions, in disputes between the
employers and the employed.   If unions are not allowed to support workmen against unfair reduction
of wages, or other oppression, the entire object of
their associations falls to the ground. But the power
of interference should be exercised with great caution
and forbearance. For *strangers* to interfere between
a master and his men, is as delicate an office, as
for strangers to interfere in the disputes of a married
pair. It may be beneficial, once in a hundred times,
but the chances are, that it tends to widen breaches,
foment quarrels, and interpose obstacles to their
mutual happiness and prosperity.

Let us now consider how the institution of trade
societies affects the community.   Hitherto, I have
only considered the relations they establish between
employers and the employed.   Their chief object, as
before explained, is the maintenance of high-priced
labour.   Society has seldom an interest at variance
with the attainment of this end.   The contest is between profits and wages; in other terms, whether a
greater or less sum shall go into the pockets of the

master or workman. **Buyers of commodities are in** the same situation in respect of profits and wages, as farmers are in respect of rent and tithe. If the farmer were exonerated from tithe he would have an additional sum forthwith to pay for rent, to an exactly equal amount. If the buyer of an article paid nothing for wages to the workman, he would have just as much additional to pay for profit to the master. Except in the particular case, when profits are at a minimum, that is, are so low, that further depression would force capital into other employment; the rate of wages has no influence on the prices of commodities. Masters always obtain as much as they can get for their goods, without regard to the wages of journeymen; if wages rise, profits fall, and the contrary, if wages fall, prices remaining unchanged. But the consumer is not affected in either case; the price he pays in the market for an article, depending on the proportion between the supply and demand, not on the proportion in which profits and wages are shared between the employer and employed.

As a consideration bearing on the aggregate happiness of the community, it is better wages should be high than profits. The number of the employed exceeds the number of employers in every occupation; if, then, either profits or wages must give way —if either masters or operatives must submit to a reduction of income, it is a less evil that the minority should undergo a privation of the luxuries, than the majority of the necessaries of life.

It has been urged against combinations, that they tend to maintain an *artificial* price of labour. But

the prices of most articles are artificially enhanced
in this country ; almost every interest is supported,
either by confederacies of the masters against the
public, or supported by protecting duties : our timber, our tea, our sugar, and even bread, are all retailed to us at artificially enhanced prices.   An artificial price of labour, then, is not an exception, but
in accordance with the general system.   The trade
unions, however, do not seek the support of protecting duties ; they do not wish that competition should
be excluded or narrowed by fiscal regulations ; all
they aim at is, not the taxing of rivals, but free
liberty, individually or collectively, to fix the price
and regulate the sale of the only article in which
they deal—their industry.

That labour does sometimes *need protection* may
be established by reference to the treatment of factory children, and I refer to this more readily, in
order to refute a prevalent error.   Legislative interference in this case has been objected to on two
grounds : first, that wages are best settled by the
master and workmen, without the meddling of a
third power ; and secondly, that masters always pay
as *high wages* as they can *afford to pay* at the current rate of profit.   The first objection I shall pass
over ; it is admitted by all, that infant labour forms
a special exception to the general rule applicable to
adults : but it is the assumption that masters pay
wages according to the profits they realize by the
sale of commodities, I shall notice.

Now, I ask whether the profits realized in the cotton, woollen, and linen manufactures, thirty years

ago, were not far greater than at present? This will hardly be denied; it cannot be denied, because the immense fortunes rapidly accumulated during the war, and the slowness and rarity with which they have been accumulated since the peace, establish the fact. Having disposed of this interrogatory, I ask another, namely—Whether factory children were treated materially better; whether their wages were higher, and the hours of working shorter from 1800 to 1815 when profits were so much greater, than in 1832 when they are so much less? Answers to this may differ: but I happen to know, of my own personal knowledge, that the poor factory child was doomed to the same merciless and unrequited toil in the former as in the latter period. Acts of parliament establish this, independently of my testimony. The 42d Geo. III. c. 73, passed in 1802 (see p. 98), and many subsequent enactments, show that parliament, nearly thirty years since, found it necessary to interfere for the protection of infants against the cupidity of their taskmasters. This, I think, fully demonstrates that the *rate of profit* does not invariably determine the *rate of wages*, and that other motives than the mere generosity of employers must occasionally interfere to compel them to a more equitable division of their gains with their workpeople.

One consequence ascribed to the trade unions, I have not yet noticed, namely, their tending to injure foreign trade, by keeping up the price of labour. Wages, as before explained, only affect commerce when they reduce its gains below the average profit of capital.   They are only one element in the prices of commodities, from which, if we suffer disadvantage, it is compensated by our exhaustless beds of coal—by superior capital, skill, and machinery—that will long enable us to undersel our rivals in the markets abroad.   When other countries equal us in these, it will be time enough to allege the high rate of wages as an obstacle to commercial industry. Of late years, we have been sustaining a national loss from *low* rather than *high* wages.   The wealth we ought to have accumulated by our mechanical improvements, has been shared in by other nations, without an equivalent return.   Our merchants have been running a race of *cheapness*, not against the foreigner, but against each other, and selling their goods greatly below the price necessary to keep possession of the markets of Germany and America. Had wages been higher, prices could not have been so far depressed by individual competition ; what the foreigner has gained, our own artisans have lost. An over-supply of labour unfortunately afforded too great facilities for an over-supply of commodities. Competition for employment enabled manufacturers to reduce wages—to increase the hours of working— make one man do the work of two—children, of adults—adding thereto a vast increase of steam power—and the result of all, an unexampled glut of commodities.

The consequences of this over-production are obvious. They are unprecedented LOW PRICES—prices that neither yield a fair profit to the master, nor fair wages to the workman—and both are dissatisfied.

It must now, I think, be conceded that I have endeavoured to state both sides of a very difficult question. The conflicting claims of capital and industry present new features for the study of the economical writer. I am not an indiscriminate admirer of the Trade's Unions : for I mistrust the honest exercise of all power, whether in governments or the people, which is not open and responsible. My chief aim has been to ascertain, by impartial inquiry, whether they are likely to be productive of more good or evil ; whether they are likely to lead to a more equitable apportionment of the aggregate income of the industrious orders, and thereby to an increase of their aggregate happiness ; and whether the machinery of their formation does not offer facilities for disseminating a knowledge of the true principles that govern the price of labour, and which I have endeavoured to explain in the preceding chapters on wages.

CHAP. XI.

EMPLOYMENT FUND-SOCIETIES.

Principle of Supply and Demand mostly regulates Profits and Wages—Social Evils of Confederacies of Workmen—Effects of a Combination of Shopkeepers—High Wages of Tailors in the Metropolis the result of their Combination—Additional Objects which Trade Societies ought to embrace—Employment Fund-Societies—Suggestions for meeting Fluctuations in Trade—Proportion Wages form of Prices—Corn-laws.

FROM the inquiries of the last chapter it is apparent trade societies for the maintenance of high-priced labour are obnoxious to serious objections. They are constantly liable to be perverted from their legitimate objects, either into arbitrary tribunals exercising an oppressive power over workmen not members of them, or into hurtful interferences with the freedom of employers. They are an attempt to establish a monopoly in the sale of labour as hurtful as monopolies in the sale of commodities. The unrestricted operation of supply and demand mostly fixes the equitable price of labour as of merchandise. Under the action of this principle the respective shares of master and workman in the prices of commodities will ordinarily be fairly apportioned. If, by improvements in machinery, or other cause, the profits of the master are augmented, the wages of the workmen will undergo improvement; because the increase of profit, by attracting capital to that channel of employment, must increase the demand for labour, which will necessarily enhance wages. On the other hand, should profits be depressed, wages would be depressed also, and this depression in the rate of profit would tend to prevent any addition to the quantity of capital already proved sufficient, and thereby to any increase of employment.

Social evils also may result from combinations which cannot be overlooked. Their natural tendency is to foment divisions and animosities in society, arraying different classes against each other, though mostly united by common interests. Supposing this divisional spirit encouraged, the whole community might become resolved into hostile confederacies, the workmen against their masters, and the masters against the public. The result would be general anarchy, a social disorganization more inimical to general order and enjoyment than the feudal system; the different classes of the industrious forming so many conflicting clans, who, like the barons and their vassals, would be engaged in a ceaseless strife of plot and counterplot, attack and defence.

Confederacies maintained by exclusive principles may be beneficial to the confederates, but hurtful to other workpeople. The brushmakers, for example, are a confederated body; they may enforce regulations which fix the wages to be paid by their employers, and to limit the number of apprentices to be taken by each master. These regulations may be advantageous to journeymen brushmakers, since they limit competition in their business; but how do they affect other classes? Whether brushes, in this particular case are kept at a higher price than they otherwise would be, I shall not inquire, but ask how other persons who have to live by their labour are affected. By the regulation respecting apprentices, and by refusing to work with non-associated journeymen, they keep out of the brush-trade many perhaps who would like to enter therein, and thereby infringe the liberty of individuals in the choice of employment. Secondly, though their combination tends to keep up wages in the brush-trade, it tends to depress them in other branches of industry; for it is obvious that as the number of brushmakers are fewer, the number of operatives forced into other trades must be greater; and as wages depend on competition for employment, they must be lower, in consequence of the exclusive laws of the craftsmen in the bristle-line.

The effect of the brushmakers' regulations is the same as if the grocers, cheesemongers, and alehouse-keepers of a town should combine to limit their numbers and prevent competition in their several businesses. Such confederacies would doubtless be very profitable to themselves, by compelling every one to go to their shops for their grocery, cheese, and beer; but it would be very injurious to the rest of the townspeople. It would obviously be a cunningly devised scheme for keeping up an exorbitant rate of profit, as the combination of brushmakers is to keep up an exorbitant rate of wages.

That combinations, when successfully executed, tend to keep up wages, may be established by comparing the wages of confederated and unconfederated operatives. Hatters, coopers, and coachmakers, for example, form associated bodies, and their wages exceed those of type-founders, saddlers, carpenters, and other branches of industry where the workmen are not associated. But the tailors afford the most striking instance of the dexterity with which they have fortified their own interests against the interests of the public and other workpeople. Cutting out is supposed to involve some sublime mysteries of art; but the chief employment in tailoring is well known to require neither great skill nor bodily exertion. Yet the wages of a journeyman tailor in London are 6s. a day, which is a much higher remuneration than is received by the generality of workpeople in the metropolis. The reason is, that tailors are closely confederated; and, by their perfect organization and discipline, they have been able to maintain their wages as high in 1833 as in 1815, when money would only purchase two-thirds of the necessaries of life it will purchase at present.

A similar conclusion might be established by a comparison of the different rates of wages paid in Lancashire and Yorkshire. Spinners and slubbers, for example, who are confederated, receive higher wages than weavers, who are not confederated.

From what has been advanced in the preceding chapter, it is plain I am not opposed to the establishment of Trade Unions; still, as they are founded on the principle of keeping up the price of labour, they ought, in my opinion, to embrace one or two other purposes, of equal or greater importance. The first of these to which I shall allude is the dissemination among themselves of a knowledge of the true economical principles, which, in a former part of this work, have been shown to govern the rate of wages. Without an acquaintance with these, and without their practical application, all their combinations against low wages and deteriorated circumstances will prove unavailing.

A *second* consideration the Unions ought to embrace is, the adoption of measures for guaranteeing workmen against the disastrous consequences resulting from fluctuations of employment. It has been already shown (chap. ix.) that the demand for labour in no branch of industry is uniform, varying with the seasons and mercantile vicissitudes. Now, it is for these periods of depression workmen ought to be provided. Upon an average of years, it is probable that the wages of workmen, in most branches of industry, are adequate to their maintenance ; but the misfortune is, that during years of full employment, no provision is made for years of slackness. The high wages of good years, the workman often spends in greater indulgence, without regard to the privations to which he will be subjected in bad years. Yet these bad years are of inevitable occurrence. By the institution of Savings-banks and Friendly Societies, future provision is made for want, infirmity, old age, and death ; but these events are not

more certain, than that a period of great commercial
and manufacturing activity will be followed by one
of corresponding depression. Why then ought not
precaution to be adopted against the latter, as well
as the former? With the exception, however, of
the tailors of the metropolis, I believe no class of
operatives make any provision for years of scarcity
of employment.

To meet so great a defect in the economy of the
working classes, various expedients may be suggested. One is, that each workman learn several
trades, so that, if one fail, he may turn to another.
A second expedient I shall beg to submit, is, that
workmen engage with their employers for such term
of years as experience has shown ordinarily covers
the brisk and slack periods of employment. This
would be analogous to the practice of hiring in rural
industry. It might be made applicable to piece-
work ; the workman conditioning to receive an average weekly sum from his employer, and the surplus
of his earnings, if any, at the expiration of his contract. Engagements of a similar nature, though for
a different purpose, are made by some masters of
Sheffield, in order to secure the services of journeymen for a lengthened period.

A *third* suggestion has been offered by a committee of the House of Commons, appointed in 1830, to
inquire into the state of manufacturers' employment. The substance of the plan of the committee
is, that societies be formed, called *Employment*

Fund-Societies, of which workmen of any trade or employment might become members; that the management of each society and its funds be vested in the members; that each member, while in work, contribute weekly or monthly a certain amount to the society; and that the amount of contributions of each person stand in his name, and not be drawn out except during his want of employment. In case of death, the amount of a member's contribution to be paid to his family or representatives, except a certain proportion, to be deducted for the general fund of the society. A member to be allowed to pay his contributions in a lump beforehand, or hold two or more shares, contributing in proportion, being entitled to receive on each accordingly, and having a number of votes in the society's meetings proportioned to the number of shares holden.

The chief advantages of a society founded on these principles would be, that a secure fund would be provided from good times, against want of work in bad times. The amount and continuation of assistance to any member would be proportioned to his own previous industry and forethought, and no idle or improvident person would draw upon the means of others. The payments would be received by little to provide against a severe practical evil, and could not be diverted or withdrawn for any other purpose. Lastly, a feeling of co-operation and fellowship among workmen would be likely to aid such societies, and a person once becoming a member, would probably continue such, for the sake of the contingent benefits arising from forfeits, deductions on deaths, &c.

In lieu of belonging to an Employment Fund-Society, a man might individually, and on his own account, make a provision for years of scarcity of work; by resolving, during a period of high wages, to deposit a sum weekly in a savings-bank, to accumulate against a period of adversity. This would be really more economical, than belonging to an association. All societies are unavoidably attended with some expenses of management, and which must be paid by the members; but these expenses would be avoided by contributing to a savings-bank. A workman in the latter would enjoy the further advantage of having a complete control, without the intervention of others, over his own fund, and he might also vary the amount of his weekly saving as most convenient. But the hazard in this case is, the fund would be liable to be violated, or not efficiently supported. Might not the workman fail to make his weekly deposit in the bank, or might not the fund itself be encroached upon for other purposes than to meet deficiency of work? These contingencies must depend on the fortitude of the party; in short, whether to belong to a society, or to raise a fund individually, is best, must depend on personal character. Both plans are good, and which ought to be preferred, can only be determined by previous habits and disposition.

I shall leave without further comment the several

suggestions mentioned, to the consideration of the
working classes, and those who feel interested in
the improvement of their condition. The objects
sought are their independence, and the guaranteeing
them against those distressing privations inseparable
from the constantly recurring fluctuations in the
market of labour. Unless, however, the working
people themselves will adopt measures for securing
their own welfare, no power on earth can do it for
them: but, before they can do this, they must be
made acquainted with the principles on which their
welfare depends. Their lot is not so favourable as
it ought to be, but it might be worse. There is a
" lower deep" still; from a cottage they may
descend to a cabin, from white bread to brown, from
meat to potatoes. They should make a stand in
time, and on sure ground; for, if once trampled
down, the spirit and power are lost to rise. There
are not wanting those to remind them how much
better off they are than their neighbours and
ancestors. They know this as well as their
teachers, they know their forefathers were serfs;
they know, too, that lords were great robbers, who
could not write their own names. What is the use
of such retrospections? Why should men be told
they were once children, and bandaged and whipped
by masters and nurses, as cruel as ignorant. Are
we never to go forward? Is the past always to be
a type of the future? The world is not so old that
all forms and fashions of society have been exhausted, and who can tell one may not be in store

which shall at least guarantee every honest man, willing to work, not merely from want, but meanness.

I am a great admirer of political economy, but do not implicitly adopt all its dogmas. National happiness is more important than national wealth, very unequally apportioned. Repudiating with contempt the idea that the *rich* are in a conspiracy against the *poor*, and that they do not wish to improve their condition; still, I think that in all fiscal and domestic measures, the maxim should be acted upon, that it is better 100 persons should live comfortably, than one luxuriantly. High wages are therefore more important than high profits; it is better—should they ever be at issue—the people should be happy, than foreign trade prosperous. On this point I concur with the working man's best friend—though long and strangely belied—who has declared that he " really cannot conceive any thing much more detestable, than the idea of knowingly condemning the labourers of Great Britain to the rags and wretched cabins of Ireland, for the purpose of selling a few more broad cloths and calicoes."— (*Essay on the Principle of Population*, b. 4, c. 10.) But it is quite unreasonable to urge the influence of high wages on the sale of manufactures, so long as masters tolerate such a stumblingblock in their way as the corn-laws. Dear provisions must produce one of two effects—they must either lower the condition of the working classes, or raise the rate of wages. Nobody can wish the former result, there-

fore every one must protest against cheap labour,
while there is dear bread.*

* I have no wish to disguise the importance of *cheap* labour.
The vast extent to which machinery has been applied, has
tended to increase the quantity of goods manufactured, and
lower their price, whereby they have been brought within the
reach of all classes of consumers, rather than to lessen the
number of persons employed.   Lord Milton, in his " Address
to Landowners," recommending the repeal of the corn-laws,
has stated some striking facts showing the proportion which
wages form of the prices of commodities.

" In the manufacture," says his lordship, " of fine woollen
cloth, the wages paid by the manufacturer amount to about
60 per cent., upon the total expenditure incurred between the
purchase of the wool in the foreign port, and the period when
the cloth is in a state fit for sale ; in the manufacture of linen
yarn, the corresponding expenditure in wages is about 48 per
cent.

" In the manufacture of earthenware, the wages paid by the
manufacturer amount to about 40 per cent. ; that is to say, in
the conversion of the requisite quantity of clay into goods
worth 100l., 40l. are paid to the workmen, in the shape of
wages.

" It is obvious, however, that, in these three instances,
especially in the latter, a very large proportion of the remaining
charges is resolvable into the wages of labour, though, perhaps,
not to so great an extent as in the next instances I am about to
cite.   In the manufacture of pig iron, the expense of labour
upon the various ingredients employed, amounts to no less than
81 per cent. ; and, in its subsequent conversion into bar iron,
to 84 per cent.

" In the working of collieries, the expenses are almost entirely resolvable into labour ; and, in cases within my own
knowledge, the wages actually paid, exceed 90 per cent. upon
the current expenditure.   In the different branches of the steel

CHAP. XII.

RENT OF LAND.

Difference between the Practical and Scientific Inquirer—Analogy between Rent and the Interest of Money—Origin of the Appropriation of Land—Increase of Cultivation with the Increase of Population—Effects produced on Rent and Prices by Cultivation extending from richer to poorer Soils—Dr. Anderson's Theory of Rent—Rent increases with the Increase of Capital and Industry—Component parts of Rent—The Machinery of Agriculture less perfect than that of Manufactures—Rent of Land determined by the Value of Produce, and the Value of Produce determined by the Cost of raising it on the poorest Soils—Tithe, Poor-rate and Land-tax fall on Landlords—Abolition of Rent would not render Corn cheaper, nor Wages higher; it would only put Farmers in the places of their Landlords.

THE objects are widely different which engage the attention of the practical man and the scientific inquirer. Ask a farmer what rent is, or why he pays

manufacture, the following may be stated as the proportions per cent. which materials and wages bear to each other.

	Material.	Wages.
In Files (coarse)	50	50 per cent.
Ditto (finer)	25	75
Table Knives and Forks	35	65
Razors	10	90
Scissors (coarse)	15	85
Ditto (fine)	4	96

" Great as is the proportion which wages bear to the direct cost of manufacturing these articles, it must never be forgotten, a higher rent than his neighbour, he shakes his head, and smiles at the simplicity of the querist. Ask him again how rent originated, or how it came to pass that Lord Acre charges a yearly sum for the use of his land, and he is still more astonished at such apparently futile and irrelevant interrogatories. If the farmer be of an ingenuous and patient disposition, and you a monied person, he may seek to enlighten your understanding by stating what he conceives an analogous case, asking, in his turn, why you charge Mr. Needy interest for a loan of money. " Rent and interest," he may allege, " have the same origin. You have the money to lend as Lord Acre has his land to let : it is unimportant how you got your money, as it is how his lordship got his estate : it might be acquired by descent, by industry, by dexterity, or by violence ; it is all one. The law says it is yours, and the law is the arbiter of right. Mr. Needy can

that by far the greater part of the price of the material itself consists of wages ; and, consequently, that almost the entire value of our steel goods may be said to consist of the wages of labour."—pp. 30—32.

His lordship has not stated the proportion which labour forms of the expense of raising corn. From the inquiries of the Board of Agriculture it appears that in the cultivation of arable land wages are about equal to the rent paid to the landlord, and about *one-fourth* of the total outgoings of the farmer in rent, tithe, taxes, rates, seed, manure, interest of capital, &c. (Lowe's *State of England*, p. 152.) It has been stated on good authority (Mr. Place), that an increase of 1s. per head per day to every husbandry labourer above 18 years of age with a proportional rise to all below that age, and to women employed, amounts to a sum greater than the whole rental received from land.

employ the money he borrows in trade, so tha it not only yields a profit sufficient for his maintenance, but to pay the interest. It is the same with my farm; the produce is sufficient to defray all outgoings, and to leave a surplus adequate to my support, and the payment of my landlord. As to my neighbour's farm being lower rented, the reason is, it affords scantier returns with the same outlay; same as if the returns of trade were less, the interest of money would be less: or if, in place of lending your money you traded with it yourself, the interest would be merged in the profit; just as Lord Acre would lose his capacity of landlord by turning farmer and cultivating his own domain."

The analogy between land and capital appears nearly perfect, and rent is the interest paid by the tenant to the landlord for the use of the soil. To this conclusion, however, it may be objected, that capital is the reward of anterior industry, but land is the gift of nature alike to all mankind. And what, it may be replied, was the gift worth as it first came from the donor. Its value is as much the creation of industry as capital; and probably it was never thought worth appropriating by man, till it had been adapted by labour to his wants.

Were land unlimited in quantity and uniform in fertility, it would yield no rent; it would fetch no price, any more than air or water. The fertile plain of the Pampas, extending for hundreds of miles across the continent of America, is without landlord and tenant, and yields no rent to any body. Men

buy only an article that is scarce, not that which is
open to all, and so abundant as to be adequate to
their utmost desires.   Let land be limited in quantity, or disproportioned to the wants of the inhabitants, and it then begins to have a value, and the
question immediately arises, whose shall it be? First
occupancy, he who first discovered it, or set his foot
upon it, seems to have the strongest claim; or if
this be disallowed, he who first cleared it of wild
animals, or in any way improved it by his labour,
would have the best title : or perhaps the question
of ownership would be determined on the principle
of an enclosure act, by the apportionment of the land
among all the existing claimants.

The most ancient account of the appropriation of
an unsettled territory is that recorded of Lot and
Abram.   When their flocks became so numerous
that strife arose between their herdsmen for the possession of pasture-ground, Abram proposed an ami-
cable division of the country, and, addressing Lot,
said, "Is not the whole land before thee? Separate
thyself, I pray thee, from me.   If thou wilt take the
left hand, then I will go to the right; or, if thou de-
part to the right hand, then I will go to the left."
This proposal being accepted, they parted, Lot
journeying eastward, and Abram dwelling in the
land of Canaan.

In whatever mode land may have been originally
appropriated, two consequences would follow it;
first, the question of ownership would be set at rest;
whoever joined the community would be bound by

the settlement previously agreed upon, and could only obtain land by conveyance from the original partitioners. The claim of a new-comer to a share of the soil would thus be cut off; but his loss would perhaps be more than compensated to him, by the advantage of being born later, and entering into a state of society which at least had made some progress in the establishment of order, industry, and the rights of property.

The second result of appropriation would be, that land would begin to have *a value*; in other words, those who joined the community subsequent to the partition, and had no land, would be willing to buy it of those who had, or to give their labour, or other equivalent for the use of it. In this manner, rent would originate; the quantity of land being limited but there being no limit to the increase of claimants, disputes would arise as to ownership, when land became scarce; this being settled by a division of the land among the existing inhabitants, rent would ensue, as a necessary consequence of a subsequent increase in the numbers of the community.

The best land would doubtless be first occupied, and, if the quality were uniform, the rent would be uniform. If the population increased, the produce of the land first brought into cultivation might become inadequate to their support, and it would be necessary to resort to soils of an inferior description, or which required a greater expenditure of labour to raise from them an equal quantity of food. Should population continue further to increase, the necessity

x

of raising a still greater quantity of food would urge
men to the cultivation of land of a still inferior quality, or which required a still greater expenditure of
labour.   The sterility of the land last brought into
cultivation, increasing with every increase of the inhabitants, they would at length be forced on land absolutely barren, or that yielded no return for the labour expended upon it.   Here further cultivation
would   stop ;   and   the   increase   of   population
must stop too ; for, as the quantity of food raised
could not be augmented, a greater number of people
could not be supported.

In this place, it is important to trace the effect on
rent and the prices of agricultural produce, of the
gradual extension of cultivation from the richer to
the poorer soils.

Rent is "that portion of the produce of land
which remains to the owner after all the outgoings
belonging to the cultivation are paid, including the
ordinary profits of the capital employed;" * it is
the difference between the value and the cost of
raising produce.   In the most fertile lands this difference is the greatest, and it becomes gradually less,
supposing the price of produce to remain stationary,
as cultivation extends over inferior soils requiring a
greater expenditure of labour.   But an advance of
price is an indispensable preliminary to the extension
of cultivation.   If the rich lands only defray the
charges of culture, no one will venture to cultivate
the poor lands.   Let, however, the price of pro-

* Malthus's Definitions in Political Economy, p. 238.

duce advance, and lands of the next inferior degree of fertility may leave profit to the cultivators; and should prices continue to advance still higher, it may be profitable to cultivate land even of the third degree of fertility, or land requiring treble the outlay of the first, and double the outlay of the second sort brought into cultivation. During this progression, the rent of the rich land would advance with every advance in the value of produce. It is plain there could not be two prices for the same article, and the price would be determined, not by the expense of raising produce on the rich, but on poor land; for, unless the outlay on inferior land could be realized, it would not be cultivated: but as the expense of raising produce on rich land had remained stationary, while its value had augmented, the surplus or difference between the two constituting the landlord's share, or rent, would have increased. The advance of rents, therefore, has been caused by the advance of prices consequent on the increased competition for food of an increasing population. It follows the position of the economists is perfectly well established. High rents have not produced the high price of corn, but the high price of corn has produced high rents.*

I have thus endeavoured to explain (perhaps imperfectly and with some deviations from my predecessors) the theory of rent. It appears to have been first partly propounded, accompanied with a

* *Principles of Political Economy*, by David Ricardo, Esq., p. 62.

considerable admixture of error, by Dr. Anderson,
in 1777,* soon after the appearance of the first
edition of the *Wealth of Nations.* Anderson's ideas
were promulgated afresh by Mr. Malthus and Sir
Gilbert West, in 1815; and a new version of them
given by the late Mr. Ricardo, who was followed by
Mr. Mill, Mr. McCulloch, and the economical
writers in the *Encyclopædia Britannica.* Afterwards
the subject was taken up by Colonel Thompson, in
his *True Theory of Rent,* who successfully, I think,
pointed out the fallacies into which Mr. Ricardo and
his followers had fallen, and demonstrated that the
cause of rent is substantially that mentioned by
Adam Smith, namely, " the limited quantity of the
land in comparison with the competitors for its produce."   Dr. Chalmers, in his late work on *Political
Economy,* concurs in this conclusion. To enter into
the controversy would not suit my pages; but as
Mr. Ricardo's doctrine was made the foundation of
erroneous conclusions on tithe, wages, and profit,
it may be useful to point out its fallacy, and which
will be easily apprehended after the preceding exposition.

Mr. Ricardo's position was, that rent had its origin
in the *varying* fertility of land, and, of course, if
land had been of uniform quality, no rent would
ever have been paid.   Rent, however, as before explained, is only the difference between the value and
cost of raising produce.   Keeping this in mind, let

* *Principles of Political Economy,* by R. J. McCulloch, Esq.,
second edition, p. 430.

us suppose the land of a country limited in quantity, and all of uniform quality; let us suppose further, that from the increase of population, there is an increase in the demand for food, and of course, an increase in the price. Now, the effect of this increase in price, must necessarily be, either to create rent for the first time, or to increase its amount. If produce, prior to the increase in value, only just defrayed the charges of raising it (and it could not do less than this), it must now exceed it, leaving a surplus or rent to the landlord; or, if it before left a surplus, it must now leave a greater; and either alternative is wholly independent of the *varying* fertility of the soil, arising as it does solely, from the increased consumption of a commodity, of which the supply is limited.

The error of Mr. Ricardo has been properly characterized by Colonel Thompson, as the "Fallacy of inversion." It confounds the effect with the cause. It is not because of the existence of inferior soils, that the superior pay a rent; but it is, because the superior pay a rent, that the inferior can afford to be cultivated.

A gradation of fertility is a secondary cause of a gradation of rent, or of inferior land yielding inferior rent, and nothing more; since the primary cause of gradation of rents is the necessity, arising from the augmented competition for food, which compels recourse to less productive lands than those first occupied.

By further endeavouring to elucidate this long

contested theme of economical writers, I should er-
haps only obscure it. So far as it is applicable to
this country, it is a *theory* only; since it is well
known, that the price of corn in England, neither
depends on the varying fertility of the soil, nor the
increase of population, but on acts of the legislature.
Various important conclusions, however, may be
drawn from the preceding inquiry into the nature of
of rent, and, with a brief enumeration of them, I
shall conclude the chapter.

1. The progress of rent is a necessary consequence of the progress of society. An increasing
population creates the necessity for an increasing
supply of food, and an increasing opulence affords
the means to purchase it at higher prices, which
tends to improve and extend the culture of the soil.
Better modes of husbandry—better implements—
improved roads and canals, for the conveyance of
produce to the best markets—reduction in the prices
of labour—diminution in poor-rates, taxes, tithes,
and other charges on land—all are in favour of the
landlord. They lessen the expense of raising and
disposing of agricultural produce, and thereby enable the occupier, or landlord's agent, to realize a
greater surplus or difference between the outgoings
and income of his farm. All these circumstances
are *extrinsic* to the owner of the soil as such; if,
however, by arbitrary legislation he compels the
consumer of his produce to pay a monopoly price
for it, the question is altogether altered. But in the
natural progress of things he is wholly passive; he

receives his rent for the use of his land as the capitalist receives interest for the use of his money. If his *agricultural machinery* has become more productive, so has the cotton and linen manufactures by the agency of the steam-engine, power-loom, and spinning jenny. He has both gained and lost by social improvement—he has gained a greater territorial revenue, and lost the power and pageantry of feudality.

2. Rent is a *complex* term, it is not only a payment for the use of the natural properties of land, but also includes the profit of capital expended in its improvement. The soil of Britain was once not more valuable than that of the Illinois. It has been enriched by centuries of labour—by the discoveries of science—and by being the site of an opulent manufacturing community. The owner of land is the owner of all these : whoever buys land buys the wealth accumulated upon it, and the revenue he purchases or inherits consists chiefly of profit arising from anterior industry. Hence, the objection made to a tax on rent, since it is a tax not only on income, derived from the natural fertility of the soil, but also on the profit of money laid out in agricultural improvements, in fencing, draining, and road-making : it operates like a tithe to the restraint of good husbandry and enterprise.

3. The earth has been compared to a machine, or gradation of machines, out of which food and raw materials are fabricated. But the machinery of agriculture differs from the machinery of manufac-

tures; in the former the best machines, or most
fertile soils, are first brought into employment, and
necessity only compels recourse to those of less productive power; in manufactures on the contrary,
the *worst* machines are commonly those first invented, and experience continually adds to their
efficiency. The commodities produced also differ in
relative importance. Agricultural industry is chiefly
occupied in producing the *necessaries*—manufacturing industry the *luxuries* of life. The former
will always create a market for themselves. Corn
and meat can never long be a *drug*; if there be a
lack of consumers of these, a few years of plenty
and cheapness will soon call them into existence.
Cheapness of provisions will even stimulate the demand for woollens, silks, and calicoes; but food is
of more indispensable utility than clothes. Men
have been found to live without the latter, never
without the former.

4. The rent of land is determined by the value or
price of its produce.

The owner of the soil will exact as much for the
use of his land as he can get, as a capitalist will for
the use of his money. If produce rise in price, the
profit of farming will rise. Capital will flow into
that channel of employment; there will be increased
competition for land; higher rents will be offered,
and, as just remarked, the landlord will take the
highest. The contrary effects obviously follow, if
there is a fall in the price of produce.

5. As rent is determined by the value of produce,

so the value or price of the whole produce is determined by the expense of raising that portion of it which is raised on the poorest land in cultivation.

There cannot be *two prices* for the same article, quality and every thing else being the same. Corn grown on the richest will be sold at the same price as corn grown on the poorest land; that is, at the highest price the grower can get. But this price must, at least, be adequate to defray all the charges of raising it on the most expensive soils : no one would cultivate such soils *at a loss ;* they would be abandoned, unless they yielded the ordinary profit of capital, and defrayed the outgoings in labour, manure, and implements of husbandry. The supply of corn would thus diminish, and this diminution would go on till either prices rose to be remunerative to the grower on the least productive land, or, which is the same thing, till cultivation was limited to land of that degree of fertility, upon which the outlay did not exceed the value of its produce.[*]

6. From what has been previously explained, it may be easily inferred how tithe, land-tax, poor-

[*] In the last two propositions, and, indeed, through the chapter, it must be borne in mind that I am endeavouring to elucidate the general principles which influence rent independently of artificial institutions. In England, rent has rarely been left to be determined by the natural rise and fall in the value of agricultural produce. Although the legislature has long ceased to fix the income of the labourer, it has not ceased to fix the income of the landlord. Rent, too, is influenced by local circumstances—proximity to towns, roads, and canals, and the terms of leases.

rates, and all imposts levied on land or its produce, ultimately settle on the owner of the soil.

Rent is the residuum or landlord's share left after the tenant has deducted from the value of produce all outgoings, including a reasonable profit and maintenance for himself.   As the value of produce is determined solely by the proportion between the supply and demand, neither landlord nor tenant has any control over the income received by the latter, to meet all outgoings.   Should, therefore, the outgoings increase, by the imposition of a tax, tithe, poor-rate, or other assessment, there is no way of meeting this augmented outlay, except by *saving* in some branch of expenditure, in the wages of labour, in the profit of the farmer, or in the rent of the landlord.   But suppose wages are already reduced to the lowest point compatible with the subsistence of the labourer, and that to reduce them lower would drive him to acts of outrage that endanger the security of property; why, then, it is plain there can be no reduction of outgoing under this head.   Will the farmer bear a reduction of income?   Not if his profits are already as low as those realized in other branches of industry; he will throw up his farm first, and transfer his capital and industry to another occupation.   But rather than the farmer should do this, the landlord most probably will submit to reduction in his rent : thus the additional burden will, at last, fall on the owner of the soil, and he will be constrained to bear it, for this simple reason, that he can throw it on *nobody else*—unless he is powerful enough in the State to throw it on the consumer by the enactment of a corn-law.

Because agricultural charges are borne by the owners of the soil, it must not be inferred that a reduction of them benefits the landowners exclusively, and not the community. This would be a pernicious error. Land may be of so poor a description, and require so large an outlay of labour and manure, that at existing prices it leaves only the average profit of capital. If to the charges on such land a tithe or poor-rate be superadded, it must necessarily remain uncultivated ; because, if the profit was only an average one before, it must now be less, or swallowed up altogether in the new assessment. Wages, in consequence, will be less than they were before, because the demand for labour is less : and agricultural produce will be *dearer* than before, because the quantity produced, and brought to market, has diminished.

7. The abolition of rent would not render *corn cheaper* ; it would only abrogate a class of society whose subsistence is chiefly derived from that species of income, and substitute in their places another order of men, who, from habits and education, are perhaps less qualified even than country gentlemen to execute the duties of legislators and magistrates.

As much corn will be grown, as can be grown at the existing prices, leaving the average profit of capital to the grower. But the prices of corn depend on the quantity brought to market ; and as the payment of rent has no influence on the harvests, neither rendering them more abundant nor deficient, it can have no influence on prices. Whether a farmer grows corn on his own land, or on land he rents, he will ask the same price for it; that is, the highest price he can get, or which, from the competition among buyers, they will be disposed to give. The abolition of rents, therefore, would only tend to enrich the farmers; it would enable them to keep a bailiff, steward, or tenant, to do their work; in short, to take the places of their landlords, without in the least benefiting the consumers of their produce.

8. The abolition of rents would not tend to raise wages.

Whether a labourer is hired by a landowner or his tenant, he is hired at the lowest wages he will submit to work for. If the farmer's rent were remitted, he would continue to go to market on the same principle; that is, of having all his work done at the lowest price. Conscience does not enter into these bargains; they are all regulated on a principle of business; that is, of saving all that can be saved, and gaining all that can be gained. This is seen in Ireland, where, from the redundancy of labourers, they are sometimes forced to work for 2*d*. or 3*d*. a day, and masters are not ashamed to give this miserable pittance. The legislature tried to remedy a similar evil centuries ago, but their efforts were found futile or mischievous, and they found that the only cure for an overstocked market of labour was to lessen the supply.

CHAP. XIII.

TENDENCY TO OVER-POPULATION.

Mankind increase faster than Food—Limit to the Increase of
the Species—Farther increase in all Countries checked by
Poverty or Prudence — Religious Objection answered—
Remedies of Over-Population—Natural and Artificial Checks
—Deterioration of Society by the Operation of the Natural
Check of Misery—Reasons for Marriage in preference to
Concubinage—Circumstances which make Marriage an Evil
—Scriptural Injunction, " Be Fruitful and Multiply," consi-
dered—Obligation to maintain Children—Policy of further
Legislative Restraints on Marriage—Decrease in the num-
ber of Marriages—Proposals for divesting Wedlock of its
impoverishing Consequences—Emigration an unobjectionable
Remedy of a Redundant Population—Symptoms of an Excess of People described—Question of the Relative Increase of Population and Capital during the last Thirty
Years—Decrease of Mortality—Over-Population results from
defect of Moral Culture—Importance of the Subject, and the
Poor more interested in it than the Rich—A Popular Knowledge of the Principles of Population the only permanent Remedy of Poverty and low Wages.

THE history of man affords indubitable evidence
of the rapid tendency of mankind to increase, and
those who adopt the authority of the Scripture can
hardly refuse assent to the theory of population.
Adam and Eve are the parents of the human race,
and by the descendants of a single pair the whole
earth has been peopled. Upon this fact the reli-

gious might found their faith in the prolific nature of our species, but the narrative of the Bible is corroborated by the testimony of history.

Romulus and Remus, aided by a few followers, founded the Roman empire. The states of Italy and of Greece, and the nations of Asia, were the offspring of a few exiles, or colonists, driven from their homes by crime or want, or internal dissensions. In more recent times America offers a striking example of the progress of nations. Almost within the cognizance of the existing generation this great continent has been discovered, reclaimed, and comparatively filled with inhabitants. Individuals, no less than nations, attest the principle of population. Sterility is the exception, not the rule of life. Of the thousands united by marriage, within immediate observance, how few there are who do not leave behind them a progeny treble their own number, and with similar powers of propagation.

This great law of nature is not limited to man, it extends in equal force to the animal and vegetable creations. A couple of rabbits, or flock of sheep, would fill the whole earth, if their increase were not checked by want of food, or space or climate. If the earth were vacant it might be sowed and overspread with a single grain of wheat, or with a single plant, as fennel, or henbane. In all these cases the law of increase is the same, whether as affects man, or animals or vegetables; they all increase in a geometric ratio, and the necessity that limits their indefinite multiplication is the impossibility of obtaining an indefinite amount of subsistence.

The propagation of plants and animals is limited by the bounds of the earth, and these again limit the propagation of man, dependent as he is upon them for subsistence. If the supply of food could be indefinitely extended, the numbers of mankind might be indefinitely multiplied. But though the produce of the earth, in a given space, may be increased by additional labour and improved modes of culture, this increase is not proportionate; a a double expenditure of labour on the soil will not obtain a double produce, nor a treble expenditure a treble produce: the increase obtained continues to bear a less and less proportion to the labour expended. There is, however, no diminution in the procreative power of man; as his numbers augment there is no proportionate diminution either in inclination or ability to propagate his race. The procreative power is a *constant* quantity, while the supply of food is a quantity constantly decreasing. It follows that we are reduced to one of two alternatives; either to the necessity of controlling the natural tendency of man to increase, or of submitting to live on a quantity of food constantly diminishing. But this must have its limits; for if man continue to multiply at a uniform rate, and the supply of food to diminish, he will at length reach that minimum of allowance inadequate to support life, and further increase be checked by absolute starvation.

Man is seldom placed in circumstances which admit of the full development of his procreative energy. In civilized communities he is restrained by prudential motives; among savages the sexual passion is unchecked, but the evils inseparable from a state of nature tend either to lessen the number of births, or cause premature mortality. The power, however, of every nation to people up to and exceed its means of support is fully evinced in the rapidity with which the ravages of war, of famine, and epidemics are supplied, and the speed with which newly-settled countries, abounding in the means of subsistence and employment, are peopled.

In rude or refined states of society the number of consumers is mostly commensurate to the existing supply of food; were there any discrepancy the chasm would be speedily filled by the activity of one of our strongest passions, aided by the facilities abundance would offer for the nurture and maintenance of children. But though nations increase up to the limit of subsistence, this limit itself varies with the degree of refinement, which has fixed among them different standards of living. The limit of subsistence to a Norwegian is the bark of the linden-tree; of a New Zealander fish and worms; of a South American the fruit of the banana; of a Chinese a dish of rice; of an Irishman a bowl of potatoes; while an Englishman, more elevated than any, fixes the necessaries of life in animal food, beer, and wheaten bread.

Higher is the standard of subsistence which the

habits of a community establish, and the further it
is removed from the extremity of famine. Every
advance in the scale of enjoyment and subsistence,
whether in respect of diet, clothing, or habitation,
is a remove from destitution, on which we may fall
back when necessity compels a retrograde movement. A nation, the general diet of which consists
of animal food, may resort to vegetables; if its diet
is corn, it may fall back on pulse or potatoes. But
perilous is the state of a people, no less than that of
an individual, driven to subsist on their last resources, beyond which there is no retreat!

Not only is it important the standard of national
subsistence should be high, but also that it should
mainly consist of commodities, the supply of which
is least liable to fluctuation. Thus corn is a much
better article of general diet than potatoes; the
latter being more perishable — more liable to be
affected by the seasons—and, moreover, not being
generally produced by other countries, a supply of
them, in the case of dearth, cannot be so readily
obtained.

The moral, like the physical world, is governed
by immutable laws, and it is only by the exercise of
a knowledge, the fruit of lengthened experience,
that man can escape the evils inseparable from his
condition. One of the great ends of nature is the
perpetuation of her works, and for this purpose she
scatters abroad the seeds of life with a liberal and
almost careless profusion. Few of her productions
appear destined to reach maturity; by their multi-

plicity, she provides for the casualties to which the early stages of existence are exposed. From this alone might be demonstrated the tendency of population to become redundant in civilized communities. In the savage state, myriads perish on first entering into life, or shortly after; the healthy, well-formed, and robust, only surviving to manhood. In civilized states the principle of increase is not less energetic; but the chief accidents of infancy are averted by the discoveries of science. Thus the ratio of mortality is diminished, while the principle of increase is unabated. Under such circumstances, it is evident population must increase faster than the means of subsistence; for though the latter may augment, it will, unless aided by some fortunate discovery of science, or other accidental occurrence, be in a ratio constantly decreasing, while the ratio of increase in the number of consumers of food will continue undiminished.

It is no argument against the tendency of mankind to increase beyond the means of subsistence, that the number of people in most countries is stationary. The reason is, that they are kept back by the operation of the natural and moral checks to which I shall soon advert. " Every body," Mr. Mill most justly observes, " knows the fact, that in the greater number of countries the population is stationary, or nearly so. But what does this prove, so long as we are not informed by what causes it is prevented from increasing? We know well that there are two causes by which it may be prevented from increasing, how great soever its natural tendency to increase. The one is *poverty;* under which, let the number born be what it may, all but a certain number undergo premature destruction. The other is *prudence;* by which either marriages are sparingly contracted, or care is taken that children beyond a certain number shall not be the fruit."*

Experience has proved that population, when permitted its full development by an abundant supply of food, can double itself in *fifteen years:*† but as in no country this rapid increase takes place, it may be inferred that the number of the people in every community is kept back by the constant operation, either of the natural check of misery, or the less afflictive preventive of moral restraint.

It has been objected to the doctrine of population, that it impugns the goodness and wisdom of the Almighty, to assume that *misery* is the natural check to the increase of mankind beyond the means of subsistence. This has been well answered in the *Supplement to the Encyclopædia Britannica.* God has given to man his reason as well as his passions; a propensity to propagate his species is one of the latter, but, like his other appetites, the indulgence of it must be subordinate to his understanding, otherwise it will be productive of evil to himself and society.

---

* *Elements of Political Economy,* 3d edit., p. 50.

† *On Political Economy, in Connexion with the Moral State and Moral Prospects of Society,* p. 580. By Thomas Chalmers, D.D. 1832.

II.—REMEDIES OF OVER-POPULATION

From the inquiries of the preceding section it may be concluded that in old settled countries, the natural tendency of mankind is to increase faster than the means of subsistence ; that the effect of this is to lessen the average share of food which can be procured for each individual ; and that as a diminution in the physical comforts of a community is productive of moral and intellectual degradation, the general condition of society will be deteriorated.

For this calamity the remedies are of two kinds : first, those which nature herself imposes ; and secondly, those which are the suggestion of human reason. In the operation of the first class of remedies, the evil may be said to be left to cure itself ; in fact, they are not remedies, any more than the conduct of a man who, suffering under a grievous malady, should prefer leaving the disorder to its own course, rather than resort to the advice of a physician. The second class of remedies may be considered *artificial*, but, in truth, they are as much in nature as the other ; for any conduct which is the result of knowledge and experience, may as properly be termed *natural* as that which results from mere passion, ignorance, and want of forethought. The proper test of the two sorts of remedies is their influence on social happiness, and by this test I shall try them.

The effect of a great disproportion between

numbers and food, is *general misery*, and this misery, either by lessening fecundity, or increasing mortality, is the circumstance that restores equilibrium between numbers and subsistence, and the *natural* check of over-population. But the evils entailed by such curative process are most afflictive. A community suffering under the pressure of physical want, would be regardless of moral and intellectual culture. General pinching and privation would engender general selfism; the more liberal arts and sciences would be neglected, and benevolence and philanthropy would be lost sight of in the scramble for animal subsistence. Mr. Hume, in one of his Essays, alludes to the deteriorating effect of misery on individual character. A prosperous man will mostly be found more accessible to virtuous emotions than one who has been soured by want and disappointment. Every one knows that it is a more favourable moment to ask a favour of a person when full than fasting; after dinner, when the heart has been mellowed by a good repast, than before. Narratives of shipwrecks, the history of the French campaign in Russia, and traits of character exhibited in our peninsular wars, testify how the noblest natures may be subdued by the constant pressure of cold, hunger, and fatigue, and rendered callous to every claim, save that of self-relief and preservation. The same causes will influence the character of a whole community suffering under the misery produced by redundant population. It is a struggle for existence, in which moral and social ties are disregarded in the conflict for food, profit, and employment. The debasing effects of want and indigence, may be remarked in the different demeanour of the several classes of society. Prudence and forethought are mostly proportioned to the degrees of comfort enjoyed. The lower we descend in the social scale, the greater is the recklessness we find of future consequences. In marriages and in domestic economy the middle classes are more saving and considerate than the working classes. A labourer is generally less prudent than the little tradesman, the beggar less prudent than the labourer. All this results from obvious and intelligible causes. Extreme privation stupifies the understanding; it destroys the mental reflection, which induces a person to deny himself an immediate but perishable relief, for the sake of a future and more enduring advantage.*

Leaving, therefore, the natural remedy of MISERY to over-population, as inconsistent with the happiness as the forethought of a civilized community, let us see if reason suggests any preventive less demoralizing and destructive. It must be borne in mind

---

* The fact is stated by Colquhoun, and quoted by Mr. Barton (*Inquiry into Depreciation of Labour*, p. 30), that "the chief consumption of oysters, crabs, lobsters, pickled salmon, &c., when first *in season* is by the lowest classes of the people. The middle ranks, and those immediately under them, abstain generally from such indulgences, until the prices are moderate." This abstinence of the middle classes, may be also ascribed to their better information; knowing that when provisions are *highest* in *price*, they are the *worst in quality*.

that I am pursuing this investigation without reference to the state of this country; whether we are suffering from an excess of people will form an after subject of inquiry.

The first condition of any preventive is, that it should be practicable; that is, consonant to the usages, feelings, and education of those for whom it is intended. Any suggestion of an opposite description, would be void of utility. For instance, to recommend infanticide, abortion, or any artifice to frustrate conception, might be positively mischievous, since, by the disgust it would excite, like an indecent attack on the established religion, it would prevent the temperate investigation of a subject of national importance. But in recommending abstinence from marriage for a season, or emigration, there is nothing to shock the public mind, both being in accordance with the existing practice of individuals.

In respect of marriage, it is laudable or not, according to the state of society, and the circumstances of individuals.

The reasons urged in defence of the institution of marriage, in preference to concubinage, or any other mode of sexual intercourse, are derived from the organization of the sexes — its tendency to promote the domestic comfort of individuals, especially females—to the production of the greatest number of healthy and well-educated children, and their settlement in life—to the peace of society, in cutting off a fruitful source of contention, by assigning one

woman to one man, and protecting his exclusive
right, by the sanctions of morality and law—to the
better government of society, by distributing the
community into separate families, and appointing
over each the authority of a parent—and lastly, to
the encouragement of industry.

These reasons have all the consequences assigned
to them, but in urging them, Dr. Paley has left out
of view the political economy they involve. In the
United States of America, marriage unquestionably
conduces both to domestic happiness and national
power, and of its utility there can be no dispute;
but in old and fully-peopled countries, the results
are different. One of the most certain and important
consequences of marriage, and that for which it has
been most highly extolled, is its tendency to increase
population faster than under any other system: this
is an advantage or not, according to circumstances;
in countries over-peopled, where individuals have
not a reasonable prospect of being able to maintain
a family, it is a source of positive misery and demo-
ralization, as will be apparent from the following
reasons:

1. By leading to a family, and thereby rendering
two persons poorer than they would be in a single
state, it is inimical to domestic happiness.

2. It is unfavourable to virtue, since it is constantly observable that indigence, no less than excess
of riches, tends to deprave the character.

3. It is not favourable to domestic peace and
enjoyment, because it augments the pecuniary diffi-

culties of individuals, and thereby sours the temper
and foments quarrels.

4. It is a source of strife, hatred, and uncharitable-
ness; for a sharp competition for food, profit or
employment, inevitably leads to ill-will and contention.

5. It is a source of weakness to the state, since a
number of people, who cannot obtain employment,
consume without yielding equivalents in return;
they are a burden in lieu of a benefit, by exhausting
national resources.

It is thus apparent how the entire question of the
policy of marriage is inverted by the single circumstance of a redundancy of people, which causes
them to crowd and interfere with each other's means
of employment and subsistence. Without the ready
means of rearing and supporting offspring, it may
be doubted whether any advantages connected with
matrimony, compensate for the anxieties and inconveniences with which it is accompanied. Unaided
at least by this, its choicest sweets are converted
into the bitterest poisons. And even facilities for
the maintenance of a family would often be found
insufficient to compel men to marry, were they not
frequently constrained by the positive institutions of
society. The Spartans obliged their citizens to
marry by penalties, and the Romans encouraged
them by the *jus trium liberorum*, and the disabilities
to which the childless man was subjected in their
laws of inheritance. In modern times morals, laws,
and religion combine to urge men to enter into the

connubial state. A single life is at best deemed one
of suspected purity, and forms a constant theme of
ridicule, if not opprobrium. Even our fiscal regulations are framed in stern defiance of the doctrines of
Mr. Malthus, and the unfortunate bachelor perse-
cuted by partial taxation. But the most weighty
obligation is that derived from the Scriptures, which
enjoin men to " Be fruitful and multiply, and
replenish the earth." Upon this injunction I think
two observations may be offered that tend to impugn
its present application and authority.

First, were not the command to be " fruitful and
multiply," forming, as it did, part of the Jewish
code, abrogated by the subsequent Christian dispensation.

Secondly, is the popular interpretation of the
words consistent with their spirit and literal import.

The object of the Almighty was, doubtless, to
augment human happiness, and when the earth was
desolate and uncultivated, " to increase and multiply," tended directly to this purpose; but if the end
has failed, may not the obligation have ceased? We
must take the precept in its entierty, " be fruitful,
and multiply, and replenish the earth;" but, in many
parts of the world, to " be fruitful and multiply,"
is not to replenish, but to impoverish the earth.
Hence, it may be concluded, that the celebrated
passage of the book of Genesis was not intended to
be either of permanent or universal application.

The moral considerations involved in this inquiry,

may be disposed of with less hesitation than those derived from Scripture. Conventional notions of utility may be always adapted to the varying exigencies of the social state. Rome and Sparta, which were intoxicated with the passion for military glory, might seek to augment the number of their citizens, for the purposes of war and devastation ; but it ought to be the glory of a Christian community to cultivate the arts of peace. In newly-settled countries, a large family is a real treasure ; but, in the crowded cities of Europe, especially in our own manufacturing districts, it too often only adds to the vice and misery previously existing.

Marriage is a voluntary act, and it ought to be a deliberate one : its natural consequences are not involved in mystery, they are known ; whoever, therefore, enters into this state, is bound by its obligations. The first, and most imperative of these is, unquestionably, the maintenance of the children that result from the union. Without a reasonable prospect of being able to support his offspring, no man can have any more right to marry, than he has to contract a debt he has not a reasonable prospect of being able to pay. That the nuptial tie is not obligatory on all, may be established from the examples of Moses, Jesus Christ, and many eminent individuals, who either have postponed, or never entered into that state, solely from prudential motives.

In a country suffering from want of employment, the question may be started, how far it would be politic for the legislature to interfere, either by prolonging the period of life, when persons are eligible to marry,* or by requiring security from those who marry, that their children shall not become chargeable to the community.

In England, the marriage contract is both a religious and civil ceremony. So far as the latter is concerned, it is, and always has been, deemed a proper subject of municipal law. The age of the parties, the consent of parents or guardians, the period that shall elapse from the publication of bans and the celebration of marriage, and the place where the nuptials shall be solemnized, are all matters of

---

* A delay of two years in the average age of marriage, would in twenty years, in the estimate of Mr. Barton, completely remedy the excessive growth of population. (*Statement on Population*, p. 15.) On the other hand, Dr. Granville stated, in his evidence before a committee of the House of Commons, that it is immaterial whether marriages are *early* or *late*; as this circumstance has no influence on the number of children. According to this gentleman, if a couple marry early, after the first seven or nine years, an interregnum intervenes, during which, child-bearing ceases; but if they marry late, no such interruption occurs, and the family continues to increase at a uniform rate. An opinion so unusual, can only be admitted after the most careful and extensive inquiry. I have, myself, a strong prepossession in favour of the efficacy and utility of late marriages. Facts founded on limited induction, are often more misleading than general propositions that are founded on no facts at all. The author of an *Inquiry into the State of the Manufacturing Population*, p. 16, alleges, that the fecundity of females employed in manufactures, is *less* than that of those employed in agriculture. But I am at a loss to reconcile this statement with the rapid increase of our manufacturing population, and the greater mortality which prevails among them.

statutory regulation. In the case of an illegitimate child likely to become chargeable to the parish, the putative father is bound to give security for the maintenance of his offspring. Why the law should interfere to guarantee the community against loss from a *single*, and as one may say, casual child, born out of wedlock, and not against the greater loss that may be incurred, by the maintenance of an *indefinite* number, born in wedlock, cannot be easily reconciled to reason. Marriage is not a contract between a man and woman for their mutual pleasure only, there is a third party to the contract, namely, the public, which, as it does not derive any direct advantage from the union, it seems reasonable, should be protected from indirect loss.

In 1808 the government of Berne, afflicted with the increasing misery of the people, arising out of their increasing numbers, issued an ordinance, that " no person who receives relief from his parish shall be allowed to *marry without their permission*, unless he previously repay the full amount which has been expended upon him." In Sweden the magistrate is empowered to interdict the marriage of a party not possessed of probable means for the maintenance of a family. According to Mr. Loudon (*Ency. of Agriculture*, p. 88) the guild companies of Germany exercise a prohibitive power over the marriages of their members, lest, I presume, it should tend to reduce the wages of journeymen. In most German states people are obliged to have the permission of the civil magistrate before it is

legal for the clergyman to celebrate a marriage; and
the permission seems to be given or withheld as the
parties soliciting it are thought to be capable of
maintaining a family. The chamber of deputies of
Wurtemburgh, in the course of the present year, have
been occupied in framing a measure for restricting
marriages between persons who have no certain means
of subsistence. In the British army, I believe, a
private soldier cannot marry without the assent of his
commanding officer. The members of the royal family, descendants of George II., cannot marry until
they attain twenty-five years of age without the consent of the king; nor even then without twelve
months' notice and the approval of parliament.

Notwithstanding these examples, I should greatly
doubt the policy of more restrictive marriage laws in
this country. The heart, rather than the understanding, is often the propelling motive in these
unions, and on this account it is likely the English,
more than any people, would be impatient of measures that bore the semblance of restraint. If marriages be too frequent, institutions among ourselves
of the nature of Temperate Societies might be beneficial. When the conduct of individuals can be influenced by improved moral culture, it is less objectionable, and often more efficient than legislation.
Public opinion is a more potent and watchful corrective than magisterial coercion, and a system of popular instruction that would early inculcate a love of
independence, a taste for the comforts and enjoyments of life, and a humane aversion to be the au-

thor of an unprovided family, form the best securities against improvident marriages. The " *immorality* of marrying without the means of supporting a family" is a doctrine of recent promulgation, and can hardly yet be considered generally impressed on the understandings and feelings of the community. Only a few years have elapsed since our most eminent statesmen and writers taught that to marry, and *marry young*, was meritorious. The sentiment of moral approbation thus associated with the act by long habit cannot be suddenly obliterated from the minds of the people by telling them that political economy has discovered that to be wrong which was formerly accounted innocent or laudable. Even now there are symptoms that the exhortations of the Malthusians have not been wholly without fruit. It is an undoubted fact that the number of weddings has been diminishing of late years. The rapid increase of population has been mainly caused by diminution in mortality not an increase of marriages. Within the last thirty years the proportion of marriages to the number of people has gradually decreased, as is shown by the tables of Mr. Rickman prefixed to the Returns of Population for 1831. In 1800 the weddings in England were as 1 to 123 of the population; 1810, as 1 to 122; 1820, as 1 to 127; and in 1830, they had fallen to 1 in 129.*

* Mr. Barton was, I believe, the first writer who called public attention to the decrease in marriages. Those who ascribed the increase of population to the increase of weddings ought in fairness to have first ascertained whether such increase had really

Although the number of marriages has decreased, yet, owing to a greater proportion of the children born being reared than formerly, they have been sufficiently numerous to cause a vast increase of population. The diminution in their number, therefore, does not detract from the policy of discouraging improvident unions. But in addition to the reasons already urged against restrictions on marriages, there are others to which I have not adverted.

Apart from the poverty occasioned by large families in densely-peopled countries, the general opinion appears to be, that matrimony is most favourable to virtue. The idea of making chastity the rule of a community has been abandoned by all men in despair. Nothing less than the power of a superstition, which has in great measure ceased to influence European society, would be adequate to

taken place. The members of the Royal Society were more wary in their dealings with Charles II., when he proposed to them the question, " For what reason is a dead fish heavier than a living one?" They *weighed the fish* and found that the waggish monarch had deceived them.

As the condition and intelligence of the working classes approach nearer to those of the class immediately above them, it is probable that not only the number of marriages but of *births* in each family will diminish: but of the children born a greater proportion will attain maturity. Among the poor a larger number of women become pregnant, and a larger number miscarry; while among the rich a smaller number of women become pregnant, and fewer miscarry. (*Parl. Report on Friendly Societies,* Sess. 1825, p. 86.) Among the poor of the metropolis, Dr. Granville states that one woman in three who are pregnant invariably miscarries.

control the strongest of human passions. A virtuous celibacy, therefore, is hopeless, and *matrimony* or *vice* the only alternative. To meet this dilemma a class of philosophers has appeared, who have sought to divest marriage of its impoverishing consequences. I am venturing on delicate ground I am aware, but I do not see how I can discharge my duty to our present subject without some notice of a matter that has excited considerable attention. The speculations to which I am alluding have certainly given a shock to the public mind, hardly less than that it received on the first publication of the celebrated *Essay on the Principle of Population.*

The theory that has been put forth may, perhaps, be collected in the subjoined extracts from the writings of its most logical and philosophical expounder.

" There are two modes in which *artificial means* may be employed to make population and capital keep pace together: expedients may be sought either to *restrain* the tendency of population to increase ; or to *accelerate* beyond its natural pace the increase of capital."—*Elements of Political Economy*, p. 57.

" If we may thus infer that human happiness cannot be secured by taking *forcible* methods to make capital increase as fast as population ; and if, on the other hand, it is certain, that where births take place, more numerous than are required to uphold a population corresponding to the state of capital, human happiness is impaired, it is immediately seen, *that the grand practical problem is, to find the means of limiting the number of births.* It has also appeared, that, beyond a certain state of density in the population, such as to afford the benefits of social intercourse and of combined labour, it is not desirable that population should increase. The precise problem, therefore, is to find the means of *limiting births* to that number which is necessary to keep up the population without increasing it."—*Idem*, p. 65.

" The result to be aimed at is, to secure to the great body of the people *all the happiness which is capable of being derived from the matrimonial union, without the evils which a too rapid increase of their numbers involves.* The progress of legislation, the improvement of the education of the people, and the decay of superstition will in time, it may be hoped, accomplish the difficult task of reconciling these important objects."—*Idem*, p. 58.

" It is perfectly evident, that so long as men are produced in greater numbers than can be fed, there must be excessive misery. What is wanted then is, the means of preventing mankind from increasing so fast ; from increasing faster than food can be increased to support them. To the discovery of these means, the resources of the human mind should be intensely applied. *This is the foundation of all improvement.* In the attainment of this important end, it is abundantly plain that there is nothing impracticable. There is nothing which offers any considerable difficulty, except the prejudices of mankind." —*Supplement to the 4th, 5th, and 6th Editions of the Encyclopædia Britannica.* Art. *Banks for Savings*, p. 93.

" What are the best means of checking the progress of population, when it cannot go on unrestrained without producing one or other of two most undesirable effects,—either drawing an undue proportion of the population to the *mere raising of food,* or producing poverty and wretchedness, it is not now the place to inquire. It is, indeed, the most important practical problem to which the wisdom of the politician and moralist can be applied. It has, till this time, been miserably evaded by all those who have meddled with the subject, as well as by all those who were called upon by their situation to find a remedy for the evils to which it relates. And yet, if the superstitions of the nursery were discarded, and the *principle of utility kept steadily in view,* a solution might not be very difficult to be found ; and the means of drying up one of the most copious sources of human evil, a source which, if all other sources of evil were taken away, would alone suffice to retain the *great* mass of human beings in misery, might be seen to be neither doubtful nor difficult to be applied."—Art. *Colony*, p. 261.

"A *parent* has considerable control over the *subsistence fund* of his family, and an *absolute control over the numbers* to be supported by that fund."—*Illustrations of Political Economy.*

"There is a choice of three things. First, to abstain from *breeding more children than are wanted.* Secondly, to destroy the supernumeraries at the period of birth, as is practised by the Chinese. And, thirdly, to go on suffering the overplus to perish by starvation, as *is the case at present.* To accomplish the first, education is requisite; because *uneducated people,* as they approach the nature of inferior animals, will persist in gratifying their appetites, wholly regardless of consequences; *educated* people, on the contrary, are amenable to the feelings of humanity. The second proposition is mischievous, because the habit of destroying life destroys all the finer susceptibilities in which the rational happiness of human beings consists. The third we are now enduring."—*State of Society,* p. 44, 45.

Leaving the political and domestic economy of marriage, I shall advert to the next unobjectionable remedy of an over-crowded community, namely, EMIGRATION, by which I mean a national plan of colonization, as explained on a previous occasion (p. 111). This appears nature's own prescription, and is that by which she has peopled and reclaimed the earth. When the vessel is too full it flows over; when population is so dense that it can neither be fed nor employed, it naturally spreads over a wider surface. Capital and industry are sources of discontent and inconvenience, not of national wealth, unless they can be productively employed.

The principle on which emigration may be defended is this: on one side is a fertile and extensive territory, useless to man for want of cultivation; on the other, a surplus of capital and labour alike valueless for want of objects on which they can be profitably employed, bring them together, and they co-operate for the production of utility, like two chemical fluids which, separate, yield neither heat nor colour, but united afford both.

' The chief objections against emigration are, 1. its hardship; 2. its inefficiency; 3. its expense. I shall submit a few brief observations on each, bearing in mind that a systematic plan of colonization is meant, though the term emigration is used.

' With respect to the first it would be as cruel as unjust either to force or seduce a man from his fatherland without regard to his future location and welfare. No such hardship, I believe, was ever intended. The object sought is to remove the industrious from a country where their labour is unprofitable, where they are ill-fed, ill-clothed, ill-lodged, and dependent withal, to another where they shall be emancipated from these evils, and be enabled to transmit the inheritance of freedom and comfort they acquire to their children.

Those who do not see hardship to individuals in emigration, object to its *efficiency*. They admit it might afford *transient* relief to the mother country, but they are apprehensive " the vacuum " it made, would be soon filled up. These are the ultra Malthusians, who can see no good in the poor-laws, nor in the repeal of the corn-laws, nor of taxes, nor of tithes; all these they allow would yield momentary ease, but the cup of misery would speedily refill, unless the activity of the breeding tendency of our race was controlled. They are right in their principle, but extravagant in its application.

First, ought a community to stand still amidst its difficulties, and make no effort to remove them? Even transient relief would be a point gained. If the emigrants were made more happy, and those they left behind less miserable, it would be a reduction from the quantum of wretchedness previously existing, and were it only to continue for *a season*, it would be worth a sacrifice. No man would refuse to eat a dinner to-day, because he may be hungry to-morrow. It would have other advantages; it would give *time for reflection*. The established habits of the people would not at once alter; they would not at once, because there was more space, begin to marry earlier and breed faster than before; they would have leisure to look back upon the evils they had escaped, and having tasted the sweets of better circumstances, might be disposed to adopt measures to perpetuate their enjoyment. The mere fact of a number of people annually leaving the country in quest of employment, would be a sort of practical and trumpet-like preaching through the thousand-tongued press, that would do more to show the real state of society, and enlighten public sentiment on its causes, than could be effected by the most zealous and well-directed labours of economical writers in a century. I say nothing of the capital

and industry that would be called into activity by
the mere preparation, provision, and transport of
a large body of colonists.

After all, it is only the straitened and redundant
portion of the community that ought to emigrate.
Those who are employed — those whose circumstances are comfortable, are already in their proper
sphere, and it would be unwise in them to put their
good fortune to hazard ; but the removal of the
able-bodied, who are permanently unemployed, benefits both them and those they leave behind : from
miserable paupers they become independent yeomen.

Lastly, as to the *expense*. To advance twenty or
thirty pounds to remove an unemployed labourer,
looks a great sum, but what is it to the expense of
his permanent maintenance. Mr. Barton informs
us, that in his own parish, a statement was drawn
out from the poor-books of the sums paid to one
labourer, during the course of a long life, and they
were found to amount to more than *seven hundred
pounds !* How much cheaper, then, to the whole
community to advance at once a million or ten
millions of money, than to support permanently a
vast body of unemployed people. The interest
of even ten millions at five per cent., is only
500,000*l.* a year. To support one million of persons at only a penny a day, would cost in round
numbers 1,500,000*l.* a year.

We can never hope to get rid of the most objectionable part of our poor-laws, namely, the main-

tenance of an *able-bodied* labourer, unconnected with a system of emigration. We cannot justly deprive him of his existing claim, without first offering him something in exchange. The parish cannot refuse him relief, without offering him the alternative of work either at home or abroad, whereby he may support himself.

III.—SYMPTOMS OF OVER-POPULATION.

It is difficult to ascertain the precise circumstances which indicate a permanent excess of population. From our preceding inquiries it is evident that the demand for labour in all the great branches of national industry is subject to fluctuation; in agriculture it varies with the season of the year; in commerce and manufactures it varies, not only with the season of the year, but with the alternate briskness and depression of trade to which these pursuits are periodically liable. An occasional excess of workpeople arising from these causes, is no proof of over-population, it merely indicates a reserve of labour essential to the effective cultivation of rural and manufacturing industry, and without which, the supply would not be constantly adequate to the demand. By an excess of population is meant a permanent excess; such as tends to the diminution of national wealth, and the deterioration of the circumstances of the great body of the people.

The circumstances symptomatic of an excess of this description are the following :

First, a general and permanent depression in the rate of wages. Wages may fluctuate from the periodic causes to which allusion has been made, but they can only be permanently depressed by the constant pressure of an over-stocked market of industry; in other words, by the supply of labour exceeding the demand.

Secondly, a low rate of profit is a sign of redundancy. The general tendency of high profits is high wages, and the contrary. When profits are low, it shows that the channels for the employment of capital are full, and consequently that the supply of labour equals or exceeds the demand which can be advantageously called into action.

Thirdly, a tendency to emigrate indicates an excess of people. Dr. Smith has remarked, that "man is the least exportable of all commodities; necessity alone will induce him voluntarily to abandon the soil, climate, habits, laws, and institutions, to which he has been accustomed." We may be assured, therefore, if the industrious emigrate in considerable numbers, it can only arise from the necessity of finding out new sources of employment and subsistence; from a conviction of straitened circumstances, resulting from diminished wages and profits; in other words, from a redundancy of capital and industry.

Fourthly, the frequent and general occurrence of typhus, puerperal fever, cholera, dysentery, and other diseases, mostly originating in low diet, insufficient clothing, and unwholesome lodging, to which the people have been compelled to submit from extreme reduction in the price of labour.

Fifthly, the prevalence of outrages against property, and of political discontent and agitation. In ordinary times, the general disposition of the people is to refrain from politics as an unprofitable pursuit; and no abstract question of government, nor even existence of positive abuses, would be sufficient to overcome their apathy, were they not accompanied by circumstances more nearly affecting their individual condition. But if they find their comforts and enjoyments greatly curtailed, whether it arises from the visits of the tax-gatherer, or from the excess of labour and capital, then they are prompt to listen to representations of the misconduct of their rulers.

Sixthly, an increase of crimes against property, arising from general poverty and privation.

Seventhly, an increasing rate of mortality among the people.

With the exception of the last, all these symptoms of population increasing faster than the means of support and employment apply to England. The returns of population tend to confirm this conclusion. During the last thirty years, population has continued to increase at nearly a uniform rate, and the average annual increase in the number of the people in Great Britain has been about one and a half per cent. The rate of increase per cent., and the amount of the four decennary periods of enumeration will appear from the subjoined summary of Mr. Rickman.

POPULATION.

	1801.		1811.		1821.		1831.
England . . .	8,331,434	14½	9,551,888	17½	11,261,437	16	13,089,338
Wales	541,546	13	611,788	17	717,438	12	805,236
Scotland . . .	1,599,068	14	1,805,688	16	2,093,456	13	2,365,807
Army, Navy, &c.	470,398	—	640,500	—	319,300	—	277,017
	10,942 646	15¼	12,609,864	14	14,391,631	15	16,537,398

Now, the question is, has the capital and productive power of the community increased in as great a ratio as the population. This could only be answered by a statistical investigation of the progress of agriculture, commerce, and manufactures, as indicated by the passing of enclosure bills—bills for internal improvements—by the amount of exports and imports—and by a comparison of the prices of commodities.

One of the most satisfactory reasons for inferring that the people have not increased faster than the national resources is the *rate of mortality*, which, during the last half-century, has decreased in a remarkable degree. In the year 1780, the average rate of mortality was 1 in 38 of the existing population; in 1790, 1 in 45; in 1800, 1 in 48; in 1810, 1 in 54; and in the ten years ending in 1820, 1 in 60. Such a decrease of mortality is wholly irreconcilable with any great deterioration in the physical circumstances of the people; though it is important to remark, that the decrease in mortality has been partly produced by the discovery of vaccination—improvements in the science and practice of midwifery, by the substitution of accoucheurs for females—better modes of nursing and treating children—better habits in the people—together with the diffusion among the community at large of more correct knowledge of the arts conducive to health and longevity. The average term of existence, especially among women, it is well known has greatly extended of late years; and the assurance offices have been obliged to raise the terms on which they grant life annuities.*

Upon the whole, though there exists no ground for indulging in the exaggerated apprehensions which prevailed, respecting the increase of population some years since, there is no reason for thinking we are not sufficiently numerous, either for external defence, or social happiness. The decline of wages and profits, and the sharpness of competition, in every walk of life, must bring home, to the conviction of every man, that if the vessel does not overflow, it is at least, full enough for the general good of society. We may, therefore, safely abandon the policy of the statesmen of the last century, who were for granting " premiums for large families," and who considered

* In addition to the causes mentioned in the text of diminished mortality, another is (though still very imperfect) the improved *medical police* of large towns. Prior to 1750, London required an annual supply of nearly 11,000 persons to fill up the void left by the excess of deaths over the births; whereas, of late years, it has not only kept up its own numbers, but yielded annually a vast surplus of people. (Barton, *On the Depreciation of Labour*, p. 110.) Great cities were formerly denominated the *graves* of mankind; but now they are, as well as the country, the *cradles.*

an increase in population, identified with the increase
of national power.

It is satisfactory to think, that, beside the checks
to population, arising out of misery and vice, there
are others less afflictive to the feelings in the diffusion
of knowledge, a taste for luxuries, habits of forethought, and personal dignity : the increase in these,
mostly keeps pace with the increase in the means of
subsistence, and those causes, which are likely to
give an impulse to the increase of population. With
the enlightened, the anxieties, expense, and restraint attendant on families in densely-peopled
countries, will mostly operate as a sufficient restriction on improvident marriages ; and it is only among
the ignorant and unthinking, such indiscretions are
to be apprehended. So that the spectre of population resolves itself into a defect of moral culture, and
a degraded standard of living: social evils, which all
classes have a common interest in correcting.

While there is in this, much to allay apprehension, it ought not to be concealed, that the science
of population is of the utmost importance to the
wellbeing of society. There is a natural tendency
in man to increase his species, but there is no cor-
respondent natural tendency in the earth to increase
his food ; so that the tendency of population to increase faster than subsistence may be considered an
axiom of social economy. Hence, the opinion that
the resources of any country are indefinite, so that
the increase in them will always keep pace with the
increase of the people, is a pernicious error. In

England for instance, it is sometimes alleged that there are resources for the maintenance and employment of a much more numerous population. Perhaps it is so if every individual were to apply himself solely to the *raising of food*. But no rational person would desire that the entire community should be occupied in spade husbandry, or other manual occupation. Without, however, a social change of this nature, it is probable neither the food nor employment derived from our own soil could be greatly augmented. Commerce and manufactures may admit of extension, but the legislative protection afforded to agriculture, and the stimulus of paper-money prices have, I apprehend, left neither in the enclosure of wastes, nor in more expensive modes of culture, any great scope for increased production. Ireland is differently circumstanced, and industry, capital, and internal peace, may effect the most salutary improvements.*

* On the culture of English wastes, Mr. Barton says, "Every one knows who has attended practically to this subject that such undertakings have in many cases been productive of loss to the undertakers. In the South Downs of Sussex, in my own immediate neighbourhood, there are considerable tracts which were once ploughed and have been subsequently allowed to return to a state of nature. The traces of the plough are distinctly visible on many parts of these downs, and there are some parts that have been in tillage within the memory of man. *Why were these abandoned?* Evidently because the annual produce did not equal the annual cost: the corn consumed by the men and horses employed in working the land was more than the corn grown on it." —*Statement of the Growing Excess of Population*, p. 17. See on the same subject, Mr. Cobbett's *Tour in Scotland*, pp. 22, 23.

Granting a country is possessed of latent resources, the position I wish to inculcate is that these resources ought to be *first elicited.* *Subsistence ought to precede population, not population subsistence.* In this respect the policy of nations and the good conduct of individuals coincide. While a just and prudent man would not think of marrying till he had a fair prospect of the means for maintaining a family ; so no statesman would think of encouraging an increase of people till he had ascertained from the high price of labour and cheapness of provisions the existence of resources for their maintenance and employment: in the latter case, however, no encouragement would be necessary, as population agreeably with the law already explained would start forward.

The RICH are only indirectly but the POOR are directly interested in the doctrine of population. The former are the *buyers* of labour, they profit by the diminution in its price, caused by the competition for employment, and they are only affected by the increase in the numbers of the people, when that increase has been so excessive and productive of misery so intense, as to endanger the security, and lessen the enjoyment of their possessions.

By exercising a control over their numbers, the industrious have a complete control over the wages of labour. Fluctuations in the amount of capital cannot affect them ; whether society is stationary or retrograde in wealth, they can always preserve their condition unimpaired, by proportioning the supply of the commodity in which they deal to the demand.

On the other hand, without the exercise of this con-
servative power over their numbers, no enlargement
of national resources can permanently improve their
circumstances.   Every addition to the means of
employment and subsistence would only call into
existence a corresponding number of claimants to
participate therein, and the share of each would not
be augmented.   Society would be *more numerous,*
but not more *happy.*   Even the best schemes for
their relief and employment, devised by the wisest
and most philanthropic individuals, must prove
illusive, unless seconded by their own co-operative
agency.   One pauper relieved would only make way
for another ; one body of emigrants removed this
year, a fresh supply to an equal amount would offer
themselves next ; while one swarm of unemployed
labourers is being located on the waste, another is
growing up to maturity equally destitute.   It is the
waves of the sea following each other in endless
succession.

I conclude therefore that all remedies are transient
—all projects for improving the condition of the
working classes vain, unless accompanied by the
exercise of that prudential virtue in individuals, and
that policy in the state, which shall induce both to
concur in limiting the number of the people to the
means for their employment and support.

CHAP. XIV.

POOR-LAWS.

Right of the Poor to Parish Relief—Their Claim to a fourth part of Tithe—Queries of the House of Lords relative to able-bodied Poor—Eleven Objections to Poor-laws answered—Under an improved System, Pauperism has declined relatively to the Population—Poor-laws not tended to increase the Number of People—Not fostered improvident Habits—Example of Scotland considered—Working Classes of England, and other Countries—Principles and Policy of the Poor-laws stated and defended—Obligations they impose on the Rich to interest themselves in the state of the Poor—Mendicity, or Poor Assessment the only alternative—Impotence of general System of voluntary Charity—The Poor often the chief Obstacle to the adoption of Plans for their own Benefit—Their Condition can only be improved by the Intervention of the Affluent—Obligations imposed by the Laws of Infanticide—Provision for the Poor in other Countries—Utility of the Poor-laws proved by Experience—Description of Persons who ought to be entitled to Parish Relief—Police as well as Charity, the object of Poor-laws—Suggestions for Improvement of Poor-laws—Law of Settlement—Unequal size of Parishes—Unequal Pressure of Poor-rate on real and chattel Property—Mendicity in the Metropolis—Practical Hints relative to the Poor and Administration of the Poor-laws.

THE term Poor is usually applied to that class of persons who are unable to maintain themselves, either from inability to procure employment, or from sickness, old age, or other bodily incapacity; whether this is the description of persons originally intended to be embraced by the poor-laws has been much disputed, but it is the description which is now generally recognised in their practical administration.

In the outset of this inquiry, it may be convenient to advert to the only abstract part of the subject we shall encounter, namely, the *right* of the poor to a compulsory maintenance. If there be any social obligation to find employment or relief for those who could not otherwise obtain it, such obligation must be derived either from the laws of nature, or the institutions of society.

The land is unquestionably the people's, in their aggregate capacity, and every one has a natural claim to live thereon. But in a state of society, man's natural claims are merged in his civil immunities, and the rights of each person are prescribed by the laws. In a state of natural liberty, every individual may claim the right to do what he likes, or what he *can;* his right to the enjoyment of this female, or of that piece of land is only limited by his power to defend his pretension against all other claimants. But in civil society, the natural rights of mere force have been superseded by the rights of property, of marriage, and personal security. It follows that the rights of the poor cannot be determined by reference to the natural state of man, which has long since ceased, but by reference to existing social institutions.

What then are the social rights of the poor ? If

a man has not the means of maintenance, and society will not relieve him, he must starve. · But the question is, *Will he starve?* Certainly not. Self-preservation will be more imperative with him than respect for civil institutions. If he cannot live in society, he will have ceased to have an interest in its existence; the social compact (if it ever existed) will, in respect of him, be dissolved ; and mendicity, or theft with its penal consequences, will be a less evil than death by hunger. Rather than he should be reduced to this extremity, in which he has a paramount interest in the violation of the laws, it seems expedient a *legal provision* should be established for his relief, and to this, though a pauper has no claim as a matter of right, and except as guaranteed to him by the law, yet society concedes it to him as a lesser evil adopted for its own conservation.

In lieu of founding the right of the poor for relief on their *original share in the soil* of the country, it has been attempted to establish their claim to parish aid as the compensation they received for the losses they sustained at the Reformation, in consequence of the new disposition of ecclesiastical property. That the poor were originally entitled to a fourth, or some other fraction of the tithe, is an opinion countenanced by many eminent authorities. Dr. Burn, in his *Justice of the Peace*, published in 1754, admits the maintenance of the poor was anciently an ecclesiastical duty; that a fourth part of the tithes of parishes was originally set apart for this purpose, and distributed by the bishop with the assistance of the churchwardens and other principal inhabitants; and that afterwards, when the tithes of parishes became appropriated to religious houses, these societies contributed towards the relief of the poor. Blackstone agrees in this view of the subject, and admits that the relief of the poor was among the " purposes for which the payment of tithe was originally imposed" (*Commentaries*, b. i. chap. ii.) And indeed the fact of the ancient fourfold division of tithes is confirmed by the existing practice in several parts of Ireland; the Bishops of Clonfert and Kildare continuing to receive their fourth or *quarta pars* of tithes in several parishes of their dioceses.

But admitting all this, it goes little way to establish the *right* of the poor to relief, except such as they derive from existing laws. Next to founding the claim to any immunity on *natural* right, the most puerile expedient is to seek to establish it upon some usage existing centuries ago, and which has been superseded by subsequent acts of legislation acquiesced in for ages by the whole community. Existing laws alone prescribe individual rights, and the laws have wisely provided in order to prevent unceasing strife and litigation, that various claims shall be for ever foreclosed unless enforced within determinate periods; as, for instance, a claim to debt and other chattel interests cannot be established unless enforced within four, five, or six years, and even a right to real property is lost if forty years in abeyance. How valueless then must be any claim to tithe founded on their apportionment and appro-

priation in the thirteenth and fourteenth centuries!
The nobility might almost with as much justice seek
to re-establish their claim to the *personal* services of
the poor—to reduce them a second time to serfship,
as the latter found a proprietary claim on usages,
contemporary with the feudal system.

It is quite an error to suppose a *compulsory* poor-
rate was imposed as a compensation or substitute for
any loss the poor sustained at the Reformation. The
celebrated act of 1601 was not passed till seventy
years after the dissolution of the monasteries, and
was intended to meet the overwhelming evil of vagabondage and mendicity which proceeded much more
from the abolition of vassalage than the suppression
of the religious houses. The poor-rate is in fact the
price paid by the community for the emancipation
of all its members from personal bondage. While
feudality continued, the poor were unknown as a
body; beggars and vagrants there were seeking casual relief from conventual and other bodies; but
there was no *national* poor; they only began when
villanage was abolished and villains acquired the
rights of freemen without the habits of industry and
forethought which their new condition required, and
which it became necessary to supply the place of by
a parish assessment for their relief.

The description of persons intended to be embraced
by the 43d of Elizabeth has been much disputed,
and some writers have contended that the poor have
sustained an injustice, either by the interpretation of
this statute, or the acts subsequently passed for im-

proving its practical administration.   The clause in
the act bearing on this point is the following, and
concisely describes the persons to whom, and the
mode in which parochial aid shall be given :

" The churchwardens and overseers, with the consent of two justices, shall take order, from time to
time, for *setting to work the children* of all such
whose parents shall not, by the said churchwardens
and overseers, or the greater part of them, be thought
able to keep and maintain their children ; and for
setting to work all such persons, married or unmarried, having no means to maintain them, and using
no ordinary and daily trade of life to get their living
by ; and for the necessary relief of the lame, impotent, old, blind, and such other among them being
poor and not able to work."

The duties of parish officers clearly appear, then,
to have been restricted to the three following specific
objects : 1. Setting to work the *children* of all those
whose parents are unable to maintain them.   2. Setting to work all persons having no income to maintain themselves, and using no ordinary trade to get
their living by.   3. The necessary relief of the lame,
old, and others being poor and unable to work. Thus
it clearly appears this was an act for *enforcing industry*, not for encouraging *idleness*.   No one was
to be relieved, either child or adult, except, if able,
by *setting to work*.   The modern practice of granting money allowances without equivalent labour to
able-bodied persons, and thereby creating a band of
parish pensioners, was certainly never contemplated

by the authors of this celebrated piece of legislation.

Upon this point has arisen the great difficulty in
the administration of the poor-laws, namely, whether
a parish is bound to relieve or find employment for
all able-bodied persons, who are willing but unable
to procure work.

Now this is a case, I apprehend, which was never
contemplated by the act of Elizabeth. Between the
age of Elizabeth and the present exists this important
distinction; the difficulty in the former was, as has been
shown in the preliminary history of the poor, to compel
men to work; the difficulty is now to find them work
to do. The idea of an able-bodied person willing to
labour but unable to get employment was never entertained by Lord Burleigh and his contemporaries.
The object of their great measure was to meet the
evil of idleness and vagabondage which grew out of
the decline of feudality. Hence I conclude that the
obligation (if it exist) of parishes to relieve or find
employment for able-bodied paupers has grown entirely out of the altered circumstances of society, and
that as these circumstances did not exist in the time
of Elizabeth, the act passed in her reign could not
have been framed to meet them. Whether the law
imposes this obligation, it would be presumptuous in
me to offer an opinion, when the highest authorities
are in doubt on the subject; but I shall, in the sequel,
endeavour at least to establish its *expediency.*

* A solution of the legal difficulties involved in the statute of
Elizabeth would probably lead to important modifications in the

II.—OBJECTIONS TO THE POOR-LAWS.

Upon hardly any question of national interest has there been so much discussion as the poor-laws; individuals the most enlightened have wavered in their opinions, and even now, the public mind is divided on their policy. After much inquiry, I think, the reasons in favour of their institution preponderate; and that, of a choice of evils, they are the least. The argument which weighs most with me, and which I shall endeavour to illustrate in the sequel, is a conviction, that the poor-laws, under judicious

administration of the poor-laws, as may be inferred from the following questions submitted by a committee of the House of Lords to the judges:

" 1. Does the 43d Eliz. c. 2, or any other law, authorize magistrates to order any relief to be given to poor persons who are not able to work, or to afford them any assistance except by procuring some employment for them where employment can be obtained?

" 2. If it be satisfactorily proved that employment cannot be procured within a reasonable distance of the parish to which able-bodied persons belong, will magistrates in such cases be authorized to *order relief?*

" 3. When able-bodied poor persons can maintain only a part of their family by the wages of their labour, are magistrates authorized to order any relief to be given to them for the maintenance of such of their children, not being able to work, as they cannot maintain?"—*Third Report of the Lords' Committee on the Poor-laws,* April 22, 1831.

The Report of the House of Commons in 1828, on the Employment and Payment of able-bodied Labourers from the Poor rate, drawn up by Lord J. Russell, contains valuable elucidations of the main points comprised in these queries.

administration, may be made more effective, than any other system which has yet been devised for reducing to their lowest amount, if not entirely extirpating the evils of indigence, and rendering the poor independent of gratuitous aid. If this result be attainable, it obviates the strongest objection against them; before, however, enlarging upon it, I shall submit a few remarks on the arguments usually urged against a compulsory provision for the poor.*

I. It aggravates the evil it is meant to alleviate, by fostering an indigent class.

Now, the practical answer to this is, whether, under the administration of the poor-laws, the number of paupers has increased, relatively to the rest of the community. During the last thirty years, population has increased at the rate of one-and-a-half per cent. per annum; and the point to be ascertained is, whether pauperism has increased in a

* Public opinion began to set strongly against the poor-laws, after the publication of Sir F. Eden's great work, in 1797, and the *Essay on Population*, by Mr. Malthus. There has been lately a reaction; it began, I believe, with Mr. Black, the intelligent editor of the *Morning Chronicle*, who showed, that, without the pressure of parish assessment, the rich would concern themselves little about bettering the condition of the labouring classes. The question of poor-laws for Ireland, and the Reports of the Poor-law Commission, are likely again to bring the entire system under consideration. From what I have seen of the Commissioners' Reports, they appear directed more against abuses in the practical administration of the poor-laws, than the general policy of their institution.

higher proportion. If pauperism has only kept pace with population, it is a presumption, the evil has not been aggravated by poor-laws. Of the relative increase of pauperism, we may form a conclusion from statements laid before parliamentary committees. From the tables of Mr. Nimmo (*Parl. Papers*, vol. vii. Sess. 1830), it appears the number of paupers, in proportion to the whole population, is only about the same at present as in 1688, and is considerably less than at several intermediate periods from that time. Here follows a summary of the relative progress of Pauperism and Population, from 1688 to 1831.

Years.	Relieved.	Population.	Ratio.
1688	563,964	5,300,000	9·4
1766	695,177	7,728,000	11·3
1784	818,151	8,016,000	9·8
1792	955,326	8,695,000	9·7
1801	—	8,872,980	
1803	1,040,716	9,168,000	8.8
1811	—	10,791,115	
1813	1,361,903	11,028,425	8·0
1814	1,353,995	11,147,080	8·2
1815	1,275,974	11,265,735	8.8
1821	—	11,977,663	9·3
1831	1,275,974	12,300,000	9·6

From this representation it is clear, pauperism has not augmented relatively to the population during the last one hundred and forty years, and that the total number of persons relieved, occasionally and permanently, has fluctuated between 8 in 100 to 12 in 100 of the entire community.

In the year ending 25th March, 1831, the expen-

diture of poor-rates in England, had decreased one
per cent.; in the year ending 25th March, 1832, it
had increased three per cent.: the inorease in the last,
arising probably from a more lenient administration
of the poor-laws, owing to the disturbed state of the
rural districts.   The poor expenditure has increased
much more rapidly in Wales than England during
the last two years.

There is another, and perhaps more authentic,
mode than that adopted by Mr. Nimmo, of ascertaining the relative increase of pauperism.   The
earliest *official* returns of the amount of the poor
assessment, are for the year 1748; but as the pressure of the poor assessment varies with the price of
bread, it is not an accurate criterion of the prevalence of pauperism ; the only safe criterion, is the
poor assessment converted into *equivalent* quarters
of corn, at the average market-price.   For the application of this test, the subjoined statement has
been drawn up ; it exhibits, at different periods, the
amount of the sums *solely* expended in the relief of
the poor (exclusive of county rates, law charges,
militia expenses, &c.), the price of wheat per quarter, with the number of quarters at that price, equivalent to the poor expenditure, and the increase per
cent., as measured by corn, during each intervening
period.   The imperial bushel was adopted in 1826,
and the equivalent number of quarters in 1830, in
that measure, was only 2,099,831, which I have
reduced to the Winchester, to correspond to the
standard of the preceding items.   The data have

been chiefly taken from *Parl. Paper*, No. 52, Sess. 1830.*

Years.	Expended in Relief of the Poor.	Price of Wheat per quarter		Equivalent Quarters of Wheat.	Increase per Cent.	Increase per Cent. per Annum
	£	s.	d.			
1748	689,971	27	11	494,307	—	—
1776	1,530,800	45	—	680,355	88	1 $\frac{1}{3}$
1803	4,077,891	56	5	1,443,101	112	4 $\frac{1}{4}$
1820	6,958,445	65	7	2,122,016	47	2 $\frac{11}{17}$
1830	6,829,042	64	3	2,167,890	2$\frac{1}{7}$	0 $\frac{1}{7}$

This statement presents a brief, but lucid view of the working of the poor-laws for the last eighty-two years. The period of the greatest increase of pauperism appears to have been from 1776 to 1803,

* It is calculated, that two-thirds of the expenditure in the relief of the poor vary with the price of corn. But if we compare dear and cheap years, we shall find that two-thirds of the poor expenditure do not vary with the prices of corn. The average expenditure in the three years 1812-13-14, was 6,400,000l., with corn at 107s. per quarter; the average expenditure of the three years 1827-8-9, was 6,300,000l., with corn at 57s. per quarter; but, supposing pauperism to have been stationary in the interval of fifteen years, and the cost of the poor to have declined with the cost of corn, the poor expenditure in the latter period, ought to have amounted to 4,300,000l., in lieu of 6,300,000l. This difference is not to be accounted for entirely, as one writer has supposed (*Hints on the Practical Administration of the Poor-laws*), by the increase of pauperism; but by the fact, that parish allowances do not vary with the prices of corn: in cheap years, the poor receive too much; in dear ones, not enough.

when it increased 112 per cent., or at the rate of $4\frac{4}{27}$ per cent. per annum. In this interval of twenty-seven years, were the war with America and the first French revolutionary war. The interval from 1803 to 1820, included the second French war, and pauperism increased 47 per cent., or $2\frac{13}{17}$ per cent. per annum, a sensible diminution in the rate of increase, compared with the preceding period. From 1820 to 1830, a period of peace, pauperism increased $2\frac{1}{4}$ per cent., or not exceeding $\frac{4}{17}$ per cent. per annum.

My conclusions from this representation are, that during the war, neither the attention of the public, nor the legislature, was fixed on the poor-laws, and consequently, they were lavishly and unwisely administered. After the peace of 1815, they were a subject of anxious inquiry and discussion; in the year 1817, a committee of the House of Commons, of which, Mr. W. Sturges Bourne was chairman, made a very elaborate and able report on the tendency and administration of the poor-laws. Though some of the positions in this report may be disputed, it abounded in many salutary suggestions, and upon it was founded the important act of 1819, by which parishes were empowered, among other improvements, to appoint managing vestries and assistant overseers. The effect of these, and other alterations in the mode of keeping and auditing parish accounts, was signally evinced in the subsequent ten years, during which, pauperism increased at a less rate than *one quarter per cent.* while population increased at the rate of *one and a half per cent.* per annum. From the inquiries of the parliamentary committee of 1817, it appeared that the increase in the *gross* amount of the parish assessment, from 1776 to 1815, had arisen in a much greater degree from the increase of law charges, removals, church rate, and county rate, than from the increased expenditure in the *maintenance* of the poor.

Were we to inquire I feel confident we should find that the income from poor-rates has not increased in a ratio with the national income, or with the rental of the country, or with the incomes derived from profits and wages. Such comparisons are superfluous. Enough, I think, has been adduced to demonstrate that an increase of pauperism is not inseparable from the principle of the poor-laws; but that under judicious administration they may be made subservient to a diminution in its amount, as is shewn by pauperism having declined relatively to the increase of population. The attempt to back out of the vicious system which was suffered to creep in during the war has not been unaccompanied with evil. A sharper administration of the poor-laws, combined with reductions in wages, have doubtless been the main causes of the incendiarisms and insubordination in the rural districts. Paupers, like any other class, are tenacious of advantages they have once possessed. But the allowance system, and other abuses, which appear either to have originated or been greatly extended in consequence of the high price and fluctuating value of bread from

1795 to 1815 may, I apprehend, be removed in conjunction with a national plan of emigration, or other alleviating circumstance, without leaving behind the revengeful feelings lately manifested. Let us proceed to the next objection against poor-laws.

II. That they encourage *improvident marriages*, and cause the poor to rely on the parish rather than their own good conduct.

Any system which should have this tendency would be justly objectionable. Self-dependence—dependence on their own forethought and industry—not the parish—are the only guarantees of the happiness of the working classes. I doubt whether the poor-laws have tended to diminish this self-dependence. I do not believe, for instance, and the opinion is confirmed by the testimony of many witnesses before parliamentary committees, that any man was ever induced to marry from knowing that the parish would relieve him, provided he was unable to maintain his family. Bad as the administration of the poor-laws may have been, the prospect of a workhouse or parish allowance has never been so inviting as to encourage any one to marry upon the strength of it. The workhouse when any one had so much thought about the future as to contemplate it as a resource to fall back upon for himself and children, would certainly operate rather to check than to promote matrimony. In short, the poor-laws have prevented the labouring classes from being so far depressed as to be altogether reckless of the future, from a conviction that their lot could not be worse ; and the consequence has been more prudence on the subject of wedlock. This view is confirmed by the decrease in weddings (*see* p. 335,) during the last half-century, and this decrease, be it remembered has been unaccompanied with any increase of illegitimate births.

The distinction made between the *married* and *single* in granting allowances for children appears a sort of bounty on marriages ; but, without defending this practice I should hardly think it has tempted many to marry. Marriages have been sometimes promoted by the reprehensible conduct of parish-officers, who, in order to evade the settlement of a female pauper or her illegitimate child, have effected *a match*, and thereby in lieu of one claimant have burdened the community perhaps with half-a-dozen.

To general imputations of improvidence against the working classes it is sufficient to refer to the progress of savings-banks and friendly societies.

III. They have given an artificial impulse to population, increasing it beyond the means of permanent employment and subsistence.

This is one of the greatest misrepresentations to which the poor-laws have been exposed, and is entirely controverted by facts. About the period of passing the act of Elizabeth in 1601, there are symptoms of population being on the increase (see p. 58) ; but during nearly the whole of the 150 years that subsequently elapsed, it remained either stationary or slowly augmented. It was only about

1770 that population made a start, chiefly from our unrivalled mechanical inventions, and consequent rapid extension of commercial and manufacturing industry. Down to 1795 the general complaint was, *not* that the poor-laws had increased population and lowered wages, but that they had diminished it, and raised wages. Mr. McCulloch cites many authorities (*Political Economy*, second edition, p. 413) to show that this was the general impression among public writers of the period to which I refer of the tendency of the poor-laws. Mr. Young, in particular, in his *Farmer's Letters*, laments the operation of the law of settlement, as " tending strongly to prevent an *increase*" of the labouring poor, in which, he thinks, consists the " strength of the state ;" and this opinion we have seen (p. 90,) was embraced by Mr. Pitt, Mr. Fox, Dr. Price, and other eminent persons. So far as the poor-laws had any influence on population, it is likely they tended to retard rather than accelerate its increase. The notion that they offered a *bounty* on marriages has been questioned in the preceding answer; but while, on the one hand, they had no influence in this direction, it is probable that persons of property soon became convinced, after the establishment of a compulsory provision for the poor, that their interests were opposed to a rapid increase in their number; and we accordingly find it was the constant policy, during the last century, of landlords and farmers, by pulling down of cottages and other expedients, to throw every obstacle in the way of poor persons marrying and settling in their parishes (*Farmer's Letters*, pp. 300—302), lest it should contribute to the increase of their rates.

The objection I am considering is quite irreconcilable with the progress of population in Scotland and Ireland : in the former, a compulsory poor-rate has made little progress, yet population has increased as fast as in this country ; and in the latter, there is no provision for indigence, and population has augmented at a far more rapid rate than in England.

IV. Had the poor not been tempted to place a deceitful trust in parish assistance, their natural sagacity would have led them to act with prudence and consideration, and prevented them multiplying their numbers beyond the demand for them.

I have partly replied to this objection in the last, by remarking that population has not increased faster in England than in other countries where no poor-laws are in operation. Those who calculate on the more efficient exercise of the *prudential virtues*, in the absence of poor-laws, are not accurately informed of the character of the labouring classes. That portion of the industrious orders who chiefly become objects of parish relief, are very little under the influence of prudence; and no system of civil polity, I fear, would be wise enough to subject them to it. As to the *future*, they never think about it at all ; they never look beyond the week, the day, or even the next meal. It is very strange, but the affluent often live under more constant apprehension of want than the needy. The apprehension of

2 B

loss of rank in society, for instance, is more terrible to the wealthy than the apprehension of famine to the indigent. Rich men often destroy themselves rather than part with their carriages and champagne; but the poor lose their mutton, their beer, and even the bed from under them, and live on. Want dulls the faculties; habit accustoms to privations. The evils of poverty do not appal those who have endured these evils from infancy. Order and cleanliness, the luxuries and conveniences of life, do not appear essential to those who never enjoyed them. Before men can be made apprehensive of the future, they must be made comfortable for the present. It is the pressure of actual, not the dread of prospective evil, that absorbs the attention of the poor, and forms the incentive to industry.

V. In Scotland there are no poor-laws, and the working classes are more moral and independent than in England.

This is slightly incorrect, both in fact and inference. 1. There are poor-laws in some of the towns of Scotland, and where there is no compulsory assessment for the relief of the poor, there are voluntary contributions. 2. The two countries do not admit of exact comparison. Scotland may be considered a *young* country, which only began to develop its resources after thorough incorporation with England, subsequent to the rebellion of 1745 : since then it has been in what Adam Smith calls the progressive state, the most favourable of any to the industrious classes; but let it advance to the stationary, when capital and labour are redundant, and it will lose its points of superiority. 3. The moral superiority of the Scotch may be conceded to their parochial schools, but their superior independence of character may be doubted, and in the opinion of many is not attested by the numerous specimens which appear in the south of England. Poverty, however, it is admitted, is not favourable to independence of demeanour, and it is possible "the Saxon" may have lost something of his ancient "pride of port," though this may be more justly ascribed to the reduction of wages than the influence of the poor-laws.

VI. The right of the poor to a maintenance is inconsistent with the rights of private property; since, as there is no limit to the increase of the poor, they may ultimately become so numerous as to absorb rents, tithes, and profits.

A speculative apprehension never likely to be realized! An assessment for the poor is no more inconsistent with the right of private property, than a church-rate or government tax, and like these will continue to be paid as long as people are able and willing to pay it and no longer. That it will not continue indefinitely to increase is proved by experience. The poor-rates attained their maximum anterior to 1820, since which they have not increased in the same ratio as population.

VII. They weaken the natural affections, and supersede the obligation imposed on the members of a family to co-operate for their mutual support in old age and misfortune.

A commentary wholly at variance with the text. The very charter of the poor-laws, the 43d of Elizabeth, enforces the ties of nature by requiring parents and grand parents to maintain their children through infancy, disease, and accident; and *vice versá*, children are bound to support their distressed parents in need, if of sufficient ability. The practice accords with the law. It is deemed the consummation of baseness, of pride, and meanness for a rich man to suffer his poor relatives to be dependent on the parish, or live or die in a workhouse; and a dread of this salutary opprobrium has often prevented a fate which mere consanguineous ties would have been too feeble to accomplish.

VIII. It has deadened private benevolence, and "the charity of law has superseded the charities of both home and neighbourhood."

A sufficiency of objects to keep alive benevolence, in addition to those within the scope of the poor-laws. But what kind of benevolence is intended by Dr. Chalmers? If that of almsgiving, it is the parent of mendicity, vice, and imposture; if that of Christmas doles, it is often only the ostentation of humanity, which at once flatters pride and generates servility. Where benevolence is more pure it is a virtue of irregular exercise—often difficult to rouse into action—too late frequently for its office—in excess, or unequal to its purpose. The "charity of how" is much more regular and discriminative; it is proportioned to the emergency—its offices are those of duty and necessity, which neither confer favour nor impose obligation.   Under such a system the charities of "home and neighbourhood" must assuredly be cemented, binding as it does in a common interest and prescribed locality the rich and poor, the prosperous and unhappy.

IX. They degrade and demoralize the working classes.

A popular error, propagated from writer to writer and talker to talker without inquiry or reflection. It can be no disgrace to receive what the *law allows*. If it be unpleasant to take what no services have earned, the poor have the rich and noble, and the spiritual to keep them in countenance.   But to the point.—Ask travellers where they found most meanness and mendicity, or if they found the workpeople in any country more independent than in England? They are dutiful and respectful; but not servile: they have not the coarseness of the American "help," nor the suppleness of the Italian, but domestic servants and operatives mostly know their office and fulfil it.   By whom are the mean and laborious offices of life chiefly performed?   By the foreigner, Frenchman, German, or Irish.   It is certainly one alleviating circumstance in the mass of vagrancy which overflows into this country from abroad, that the spectacle of comfort, dress, and manners it presents, has no tendency to render either an Englishman or Englishwoman more dissatisfied with the

community to which they belong. Our labourers
have long complained of the depressing competition
of Irish immigrants; but, from the appearance of the
streets and suburbs of the metropolis, they are
threatened with new rivals from the plains of Italy,
the Tyrol, and the Hartz mountains.

It has been the abuse I apprehend, not the principle
of the poor-laws which has degraded the working
class; and one of the greatest abuses was the making
up wages out of the rates. Doubtless a farmer would
sometimes employ a servant on these terms when he
could not at full wages, by which he was kept from
total idleness. But the practice is pernicious, and
breeds confusion of all sorts. It confounds wages
with charity—the master with the overseer—the industrious with the idle, in short it confounds every
thing which it ought not to confound, except the
married and single, between which it unfortunately
makes a distinction.

If we could accurately compare the state of England
with other countries, I have little doubt but we should
find that our poor are maintained in a less expensive
way to the community, and also in a mode less tending to degrade and demoralize them. The country
next to us in intelligence and freedom certainly does
not offer any enviable example. From recent statistical returns of Paris it appears that one-third
of the inhabitants die in poor-houses and hospitals;
and that of 25,000 births 10,000 are illegitimate;
and of the illegitimate births one-half are found-
lings.

X. Any amount of poor-rate is sure to be inadequate to its object, and always leaves a surplus of distress for which there is no provision, and which surplus equals what would have accrued, had there been no compulsory provision for the poor at all.

This is a formidable objection, and would be fatal to the policy of the poor-laws were it well-founded. The object of the poor assessment is to mitigate distress, but if for the distress it relieves an equivalent portion is generated, the tax imposed on society is a useless burden —it is worse ; for, according to the supposition, social distress would be doubled, one-half of which would be provided for, and the other destitute ; and thus the effort under such a system would be as vain as the attempt to destroy the Hydra.

My *first* answer is, that it is not peculiar to the poor-rate that it may be inadequate to the object for which it is raised, any more than any other fund raised and set apart for a specific purpose. If the expenditure be lavish and injudicious, it may exceed the income ; so may the expenditure of the state, a corporation, or even a private individual. That the poor-rate will not continue indefinitely to augment is proved by the fact that it has, relatively to the population, already begun to decline under an improved system of management.

The *second* part of the objection is grounded on the supposition, that for every pauper relieved a new claimant is called into existence.   Now, it is unan-

swerably true, that we make no progress towards the
extinction of indigence, if we merely provide for its
relief without adopting precautions against its renewed growth. We only prune, not root out, the
tares of want and poverty, and multiply the dependent classes of society. But no man of sense
would countenance a system of poor-laws so vicious-
ly administered. The legitimate purposes of a poor
assessment I take to be the raising of a provisional
fund for meeting, in the least objectionable way, a
positive evil, inseparable from the existing knowledge
and habits of society ; that this fund ought to be so
disbursed as to leave no one an excuse for being either
a beggar or a thief ; and at the same time so sparingly disbursed as to make it the interest of no person
to be a pauper rather than live by honest labour.
The object of the poor-laws is to relieve real and
unavoidable distress, not distress wantonly and
wickedly created ; and if the poor-laws are perverted into the fostering of the idle and dissolute, the
fault is not in the laws but their administrators, who
apply the poor when they ought to apply the
vagrant laws.

XI. People work from necessity, not choice ; it
follows, if there be any fund to which they can resort
without labour, it will always be resorted to ; and, in
illustration of this, reference is made to the Bedford
charity and the Foundling Hospital.

This, I must again repeat, is arguing against the
use from the abuse. If a fund intended for a good

purpose be perverted to a bad one, the fault is in those having the management of it. The idle and dissolute will live on the industrious and deserving, if they can ; but it is the fault of individuals or of society if they succeed. The poor-rate was intended for the distressed ; but if it is wasted on vice and improvidence, the opprobrium rests with the parish officers. The worthless of society will not labour, if they can live by standing with their arms folded at the corners of streets, by touching their hats to passengers, by holding up a bunch of matches, or by exposing infants to the inclemency of the weather ; but it arises from defective information in the community if such vagrant artifices are successful.

I have thus endeavoured to answer the chief objections against the poor-laws ; others have been urged, but they are only branches from the more general propositions which have been noticed. Nearly the whole of the objections against a compulsory poor-rate may be resolved into three sources : 1. An imperfect knowledge of the history of the poor-laws, especially of their operation during the ten years from 1820 to 1830. 2. A misapprehension of their influence on the habits and character of the labouring population. 3. Objections have been raised (and this has been the most fruitful source of misstatement) which apply only to a vicious and defective administration of them, not to the legitimate purposes of their institution.

I shall next proceed briefly to state these reasons

which appear to me unanswerably to establish the utility of a compulsory poor-rate, as a branch of the civil institutions of a well-ordered community.

III.——PRINCIPLES AND POLICY OF THE POOR-LAWS.

The *first* condition of any remedy for social destitution is that it shall be available and adapted to the removal of the evil. Better habits in the people might perhaps form a substitute for the poor-rate; but suppose from defective education or other cause those habits do not exist, why then such substitute becomes wholly inapplicable. For evils which now exist, we must apply remedies that are now applicable, not those applicable only to a state of society differently constituted from the present. When prudential habits have been universally established, we may trust to them for averting the evils of indigence; till then we might as well expect the filth and mire which accumulate in our streets and highways to be removed without the aid of the scavenger.

A mass of destitution is constantly being generated in society; it arises from fluctuations in employment, from changes of the seasons, from disease, old age, orphanage, infirmities of nature, vice and improvidence. Part of this destitution may be foreseen, and provided against; part of it results from calamities, which no forethought could avert. The question is, not as to its origin, but as to the best mode of dealing with it. So long as society exists in its present form, or any other of which the world has yet had experience, the poor form an inseparable adjunct to it, and how they shall best be dealt with is the subject to be investigated.

Where there is no public provision for the relief of indigence, it would be inconsistent with humanity, to deny to the wretched the liberty of craving alms from their more fortunate fellow-creatures. The conservation of society demands, that neither ignorance of the laws, nor the pressure of want, shall justify their violation ; and no man, however urgent his necessities, shall, with impunity, seize on the property of another; but it would be a great stretch of this principle, unwarranted by the same social interests, to interdict to distress, what charity may be voluntarily disposed to bestow! One is a crime of the deepest dye, the other, in its own nature, scarcely appears a crime at all, and can only be so construed from the necessity of its exercise having been superseded by civil institutions. Unless distress be allowed openly to manifest itself, neither its intensity nor extent can be known ; measures of alleviation will not be adopted—its origin investigated ; nor can these salutary reflections be excited in the beholder, tending to warn him from errors by which the calamities of others have been produced.

All these reasons, however, for the open toleration of MENDICITY, in countries where there is no provision for the destitute, have been superseded in England. Hence, the institution of poor-laws, dispenses with all pretext for *begging* for subsistence.

Every Englishman has his parish, and every parish is bound to find work or food for those unable to get employment; to bring up to useful trades, the children of the destitute; and to provide for the lame, impotent, blind, and others, being poor, and unable to provide for themselves.

Under these humane provisions, the rich and poor are bound up in a common fate, and reciprocal ties of obligation; neither prosperity nor adversity can visit one, without operating a corresponding influence on the other; the rich have an interest, paramount to the poor themselves, in every circumstance influencing their condition; and with their numbers, employments, education, improvidence, and vices, they are necessitated to feel a concern, and apply to their consideration, whatever superior knowledge or forethought they possess, in order to the permanent security of their own enjoyments.

Either mendicity, open and tolerated, or poor-rates, is the only alternative. In a manufacturing community like England, where the demand for labour is subject to great and unceasing fluctuations, the consequences of the former, in the absence of poor-laws would be frightful to contemplate. To the cases of real distress in our streets, would be superadded an immense mass of imposture, which in the absence of any legalized system for its detection and exposure, would increase to an extraordinary extent. Under the poor-laws, an Englishman does not need the public exhibition of distress, to be apprized of its existence; he knows it from the amount of his

poor assessment, and thus, without the spectacle of
want and wretchedness in the public thoroughfares,
he is possessed of an infallible barometer for ascertaining the condition of his less fortunate fellow-
creatures.

In the absence of public provision for the poor, it
cannot be supposed no efforts would be made for the
mitigation of distress; it would be the work of individuals, of voluntary associations, and parochial committees without number. Subscriptions would be
opened, collections made from house to house, charitable bequests from the dying would be solicited:
all this would be done without co-operation, without
uniformity of principle, without responsibility; and
the consequences would be, an inconceivable amount
of fraud and mismanagement; the waste, labour, and
expense would be greater than under the existing
system of assessment; and what would be worse, as
the exertions and sacrifices were *voluntary*, the burden would fall exclusively on the benevolent, while
the reckless and hard-hearted would be exempt from
all contribution either in purse or person.

Without poor-laws, the great bulk of society must
remain in a state of hopeless and irreclaimable misery.
But misery is incompatible with moral and intellectual culture: it is incompatible with personal and
proprietary security; it is incompatible with public
liberty and freedom of discussion. The greatest improvement in government—that of producing a conviction of the advantages it confers on the whole
community, in lieu of mere coercion, could never be

realized. A mass of social wretchedness would always form the *pabulum* of sedition; it would always form the combustible mass which the arts of the demagogue could kindle into the flames of discontent and agitation. Hence, in place of *public opinion*, a barrier of force and delusion—of standing armies, of well-paid ecclesiastics, and sinecure placemen, would be necessary to shield the ruling few against the ignorant and destitute many.

It is only by the exertions of the affluent, operating through the instrumentality of the poor-laws, that any great improvement in the condition of the labouring classes can be effected. The poor are too depressed, and too inert, to make voluntary efforts for bettering their lot. In all ages, and all countries we find they remain stationary, unless acted upon by the upper strata of society. In England, the course of social improvement has been *downwards*. Villanage was not abolished by the serfs, but chiefly by the interference of the rich and educated clergy. The foundations of civil liberty and constitutional government were not laid by the oppressed burghers of cities and towns, but by the feudal barons of the age of Magna Charta. In like manner, it is chiefly by the example, and almost coercive interference of the opulent and intelligent, that the state of the poor of our own day can be alleviated. The middle classes suffer from their vices and misery, and have, by the exaction of an assessment for their relief, a direct interest in inculcating in them right principles of conduct? and thus, a duty imposed upon them by justice and humanity, is further enforced by the excellence of a civil institution.[*]

Without a public provision for the needy, our laws would be inconsistent. Society, by its watchfulness over population, by its severe enactments against infanticide, abortion, and whatever may frustrate the multiplication of its members, tacitly binds itself to their general sustentation. A compulsory assessment for the more unfortunate may be considered a temporary provision raised for their maintenance during pupilage, till such time as they have become better acquainted with their real interests, and have acquired knowledge more suited to their domestic happiness and social importance.

Our poor-laws are often written and spoken of as if nothing analogous to them existed in any other country. " In Scotland," says Dr. Chalmers, " a sound interpretation of the law would educe as valid a right to relief from the statute-book of Scotland as

[*] The poor have been mostly found the great obstacle to the adoption of plans for their own benefit. Their hostility to the Reformation, is a case in point, and has been before remarked (p. 40). According to M. de Bussiere (*Voyage en Russie*, 1829), the abolition of slavery in Livonia, was resisted by the peasantry. The colliers and salters of the north were bondsmen till the year 1775, and did not feel grateful when their fetters were knocked off by the 15 Geo. III. c. 28. They were so far from desiring or prizing the blessing conferred on them, that they esteemed the interest taken in their freedom, to be a mere desire on the part of their proprietors to get rid of what they called head and Larigald money, payable to them when a female of their number, by bearing a child, made an addition to the *live stock* of their master's property.

from that of England." In France, besides numerous hospitals, a revenue is raised for the poor by
octrois, or dues on wine, cider, spirits, and other
articles of consumption, paid on their introduction
into towns. These are exclusive of winter collections, and occasional issues from the public treasury,
on the application of mayors and local magistrates.
In Denmark, Sweden, Norway, Switzerland, and the
Netherlands, a provision for the poor was made on
the extinction of feudality. In Prussia, Austria, and
I believe nearly the whole of the German states, not
only is a provision made for the relief of the poor,
but their education. Lastly, in the United States,
there are both paupers by law, and beggars and vagrants by connivance, as in England. In Boston
only (*North American Review*, No. 72, p. 181),
there are 2000 persons "who get their daily bread
by begging or fraud."

Experience is considered the best test, and the
English system of poor-laws will not suffer by its
application. The 43d of Elizabeth has been in operation since 1601, and what have been its results?
May not our population be advantageously compared with that of any other country in Europe?
Is the number of workpeople more disproportioned
to the means of subsistence and employment than in
Ireland, France, Germany, Holland, and Italy? Are
they less brave, less cleanly, less moral, less prudent,
less manly and independent? in short, do they not
possess every domestic and social virtue in at least
as great perfection as their neighbours? To these

questions I know every traveller will answer in the affirmative; and those who are not travellers will be able to answer in the same manner from the specimens of foreign production which are seeking to establish themselves amongst us.

Degraded as a pauper may be, he is at least an improvement on the beggar; and every one knows that mendicity is the only alternative in place of pauperism.

Had poor-laws been introduced into Ireland, would she have been in her present state? Many of her calamities have doubtless resulted from faction, misgovernment, and degrading superstition; but can it be supposed the gentry and priesthood would have suffered, nay, encouraged, her population to increase at such a fearful rate—to multiply in filth and rags—had the indigent, those who could neither obtain employment nor food, had a legal claim on their estates and income? Most assuredly not: they would have been incapable of such recklessness, such suicidal infatuation.

The different rates at which capital and population have increased in England and Ireland, during the last century, is chiefly ascribable to the difference in their civic economy, in the institution of poor-laws. Though capital has increased in Ireland, it is generally supposed by the best informed that it has not increased more than one-third or one-fourth so fast as in England; while on the other hand, the rate of increase of population in Ireland has been nearly quadruple the rate of its increase in

England. In 1730 the population of England and Wales was 5,796,000 ; in 1831 it had increased to 13,894,571, or rather more than doubled. In Ireland the population in 1731 was estimated at 2,010,221 ; in 1831 it amounted to 7,734,365, which has been almost a fourfold increase in the last century. The permanent surplus of labouring people has been estimated (*Parl. Papers,* vol. viii. p. 4. Sess. 1830) at one-fifth, and by Mr. Ensor at one-fourth of the entire population.

In short, Ireland affords an illustration of the main proposition I have sought to establish in favour of the poor-laws, namely, that the poor will either deteriorate or remain stationary in their degradation, unless acted upon by the classes immediately above them ; and the classes above them will never interest themselves about their welfare, unless stimulated thereto by the pressure of a compulsory assessment ; in other words, till they find their own security and enjoyments endangered by the misery and predial agitation by which they are surrounded.

IV —PERSONS ENTITLED TO PARISH RELIEF.

Having, in the last section, endeavoured to establish the policy of a compulsory provision for the poor, I shall next submit a few remarks on the description of persons to whom it ought to be restricted. Many who are in favour of a poor-rate are still inclined to keep the amount at a minimum, and

for this purpose have submitted the following suggestions : 1. That no case of distress shall be eligible
to relief unless it be casual, unavoidable, and such
as ordinary prudence could not foresee and avert.
2. That able-bodied labourers shall not be eligible
to relief merely because they cannot obtain employment.   3. That neither a wife nor child *per se*
shall constitute a claim to parish allowance.

Under the first class of exclusions, a claim, on account of old age, would be rejected ; since that is a
calamity which comes on a man by degrees, and can
always be foreseen.   Secondly, mere want of employment is often nothing more than one of those
occasional depressions in demand for labour arising
out of the changes of the seasons, or vicissitudes of
trade, which are of periodical occurrence, and which
workmen ought to be provided against.   Thirdly,
marriage is a voluntary act, for which the parties
have nobody but themselves to blame, and consequently cannot reasonably expect to escape the
burden they have deliberately brought upon themselves by throwing it on the shoulders of others.

It is obvious that all these cases of exclusion from
parish relief are founded—first, on the consideration that they are all cases of distress, which, by the
exercise of the prudential virtues, might be avoided :
secondly, on the consideration that by leaving such
cases of distress to what may be termed their *natural*
punishment, a powerful motive is created for the
exercise of the forethought by which they may be
avoided : and thirdly, that a public provision for

such cases of distress is really granting a bounty on imprudence.

My first remark on these deductions is, that before we rely on the prudential virtues as a provision for any description of indigence, we must be sure that such prudential virtues exist. If the habits of the poor are such as clearly indicate they do not exist, then they can neither be a remedy nor preventive of that specific evil for which the poor-laws provide. It is an error on which I have before enlarged, to suppose either that the poor-laws encourage an improvidence which would not prevail in the absence of such an institution, or that the absence of them would call into exercise an increase of prudence not before in operation. The class to whom the poor-laws are available, and for whom, in truth, they were intended, are never influenced by prospective considerations, they neither look backwards nor forwards: they form no useful resolves for the future from experience of the past, for they are equally regardless of both. It is among the working classes as it is indeed among every other class of the community, a certain portion of them are wholly reckless of consequences; either from defect of education or defect of nature, they have no habits of calculation and forethought; they live, every day as if it were their last, and never think what to-morrow may bring forth. This description does not apply to the whole of the working, any more than to the whole of the middle or upper orders of society. Perhaps of the entire class of operatives and labourers not more than one-fourth ever burden the parish at all; the remainder, by superior economy, management, and saving, make a provision for all the casualties to which they are exposed from sickness, age, or want of employment. It is not for these the poor-laws were designed, but for the smaller portion who are unfortunately not endowed with similar habits, and whose existence I contend in society is wholly uninfluenced by the poor-laws, but for whom I think it is better a compulsory provision should be made, than they should be left to resort to those extremities which without it would be their only resource.

The poor-laws have not been instituted for the relief of the destitute merely, but for the general *peace and security* of the community. They are not only an institution of charity but of POLICE, to shield society from the evils of mendicity and crime. If we exclude the aged in distress, or the able-bodied in want of work from the scope of their operation, we fail to obtain one great object of their establishment. Cases of distress will arise from these causes, and how are they to be met? The sufferers will not *starve;* therefore they must either beg or steal, or be relieved. If we tolerate the first in ever so limited a degree we open a door for the admission of the greatest evil the poor-laws were meant to exclude; and if mendicity be allowed in conjunction with a poor-rate the community is at once afflicted with both. Therefore I say let there be no pretext either for begging or stealing; let the poor-laws embrace every case of absolute destitution whether it arise from old age or want of employment; if the latter is occasioned by idleness or criminal misconduct there are laws to punish the offender, and it is the fault of the magistrate or parish officer if they be not enforced.

Whether the destitution for which the poor-laws provide arises from improvidence or unavoidable necessity, is not so important a consideration as that persons and property should be shielded from all pretext of violation; and the security of these, and the justice and humanity of the laws by which they are guaranteed I esteem wholly incompatible with any large portion of the community being in a state of extreme misery without resource or means of alleviation.

It will now be seen that I am a decided advocate of the famous national institution of the Elizabethan age; but though an advocate of the policy of the poor-laws, I am neither an advocate of the abuses in the laws themselves, nor in their practical administration.

V.—IMPROVEMENTS IN THE POOR-LAWS.

The *law of settlement* interferes with the free circulation of labour from one part of the country to another, and has long been the reproach of legislation. Why should a man's claim to relief depend on the circumstance that he was born here or his mother there; or that he was apprenticed in this place or resided a year in that. What puerile distinctions —profitable only to lawyers—for the inhabitants of the same community, living under the same laws, and under the same government. An Englishman is an Englishman, whether a native of Cornwall or Westmorland, and he ought to be eligible to relief as much in one place as the other.

The enormous number and complexity of the poor-laws, chiefly arise from the conflicting rights of settlement; they are the source of endless disputes, and the most costly portion of parochial litigation, and by the frauds, tricks, and conspiracies to which they give rise among parish officers, and the cruelties sometimes perpetrated in the removal of paupers, contribute greatly to bring into disrepute, this branch of our civil institutions. This is by no means the extent of the evil. The practice of *hiring for a year*, by which the master became bound to maintain his servant for a twelvemonth, in sickness or in health, is not so common in husbandry labour as formerly; either there is no legal hiring at all, or the servant is engaged for a term less than a year, by which his claim to a settlement is evaded. A similar practice, and for a similar purpose, prevails in the letting of houses; if the rent exceeds ten pounds per annum, they are often let for a shorter term than a year, or a private understanding is entered into with the tenant by the landlord, regulating the mode of paying the rent, so that the claim of the former, in consequence of his occupancy, may be frustrated. In some towns (Hastings to wit), printed

directions are circulated among the inhabitants, instructing them in the *art* of hiring servants, letting
houses, and managing apprentices, so that no settlement in the parish may be created: thus, some of
the most salutary usages of life, and even the management of property, are superseded and interfered
with by the settlement laws.

In lieu of the existing diversified claims, it would
be better to substitute a uniform principle, and
what better could be adopted, than that which should
found the right to parochial relief of all male adults,
solely on *residence* in one parish for a determinate
period ; leaving children and married women to derive their settlements from their parents or husbands,
as at present.

The *unequal size of parishes* is another obstacle
in the practical administration of the poor-laws. The
magnitude of parishes is neither founded on property,
population, nor territorial extent. In the North, the
area of parishes is quadruple what it is in the south
of England. In some parishes there are no inhabitants,
in others, not more than a dozen or a hundred ; in
others again, a hundred thousand and upwards.
These discrepancies should be reconciled. A legislative measure which would new-model the parochial
divisions of the kingdom, would be of immense social
benefit, not only in the administration of the poor-
laws, but as the basis of national police, judicature,
and municipal government.

The unequal pressure of the poor assessment ; and
the disproportionate weight with which it falls on real

chattel property, forms a just subject of complaint. Professions, manufactures, and trade are among the principal sources of revenue; yet, the maintenance of the poor scarcely touches them, which is the less defensible, when we consider that the two last are the most fruitful sources of pauperism. The nature of this evil will be evident, from the following statement, exhibiting the allocation of the rates levied, in the year ending March 25th, 1826, showing the proportional parts raised on land, dwelling-houses, &c.

Property.	Amount Levied.	Parts of 1000	
Land	£ 4,795,482	688	
Dwelling-houses . .	1,814,228	261	
Mills, Factories, &c.	259,565	37	
Manorial Profits . .	96,882	14	Parl. Pap. No. 52,
Total . . £	6,966,157	1000	Sess. 1830.

The chief argument relied upon in the defence of this allocation of the poor and county rates is, that the possessors of property bought or inherited their possessions subject to the poor assessment, and they have no more right to complain of its pressure or inequality, than they have to complain of the pressure or inequality of the land-tax, or other fixed burden with which their estates are charged. The assessment too, is said to be expedient as well as just : for the owners and occupiers of land and houses are those only, who have the power over the *increase of population ;* and, by laying the burden of providing for and managing the poor wholly upon them, they are prompted, not only to take measures for economizing the funds for their support, but to prevent a too rapid increase in the numbers of the labouring classes.

Passing over the latter part of this reasoning, I may observe, that the former part does not exactly meet the objection. The poor-rate is a variable assessment, and many estates have suddenly become liable to a great additional charge, solely from the circumstance of being in the neighbourhood of newly-created commercial or manufacturing establishments, which have drawn to the spot a great increase of workpeople. These establishments may yield princely revenues to the owners; they may realize immense profits from the labours of the persons they employ; while the owners and occupiers of land and houses in their vicinity, who do not benefit by them, are almost exclusively sufferers from their existence, in the increased burdens they entail upon them in the maintenance of the diseased, aged, maimed, and impotent, that they multiply in their parishes.

A poor rate, assessed in proportion to the number of persons employed by the owners of mills, factories, and mercantile establishments, would tend to adjust the unequal pressure of the poor assessment. But to this modification it has been objected, that it would operate as a *tax* on workpeople, and thereby discourage their employment.* It may be further remarked in favour of the commercial and manufactur-

---

* Report on the Poor-laws, *Parl. Papers*, vol. vi. 1817.

ing classes, that if their establishments tend to increase the poor-rates, they more than compensate
the owners of property, by the increased value they
give to land and houses in their neighbourhood.

It has been proposed (*Quarterly Review*, No. 96)
that the parish assessment should be levied on one uniform rate ; say in proportion of full rental for lands,
and three-fourths of rental for buildings; or three-
fourths the rack rental of lands, and two-thirds
buildings.   At present, every parish has a different
principle; so that parliamentary returns of poor-rates
can only give deceptive information as to the real
proportion of the sum raised, to the value of the
property assessed.

Another suggestion for the improvement of the
poor-laws has been thus set forth :

It would be of the greatest advantage, some alteration
should take place in the law, so as to allow the *owner* of rated
property, or his agent, considerable power in laying on the rate,
and administering it when raised; in which case, the owner
should contribute a certain proportion of the rate : at present it
is under the sole control of the occupier, who pays the whole.
The tenant occupier has not the same permanent interest in the
proper management of the rate as the owner has : if the *rates increase, the tenant on each fresh letting will make this a ground for
a diminished rent*, and often thinks it is his interest to keep
wages as low as possible, however high the rates may thereby
be raised ; and this accounts for some of the abuses prevalent in
several counties of the south of England.   If the owner paid a
proportion of the rate, its increase would be a salutary warning
to him, that some attention to the subject was necessary, and
his interest would direct him to improve the condition of the
workmen, as the only true and permanent mode of keeping the

rates low. In ordinary cases, and in agricultural districts, it is a general rule, that rates and wages vary inversely to each other : if wages are high, rates are low ; and if rates are high, wages are low.   In Scotland, the rate is laid on by the heritors only, or their agents, in conjunction with the clergymen, and paid in equal portions by heritor and occupier, and expended by the minister and kirk session.—*Hints on the Practical Administration of the Poor-laws,* p. 4.

Whether the advantages of this alteration would countervail its accompanying evils, it is difficult to determine; it appears liable to three objections : 1. By letting a new class into the working of the poor-laws, it might impede and complicate their practical administration.   2. The tenant-occupier is on the *spot ;* he is in immediate contact with the poor; is acquainted with their habits and character, and is likely to manage them more judiciously than the landlord or his agent, who is probably an absentee from the parish, and moves in a more elevated sphere of life.   3. It would not create additional interest in the welfare of the labouring classes, not now substantially possessed by the owners of property.   The writer admits that an increase in parish rates is made a ground, on the part of the tenant, for the payment of a diminished rent; so that the owner is indirectly interested, at least, as much as if he paid a portion of the rates in all the circumstances that influence the condition of the working classes.

One advantage, it must be conceded, would result from the greater interference of the landlords in the management of the poor.   They would bring a wider experience and more general principles to the task than is now usually combined in the practical administration of the poor-laws: but even this they have opportunities for communicating to their tenants on the rent-day, or in their more appropriate functions of magistrates.

It is unnecessary, however, to dilate further on this proposition; as government has appointed a commission expressly for the purpose of considering the improvements of which this branch of public economy is susceptible, no doubt the suggestion I have just noticed will obtain a due share of consideration.

VI.—PRACTICAL HINTS RELATIVE TO THE POOR AND THE ADMINISTRATION OF THE POOR-LAWS.

I have now stated the chief reasons I have to urge in favour of the poor-laws, and suggested some alterations in them. The general conviction at which I have arrived is, that under an enlightened administration they might be made more conducive than any other system to the diminution of indigence and its consequences, pauperism and mendicity. To show how these ends may be attained, I shall submit a few suggestions, according to which, in my opinion, the relief and management of the poor might be improved.

1. The parish allowance ought never to compete with, or be an equivalent for the fair wages of labour. It ought to be the interest of *no person* who can get employment to be a pauper; the lowest wages of the

lowest labourer ought to be better than parish pay.
Upon this principle, the parish would never be a covert for idleness and imposture ; the able-bodied
would never seek it to augment their comforts and
ease, in preference to a dependence on their own industry ; and it would become what it ought to
be, only a resource for those who are willing, but
otherwise unable to maintain themselves.

2. Parish allowance is nothing more than a *charitable dole*, and the person who is reduced so low
as to be necessitated to accept the gratuitous bounty
of his fellow-men, cannot justly claim the full exercise of his *personal rights*.   As he is maintained by
the public, he can have no right to prescribe the
mode of that maintenance, either as respects his
clothing, diet, lodging, habitation, or employment.
Whatever regulations a parish may consider it expedient to frame in respect of these, in order to economise the parochial expenditure and lessen the rates,
they have perfect right to enforce, provided such regulations are unaccompanied with any hardship inconsistent with the legal objects of the poor-laws, to
grant relief to the destitute.

3. Two essential points to be kept constantly
in view are, first, not to augment the number of the
pauper or dependant class of labourers ; and secondly, not to resort to any expedient for creating
employment, which may lessen the amount of work
already in existence for the employed and independent class of workpeople.   The first would be a
direct aggravation of the evil against which society

is contending; and the last would be curing one inconvenience by the creation of another of equal magnitude.   Home colonization is liable to the former objection, inasmuch as it tends to establish, under an organized and permanent system, an intermediate grade of pauperism, while the object is to reduce pauperism to its lowest amount.   New employments, however, might be found which would neither augment the mass of pauperism, nor interfere with the employed labourer.   In both town and country parishes there is a great deal of work, and many undertakings that are not entered upon from unwillingness to pay the current wages of labour ; but it would be better for parish officers to contract for the execution of labour of this description at less than its current price, as a temporary means of finding employment for their paupers, than that they should be kept in total idleness.   No one can have observed the state of the roads, footpaths, courts, lanes, alleys, and sewers, of the metropolis, without being convinced of the immense quantity of additional labour that might be exerted with benefit to the public.   Parishes, with unemployed paupers on their hands, and without any of the work to execute to which I allude, might enter into agreements with adjoining parishes differently situated.   In improving the estates of gentlemen, and on the property of most private persons, more or less of this sort of work might be found.   The principle of such employment must be strictly adhered to, the parish must not be a competitor with either the employer or the employed in the market of labour; it must give less remuneration to the pauper than the regular workman receives; and it must execute no work at the under price, except such as without its interference would have remained unexecuted. A parliamentary committee might be usefully employed in examining witnesses, and making inquiries into the best mode of creating additional employment beneficial to the community. If the field for their exertion is not so extensive in England, it is well known to be almost boundless in Ireland.

4. The circumstance of an applicant having money in a savings-bank, or being entitled to the benefits of a friendly society, ought not of itself to disqualify him for parish relief. The idle and dissolute ought not to be alone eligible to a public provision from which the frugal and provident are excluded. Such a principle holds out a salutary encouragement to the industrious, and is not likely to be abused; as no person who had been considerate enough to become either a depositor in a savings-bank or member of a benefit society, would become a claimant on the parish without pressing necessity.

5. The maintenance of a *high price* for labour has been proved to be the main source of happiness and independence to the poor; all other schemes of alleviation are illusive or transitory, and tend only to multiply and degrade them. Keeping the market under-stocked with labour is the philosopher's stone, that gives them the command of a commodity which they can always transmute into money, food, or

raiment. Whatever, therefore, has this tendency whether it arise from regulations among the industrious themselves, or from opening new channels of trade and employment, or from schemes of emigration, and backwardness to enter into the married state, ought to be encouraged, as effective means for relieving and improving the state of the working classes.

6. As a corollary to the last principle, it may be urged that the policy of legislators and magistrates ought to incline to a *high* rather than a *low* rate of wages. Wages that do not afford to the working classes a command over the necessaries of life, tend to generate habits and feelings, not only inimical to their own improvement, but to the peace and security of the community. Hence combinations among masters to reduce wages, or attempts by manufacturers, tradesmen, and shopkeepers, to undersell each other, by reducing the wages of their servants, ought to be discountenanced by the general feeling of society, as inimical to the common weal. No regard for the advancement of foreign commerce should be allowed to interfere with the operation of this principle : " for where," as justly observed, " is the national advantage of an extension of foreign trade, which fills our workhouses with idle paupers, for the sake of clothing the continental peasantry with cheap calico."

7. Next in importance to keeping wages high is keeping food *cheap*. Hence the objectionable nature of taxes that keep up the price of bread, malt,

soap, and other common necessaries of the industrious classes.   Mr. Pitt used to say that the high
price of labour in England arose chiefly from the
excise ; three-fourths of the wages of a poor man
passing into the exchequer.

8. The administration of the poor-laws ought to
be confided to paid officers who have no personal
interest to serve incompatible with their duty.   They
ought also to be well versed in the principles of the
laws they administer, and familiar with the habits
and manners of the labouring classes.   Every order
of society has its characteristics, with which those
only can be familiar who belong to it, or at least
have had an opportunity for their observance.   It
would be thought absurd to make a landsman a captain of a ship's company, or a civilian commander
of a regiment of soldiers ; it is quite as preposterous
to choose many persons who are chosen for overseers—an office, the duties of which are as complex,
and require as much tact in the execution as those
of a police justice in the metropolis.   Hence arises
the utility of permanent overseers, paid by the
parish, and responsible to the parish for their conduct.

9.   Magistrates ought to use great caution in
ordering relief, lest they countenance imposture or
interfere injudiciously with the duties of parish officers.   The latter too require almost as strict watching as the paupers themselves.   The proneness of
parish officers to jobbing—reciprocal connivance at
each others misdeeds—lavish charges for pretended

parochial services—waste of the parish funds in sumptuous entertainments—are notorious delinquencies, requiring unceasing vigilance in the vestry and auditors.

10. The defective state of national police hardly admits of proceeding with either humanity or efficiency in the extirpation of *common begging;* but it is certain that without the enforcement of the Vagrant Act we shall be overrun with mendicity as much as if we had no poor-laws whatever, and thus a main purpose of their institution be frustrated. From the inquiries of a parliamentary committee, in 1815, it was ascertained that gross and monstrous frauds are practised by mendicants in the metropolis; the success of which affords a direct encouragement to vice and idleness, as much more is gained by importunate solicitations in the streets for charity than is earned by the industrious artisan by his utmost application to the work in which he is employed. As the number of beggars has not decreased, and their craft is carried on upon nearly the same principles, I shall insert a digest of the results of the committee's inquiries, from the Report on the State of Mendicity in the Metropolis.—*Parl. Pap.* *No.* 396, Sess. 1816.

Beggars on being searched when brought before the magistrates, a great deal of money has been found about them, in their pockets and in their clothes.

Beggars make great profits by various practices, such as changing their clothes two or three times a day, and getting money intended for others. Clear proof that a blind man, with a dog, got 30s. in one day. Another man got 5s. a day; he could, with ease, go through sixty streets in a day.   Another got 6*s.* a day.

A negro beggar retired to the West Indies with a fortune, it was supposed, of 1500*l.*

Beggars gain 3*s.* or 4*s.* a day by begging shoes.

A woman alleged that she could go through sixty streets in a day, and that it was a bad street that did not yield a penny.

Children are made use of to excite compassion.

Beggars are furnished with children at houses in White-chapel and Shoreditch; some, who look like twins, frequently carried on their backs.   Children frequently sent out to beg, and not to return with less than 6*d.*

A girl of twelve years of age had been six years engaged in begging; on some days got 3*s.* or 4*s.*; sometimes more, usually 18*d.* or 1*s.*; on Christmas-day, 4*s.* 6*d.*

One man will collect three, four, or five children from different parts, paying 6*d.* or 9*d.* each, to go begging with them.

A woman with twins, who never *grew older*, sat for ten years. Not once in a hundred times twins are the children of beggars.

A night school, kept by an old woman, for instructing children in the language of beggars.

In the neighbourhood of St. Giles's thirty or forty houses, apparently crowded, in which are not less than 2000 people, one-half of whom live by prostitution and beggary: the remainder Irish labouring people.   The rector of St. Clement Danes described them as living very well: especially if they are pretty well *maimed, blind*, or if they have *children*.

The *begging walks are sold.*

Worthy persons, however distressed, will not have recourse to begging.   Street-beggars, with very few exceptions, are utterly worthless and incorrigible.   Beggars evade the Vagrant Act by carrying matches and articles of little intrinsic value for sale.   Out of 400 beggars in St. Giles's, 350 are capable of earning their own living.

11. The principles of the poor-laws are intimately connected with those of police and popular instruc-

tion; in lieu of fostering vice, idleness, and improvidence, they ought to be so administered as to be instrumental in their prevention and discouragement.

12. In granting and apportioning allowances the utmost discrimination is required. The really unfortunate should be promptly relieved, but the clamours of idleness and profligacy firmly resisted. Improvident workmen are a prolific source of pauperism; many of these have high wages sufficient to enable them to make a provision for periods of sickness or scarcity of work, but they are wasted in folly and extravagance, and immediately they are unemployed they fall upon the parish. Relief to these should be afforded by way of loan as directed by 59 Geo. III. c. 12, s. 29, and steps taken to recover the loan when the borrower is in circumstances to repay it.*

13. Suggestions of economy and better management may be frequently offered with advantage, and all useful institutions, especially intended for the benefit of the working classes, as infant schools, savings-banks, and friendly societies, should be encouraged and recommended. By acting on these and similar maxims the most beneficial results have

* Mr. Kershaw, one of the overseers for Greenwich last year, gave me the following classification of their paupers: 1. Improvident workmen of the description mentioned in the text. 2. Tramps, chiefly Irish. 3. Hereditary paupers. 4. Sailors' and fishermens' wives. 5. Illegitimate children. 6. Regular pensioners to whom allowances are paid. 7. Hospital paupers. 8. Lunatics.

been obtained, as witness the reductions in the parish expenditure of Liverpool, Southwell, Maidenhead, and Hatfield. In Liverpool the following change was effected, though the population had increased 10,000 in the interval: in 1821, 4717 paupers cost 360,136*l.*; in 1827, only 2607 paupers cost 193,956*l.* — *Evidence of Mr. Ellis before Poor-law Committee,* 1828. See also Mr. Day's *Inquiry,* p. 22.

The settlement law and the tendency of the allowance system have been before noticed p. 89 & 390. I shall conclude with an abstract of the *Hints on the Administration of the Poor-laws,* contained in a tract published under the superintendence of the Society for the Diffusion of Useful Knowledge.

1. A permanent overseer should be chosen, acting under the control of the annual overseers; and if the parish be large, a select or managing vestry.

2. An efficient workhouse and poor-house should be established; they are often united, but are better separated for the purpose of classification.

3. The aged poor are mostly depraved and incorrigible; parish children should be kept separate from them, instructed in arts likely to be useful in after life, and educated upon the plan of the infant schools, where health, recreation, and tuition, adapted to their years, are promoted.

4. Parish officers should keep constantly before them the 43d Eliz. c. 2, s. 1 (see page 356), bearing in mind that the fundamental object of the poor-laws is *setting to work* all who are able, and not maintaining any in idleness; many even of the infirm poor may be able to do some work, and so much work should be required from each as is compatible with health.

5. Parishes are liable to much imposition, and careful inquiry should precede and accompany allowances to out-dwellers.

6. To every applicant the parish should have the option of

granting an allowance or a residence in the poor-house.[*]   There is nothing the idle and disorderly dread so much as the strict discipline, scanty fare, and hard work, that ought to be enforced in every workhouse.   Relief, however, may be sometimes granted to the infirm who reside with relatives or friends; so also that temporary assistance which the able-bodied poor occasionally require may be often most advantageously afforded at their own houses.

7. An offer of the poor-house will cause many applicants to shift for themselves, or if they accept an abode there, leave it after experiencing its regulations; so that the expense of the poor-house is not to be estimated by the cost of its inmates alone, but by the saving it effects in restricting the application of the parish rates solely to the necessitous.

8. The granting of allowances in aid of wages, and in consideration of children, tends to lower the price of labour and stimulate population by the encouragement it offers to marriage.

In conclusion I shall remark, that though it is unlikely " the poor will ever cease out of the land," yet a large portion of existing pauperism might have assuredly been averted by better habits in the people and more wisdom in the classes immediately above them. The poor are not wholly to blame for their vices. Without instruction in the principles which influence their condition, without examples of economy, order, and forethought in their early years, they have not

* The granting of allowances in place of an abode in the workhouse is reckoned in the *Parliamentary Report of 1817* (p. 7) among the chief causes of the increase of pauperism. The allowance system began in 1795, under 36 Geo. III. c. 22, extended by 55 Geo. III. c. 22, and is unquestionably the bot-bed of fraudulent pauperism.   But by a reference to the statement, page 363, it will be remarked that pauperism had made rapid strides prior to the prevalence of the allowance system.

an opportunity to become in after life any thing more than children in understanding, and it not unfrequently happens that the most kind and generous hearts among them are those least gifted with the saving virtues by which the miseries of future penury and want may be averted. They are the orphans of society to whom every indulgence compatible with their own welfare should be extended. If they have been ignorant of their duties, the rich have neglected theirs. How can it be supposed the labouring man, doomed to unceasing toil, can discover those hidden causes of poverty which for thousands of years escaped even the scrutiny of the philosopher. It is not parish officers, clergymen, and magistrates only to whom the weal of the poor ought to be confided; upon every employer of workpeople is imposed a solemn duty next to that he owes his own family, to learn himself and explain to those dependant upon him, the origin of social distress arising from bad habits, excess of population, changes of the seasons, and periodical vicissitudes in trade. It is only in this manner popular education can be made universal, and knowledge really useful disseminated through the community.

PART III.

POLITICAL PHILOSOPHY.

CHAP. I.

INTRODUCTION.

Progress of Political Philosophy—General Principles—Rousseau, Godwin, Bentham, Mill, Paley, Burke, and Paine—Effects of the French Revolution on the Practice of Governments—Misapplication of Abstract Propositions.

SOCIETY is now about five or six thousand years old. Its institutions, laws, manners, and usages, are the results of that lengthened term of experience. It is in human nature to seek to replace evil by good, to substitute something better in lieu of the worse which preceded it; what, then, we now possess, defective as it may be, is the fruit of all the generations that have gone before us.

I mention the age of society to contrast it with the age of an individual, and to show how mistaken that man must be who thinks that within the short

span of his own existence, within the contracted
sphere of his own observance, and by the help of his
own single faculties, he can devise any system, or
propound any idea, that shall not supersede, but
even materially alter the social fabric which is older
than the pyramids, and nearly as aged as the hills ;
and which has descended to us as the product of all
the wisdom that has successively appeared at Thebes,
Athens, Rome, London, and Paris. Yet individuals
have laboured under this delusion, who thought they
were wiser than nature and all her works, though
themselves but an atom—a short-lived atom—in the
universe !

This retrospection is not introduced to imply that
establishments of any kind derive authority from age,
or to recommend mere antiquity in place of principle, but to suggest two useful considerations—one
corrective, the other consolatory. First, it must
show the error of those who think immediately, and
by their individual efforts, to alter the moral and
political institutions of mankind ; those institutions
that have been the growth of centuries, and the
creation of successive races of men as far beyond
their contemporaries in benevolence and science as
they themselves can assume to be. Secondly, it
must be consolatory and encouraging to future perseverance to think that every endeavour at social
improvement may not be fruitless ; that its apparent
insignificance may only result from the greatness of
the undertaking ; and that the smallest additional
amendment to the vast and complicated pile of

human association, may be a service of inestimable price. A philosopher, who, by the labours of a long life, has succeeded in removing a single error in education, morals, or jurisprudence, has done enough to entitle him to be enrolled with honour in the calendar of man's benefactors.

It is, doubtless, experience of the deceitfulness of the more general and dazzling schemes of social improvement that has tended to make new systems of political philosophy as little fashionable as new systems of physical science. They promise much, and perform little. They assume to embrace the present, and lay the foundations of the future; but they are often only the illusions of a mental phantasmagoria, and vanish from the touch when submitted to the test of utility. It is sufficient for each generation to contend with the evils that immediately environ it; leaving posterity to do the same, and to adopt their own remedies. Every project is an experiment, all the effects of which actual trial can only manifest; there is a risk of loss as well as gain; and why should any age run this risk without a present and well-defined necessity for sake of a future that may never come, or come in a shape wholly different from anticipation?

Philosophers are often as extravagant in their way as the empirical teacher, and require to be as narrowly watched. They discover a valuable principle, but bring it into discredit by their eagerness to compass all things within its influence. They are bigoted in their science as enthusiasts are in religion, and

frequently as intolerant in the maintenance of their
dogmas. Like the Pope of Rome, nothing less than
universal faith will satisfy them : within their pale,
there is salvation ; without it, nought but perdition.
They are right, so far as they can see ; but the misfortune is, there is something beyond which they cannot see, and which their theory does not embrace.

The abandonment of the school philosophy, which
was founded on no induction whatever, but simply
on the conceits of the mind, was an important step
in the progress of knowledge. Next to that is the
practical wisdom which limits the application of
principles to their legitimate issues : the error of the
schoolmen was to build on no foundation at all ;
the error next in degree is to build on one too narrow. The practical evil of dogmatism in social philosophy is the ambition to solve all moral phenomena
by the application of one exclusive principle, while
the complicated interests of life require the co-operative agency of many. It is difficult to say whether
the abstract propositions of ROUSSEAU have done
more harm or good to European society. His *Social
Contract* contains useful maxims depreciated by
tinsel paradoxes. I cite one of the latter for illustration : " *Man* is born *free*, yet is every where *in
fetters*" (b. 1, c. 1). Here we see how many truths
are sacrificed to a bold assertion. No *man* was ever
born at all, unless Adam can be considered such,
who proceeded in full maturity from the hands of
his Maker. Secondly, how is " man born *free* ?"—
what is the freedom he derives from birth ? Born

on the banks of the Neva, his birthright is to be punished with the knout, at the pleasure of the czar; or on the Bosphorus, to be bow-stringed at the command of the sultan? Then where are the "fetters" that bind us? May not a Londoner or Parisian be *levant* or *couchant*, just as he pleases? may he not do whatever he lists, provided it does not injure other people?—and would even a savage—the favourite biped of the Genevese philosopher—be able with impunity to do more?

Ah, John James Rousseau, how much better you would have been occupied, if, in place of grinding such startling abstractions, you had aided your contemporaries of the *Encyclopædia*, in pointing out fiscal, judicial, and ecclesiastic abuses; and in demonstrating the utility of religious toleration, of freedom of inquiry, and popular education; and which, in spite of your eloquence and egotism, they were mainly instrumental in establishing!

The mantle of Rousseau has been taken up by some of our own countrymen, but the spread of popular knowledge abates the power of philosophical enthusiasm as well as religious fanaticism.

Mr. GODWIN poured out in sixteen months (Preface, p. 7, 2d edit. 1796) his *Inquiry concerning Political Justice*, as he would a novel from the fulness of the heart and imagination, almost without reference to a single fact, authority, or standing principle. What has been the result? A congeriei of impassioned notions which portray the author much better than society either as it is, can, or probably ever will be.*

Social errors and abuses that abridge happiness are many, but he would be a rash surveyor who should pull down a building to come at the cobwebs and decayed timber. " The talent for destroying," says Mirabeau, " is the reverse of the art of reforming; it is the heroism of the suicide. An ignorant surgeon will amputate the limb, which the science of Esculapius would have cured." — *L'Ami des Hommes*, p. 143. Society is only another term for laws, manners, and usages; they are the fruits of experience, each of which has been devised to remedy a specific and pre-existing evil. The institution of marriage, the rights of property and of persons were doubtless intended to obviate the evils of promiscuous intercourse, of injustice, and oppression. To abrogate them would be to abandon the chief conquests civilization has made from the waste of barbarism, it would be like suffering the earth to return to a state of desolation after being reclaimed and fertilized by human industry.

The minds of Godwin and Jeremy Bentham pre-

* Mr. Godwin still lives, and far be it from me to offer any unpleasant observation on so extraordinary, independent, and elevated a mind. But his work on Population, as well as his Political Justice, show that he is not an inductive philosopher. His power is in Caleb Williams, Fleetwood, Mandeville, and other creations of the imagination, by which he has delightfully interested the writer of this with innumerable others in Europe and America.

sent a singular contrast. They are the extremes of two opposite systems. During their protracted terms of existence they may be said to have flowed down side by side, like two parallel streams, without ever mingling together.* One has been the expounder of sentiment, the other of reason. The intellect of Mr. Bentham was purely inductive; but if I may venture an opinion on so great an authority, I should say his deductions were sometimes derived from too limited a circle of facts. He included in his moral equations the chief impulses of our nature, but he left out minor and perhaps inappreciable quantities which in actual life determine the course of human actions. Let us try this observation by an example from the writings of one of his most distinguished disciples.

" The position," says Mr. Mill, " which we have already established with regard to human nature, and which we assume as foundations are these: that the actions of men are governed by their wills, and their wills by their desires; that their desires are directed to pleasure and relief from pain as *ends*, and to wealth and power as the principal means; that to the desire of these means there is no limit, and that the actions which flow from that desire are the constituents whereof bad government is made."
—*Sup. to the Ency. Brit.*, art. *Government*, p. 496.

* This is literally as well as metaphorically true. Mr. Godwin often sought an interview with Bentham, but the latter declined, calling the author of *Political Justice* an " ambidexter," or some other hard name.

Now these deductions are all important and all true, but I doubt whether they embrace the *whole* truth.   For instance, it is difficult to reconcile one's practical observance of the world with the affirmation that men's desires are directed to pleasure and relief from pain as *ends,* and to wealth and power as the principal means.   A large portion of mankind seem to live without *ends ;* they are carried through life by the mere impulse of habit or appetite, and beyond that never calculate.   Wealth is toiled after, not with a view to present or future gratification, but merely from the habit of accumulation, a restless desire to repeat to-day the routine of yesterday.   Power is sought not as an instrument of indulgence, or means of making others subservient to our desires, but often only to establish an opinion, reduce a principle to practice, or to better or injure some class of society with which personally we are wholly unconnected.   How many there are who really seem to court *pain* rather than *pleasure ;* they abandon security, repose, and indulgence, for danger, hardship, and privation ; while again others are intently occupied in efforts to possess themselves of the very advantages the former relinquish.   Emulation and fame are great motives to exertion ; we make prodigious sacrifices to induce men to talk of us whom we can never hear, nor see, nor know.   " The object of all," said Frederick the Great, " was *pour faire parler de soi.*"   In what does the pleasure or pain of this consist ? It consists, I apprehend, in neither, but it is the action of another principle of our nature, solely intended to put us in motion like the principle of gravity to move bodies. Posthumous fame can in no sense be considered a pleasure to the owner, because he to whom it appertains is wholly unconscious of its existence. Yet many live for this alone. May we not conclude, then, that other impulses in addition to pleasures and pains influence human conduct? It is true, the motives I have indicated may be included under the heads of pleasure and pain, but to this extension of application I must object : if the ordinary understanding of words is not adhered to, if writers may be allowed to give their own arbitrary interpretation of their meaning, there is no sort of paradoxes a little verbal ingenuity may not establish. Language is perverted from its office, and confusion and misapprehension introduced into all our reasonings.

Beside the writers who have sought to reduce political philosophy to a few general principles, there are others who have endeavoured to give it a more practical form, by combining theory with the institutions of life.

The principal and most recent of these is Dr. PALEY. Had not Paley been a churchman, and it has been said a worldly-minded churchman too, he would have made an unexceptionable teacher of ethical and social science. His style is clear and strong ; his illustrations apt and striking ; his judgment searching and judicious : but his theology often fetters his mind and perverts his applications. He labours to execute a task which is hardly within the reach of human power to accomplish, namely, to reconcile the deductions of reason with the precepts of revelation. The shrewd and practical sense of Paley is evinced in the manner he has availed himself of the writings of Rousseau, in his *Principles of Moral and Political Philosophy ;* having incorporated many of the most valuable propositions of that singular author, divested of their extravagance and affectation.

The writings of Paley were, perhaps, as appropriate to the state of society in England as those of Dr. Franklin were to the circumstances of America. One wrote for an old, the other for a new community : the situation of the latter is like that of a friendless individual commencing life ; success depends on industry, frugality, probity, and perseverance ; order, economy, a saving of time, and a saving of money, constitute the stamina of the philosophy of Franklin, and it was suitable to the condition of his countrymen. Both Paley and Franklin were men of eminent benevolence ; they saw the evils which afflicted their fellow-creatures, and endeavoured by simple and efficacious precepts to alleviate them.

The fate of EDMUND BURKE has been unfortunate. Nature intended him for a professor of wisdom, while accident or the necessities of his fortune constrained him to be a politician : the result has been, that he does not hold a distinguished rank in either capacity. As practical statesmen, Mr. Fox and Mr. Pitt were superior to him ; while he was superior to them as the oracle of general principles : but so conflicting are the latter in his writings, and so distorted by his imagination and eloquence, that few think of resorting to them as authority. The transition from private to public life has mostly an extraordinary effect, and Mr. Burke was not exempt from its influence; in the former, when uninfluenced by passion, connexion, and personal interest, general maxims are advocated as the rule of conduct; in the latter, when the application of them has become impracticable or inconvenient, they are decried as the exception.

By a natural association of ideas one is carried from Mr. Burke to his celebrated opponent and contemporary, the author of the *Rights of Man*. The intellectual powers of THOMAS PAINE must have been considerable, to enable him to give even transient popularity to schemes of government, founded on a few abstract principles, without reference to the previous habits, education, and institutions of society. He saw the pendulum of the clock, but not the other mechanism, by which the permanence and steadiness of its motion are maintained. For the practice he gave the theory of civil immunities. On the other hand, in the writings of Mr. Bentham, forms of government are considered a practical question; the extent of popular rights and system of rule are considered *means to an end*, which may vary with the circumstances of communities, provided the end itself be attained,—the greatest happiness of the greatest number. The error of Paine— if error it be—was an error of inexperience, common among the most enlightened and best intentioned at

2 E 2

the time he wrote.   It may be doubted whether this
ingenious writer was so steadfast in his political
principles as some of his followers have been in the
adoption of them.   After the publication of his
Rights of Man it is well known he became obnoxious to the jacobins by his *moderation* in voting
against the death of Louis XVI.   His opinions appear not to have been reiterated in any subsequent
production of his pen, and it is impossible to ascertain how far they may have been modified by experience and reflection.   It is not impossible he may
have lived to be little more than a WHIG in politics ;
and had the apostle of republicanism encountered
in America the apostle of Chivalry, the long interval that once divided them, I doubt not would have
been found greatly abridged by mutual approximation.

It detracts much from the value of all writings on
the philosophy of politics anterior to the nineteenth
century, that their authors had not the full benefit
of the experience which the French revolution
afforded.   That great struggle was a series of experiments in the art of governing mankind, and solved
a hundred problems, which before had only been
matters of paper speculation.   In social science it
has been as important as the compass in navigation,
and has enabled men not only to see the goal to be
attained, but the dangers to be avoided in reaching
it.   Two results of great value may be satisfactorily
deduced from the truths it elicited.   First, that the
science of government is a practical question,—a
system of rules not to be derived once and for ever

from the mind of any individual, however ingenious, but to be gradually adapted to the character, usages, and knowledge of the people for whom they are intended.

A second deduction may be made more important to public happiness than the first. Before the French revolution, the general impression was, that the people were made for the benefit of the government not the government for the benefit of the people The inversion of this position has been fruitful practical advantages. Rulers were wont to be occupied solely with themselves, not with the communities they governed. Wars for ambition or pastime—family alliances—an extension of territory—the ostentation and trickery of diplomacy—with the intrigues of senators, ministers, and mistresses, for places, honours, and pensions, formed the staple, but costly and unprofitable, trifling of public authorities, both at London and Paris. This has been all changed. Judicial and fiscal improvements—popular education—the freedom and advancement of commerce—population, and the proportion it bears to subsistence and employment—national police—the slavery of negroes—the immunities of corporations—church establishments, and their social usefulness, form the subjects of investigation, to which both the executive and legislative powers are compelled to devote themselves.

The most rational and able disquisition of Mr. Burke, is his *Thoughts on the Present Discontents;* it contains clever writing on men, their motives and machinations, but it is all blank on the im-

portant questions I have enumerated.   The truth is,
they were neither thought of, nor understood, by
the public men of the last century.   Government
was considered a sinecure or appanage of the great,
with which the people had no concern—a splendid
prize for clever men to aim at, and a toy or play-
thing of hereditary imbecility.   It is so no longer; it
must be a productive machine, and that it has been
made such, is a triumph we owe to the French revolution.*

---

* Having frequently, in the course of this chapter, used the
terms, "abstract proposition" and "general principle," (see
p.' 411) it may be proper to explain, more particularly, what I
mean by their misapplication'; lest it be inferred, I wish to
countenance empiricism in place of science.

A general principle, is only another term for a rule or law,
by which moral and physical phenomena are regulated.   It is a
general principle, that a bullet discharged from a gun, will, by
the joint action of gravity, and the force of expulsion, describe
a parabolic curve, and if mathematicians know the angle of pro-
jection and velocity, they can calculate its time of flight, its
range, and the greatest height to which it will rise.   This is the
general principle, or theory of projectiles.   But it applies only
to a vacuum or free space, not to the passage of bodies through
a resisting medium like the atmosphere. Marshal Gerard would
never have reduced the citadel of Antwerp, had his shells only
been directed by the general principle, or theory, of gunnery.

Again, it is the interest of every one to lead a virtuous life,
and refrain from crime. This is the general principle of morals.
But we are afraid to trust to its operation in actual life, and,
therefore, enact laws to punish offences.   The reason is, that
all men are not sufficiently enlightened to appreciate their own
interests, and if they were, they have not all sufficient control
over their passions, to enable them to follow them.   Ignorance
and passion thus render the application of the general principle

CHAP. II.

NATURAL AND CIVIL LIBERTY.

THE natural liberty of man consists in freedom to do all he wills, and has power to do; civil liberty, in freedom to do all the law has not prohibited. The basis of natural liberty, is the exclusive good of the individual; the basis of civil liberty, is the good of the individual too, but it is an equal good, consistent with the possession of the same good, by every other person.

In exchanging the natural for the social state, man obtains two advantages—a knowledge of his rights, as prescribed by the law, and security for

of morals impossible, and human conduct is necessarily controlled by the artificial institutions of society.

It is the same with other general principles; they may be true in the *abstract*, but in real life, additional circumstances may interfere, to counteract their operation and cause them to be productive of results different from those anticipated. Just as in the flight of a shell, when opposed by the resistance of the air, it describes a very different curve from a parabola; and the conduct of an individual, while biassed by his passions and ignorance, would, without the restraint of law, and public opinion, be much less virtuous than it is, though it might be contrary to his self-interest to be so.

their enjoyment, as guaranteed by the common interest of all who belong to the same community.

Were there no civil rights, all men would equally possess the natural rights to live, to the produce of their labour, and to use, in common, the light, air, and water. These are as much the property of each individual, as his person : but the only security for their exercise, would be, the power to defend them. In the absence of law, there would be no transgression ; the strong might overpower the weak, or the artful, with impunity, circumvent the unsuspecting. A state of nature, therefore, is a state of great inequality ; as much so as men's abilities and physical power. It follows, that it is civil, not natural liberty, which introduces equity among mankind, by making the law, not force, the shield and arbiter of right.

The natural right of a man, to do as he desires, and can, supposes the same right in every other person : but the exertion of so many independent rights, would often cause them to clash and destroy each other. A law that would restrain all, might be beneficial to all ; because each might gain more by the limitation of the freedom of others, than he lost by the curtailment of his own. Natural liberty is the right of every one to go where he lists, without regard to his neighbour ; civil liberty compels him to go on the public road, which is most convenient to himself, consistently with the enjoyment of the same convenience by other persons. The establishment of civil liberty, is the enclosure of the waste, by which each surrenders his right of common, for the quiet possession and culture of a separate allotment.

The transition from the natural to the civil state, subjects man to responsibilities to which he was not before liable. In the former, he indulges his appetites, solely with reference to himself; in the latter, he can only indulge them, with reference to the society of which he is a member : and this he is bound to do, first, by the criminal restraint which the law imposes on actions of importance; and, secondly, by the moral restraint, which public opinion imposes on those of lesser degree.

As the natural was the first state of man, it may be inferred that this state would have continued, had not a persuasion arisen, that social order would be more conducive to happiness. As the public good was the motive, so it must continue the end of civil society; and for this reason : that there is no obligation imposed on mankind, save their advantage, to maintain the social in preference to the individual state of existence. And upon this principle the laws of a free people are founded, namely, that they shall impose no restraints on the acts of individuals, which do not conduce in a greater degree to the general good; by which it is implied, 1. That restraint itself is an evil; 2. That this evil should be overbalanced by some public advantage; 3. That the proof of this advantage lies upon the legislature, or those imposing the restraint; 4. That a law producing no real good is an evil of itself, and a sufficient reason for its repeal, without further proo.

of its bad effects. The application of this last condition to the English Statute Book, would tend much to its amelioration; it contains a vast number of dormant acts of parliament, and the fact that they are acts, is a sufficient reason for their abolition, without proof of positive mischief from them.

Whether man has benefitted by the introduction of civil society is a moral problem, which, like other problems not mathematical, can only be solved by inferential testimony. Two reasons make strongly, and, I think, decisively in favour of the affirmative conclusion. First, mankind had their *choice*, and it is contrary to human nature, to suppose that they would voluntarily have left the natural state, had not experience shown them that the social was better. Secondly, by the surrender of a portion of his natural freedom, man appears to have been well compensated by civil enjoyment. Civilization only divests man of a fraction, not the whole of his primitive liberty: all those acts that are personal to himself, he may continue to indulge in as freely as the savage, subject to no other control than public opinion, which he may defy if he pleases. The law restrains public deeds, and this it does because they are hurtful to others, not to the perpetrator only. Such restraint is civil liberty, and he who seeks greater licence, can neither be just nor rational; he can scarcely be a man, but something worse.

The establishment of civil rights entirely supersedes the operation of the natural rights, which previously governed the relation of individuals. The right of revenge, of the strong to oppress the weak, and of all those powers which are supposed to appertain to the wild justice of nature, are abrogated by the institution of society. The law is then supreme arbiter: it may be a bad law, but while it continues unrepealed, it is the sole rule, the only tribunal of resort to establish a claim, or redress an injury.

It is unnecessary to illustrate further the distinction between natural and civil liberty. The first is a chimera, like the points and lines of mathematicians; but, like them, it serves as a basis for reasoning, and enables us to deduce the real from the abstract. Alexander Selkirk might possess his natural rights in Juan Fernandez, but nobody else. Two men could not live a day on a desolate island,— they could not meet at the fountain for a pitcher of water, without settling the question whether age, strength, or first comer, should have precedency; and the termination of the dispute would be the establishment of civil order between them.

CHAP. III.

CIVIL GOVERNMENT.

GOVERNMENT is the law and its administration, instituted for the maintenance of civil liberty, and includes among its functionaries, not only the executive and legislature, but the judges, magistrates, and all other public institutions established for the general peace and security. Under the authority of these is produced that state of society termed order, as contradistinguished from liberty, or man in a state of nature.

" Society," says Paine, " is produced by our *wants*, and government by our *wickedness;* the former promotes our happiness positively by uniting our affections ; the latter negatively by restraining our vices."   This is an ingenious distinction ; but it would have been more correct to say, that society is produced by the wants of man, and government by the wants of society.   Man would be helpless and miserable without the co-operation of his fellow-creatures ; and society could not subsist without laws, and their ministers for its regulation and government.

The great problem in social institutions *is* to obtain the advantages of order with the least sacrifice of personal freedom.   Human happiness consists in entire liberty of action ; that is, in the perpetual doing of what is agreeable to our inclinations. Whatever abridges this liberty is an evil, but it is an evil which may be voluntarily incurred, like the taking of an unpalatable medicine, for sake of the greater compensating advantage which results from it.   Government is that compensating advantage, the benefits of which may be easily established.

The great ends of life are *freedom, security*, and *sustenance;* in a state of nature these are all imperfectly guaranteed.   The savage is neither free nor secure ; he is the slave of every member of his tribe stronger than himself, and may be sacrificed to his lust, his anger, or revenge.   Sustenance, under which is included food, clothing, and lodging, is not less precarious than freedom and security.   The rights of property not being recognised, no one can possess any thing which he can call his own ; if he cultivate a plot of ground, he cannot be sure he will be allowed to reap the produce ; if by superior toil and ability in hunting and fishing, he lay up a stock of provisions, he cannot be certain he will not be compelled to share them with a stranger ; where things are in common, spoliation is not robbery, it is only partnership : hence there can be no industry, no provision for the future ; the gratification of immediate wants is the sole object of exertion, and any thing beyond this is an unprofitable, because it is an unsafe, accumulation.

Contrast the evils of this uncertain state of existence, with the advantages enjoyed where civil rights are recognised, or those rights prescribed by law, and guaranteed by its administration.

The general principle of civil liberty, as explained in the last chapter, is to leave every one to act as he pleases, provided he does not injure his neighbour ; the objects of law are actions which affect the community, not the individual. For example : a person has the entire liberty of locomotion, he may go to whatever place he thinks proper, but he must go on the highway, or other legal path, and not trespass over another's ground. He is also entire master of his own person, and may subject it to what discipline he thinks fit; for instance, he may, as used to be common in Catholic countries, flagellate himself, but not assault his neighbour; he may get intoxicated with impunity, provided it is done privately, and not so as to be an annoyance to the public. He has similar privileges in respect of his dwelling, and the government of his family. His house is his castle; for mere purposes of a private nature, it is wholly impregnable, and on public occasions, it can only be legally violated, in case of the more serious delinquencies. In the treatment of his wife and the bringing up of his children the law is equally scrupulous, leaving them to his own discretion, regulated by his affections and judgment, and only interfering for their protection in those extreme cases where the lien of the commonwealth on their future services is endangered.

Hence it may be concluded, that human liberty is augmented rather than diminished by social institutions; not only is a greater portion of the natural liberty of man guaranteed to him by civil order, but what is peculiar to that state is, that he is protected in the enjoyment of it.

CHAP. IV.

ORIGIN AND PRINCIPLES OF CIVIL GOVERNMENT.

Two writers, of very different powers,* concur in tracing the origin of civil government to paternal authority. Had mankind sprung out of the earth mature and independent, they would, perhaps, with greater difficulty have been brought into a state of subordination; but the dependence of infancy prepares man for the restraint of society, by combining individuals into primary communities, and by placing them, from the beginning, under direction and control. A family is the model of a political association; their chief is represented by the father, and the people by his children. A federative union of families, having a common head, constitutes a state or empire; and the disposition to govern and be governed, in domestic life, are the rudiments of social order coeval with the mature and first existence of the human species.

The most simple and, perhaps, original form of political administration, is that in which each adult or head of a family, without representation or other contrivance, directly participates, and in which the sovereign power, or power to make laws, is vested in the will of the majority. A democracy of this kind is practicable in a small community, but is attended

* Rousseau's *Social Compact*, b. i. ch. 2. Paley's *Principles of Moral and Political Philosophy*, b. vi. ch. 1.

with inconveniences in a large one.   First, it is ill-suited to the purposes of deliberation ;   secondly, the division of power among so many persons renders it slow and inefficient in its operations ;   thirdly, it causes a loss of time, as on every public occasion each individual has to leave his occupation to discuss the affairs of the community.   These disadvantages would, doubtless, speedily originate improvements for abridging the trouble of government. A form of rule in which every one takes a direct part is as ill-adapted to political society, as the labour of individuals to the production of commodities, unaided by machinery or division of employments.

As knowledge is power, and as knowledge in the early ages is derived from personal experience, it is likely public authority would devolve into the hands of the elders, who would form a council, or senate, for the regulation of the community.

This second form of government might not be of long duration.   Disputes might arise among the people as to the choice of elders ; or, secondly, the elders themselves, from mutual jealousy or conflicting interests, might disagree, and, in either case, the necessity arise for a new disposition of political power.   To obviate the first cause of dissension the elders might become hereditary in their functions, or privileged to fill up, by election, vacancies in their own body: this would be an aristocracy. The second cause of dissension might be obviated by vesting all power in a single person, and thus establish an absolute monarchy, or despotism.

These several forms of power have each their advantages and disadvantages.

The separate advantages of MONARCHY, are unity of council, secrecy, despatch; a vigilant and energetic system of police; exclusion of popular and aristocratic contentions; preventing (if hereditary), by a known rule of succession, all competition for the supreme power, and thereby depressing the hopes, intrigues, and ambition of aspiring citizens. Its disadvantages are tyranny, expense, military domination; unnecessary wars, waged to gratify the passions of an individual; ignorance of ministers and governors, selected from personal favour, of the interests of the people, and consequent deficiency of salutary regulations; want of constancy and uniformity in public councils, measures, and laws, fluctuating as these do with the character of the reigning prince, and thence insecurity of persons, property, and industry.

The chief and, indeed, almost only advantage of an ARISTOCRACY, consists in its forming a permanent legislature, which grows up, as it were, for its office, without the trouble and interference of the people, and the members of which may be supposed to be trained and educated for the stations they are destined by birth, tenure of land, or other condition, to occupy. Its disadvantages are divisions among themselves, which, from want of a common superior, may (as formerly in the Polish diet) proceed to desperate extremities; partial laws, made for the exclusive benefit and conservation of their own power and privileges ; impolitic measures, resulting from prejudice, ignorance, or disregard of the public weal ; impoverishment and degradation of all the non-aristocratic classes, by disqualifying enactments, and partial fiscal regulations.

The advantages of a REPUBLIC, or democracy, where the people collectively, or by representation, constitute the legislature, are equal laws ; exemption from needless restrictions ; regulations adapted to the wants of the people ; public spirit, economy, averseness to war ; opportunities, by popular appeal, to enforce the adoption of measures most conducive to the general interests ; facilities to each citizen for displaying his abilities, and to the commonwealth for obtaining the advice and services of its best-qualified members. Its disadvantages for the purpose of legislation have been already indicated ; its other evils are dissension, tumults, faction ; loss of time and interruptions to industry consequent on popular elections ; oppression of distant colonies not represented ; delay in public measures from difficulty of obtaining concurrence of numerous bodies ; lastly, danger of ascendancy of unprincipled writers and agitators, by the practice of artifices adapted to the prejudices, folly, and ignorance of the multitude.

A MIXED government may be established, composed of two or more of the simple forms above described, and in whatever proportion these several elements enter into the constitution, in the same degree will the evils or advantages of that system of rule predominate. Thus, if monarchy is the prevailing power, then secrecy, despatch, internal peace, will be the excellences, and profusion, caprice, military parade, and incapacity, the defects of government. A similar equation of good and bad will result from the preponderance of aristocracy or democracy in the constitution. The general rule for the construction and improvement of governments, therefore, is to proportion the ingredients to the wants of society; strengthening or weakening the regal, aristocratic, and popular branches, according as the qualities of each may become essential to the general welfare. It is important, however, to observe, that a quality sometimes results from the union of two forms of government which belong to neither in its separate state of existence. Thus corruption, which has no place in absolute monarchy, and little in pure democracy, is sure to gain admission into a constitution which divides authority between an executive and legislative; unless either one or both are under the control of a popular and incorruptible constituency.

The best form of government for a country to adopt is not a speculative question: it can only be determined by reference to the character and circumstances of the people for whom it is intended. Russia, and the United States of America, offer two striking illustrations of the truth of this proposition. We have here instances of the working of the two extreme forms of government—one a despotism, the other a democracy—and each form of rule has operated, perhaps, more favourably than any other system that could have been adopted for the benefit of its respective community. Had the institutions of Russia been more free, they would have been less favourable to her prosperity and happiness. Civilization was received from without through the instrumentality of her sovereigns, who for their own power and glory were anxious to raise her nearer to a level with the European states by which she is surrounded. But had the barbarism and ignorance of the empire been represented in the government, as they would have been by more popular establishments, the prejudices of the people would have been a stumbling-block to national improvement. As it was, the prince was every thing, and the people nothing : if he were enlightened and benevolent his impress was stamped on his courtiers and the aristocracy, and through them on their followers and dependents. In America the case is reversed, and the intelligence and independent circumstances of the people have enabled them to exercise a salutary control over the government. Had the chief magistrate of the United States been an absolute and hereditary chief, he must have been corrupted by the possession of uncontrolled and irresponsible authority ; his government would have been marked by the vices inseparable from absolute monarchy—war, costliness, and neglect of the general welfare. But the people, by the retention of political power in their own hands— by holding the reins, as it were, have kept their presidents steadily in the highway of public happiness —have protected themselves from the caprice of individual character—and afforded to the world a splendid example of a constitution administered not for the benefit of one person, or a class of persons, but for the general benefit of the governed.

In all countries popular liberty must necessarily extend with popular intelligence. It is as much in the nature of political power to devolve into the hands of those who have the most right and capacity to exercise it, as it is in bodies to descend to the earth by the force of gravity, or water to spread itself over a plain. In England power was formerly wielded by the king, nobility, and clergy, and for this simple reason, that in them was concentrated the entire property and intelligence of the community; and it was doubtless most advantageous in the existing state of society, that in these classes should be vested the exclusive government of the country. The rise of new interests into importance—the acquisition of wealth and knowledge by the productive orders, rendered necessary a new disposition of political power; and it is well known that during the last two centuries the circle of aristocratic domination has been undergoing gradual contraction by the external pressure of the popular party. Similar causes are producing similar effects on the Continent, where the ill-suppressed struggles for constitutional governments arise solely from the development of new social interests; these interests must ultimately triumph, because claims, just and expedient, must gather strength by conflict and discussion, while those by which they are opposed, having no such basis, must become weaker : and the final issue will probably be the general substitution in Europe, of representative in place of hereditary authority.

The limit which utility prescribes to the diffusion of political power among a people, is competency to exercise it. The legitimate purpose of government is the promotion of the general interest, but the general interest will not be promoted unless it be incorporated in the general government. Whatever interest is excluded will be neglected or sacrificed. These are truisms which require no metaphysical analysis to establish ; they result from the most obvious principles of human nature,—namely, the proneness of men to advance their own interests in preference to those of strangers, and this they will do as much from the bias of the understanding as the impulse of selfishness : for it is the tendency of our minds, in spite of, and even unknown to ourselves, constantly to see right and justice in the same direction that we see profit.* Upon this principle alone can we account for the treatment of factory children in England, and of slaves in the West Indies and America ; all of which afford instances

* Mr. Mill, in his *Essay on Government*, has endeavoured (if I rightly understand him) with much subtlety to establish this principle of human nature, but the common experience of mankind is enough. One of the biographers of Mr. Burke remarks, amusingly enough, that his mental organization was such that he could not help seeing that conduct to be just, which accorded with his interest or taste. Few persons can live long in the world without arriving at the conclusion, that Burke had no exclusive property in this endowment.

of both the feelings and moral perceptions of individuals, otherwise perhaps just and enlightened, being perverted by their interests. Such being the frailty of humanity, and the misleading tendency of power, the conclusion is irresistible that any interest or class of persons excluded from a share in the government must be sacrificed or neglected in its administration. The only valid plea therefore for the political disfranchisement of individuals is a manifest incompetency in them to exercise power for their own advantage. That cases of this kind may be established is unquestionable. Power in the hands of a person debased by ignorance and superstition, might be as mischievous to himself and others as power in the hands of a child or insane person. The boors and nobles of Russia were the chief obstacles to the plans of improvement of Peter the Great. In Spain and Portugal, projects for the establishment of constitutional government have been supported by the middle classes, but frustrated by the fanaticism of the peasantry. Not only is a certain degree of intelligence necessary to the reception and exercise of political power, but personal independence. By giving power to a slave, we only confer a boon on his master. The forty-shilling freeholders of Ireland were the alternate tools of their landlords and priests, not free agents for their own benefit.

In England, during the last fifty years, the extent to which the elective suffrage ought to be carried, so as to secure the advantages of good government, has formed a constant subject of political disquisition. So far as *abstract* right is concerned, no good reason can be alleged why every one should not share in the making of laws to which he is amenable. The person is not less precious than property; and laws which affect the security of the former are certainly not less important to every individual than those which affect the security of the latter. It is not, therefore, householdership, the payment of taxes, or any other property-qualification, but *legal responsibility*, which prescribes the strictly equitable limit to the right of suffrage. But the admission of such a principle is incompatible with practical government: it would entitle all, with scarcely any exception, to participate in legislation; it would embrace females as well as males; all minors would be included, of whatever age, provided they were judicially responsible: in short, none would be disqualified, except the insane, and infants of so tender age that they are unable to distinguish right from wrong. The introduction of such an unlimited scheme of suffrage, every one must disclaim. Still, were I asked why I would adopt any other principle, why disfranchise women in preference to men, or minors to majors; why allow a person to vote at the precise age of twenty-one, and not at twenty or eighteen; I confess, in answer to these inquiries, I could only give one reply, namely, that *expediency*, not strict justice, dictates their exclusion.

To this principle we are compelled to resort in the prescription of civil immunities: we cannot enforce the merely natural or abstract claims of justice which are abrogated by the first institution of society, but must content ourselves with guaranteeing the greatest happiness of the greatest number in the most feasible manner.   Upon this principle minors may be excluded from the elective suffrage, because their interests may be presumed to be identified with those of their parents; females, because their interests are merged in those of their husbands, fathers, or brothers.   How much further the principle of exclusion should be carried, is a practical question only—one of *utility*, not theory.   Whether the right of suffrage should be exercised by all male adults, or limited to householders, or to payers of a certain amount of taxes, is a consideration which must be decided by ascertaining which would be most conducive to the public good.   The end of just government is the equitable and adequate protection of *all interests*; and provided this is attained, the object for which the suffrage is exercised becomes secured. The task of legislation is a part of the labour of society; and it is only a clumsily-contrived social machinery—approaching to the organization of the primitive state of mankind—if it demand the participation and exertion of every individual.   No condition of suffrage, I apprehend, is of universal application, and adapted to all times and places. A right of suffrage appropriate to France or the United States, may be unsuited to England.   In no country is the franchise exercised without some personal or proprietary condition being annexed. Every where *full age* appears to be an indispensable qualification.   In America the slave-population, which forms a large portion of the inhabitants, is entirely excluded ; and in none of the States of the Union, I believe, is the suffrage exercised unaccompanied with residence or other qualification in the elector.   Were it otherwise, it would not be a conclusive argument for the adoption of a similar scheme of representation in the United Kingdom.   In the cheap and universal circulation of newspapers—in the independent circumstances of the industrious— and in the absence of that mass of vagrancy, poverty, and destitution, which is found among ourselves, the Americans possess advantages for the exercise of political power which unhappily do not exist in England. The distribution of property, too, is wholly different.   " We have " (says the *North American Review*, No. 72, p. 181) " no landed proprietor whose estate yields 20,000*l.* a year."   There is not, perhaps, in America, a merely landed estate the fee-simple of which is worth one year's income of several of the English aristocracy.

In France a *higher* elective qualification might be sufficiently protective of popular interests than would be adequate to the same purpose in England.   In the former, there is no richly-endowed church, nor nobility with vast territorial possessions to contend against.   There are no interests like the Bank of England, East India Company, West India planters, London brewers, or factory owners to counterpoise : these are all consolidations of wealth and influence which *it* is necessary in some degree to balance and neutralise in the composition of an English legisla-lature. Among the French, the constitution of society is essentially democratic ; there is no monied aristocracy nor landed interest : having no primo-geniture and entail laws, property is more equally divided. In the whole kingdom, it is computed there are only 107 persons possessed of 4000*l.* a year each from landed property. Hence it is that a much smaller body of electors would represent and sustain the popular interest in France, than would be adequate to a similar purpose in England : for it must be borne in mind that the excellence of a system of representation does not exclusively consist in the *number* of voters, but in the unbiassed and intelligent exercise of their suffrages, and in their being sufficiently numerous to touch on and con-stitute a fair and aliquot proportion of every social interest.

The object of representation is, that it should be a transcript of the intelligence, probity, wealth, and industry of the community. For this purpose, some *external* sign or elective qualification must be adopted in the constituent body. In England the interests of agriculture are represented by a con-stituency of freeholders, copyholders, and lease-holders ; those of commerce, manufactures, and industry, by a constituency renting houses of ten pounds yearly value. These qualifications may not be the best indications of elective fitness, but they at least show that the elector is of some standing in society, that he is not a pauper nor a vagrant. They are not meant to denote, as I conceive, merely a proprietary interest in the state, but also, by a visible symbol, the personal circumstances of the elector as to age, discretion, and settlement in life. Neither are they meant to imply that the non-electors have no interest in the state; because every one has an interest in the making of laws he is bound to obey: but they are adopted for the purpose of reducing the constituency to such a number as may not be greater than needs for the general protection of all. That they are not exclusively *property-qualifications* may be instanced in this: there are thousands of persons disfranchised though in possession of millions of income—income derived from the funds, from colonial property, from copyrights of books, from professions and trades; being affluent, it might have been thought government would have been desirous to attach these classes to its interests by granting them the suffrage: yet many of them, not being occupiers of houses, from dislike to the trouble of housekeeping or other motive, are without political power in the state; have no share in making militia laws, or laws of any other description, though bound to obey them. If the elective qualification be unjust, it is impartially so; it does not strike one class and leave another unscotched; it does not exclude all the poor and incorporate all the rich: it embraces a part of every grade of society, and omits a part; and this, in my opinion, constitutes a recommendation of the scheme; for, by means thereof, no interest is left wholly without legislative protection.

The excellence of representative government must also depend on the mode in which the elective suffrage is exercised, whether *openly* or *covertly*. The objection ordinarily made to the BALLOT is, that—it is a shelter for meanness and collusion. In this there is more of sentiment than of reason. Government at best is only a necessary evil, but having adopted such a contrivance for the general conveniency of society, the best machinery ought to be employed. The ballot is more favourable to the peace of elections, and abridges the facilities for bribery and intimidation. It imposes no restraint on the independent expression of opinion; every one is at liberty or not to avow his political predilections; but it affords protection to those whose circumstances may render an open avowal of their sentiments hurtful or inconvenient. It shelters the weak, and leaves the strong in the full enjoyment of their liberty.

Unless the free exercise of the suffrage is protected, the purpose for which it is given may be defeated. The object of the franchise is, that the elector may have a responsible organ through which his opinions and interests may be represented. But of what avail is the suffrage to a workman, leaseholder, tenant, or tradesman, if he must necessarily exercise it under the dictation of his employer, landlord, or customers. In this case the franchise is not given, it is only delegated, and the elector is merely the proxy of him who has power to control his choice of a representative. No additional interests are represented by such mock constituents, the working of the machinery of representation is only encumbered by a useless apparatus.

There is only one point more, connected with representation, I shall notice ; it is the *duration of the representative body*.   As at an early period of our history the simple business of parliament was quickly despatched, prorogation was unfrequent, and parliament was mostly elected as often as it assembled.   Later the term of duration was irregular. Charles II. protracted his second parliament to seventeen years—a term long enough to obliterate all connexion with the electoral body.   In the 461 years preceding the reign of George III. there were 202 parliaments, whose average duration was two years and a half.   In the sixty-nine years of the reigns of George III. and IV. there were only thirteen parliaments, averaging five years and one-third each.   A three years' term, as fixed at the Revolution, appears a just medium.   A lease of seven years, as Junius expresses it, gives a corrupt member six years to commit sins and one year to atone for them.   Effective legislation lies between the extremes of annual and septennial parliaments.   The short parliament has the inconvenience of frequent elections, and does not afford time to perfect sound measures of national improvement, or even to acquire the information which the responsibility of legislation needs ; while the long parliament deprives the elector of the means of repairing the error of his choice within any reasonable period of recovery, and gives to the representative the means of trading at will upon a trust, which should always be considered as held under constantly renewable liabilities to his constituents. The more the principles of representative government are considered, the stronger will be the conviction, that the elected legislature is as much entitled to have a sufficient period of trial, as the people are to possess a reasonable power of redemption and renewal in their own right.

CHAP. V.

PROGRESS AND PRINCIPLES OF THE ENGLISH CONSTITUTION.

A DISTINCTION is mostly made by political writers between constitution and government. Government has been already defined to consist of the legislature, the laws, and their administrators; and the constitution is that department of the laws which prescribes the origin, powers, and composition of the legislative body, the functions of the executive, the franchises of the people, and the form, construction, and course of judicial administration. The constitution refers almost exclusively to the acts of public functionaries; the law, more comprehensive, refers not only to these, but to the acts of the people, or that great division of the community apart from the administrative government.

Every unconstitutional act is also an illegal act,

but every illegal act is not an unconstitutional act;
that is, neither the act itself nor the perpetrator may
be so important as to contravene the general and
fundamental provisions which the constitution has
established.   It would be unconstitutional in the
crown to raise money by prerogative, but it is only
unlawful in a person to steal, or for a judge, or
magistrate, to convict contrary to established precedent or act of parliament.

Political constitutions have mostly had two ori-
gins; either they have been promulgated at once
and entire in a public act emanating from the whole
or a portion of a community; or they have been the
gradual creation of successive emergencies and
occasions, resulting from the fluctuating wants of
different ages, from the contentions and interests of
different orders and parties in society.   America,
France, and Belgium offer examples of the former
description of constitutions; England of the latter.

It was a common practice with writers of the last
century, to represent the British constitution as a
scheme of government formally planned and established by our ancestors in some remote period of
our national history.   Such representations might
be necessary, and even venial, at a time when antiquity was often considered to give a higher sanction
to authority than principle.   But a better understanding of the purposes of government dispenses
with the necessity of historical fables to establish the
justice and utility of popular immunities.   Without
fear of misconstruction it may be now affirmed, that

it is futile to revert to ages of barbarism for models of free and enlightened institutions; that the early institutions of the Britons were analogous to those of all communities entering on the first stages of civilization; that there is no distant date or point of time in history when the government was to be set up anew —when it was referred to any single person, assembly, or committee, to frame a charter for the future political administration of the country—or when a constitution so prepared and digested was by common consent received and established. The English constitution is the result of successive improvements advancing with the increasing wealth and intelligence of society. Those who entertain a different opinion rely, I apprehend, either on descriptions purely imaginary, or refer to a period too remote for authentic intelligence.

The surest test of the excellence of public institutions, and the extent of popular rights, is the *administration of justice*. The executive government may claim and exercise a transitory power dependent on the character of the sovereign or his ministers, or imposed on them by the emergency of the moment, but the judicial administration is that permanent and wide-spread division of social machinery which touches all the members of society; and accordingly as their rights are respected or violated under it, may be inferred the general existence or absence of civil liberty among the people. If we apply this test to the state of society under the Anglo-Saxons, as described by Turner and Pal-

2 G

grave, or to much more recent periods of our annals,
down even to the Revolution of 1688, as illustrated
in the State Trials, it will be found that popular
rights, in the modern sense, had hardly begun to
exist—were crudely defined, and little appreciated
in courts of justice, and courts of justice are, in
truth, the only places to look to for evidence of the
existence of general practical liberty.

Two reasons may be assigned for misapprehen-
sions on the progress of the English constitution:
first, wrong impressions as to the import and application of certain current phrases in acts of parliament and royal proclamations, to which meanings
have been ascribed irreconcilable with the contemporary state of society; secondly, the ascribing
powers to ancient institutions, designated by popular
names, which only appertain to them in their present form of administration. I shall mention one or
two examples illustrative of each source of error.

In the writs issued by Edward I. for the assem-
bling of a parliament in 1297, occurs this phrase:
" *What concerns all should be supported by all,
approved by all, and common danger should be
repelled by all.*" " No such introduction to a writ,"
says Prynne, "had been before issued:" and from it
has been deduced the right to universal representation, or the right of every one not to be taxed
without his consent. Notwithstanding this popular expression, the principle it imports never entered into the practical government of the country. For a long period subsequent to the reign of

Edward I. a large portion of the community was in a state of personal servitude, with scarcely any civil, much less political, immunities. The dispensing power of the crown arbitrarily to interfere to stop legal proceedings, continued for two centuries later, and in 1539 the commons passed the memorable 31 Hen. VIII. c. 8, declaring a royal proclamation binding on the subject like a statute of the realm. Parliaments were assembled at uncertain intervals, according to the exigences of the sovereign; the election and holding of them were probably synonymous; boroughs were admitted or excluded from representation at the royal pleasure; and though the assent of the commons appears to have been sought when greater supplies than ordinary were required, yet the continuance to a much later period of purveyance, wardship, forced loans, benevolences, and other modes of raising supplies by prerogative, shows that the people's representatives had acquired only an equivocal hold of the purse-strings of the nation. Abundant facts serve to show that this formality was often dispensed with even by princes of the Tudor and Stuart race, as in the cases of purveyance and ship-money.

An example of the second source of error may be found in the ancient constitution of JURIES. Trial by jury is justly deemed one of the most effective guarantees of popular freedom, but the ancient functions of this tribunal are as remote from the modern, as the prerogatives of Henry VIII. from those of William IV. Many who have descanted

2 G 2

on the excellence of this national franchise, confirmed by Magna Charta, appear to have supposed that it had descended unchanged from the time of Alfred.   The contrary will appear from the following extract from Mr. Palgrave's *Rise and Progress of the English Commonwealth*, pp. 243-4 : " Trial by jury, according to the old English law, was a proceeding essentially different from the modern tribunal, still bearing the ancient name, by which it has been replaced ; and whatever merits belonged to the original mode of judicial investigation—and they were great and unquestionable, though accompanied by many imperfections—such benefits are not to be exactly identified with the advantages now resulting from the great bulwark of English liberty.   Jurymen, in the present day, are triers of the issue ; they are individuals who found their opinion upon the evidence, whether oral or written, adduced before them ; and the verdict delivered by them, is their declaration of the judgment which they have formed. But the ancient jurymen were not empannelled to examine into the credibility of the evidence ; the question was not discussed and argued before them ; they, the jurymen, were the *witnesses themselves ;* and the verdict was substantially the examination of those witnesses, who, of their own knowledge and without the aid of other testimony, afforded their evidence respecting the facts in question to the best of their belief.   In its primitive form, a trial by jury was, therefore, only a *trial by witnesses*, and jurymen were distinguished from any other witnesses only by the customs, which imposed upon them the obligation of an oath, and regulated their number, and which prescribed their rank and defined the territorial qualifications from whence they obtained their degree and influence in society."

"Trial by jury" it appears, then, was not the trial of the accused by his equals; the jury only gave evidence of the fact, not a judgment on the truth or falsity of the accusation; both the law and verdict of guilty or not guilty being issues solely determined by the judge.

The HOUSE OF COMMONS has undergone quite as great a metamorphosis as jury trial. Although the history of this assembly has been traced by Gildas up to the time when Britain was occupied by the Romans, it is now generally understood, that it hardly began to exist for any useful purpose till the accession of the Stuarts. Prior to this period it could be considered little more than a commission summoned or not, at the pleasure of the crown or of the sheriff, to raise a sum of money for the public treasury, by taxing themselves and fellow-subjects. It was not a legislature in any proper sense of the term, any more—perhaps not so much—than the Court of Star Chamber, or High Commission. It was a meeting of deputies to assess taillages and scutages, not *to make laws*. That was a branch of the royal prerogative exercised by the more summary process of proclamation, not by illiterate burgesses, whom it was assumed might be great adepts in the mysteries of trade, but not sufficiently learned for

the high task of legislation.   So little did the M.P.s
of those days value the representative function, that
they considered it a task imposed, not an honour
conferred, and actually received *wages* for the discharge of so unpleasant a duty.   All sorts of eva-
sions were practised to avoid sending representatives
to parliament; some boroughs pleaded poverty,
others their insignificance, and the honourable members were almost constrained by force to appear at
Westminster, Oxford, or other place of royal residence.   The whole proceeding was analogous to
what takes place in a city taken by storm.   The
victorious general calls together the principal inhabitants, not to make laws for the government of the
town, but to determine how great a sum they can
raise to save themselves from pillage.   It was the
same with the House of Commons, and so continued
till the advent of Hampden, Pym, Hollis, Eliot, and
other master minds, claimed for the third estate a
nobler and more independent vocation.

To trace the gradual evolution of the several parts
of the English constitution, to show how the executive, legislative, and judicial powers were formerly
blended and clumsily executed, and how they became separated, defined, and secured in the exercise
of their respective functions by ages of conflict and
trial, form curious and interesting subjects of study
and inquiry.   It is the progress from chaos to order :
or it is like contemplating the reclamation of a waste
country by the embankment of its rivers, the draining of its morasses, the clearing out of its jungles,

the extermination of beasts of prey, and other operations by which it is brought into a state of security and productiveness. Divesting ourselves of the illusions of antiquity, it is impossible to conceal that the government for a long period was a simple despotism, occasionally controlled by the interference of the nobility and clergy. The first regular approach to constitutional rule, was the regal grant of Magna Charta. Doubtless the concessions extorted by the barons at Runnymede were chiefly in their own favour; but it also contained provisions which were a guide and sanction for future and more general claims of freedom. The mere conventional adoption of such an instrument denotes a progression in society. A division of political power between two orders in the state had at least begun to be formally recognised, namely, the king and aristocracy; and the idea of prescribing their respective immunities by a public law, shows a growth of intelligence and justice, and may be deemed perhaps the first visible germ of the constitution.*

* "Many parts of the great charter were pointed against the abuses of the power of the king as lord paramount, and have lost their importance since the downfall of the system of feuds, which it was their purpose to mitigate. But it contains a few maxims of just government, applicable to all places and times, of which it is hardly possible to overrate the importance of the first promulgation by the supreme authority of a powerful and renowned nation. Some clauses, though limited in words by feudal relations, yet covered general principles of equity which were not slowly unfolded by the example of the charter, and by their obvious application to the safety and wellbeing of the whole community."—*Mackintosh's History of England,* vol. i.

From the reign of King John to that of Charles I. the constitution underwent no change of decided importance, the power of the several parts of which it consisted was the subject of contention, but it was not fixed or materially altered by any public act. Important improvements, however, had taken place among the people, and the silent influence of the commonalty had encroached on the authority of the nobility.   Vassalage was at last entirely extirpated. Commerce extended, and manufactures were introduced and flourished.   Domestic comforts, and even luxuries were placed more within the reach of all classes.   But the most distinguishing feature of this long interval was the growth of an entirely new order of vast power and influence, who claimed for the first time a share in political government, namely, the MIDDLE CLASSES, consisting of the smaller freeholders and copyholders living in the country, and of merchants, manufacturers, and tradespeople living in cities and towns.   These, hitherto unknown as an independent cast, had almost imperceptibly become influential enough to contest the prerogatives of the sovereign in the legislature—make war upon him—and after triumphing over him in open battle, consolidate all authority in themselves.

p. 217-18.   Further on (p. 221) Sir James observes, "For almost five centuries it was appealed to as the decisive authority on behalf of the people, though commonly so far only as the necessities of the case demanded."—This continued in fashion till within these few years; but the public taste has altered, and it is more common now for reformers to refer to principles of utility than constitutional authorities.

Political knowledge, however, had not been sufficiently diffused to enable the victors in the civil
wars to frame and maintain a system of government
greatly superior to that which previously existed;
and, as a consequence, the power of the state fell
back into the hands of its former possessors. But the
new influence manifested in this great struggle was
never lost ; though political power reverted to the
king and aristocracy, a vast influence continued to
be exercised over public affairs by the middle orders
till the next great era of the constitution in 1688.

By the triumph of the Orange revolution, mere
absolutism was for ever struck from its pedestal.

The alteration of the succession to the crown by
parliamentary authority, and a distinct and popular
affirmation of all those questions on which the
sovereign and the commons had been formerly
divided, were important advances towards constitutional government. The BILL OF RIGHTS, however, only affirmed and defined, did not new-model
public institutions. It brought the *practice* nearer
to the *theory* of the constitution. It deprived the
crown of no power it previously possessed by law,
nor added any privileges to the people which they
did not previously possess by law. It merely bound
the king to his legal prerogatives, and secured to
the other branches of legislature their legal rights.
The great defect of the new charter of the constitution consisted in not embracing a new scheme
of representation adapted to the augmented wealth
and intelligence of the community. The conse-

quence of this omission was a long course of disastrous policy. The power lost by the crown was ingulfed by the aristocracy, who often perverted it to the purposes of war, faction, and popular delusion. In place of the Revolution being followed up by a reform in the church, corporations, and judicial administration—by the removal of religious disabilities, and the establishment of a popular system of education—government became an arena for aristocratic intrigue and contention; public abuses accumulated, and the great work of national reformation which Lord Bacon and Bishop Burnet indicated, had to be entered upon upwards of a century later.

The Revolution undoubtedly guaranteed the interests of the nobility and clergy, by whose vigorous and well-concerted exertions the change of dynasty was principally effected. One cause of its incompleteness was the despatch with which it was consummated, not leaving time for maturing a more perfect settlement, and this again perhaps is an evil inseparable from any great political movement effected with a certain degree of violence upon a sudden emergency in the face of opposition. Whatever may have been the cause of the sins of omission in 1688, it is pleasing to think that the chief of them have been at length repaired by the political party usually charged with the guilt of their perpetration.

By the acts for the amendment of the representation of the United Kingdom under William IV.

the body of the community appears to have acquired
that operative control over the government which,
since the time of the Commonwealth, it had indirectly, though often inefficiently exercised through
the medium of the press, public meetings, access to
parliamentary debates, and a fragment of representation in the House of Commons.

From the preceding brief indication of the more
important epochs and modifications introduced into
the government, I think it may be inferred that *progression* and *gradual adaptation* to the changing
circumstances of the people constitute the living
principles of the English constitution. Experience
shows that searching and even radical reforms of its
several parts are by no means tantamount to their
dissolution. Imperfection is inseparable from every
institution—executive, legislative, and judicial—imperfections in their origin, and imperfections the
produce of time from the first moment of their establishment. To remove imperfections as they become
developed and oppressive, and to create new checks
and substitutes as experience may suggest, are the
legitimate objects of reform. There is nothing novel
in this; reform, indeed, is very old-fashioned—
6000 years at least, and will assuredly continue to operate for 6000 years longer, unless
some device like Bishop Berkeley's wall of brass can
be hit upon, for limiting the number, wealth, and
intelligence of mankind.

After the successive improvements the constitution
has undergone, it may be reasonably asked, *Of*

what does the aggregate now consist—where can it be found? A Frenchman can point to the charter, an American to the Declaration of Independence, the Articles of Confederation, and general constitutions of the States, but to what can an Englishman point as the ark of his constitutional immunities? I shall endeavour to answer these questions. That we have a constitution I am confident, and a constitution adapted to the removal of social evils, so far as social evils can be removed by political government. What is very much needed is a popular and consolidated presentment of public rights—a task which might be easily executed by a committee of the reformed parliament, and which would be a service of incalculable value. The general code of laws is to the people what the constitution is to their governors—it is a rule for their conduct, and prescribes their powers and responsibilities.

The following is a summary of the principal usages and acts from which a public declaration of the kind to which I have adverted might be compiled and digested :

I. *General Constitutional Acts.* —These are Magna Charta, the Coronation Oath, the Petition of Right, the Habeas Corpus Act, the Bill of Rights, the Act of Settlement, the Acts of Union with Scotland and Ireland, the Jury Act, the Acts for the Reform of the Representation. These are all fundamental measures; the Bill of Rights especially may be considered the charter of the constitution, affirming and defining the chief conditions affecting the executive, legislature, and liberty of the subject.

II. *Personal Liberty.*—The securities for this are—1. Inviolability of the habitation. 2. Protection from arrest. 3. Relief against protracted imprisonment. 4. Trial by jury. 5. Independence of the judges. 6. Exemption from self-crimination. 7. Right of petition to parliament. All these in different degrees guarantee the freedom of individuals, or afford means of relief when it is unlawfully abridged. A few words of explanation on each may not be out of place.

In civil suits the *house* is an inviolable asylum, and in the execution of criminal process it can only be forcibly entered under the authority of a warrant issued by a magistrate, on such charge made before him as would justify him in an action for false imprisonment. Again, the *person* cannot be arrested without a warrant, unless it be by a peace-officer for an assault or offence committed in his presence; or a peace-officer may arrest without warrant on a charge of felony made to him; and any private individual may arrest an offender in the act of committing a felony, without warrant.

By the *Habeas Corpus* Act, if any person be imprisoned by the order of any court, or the king himself, he may have a writ of *habeas corpus* to bring him before any of the four courts of Westminster-hall in term time, or to the lord chancellor, or one of the judges, in the vacation, who shall determine whether the cause of his imprisonment be legal. The *habeas corpus* act of Charles II. extended only to committals in criminal cases, but by subsequent statutes of the reign of George III., the remedies it gives are extended to all miscellaneous causes of confinement ; except, I believe, confinement for an infringement of the privileges of the House of Commons. The importance of this constitutional act can only be appreciated, by reverting to those times (the reign of Elizabeth for instance) when it was not unusual to keep persons confined for years without bringing them to trial, or confronting them with their accuser. In times of great political excitement the protection of the *habeas corpus* act has been suspended. But this suspension does not enable any one to imprison without cause or reason for so doing; it only prevents persons who are committed from being bailed, tried, or discharged during the suspension, leaving to the committing magistrate all the responsibility attending an illegal imprisonment. It is common, therefore, to pass an act of indemnity afterwards for the protection of magistrates.

- The protection afforded by *jury trial*, especially in offences against government, need not be enforced, and this branch of judicature has been recently improved by the consolidatory act of Sir Robert Peel.

- In the reign of Elizabeth, and subsequently, the sovereign often interfered to stop or influence judicial proceedings by the arbitrary removal or appointment of judges for sinister purposes. For better securing the *independence of judges* it is provided by 13 William III. c. 2, that their commissions shall not, as formerly, be made *during pleasure*, but during good behaviour; that their salaries shall be ascertained and fixed, but that they may be removable on an address of both houses of parliament. Under the 1st Geo. III. c. 23, their commissions were made permanent, notwithstanding a demise of the crown.

Exemption from *self-crimination* is not so important now as formerly, when torture could be employed to extort confession, and when examinations in prison were frequently resorted to for the purpose of *getting up evidence* against the accused on the day of trial. No one is bound to answer questions before a magistrate tending to criminate himself; such evidence, if taken before a committing magistrate, is inadmissible on the trial of the accused, unless it has been freely and voluntarily tendered.

The *right of petition* to any branch of the legislature is not limited to magisterial or judicial oppression, but extends to every description of public grievance.

III. *Mutiny Act.*—The constitutional guarantee of this consists in its being an annual enactment, and is an ingenious safeguard of civil freedom peculiar to the English government. As the army, if placed at the irresponsible command of the crown, might at any time be turned against the people, it is provided that [the king cannot raise an army without the consent of parliament, and that consent must be renewed annually. Without the annual re-enactment of the Mutiny Bill no pay could be issued to the army; nor courts-martial held; or any measure of military discipline carried into effect. At the end of every year the army, without a vote of the commons for its continuance, would, *ipso facto*, be disbanded. The crown is not in the same state of dependence in respect of the navy. As the sea forces cannot be so readily made available against the nation, the king is permitted to keep them as he thinks proper, being only placed under the same restraint that applies to all subjects of finance—that of being obliged to apply to parliament in the usual way for a vote of supply.

IV. *Freedom of Opinion.*—The repeal of the Test and Corporation Acts, and the removal of the civil disabilities of Roman Catholics, completed the extinction of the formidable penal code existing at the accession of George III. To perfect the triumph of freedom of opinion, a measure has been introduced for removing the civil disabilities of the Jews. It is probable the promulgation of any opinion would not now be interfered with, provided it was not done in such open and indecent manner as to amount to a public nuisance, by the insult it offered to the general sentiments of the people. The interference of the civil power in this case would not be for the purpose of checking the spread of obnoxious doctrines, but to maintain the public peace. The sentiments of the Chief Justice of England on this subject are important; while attorney-general, Sir Thomas Denman said, "With regard to the general question of libel, my opinion is, that as long as a writer *honestly* expresses his opinions, and his opinions only—as long as it is possible to give him credit for *sincerity*—I should be greatly disinclined to prosecute."—*Mirror of Parliament*, May 21, 1832. After this declaration I think it may be concluded that government has gradually worked itself into a state of almost theoretic perfection as respects freedom of discussion.*

V. *Liberty of the Press.*—Previously to the reign of William III. the press was always more or less shackled; but the popular principle gained so much force in the constitution under his administration, that the press was at last relieved to a very considerable extent. The liberty of the press may, perhaps, be said to consist in its exemption from the interference of a licenser; except as respects dramatic compositions this liberty is possessed, but its prac-

* The statute against *Apostacy* I apprehend has become a dead letter, as I never hear of it being enforced against members of parliament, or other transgressors. By the 9th & 10th William III. c. 32, if any person *educated in*, or having made profession of, the Christian religion, shall, by writing, printing, teaching, or advised speaking, deny the Christian religion to be true, or the Holy Scriptures to be of Divine authority, he shall, upon the first offence, be rendered incapable to hold any office or place of trust; and for the second, be incapable of bringing any action, being guardian, executor, legatee, or purchaser of lands, and suffer three years' imprisonment. Such disabilities may for *once* be avoided by a public recantation within four months after.

2 H

tical benefits are abridged by fiscal imposts and the
law of libel. As respects the latter, the known
opinions of Chief Justice Denman may be *pro tem-*
pore a practical security, but a public writer does
not like to hold his freedom by *courtesy*, he seeks
the guarantee of a well-defined law. The policy
of restricting the circulation of newspapers by stamp-
duties has been keenly contested. The extension
of political power by the Reform Acts appears to
call for an extension of the means of political *infor-*
mation. Few have advocated with more good sense
than Dr. Paley the advantages to society of discussion on matters of general interest. " The satis-
factions," says Paley, " the people in free governments derive from the knowledge and agitation of
political subjects; such as the proceedings and
debates of the senate, the conduct and characters
of ministers; the revolutions, intrigues, and contentions of parties; and in general, from the discussion of public measures, questions and occurrences. Subjects of this sort excite just enough
of interest and emotion to afford a moderate engagement to the thoughts without arising to any painful
degree of anxiety, or ever leaving a fixed oppression
on the spirits;—and what is this but the end and
aim of all those amusements which compose so much
of the business of life and the value of riches? For
my part (and I believe it to be the case with most
men who are arrived at the middle age, and occupy
the middle classes of life), had I all the money
which I pay in taxes to government, at liberty to

lay out in amusement and diversion, I know not whether I could make choice of any in which I find greater pleasure than what I receive from *expecting, hearing, and relating news*—reading parliamentary debates and proceedings; canvassing the political arguments, projects, productions, and intelligence which are conveyed by various channels to every corner of the kingdom. These topics, exciting universal curiosity, and being such as almost every man is prepared to form and deliver his opinion about, greatly promote, and I think improve conversation. They render it more rational and more innocent; they supply a substitute for gaming, drinking, and obscenity."—*Principles of Moral and Political Philosophy*, b. vi. ch. 6. A reduction of the newspaper duties would be to the people like the discovery of some new and useful invention, which brings within the reach of the whole community an article of luxury or comfort that had previously been accessible only to the richer classes.

VI. *The Executive.*—The constitutional maxim that " the king can do no wrong," is absurd in expression, but harmless in application. Its mischievousness is balanced by another maxim not less constitutional, " that the *illegal* commands of the king do not justify those who assist or concur in their execution;" and by a second rule subsidiary to this, that " the acts of the crown acquire not a *legal force* until authenticated by the subscription of some of its great officers." In some cases the royal commands must be signified by a secretary of state; in others, they must pass under the privy seal; and in many, under the great seal. Should, therefore, the private will of the sovereign be directed to illegal acts, they could not be executed without the co-operation of responsible ministers. Though the principal might escape with impunity, the accomplices would be liable to punishment, and a minister who had attested an illegal order would not be permitted to plead or produce the command of the king in justification of his obedience. Hence is derived the parliamentary practice of addressing the king to know by *whose advice* he resolved upon a particular measure; and of punishing the authors of that advice for the counsel they had given. The private inclinations of the king, or any disposition to *favouritism* in the choice of servants, is further restrained by the power of the House of Commons to stop the granting of supplies to ministers not possessing their confidence. The effect of this has often been to compel the king to form an administration not agreeably to his own predilection, but which, in the opinion of parliament, were best qualified to conduct the government.

VII. *Acts for the Amendment of the Representation.*—The theory of the *balance* of the constitution, that is of three equal and independent powers in the state, moving like the sun, moon, and the earth, in their several orbits, and reciprocally checking, controlling, and sustaining each other, was never, I apprehend, any thing more than a theory, and never had a practical existence in the government. Political power has always been substantially vested either in the king, lords, or commons, and was never, I conceive, contemporarily and conjointly exercised by the three estates, each possessing an aliquot and independent portion of the national sovereignty.

Up to the period of the revolution of 1688, the power of the crown was absolute, or at least so far preponderated in the government as to leave nothing like co-ordinate authority in the other branches of the legislature. The circumscription of the royal prerogatives by the Bill of Rights caused a transfer of the political supremacy of the monarch to the aristocracy. The acts for the amendment of the representation have effected a new disposition of power, and the supremacy which had been exercised by the peerage through the medium of the nomination boroughs has been transferred to the commons of the united kingdom.

That such has been the progress of public authority might be established by reference to past history, and the character of the measures now in progress through the legislature. Of the former predominance of regality in the constitution, the history of the Tudors and the claims of the Stuarts are a sufficient confirmation. The subsequent aristocratic bearing of the government has been manifested not less decidedly in the public policy pursued since the Orange revolution. Without joining in the popular clamour against the aristocracy, or thinking that their conduct has been more selfish

and arbitrary than that of any other class would
have been, possessed of like irresponsible power,
it cannot be denied that they have evinced their
political ascendancy in the control they have exercised over the crown in the choice of ministers—in
the allocation of taxes—in the objects of the wars
they have waged—in resisting the reform of judicial,
ecclesiastic, and corporate abuses—in short, in conducting the government precisely in that way which
has been most favourable to themselves, without
regard to the wellbeing of the community. The
measures in progress for the reform of public establishments in church and state testify to the new
interests incorporated in the constitution by the
reform acts, and show that the partial interests
formerly predominant in parliament have been abased
by the triumph of the democracy. The House of
Commons has exchanged places with the House
of Lords, and from being the subservient has become the controlling body ; and it is only, I apprehend by the lords quietly submitting to move in
this nether sphere, that its nominal position as one
of the three estates of the realm can be permanently
maintained. There is no general disposition in the
people, I verily believe, to alter the *frame* of the
government ; they are too well informed to put all
things to hazard—to have a sort of scramble, for the
sake of getting rid of a little pageantry and ceremony, or to achieve some paltry savings : *still,*
should the peerage unwisely become an obstacle to
the popular will, concentrated, intelligent, and all-

powerful as that will is, the result of a collision would most assuredly be fatal to "the proudest aristocracy in Europe," the programme of the days of the commonwealth would be rehearsed, and the House of Lords, as Mr. Burke observed of France, be "blotted out" of the political firmament. Such a catastrophe would be deeply to be deplored, as there is no foreseeing to what monstrosities in government it might give birth. *Forewarned, forearmed;* and as what has once happened may happen again, the following historical anomaly is subjoined :

"AN ACT FOR ABOLISHING THE HOUSE OF PEERS, passed the 19th of March, 1648 (*Old Style*).

"The Commons of England assembled in parliament, finding, by too long experience, that the House of Lords is *useless,* and dangerous to the people of England to be continued, have thought fit to ordain and enact, and be it ordained and enacted by this present parliament, and by the authority of the same, *that from henceforth the House of Lords in parliament, shall be and is hereby wholly abolished and taken away ;* and that the Lords shall not from henceforth meet or sit in the said house called the Lords' House, or in any other house or place whatsoever, as a House of Lords ; nor shall sit, vote, advise, judge, or determine of any matter or thing whatever, as a House of Lords in parliament ; nevertheless, it is hereby declared, that neither such Lords as have demeaned themselves with honour, courage, and fidelity to the commonwealth, nor their posterities (who shall continue so), shall be excluded from the public councils of the nation, but shall be admitted thereunto, and have their free vote in parliament, if they shall be *thereunto elected,* as other persons of interest elected and qualified thereunto ought to have. And be it further ordained and enacted by the authority aforesaid, that no peer of this land (not being elected, qualified, and sitting in parliament as aforesaid) shall *claim, have, or make use of any privilege of parliament*, either in relation to his person, quality, or estate, any law usage, or custom to the contrary notwithstanding."

Every one must see that government can only be carried on in accordance with public opinion ; that is, in accordance with the opinion of the metropolis and great towns of the kingdom.   What that opinion is may be derived by a more infallible test than even the composition of the House of Commons—namely, the tone of the public journals : they represent the national mind, and the direction of that mind unequivocally is to the substantial, not the illusive, removal of abuses.   The giant power that created a reformed parliament will support it in carrying through those specific measures of general alleviation for which parliamentary reform itself was conquered.

One of the consequences of past misgovernment has been such as its authors did not calculate upon. The Tories, when contracting the monstrous debt, and infolding every one in their fiscal web, were not aware of the trap they were preparing for themselves ; they were not aware that they were giving a greater political power to the people at large than they could possibly have done by the establishment of universal suffrage itself.   A large revenue can only be collected from an intelligent people while they are willing to pay it, and they will only be willing to pay it so long as public measures are in accordance with the public sentiment.   The people, therefore, may exultingly exclaim of their rulers as Cromwell of his enemies,—"*The Lord has delivered them into our hands!*" and government can only escape from this dilemma by the repeal of direct taxes, and by narrowing the circle of taxation; but these again are protective expedients, the adoption of which is next to impossible, in consequence of the pecuniary obligations in which they have recklessly tied themselves up!

CHAP. VI.

LAWS, MORALS, AND MANNERS.

PAINE truly observes, that a great part of that order which reigns among mankind has its origin in the principles of society and the natural constitution of man.* The mutual dependence and reciprocal interest which man has upon man, and all the parts of civilized community upon each other, create that great chain of connexion which holds it together. All classes and occupations prosper by the aid which each receives from the other and from the whole. Common interest regulates their concerns, and forms

* Some of my readers may feel surprised I should quote a proscribed author like Thomas Paine. The truth is, I have been lately looking over his political writings, and found more in them that is absurd than dangerous. Government, by wisely allowing them to be publicly sold, has deprived them of whatever potency they once possessed. They contain ingenious thoughts, but in the main are a jumble of conceits and impracticable dogmas, which the age has outlived.

that code of manners and usages, which has really a greater influence on social happiness than the laws themselves.

Civilization is only another name for laws and manners, and at first view it may appear that a person whose sole dependence is on his labour is not so deeply interested in their maintenance as the man of property. But this is a fallacious impression, and more attentive consideration will demonstrate, that the poor as well as the rich share in the advantages of the social state.

The first and most important benefit derived by all classes from the law is *personal security*. This is an advantage we have so long been in possession of that we can scarcely conceive the value of it, yet the times have been when it did not exist. That we now enjoy this blessing may be ascribed to various social improvements, especially the abolition of vassalage, the establishment of police, and the power of magistrates to punish criminal violence. In some of the despotic countries of Europe personal security is still inadequately secured; in Russia, and several of the states of Germany, serfship exists, and as to any redress a peasant or other inferior person could obtain for any merely personal attack, as, for instance, a blow from his landlord, the idea is almost chimerical. In England a very different degree of civilization has been attained, and no person, however wealthy or high in station, could with impunity raise his finger against the humblest individual, either in anger, wantonness, or revenge. This security is not limited to the person, it extends to the habitation. Every man's house is his "castle," and the cottage of the poor, no less than the mansion of the affluent, is protected from illegal intrusion.

The next important benefit derived from the supremacy of the law consists in the liberty of *loco-motion*. A working man was formerly restricted to the soil like cattle; if he strayed beyond the boundary of his employer he might be brought back with stripes, perhaps in bonds. His domain is now as wide as the world; wherever interest, pleasure, or curiosity may prompt him to go, he has privilege to roam without any one having the right to question or impede his progress. This is certainly liberty; and if we add to it the other advantage of personal security in its exercise, we may truly call it enjoyment, and one of the most gratifying results of civilization.

We come to a third great advantage of civil society in the *freedom of industry*. Every adult person is considered by political economists a portion of accumulated capital. A mere labourer cannot be reared from infancy to manhood without the expenditure of a considerable sum in clothing and food. If to mere sustenance be superadded a costly education, or instruction in a useful trade, then the value is still further augmented, and the owner of such capabilities possesses as productive a source of revenue as a freehold estate. The industrious classes all possess more or less property of this description, in the free disposal of which, and its bene-

ficial employment, they are as much interested as
any capitalist can be in his ships, buildings, or
machinery.   Now it is one of the advantages of civilization that industry as well as capital is protected,
and both enjoy freedom and security in their application.

As society advances the interests of the industrious will be still further promoted.   Labour is the
foundation of national wealth ; and a wise policy
prescribes that every obstacle to its development
should be removed.   Imposts which press on the
springs of industry, as well as monopolies which
restrict its freedom, must be abandoned.   Exclusive
privileges to trades may have been necessary in their
infancy, like nurture to childhood, but they become
fetters and impediments in maturity.   The policy of
entire freedom of industry is now generally recognised.   The functions of government are limited to
superintendence ; they are the stewards of the *course*,
whose duties consist in seeing fair play, and removing obstructions, leaving the prize of opulence
to the successful competitor.

Not only will freedom of industry, but also freedom of mind be established.   No errors, profitable
to the few and hurtful to the many, will be tolerated.
Every dogma and assumption must be submitted to
the test of discussion, and its truth or fallacy demonstrated.   As the end of government is the public
good, no partial interests, bolstered up at the expense of the general interest, will be suffered to
exist.   Thus, by the progress of knowledge, laws and

institutions will be made to contribute to their legitimate purposes—the general happiness of the community.

The manifest tendency of the improvements in the English government now in progress is to identify its interests with those of the people, to divest it of every thing like a corporate and exclusive interest separate from that of the community. This is the end mainly sought to be accomplished by the enforcement of public economy; it is not thought that society will be materially benefited by the saving of one or five millions in the national expenditure; but the reduction of lavish salaries, and unmerited pensions and sinecures, divests power of its corrupt and extraneous support—support extraneous and opposed to the interests of the people, and which has caused its agents to look more to the emoluments of administration than the public welfare—and which corrupt and extraneous support has naturally tended to render the instruments of authority uneasy at, and averse to, the freedom and enlightenment of the people, lest it should disturb or shorten the term of enjoyment of their factitious advantages. When government is based on the general interest, it must be favourable to every change and every measure which tends to the benefit of that interest.

The same reasoning applies to the reform of the judicial administration, the established church, and corporations; it is not merely the saving which is to accrue from the abolition of legal fees, tithes, and municipal corruption, but the taking away the pabulum and vicious motives which support interests exercising great influence in society, and rendering them favourable to, and not jealous of and opposed to, the common weal.

Leaving law and government, let us advert to the subject of MORALS.

The basis of morality, like that of law, is utility. Moral obligations result from experience of the evil consequences of their violation. They differ from laws in being left to the cognizance of individuals, and not being enforced by public authority. They also differ in their consequences. Criminal actions affect society; immoral ones chiefly the authors. Though the latter are less atrocious they are often more hurtful to the perpetrators than the former. Take theft and drunkenness for illustrations. Stealing is a crime because it renders the possession of property insecure, but the punishment of the delinquent only indirectly involves his family and connexions. On the other hand, inebriety operates very differently; it scarcely affects the community, but it is the source of ruin to the individual, and, mostly, to every one dependent upon him, or with whom he is connected.

The ties of morality bind all, but the same actions do not affect all classes alike, because their consequences are different. Actions which are only follies in the rich may amount to almost crimes in the poor. Idleness and intemperance, for example, are completely ruinous to the domestic comforts of a mechanic or tradesman, while to the opulent, however personally degrading, they are comparatively innoxious. Economy, order, and punctuality, are cardinal virtues in the industrious; in the wealthy they are of secondary consideration: they are vices in all, but poverty and destruction to some.

It is not necessary to run into an ethical disquisition, for there is no dearth of moral teachers: most men know the obligations of virtue, only they want fortitude to practise them. This can only be acquired by the formation of good habits, and a firm resolution not to incur great permanent evils for slight momentary enjoyments, and these again must be the result of sound education.

The third and last consideration is the influence of MANNERS on social happiness. The usages of society have established certain forms, founded on experience of their utility, to regulate the ordinary intercourse of individuals. Though neglect of these forms is not so great an evil as a violation of the laws, or of morals, still they cannot be disregarded without mutual inconvenience and annoyance. The pleasures and occupations of the higher classes resulting chiefly from social intercourse, the rules of politeness established among them are more numerous and more scrupulously observed than among the industrious orders; but no class can disregard them with impunity. Among all a mutual deference and reciprocity of feeling are essential to enjoyment. A person rude in nature, arrogant and assuming, indifferent to the comforts and conveniences of others, must be a nuisance which every

one would be desirous to shun or abate. Those
who do not sufficiently appreciate the value of the
minor virtues, have only to test them by experience,
and contrast the relative advantages of a neglect and
observance of them in society: the one is all strife,
contradiction, selfishness, and assumption; the other
agreeableness, concord, and at least the semblance
of disinterestedness—one is peace, the other war, on
the domestic hearth.

In manners, as other things, extremes are to be
avoided. The object of politeness, as well as laws
and morals, is utility. Useless restraints then are
to be shunned. Liberty is itself an enjoyment, and
no restriction on it should be imposed merely for
the sake of an unprofitable etiquette, but only for
some compensating advantage. If men were all
virtuous, laws would be unnecessary; if they were
all rational and disinterested, there would be no need
of forms of politeness: the obligations of the former
are imposed to restrain the vicious and violent, and
of the latter the selfish and low-minded.

In order to avoid running into commonplace
remarks on such old-fashioned topics, I shall conclude with two observations. The first is, that
though laws appear to claim the highest attention in
every well-ordered community, yet they are not so
vitally interesting to the bulk of society as morals
and manners. Many persons, during a long life,
never become obnoxious to the laws in any capacity;
they never violate them, neither have they occasion
to enforce them against any individual. To them

the whole apparatus of courts, magistrates, and judicial procedure are a dead letter; they benefit, it is true, from the protection they afford, but their own personal conduct is quite unaffected by their operations. Can the same be said of morals and manners? Certainly not. No one can pass through life without being gratified or annoyed by the good or ill demeanour of his neighbours, friends, and acquaintance. The relative importance then of laws, morals, and manners, must be evident; good laws are of contingent benefit to some; correct morals and manners of interest to all. The second observation applies to the different powers for enforcing the several obligations we have been considering. Laws are enforced by the state; morals and manners by individuals; a breach of one is penal, the other only disgraceful; fear upholds one, honour the other. These different species of coercion readily account for the different degress of restraint imposed by laws and manners, on the mean and high-minded, the cultivated and uncultivated portions of mankind.

CHAP. VII.

RIGHTS OF PROPERTY.

In the cultivation of the earth, two modes may be adopted : either it may be cultivated in common or individually ; the disadvantage of the former is that it makes no distinction between the weak and strong, the idle and industrious : for superior exertion and ability there is no superior reward. Under this system, the world would not be reclaimed—men will not willingly labour for others ; to stimulate exertion, rewards must in some degree be proportioned to desert. Appropriation, therefore, or the right of every one to enjoy the produce of his industry, became necessary to the effective cultivation of the earth ; each man having a portion of land allotted to him in which he vested his labour, became entitled to its produce. This was probably the foundation of property in the soil. By its introduction, no man's natural rights can be said to have been extinguished or encroached upon ; the earth before lay common to all, but unprofitable to all—by appropriation it has been made valuable to all. Farther than this it does not appear necessary to inquire into the origin of the rights of property ; their obvious utility must have forced themselves on every people on first emerging from the barbarous state.

A state of society in which there is equality of possessions, in which each man tills his own land, and raises the food and clothing necessary to his wants, appears at first sight very fascinating. It favours that feeling of independence so dear to the human heart. But if we reflect on the tendency of such a mode of social or rather anti-social existence, we shall find it pregnant with misery.

In the first place, the mere labour of society would be greatly augmented. As each person's means would not exceed his current necessities, they would not exceed the amount essential to the maintenance of himself and family, the idea of capitalists is precluded, and consequently no expedient for saving labour by machinery or otherwise, could be employed. All would be engaged in spade husbandry or other manual occupation. Such a disadvantageous mode of exertion would obviously be very unproductive; it would yield none of the luxuries, and barely the comforts, of life; people would hardly be better off than the cotter peasantry of Ireland, or the pauper colonists of Holland; and the whole of society would be literally brought under the primitive curse inflicted on our first parents. If the physical wants were supplie l with so much difficulty, the mental ones would be totally neglected. As each would be fully occupied in providing sustenance, there would be no spare time to any for intellectual pursuits. If science, philosophy, and the arts had exis ed, they would speedily fall into disuse and oblivion. Ignorance and barbarism would overspread the land. Men would become unacquainted with themselves and with the natural phenomena by which they are surrounded. Their past

history and future destiny would be alike shut from
view; they would move, as it were, in darkness—
the victims of suspicion, of mutual mistrust and
superstitious fears—a prey to all those calamities
which are known to be inseparable from savage life
when divested of the illusions of the imagination.

From such a state of universal toil and dreariness,
one naturally turns to the more cheerful appearance
which actual society presents, and one of whose
chief advantages is derived from the circumstance
that certain classes are exempt from at least the
necessity of bodily labour. Now this advantage
could not be possessed without a certain degree
of inequality in men's fortunes; in other words, the
existence of a proprietary class. Property is not
a free gift of Nature; the value even of landed
property is chiefly a product of labour; it is almost
entirely capital, or the produce of anterior industry.
But if this capital or property did not exist, there
would be no fund in reserve to maintain a class
of persons occupied in what have been very inaccu-
rately termed unproductive employments: all would
be engaged in procuring food or raiment, and none
could exclusively devote themselves to the pursuits
of literature, science, and legislation.

Besides augmenting the produce of the earth, and
creating a surplus beyond the wants of the producers, the rights of property have other advantages:
they *preserve it to maturity.* " We may judge,"
says Dr. Paley, " what would be the effects of a
community of right to the productions of the earth,

from the trifling specimens we see of it at present.
A cherry-tree in a hedge-row, nuts in a wood, the
grass of an unstinted pasture, are seldom of much
advantage to any body, because people do not wait
for the proper season of reaping them. Corn, if any
were sown, would never ripen; lambs and calves would
never grow up to sheep and cows, because the first
person that met them would reflect, that he had better
take them as they are than leave them to another."

Property also prevents *contests*. War and waste,
tumult and confusion, must be unavoidable and
eternal where there is not enough for all, and where
there are no rules to adjust the division.

Further it improves the *conveniency of living* by
facilitating the division of employments. Without
property this would be impossible, for there could
be no exchanges of commodities; in a community
of goods, every thing would belong to every body:
no one would have any production which he could
call his own, and which he would be entitled to
exchange for the production of another man. We
should thus be deprived of one of the chief advantages of civilized life. When a man is from necessity his own tailor, tent-maker, carpenter, cook,
huntsman, and fisherman, it is not probable that he
will be expert at any of his callings. Hence the
rude habitations, furniture, clothing, and implements
of savages; and the tedious length of time all their
operations require.

Upon these several accounts, we may venture,
with few exceptions, to pronounce, that even the

poorest and worst provided, in countries where property, and the consequences of property prevail, are in a better situation with respect to food, raiment, houses, and what are called the necessaries of life, than any one in places where most things remain in common.

Against the institution of property, it is urged that it is the source of *competition* among mankind. This, on reflection, will be found a recommendation. Property is mostly the reward of ability, sobriety, and perseverance. Without its stimulating agency, we should have little eminence, social, moral, or intellectual. The innate tendency of man is to repose, not to persevering exertion; and if superior application, superior enterprise, or superior endowments, were not rewarded, few would sedulously devote themselves to trade, agriculture, manufactures, and the useful arts. In pursuit of these, an honourable—not a greedy, short-sighted, and fraudulent—spirit of competition is salutary, by stimulating invention and rivalry, which tend to general cheapness, excellence, and accommodation.

For competition, Mr. Owen would substitute *cooperation*. But do not the several classes of society already co-operate in the most advantageous manner for the common benefit of the community? One class is occupied in rural industry, another in manufactures and commerce, another in science and letters. Each is rewarded, not always perhaps, but mostly in proportion to desert: but the claims of merit would not be recognised under Mr. Owen's system; the indolent would reap the rewards of the industrious, the vicious of the more deserving. This is more like *corporation* than co-operation, the principle of the old monastic institutions and commercial monopolies—associations of whose stagnating, debasing and injurious tendency the world has already had sufficient experience.

· Rousseau, the Abbé Mably, Godwin and Paine, have objected to the institution of property, the *partiality* of its advantages. They allow that it is advantageous to those who possess property, but contend that it is disadvantageous to those who have none. " It has tended," says Paine, " to make one part of society more affluent, and the other part more wretched than would have been the lot of either in a natural state." The radical difference between the civilized and natural state is, that in the latter, *all are poor*—all are in a state of discomfort, insecurity, and privation, and none are rich. But even in this state there is not exact equality of condition; all are not equally strong, dexterous, and persevering in fishing, hunting, and hut-building ; and these inequalities of endowments produce inequalities in the rewards of their exertions. In the civil or natural state, no two individuals are exactly alike, either in mental or physical qualities; they differ in their habits as in their stature, complexion and strength, and supposing an equality of possessions was at any time forcibly established, it could not possibly continue for a day or hardly an hour,—some would be more

wasteful than others, some more industrious and
inventive.   There may doubtless be institutions
which tend to aggravate the inequalities inseparable
from human nature; these institutions may have
risen from the predominance of proprietary influence
in legislation; but such abuses are wholly unconnected with the utility of the right of property, and
the progress of society must necessarily tend to alleviate them; the right of property of itself *is an*
unmixed and universal benefit.   Without its protection, the rich would become poor, and the poor
be unable to become rich, and all would sink to the
same bottomless abyss of misery and barbarism.   It
gives no exclusive advantage—it only gives general
security;   it does not take from one to give to
another, it only says to all—*labour, and I shall take
care that none shall be permitted to rob you of the
produce of your exertions.*   "It is the security
of property," says Bentham, "that has overcome
the natural aversion of man from labour, that has
given him the empire of the earth, that has given
him a fixed and permanent residence, that has implanted in his breast the love of his country and
of posterity.   To enjoy immediately—to enjoy
without labour, is the natural inclination of every
man.   This inclination must be restrained; for its
obvious tendency is to arm all those who have
nothing against those who have something.   The
law which restrains this inclination, and which
secures to every individual the quiet enjoyment

of the fruits of his industry, is the most splendid achievement of legislative wisdom—the noblest triumph of which humanity has to boast."—*Traité de Legislation*, ii. p. 37.

CHAP. VIII.

INSTITUTION OF MARRIAGE.

THE civil institution next in importance to that of private property, is the contract of marriage. Writers who have disputed the policy of property-rights have naturally also disputed the policy of matrimonial rights, and have considered the appropriation of women, like the appropriation of land, an infringement of the common immunities of mankind. The analogy between marriage and property is striking, and the chief arguments which vindicate the utility of one, are applicable to the other.

1.—Marriage is favourable to an increase in the number, and improvement in the character of females.

If an increase of women, like an increase of the produce of the earth, be conducive to the happiness of men—which no one will deny—whatever tends to multiply the number must be esteemed advantageous.

But for obvious reasons the irregularities of promiscuous intercourse are unfavourable to the multiplication of the species; even in countries where polygamy prevails it is known to operate as a check on the population; and such must be its natural tendency, for this reason, that as the two sexes are nearly equal in number, if one man has more wives than one, another must have less, so that the effect is similar, though in a less degree, to women being held in common.

Not only would the number be fewer, but they would be rendered less valuable. A woman in common would be like a field in common, or a child with many parents; there would be no concentration of care upon any particular female; all those ties and obligations which unite parties in marriage, and give them a mutual interest, would be dissolved. The effect of this would be a general depreciation of women in society; they would be treated with less attention and consideration; they would be like the air we breathe, necessary to life, but not being appropriated, they would have no exchangeable price. But as they lost their value the same pains would not be bestowed on their cultivation; their education and bringing up would be neglected: all the graces and accomplishments which add as much to the value of females as the arts of the horticulturist add to the products of the conservatory, would be abandoned, as an useless expenditure on a commodity so ordinary as women would then become.

2.—Marriage preserves women to maturity.

Without marriage the same reasons would not exist for interdicting sexual intercourse till females attain to womanhood. The chastity of the bride is her most valuable portion; in a community of women there would be no such future contingency for which the harvest need be husbanded. Females would be similarly situated to the cherry-tree in a hedge row, or nuts in a wood without owner, and which has been alluded to in the case of property; they would be of no advantage to any one, because people would not wait for the proper season of gathering them; each would be fearful of being anticipated by his neighbour, and the young be prematurely defloured.

3.—It prevents contests.

The value of women differs as much as any of the goods of life, arising from diversity of personal attractions, temper, and accomplishments. Were they not appropriated by marriage, the contests that would ensue for the possession of the most estimable would be furious and unceasing. The desire of gain frequently calls into action the furious passions of men, but the conflicts from lust would be far more dreadful. Nations have gone to war for one woman, but if the whole sex were open to contention the world would be in arms; and not unfrequently the object of contest be sacrificed in the struggle. In place of such calamities how superior is the existing arrangement! The lists are marked out, the fair are open to the competition of all—no monopoly, every one is at liberty to make proposals, and the most worthy, or most favoured, wins the prize. When two parties have agreed, the unsuccessful candidates are precluded from further interference ; and thus, by an admirable civil contrivance, is a division of the most precious of earth's products effected without violence, tumult, or disorder.

4.—It improves the conveniency of living.

This it does two ways. Viewed as a common partnership, marriage tends to facilitate and lessen the duties of each ; having a common interest it also tends to their mutual improvement and advantage. It likewise improves living by promoting independence ; each family constitutes a separate community in the state, united by a sort of federative union, and only amenable to the general laws of society in such matters as affect the general interests : we thus enjoy the advantages of natural liberty, combined with the advantages of social organization.

Having shown the analogy subsisting between marriage and property, I might advert to reasons peculiar to the former, and which do not apply to the latter : such as the example of other orders of the creation, and the necessity of the nuptial tie for the well-educating and nurture of children ; but these are topics familiar to every mind which has bestowed the slightest attention on the subject.

I shall conclude with inserting some extravagances published on the subject of marriage upwards of forty years ago by a distinguished living writer. In the introductory chapter to this Part I endea

voured to show that philosophers are often as mad
in their way as the empirical enthusiast, and that
the judicious application and limitation of general
principles to their legitimate issues, are quite as important as their discovery. Hear what an apostle of
the new light propounded on the subject we have
been considering :—

"Add to this that marriage as now understood is a *monopoly,*
and the worst of monopolies. So long as two human beings
are forbidden by positive institutions to follow the dictates of
their own mind, prejudice will ever be alive and vigorous. So
long as I seek, by despotic and artificial means, to engross a
woman to myself, and to prohibit my NEIGHBOUR *from proving
his superior claim,* I am guilty of the most odious *selfishness.*
Over this imaginary prize men watch with perpetual jealousy ;
and one man finds his desire and his capacity to circumvent as
much excited, as the other is excited to traverse his projects
and frustrate his hopes. As long as this state of society continues, *philanthropy* will be crossed and checked in a thousand
ways, and the still augmenting stream of abuse will continue to
flow."—*Enquiry concerning Political Justice,* v. ii. p. 499. Edit.
1796.

"In a *state of equality* it will be a question of *no importance to
know who is the parent of each individual child.* It is aristocracy,
self-love, and family pride, that teach us to set a value upon it
at present. I ought to prefer no human being to another, because that being is *my father, my wife, or my son,* but because for
reasons which equally appeal to all understandings, that being is
entitled to preference. One among the measures which will
successively be dictated by the *spirit of democracy,* and that
probably at *no great distance,* is the abolition of SURNAMES."—
Ibid, p. 503.

This must assuredly be the *ne plus ultra* of Uto-
pianism. The commencement of the French Revo-

lution produced an intellectual intoxication in many who afterwards lived to be sobered. Every thing *old* was deemed presumptively *bad*, and every thing *new* presumptively good. It was a rush between two extremes.

CHAP. IX.

POPULAR EDUCATION.

Object and Necessity of Education—Ought to be adapted to future Occupation—Maintenance and Choice of Employment—Branches of Knowledge constituting Popular Instruction—Domestic Economy—Art of Preserving Health—Laws and Moral Philosophy—Property and Government—Political Economy—Superstitious Fears and Apprehensions—Popular Education, a duty imposed on the State—How it may be promoted by Parish Schools, the Magistracy, Clergy, Fiscal Regulations, and Employers of Workpeople—Objections to National Education considered— Progress of Education in England—Connexion of Education with the Increase of Crime—Improvement in the Character of the People—Distinction between Moral and Physical Knowledge—Influence of Education on Happiness and Conduct of Life.

EDUCATION is acquiring in infancy the knowledge useful to ourselves and others in maturity. It is not limited to book-learning; the learning of a useful art or trade, the attainment by practice of habits of industry and application ; the mastering of a recreation or accomplishment favourable to health, innocent amusement, or general convenience : all these are alike educational acquirements, valuable as tending to augment individual and social happiness.

We have improved so greatly over the rudeness and helplessness of nature, that art and science co-operate in the pursuits of every class of society. In the forms and usages of civil life, in domestic economy, in manufactures, commerce, and professions, the improvements are almost innumerable which facilitate social intercourse, economise expenditure, multiply and perfect the products of industry. The great end of education is to place within the reach of infancy these results of experience, to increase individual power—power to augment the good and lessen the evil incident to humanity.

The contrast between a naked savage and armed man is not greater than between the untutored and educated. A person commencing his career without previous culture is shorn of his fair proportions—his term of existence is abridged, and he enters on the race of life at every disadvantage. Hence arises the obligation imposed on parents. and which natural affection prompts them to discharge. The ties of nature bind them to the maintenance of their offspring; but they are not less bound to provide them with the resources of knowledge. Without these, they only give them existence which may be an affliction unaccompanied with the means to maintain it; they are placed on the stage of life where their moral and physical powers are stunted, or not developed; and lameness, blindness, or other infirmity would hardly subject them to greater privations in the enjoyments and competitions of the world.

Society suffers as well as individuals by this omission. Education is the best branch of social police, inasmuch as it destroys the chief seeds of crime, want, and ignorance. Dr. Paley has forcibly remarked that to send an uneducated child into the world, is little better than to turn out a mad dog or wild beast into the streets. Children so unfortunately situated have not equal chances of happiness; they are mostly miserable and often vicious, either from the indigence which want of training in habits of industry and arts of life tend to induce, or from the want of some rational and inoffensive occupation.

It is unnecessary, however, at this day, to insist on the advantages of learning. The pleasure as well as the profit to be reaped from knowledge, are now generally recognised. If the time ever existed when any class of society sought an advantage by keeping the rest in ignorance, it is past, and all alike seek peace, security, and prosperity from the diffusion of intelligence. Men are divided, not upon the utility of popular instruction, but upon the kind of knowledge of which it ought to consist, and the most efficient means of its communication. My object will be to submit a few remarks on both these branches of inquiry.

A primary maxim of education is that the course of instruction should be adapted to the future occupations of life. Knowledge of any kind cannot be a detriment, but it is obvious that the acquirements most essential to the possessor in the pursuits and necessities of his station ought to be first secured. This rule is so self-evident that only the most injudicious neglect its observance.

As education ought to have a reference to the atmosphere in which we are destined to live and move—a different course of instruction is prescribed for the different orders of society. Those born to the inheritance of a fortune, or to professional or legislative duties, require a species of knowledge and accomplishment the advantages of which would not reward the cost of acquisition to those intended for a different sphere of life. Again, a merchant, manufacturer, or even an artizan, requires knowledge that would be comparatively valueless to a ploughman.

In this remark it is not meant that the pursuit of knowledge of any kind, useful or ornamental, should be interdicted to any class of the community. This would be unjust, and often hurtful to society. Individuals are constantly being found in all the walks of life with singular aptitude for pursuits quite foreign to their occupation ; and indeed it has been truly remarked, that the most valuable discoveries in the arts and sciences have mostly been made by persons not immediately, or as one may say officially engaged in their cultivation. My remark is only meant to fix a general rule, not its exceptions. I may further observe, in order to limit the scope of our subject, that my purpose is not to

2 K

treat on education generally, but only upon that branch of it applicable to the industrious orders, or what is usually termed popular education : so called, I presume, from its applying to the great bulk of the community, or as comprising that portion of knowledge which it is desirable every member of society should possess. By the industrious orders is meant those classes who have not the means of sustentation independent of their industry. Their most urgent necessity is a maintenance suited to their condition, and the knowledge which most facilitates the attainment of this will be to them of the first consideration.

During infancy the obligation of *maintenance* clearly devolves on parents, for no one can have a right to burden others with the consequence of his own act. Hence arises the guilt of those who run away from their families, or through idleness and drunkenness throw them upon a parish; or who leave them destitute at their death, when, by diligence and frugality, they might have laid up a provision for their support : also of those who refuse or neglect the care of their bastard offspring, abandoning them to a condition in which they must either perish, or become burdensome to others; for the duty of maintenance, like the reason upon which it is founded, extends to natural as well as to legitimate children.

The duty of maintenance is not limited to the period of infancy; parents are bound to look to the maintenance of their children after they attain maturity, and in this properly consists the first stage of education.

In the Working Classes this principle condemns those who do not inure their children betimes to labour and restraint, by providing them with apprenticeships, services, or other regular employment, but who suffer them to waste their youth in idleness and vagrancy, or to betake themselves to some lazy, trifling, and precarious calling; for the consequence of indulging in this unrestrained license when the relish for it is greatest is, that they become incapable, for the remainder of their lives, of continued industry and persevering attention to any thing: spend their time in a miserable struggle between the importunity of want and the irksomeness of regular application, and are ready to adopt any expedient which presents a hope of supplying their necessities, without confining them to the plough, manufactory, shop, or counting-house.

In the Middle Classes of society those parents are most reprehensible who neither qualify their children for a mercantile or professional pursuit, nor enable them to live without one. So imperative was this deemed among the Athenians, that if the father did not put his child into a way of getting a livelihood, the child was not bound to make a provision for him when old and necessitous. Even persons of fortune are not exempt from this obligation. They have duties to discharge for which they ought to be fully qualified by their previous attainments; and *if*

parents from indolence, indulgence, or avarice, permit their children to consume the season of education in hunting, horse-races, gambling, balls, or
other unedifying, if not vicious diversions, they
defraud the community of a benefactor, and be-
queath them a nuisance.*

With respect to the choice of a calling that will
be mostly determined by the condition of parents.
It is the natural desire and the right of every one to
seek to better his lot, but as the expectations of
children are mostly limited to the situation of their
parents, the duty of the latter is fairly discharged if
they enable their offspring to succeed them in their
own or similar occupation. Hence a labourer or
artisan satisfies his duty who sends out his children,
properly instructed for their employment, to husbandry, or any branch of manufacture. This is the
general rule. But where the child shows a marked
propensity or talent for a pursuit (as was the case
of Cooke, Ferguson, and Franklin), it ought always
to be consulted, and provided it is neither vicious
nor criminal, and in the power of the parent, ought
to be encouraged and promoted.

As happiness is the universal aim, and as health
and virtue conduce more thereto than riches or
power, or any other object of desire, whatever has
the smallest influence on these, claims a parent's

* These remarks are abridged from Dr. Paley, who was well
versed in the practical philosophy of life, and I know no reason
why we ought not to avail ourselves of the good, provided we
shun the evil, in the works of so sensible an observer.

first attention. In respect of health, agriculture, and all active rural and out-of-door employments are mostly preferred; but recent inquiries show that crowded towns, like the metropolis, and sedentary occupations, are not so unfavourable to longevity as had been supposed. Intemperance, protracted hours of labour, without intervals of relaxation, and mental anxiety, are the great destroyers of life: these it is often in the power of individuals to modify and without it length of days is not to be expected in any situation. In respect of virtue, a course of dealing in which the advantage is mutual, in which the profit on one side is connected with the benefit of the other (which is the case in trade, and all useful arts and labour), is more favourable to the moral character than callings in which one man's gain is another man's loss; in which what you acquire is acquired without equivalent, and parted with in distress; as in gaming, and whatever partakes of the nature of gaming—as in the prizes and plunder of warfare. A business like a retail trade, in which the profits are small and frequent, and accruing from the employment, furnishes a moderate and constant engagement to the mind, and so far suits better with the general disposition of mankind than engagements which are supported by fixed salaries, or wherein the profits are made by large sums, by a few great concerns or fortunate speculations; as in many branches of commerce and foreign adventure, in which the occupation is neither so constant nor the activity so kept alive by immediate encouragement. For security personal industry exceeds trade, and such as supplies the wants of men is better than that which ministers to their pleasures.

These appear the most essential considerations in reference to maintenance, or the physical part of education. We next proceed to what is intellectual, and bears on the adult period of life. This branch of the subject is extensive, embracing all the knowledge appertaining to the interests of the industrious orders, and which a national scheme of popular instruction ought to comprise; much of this knowledge, I trust, has been afforded in this publication, but a great deal has been necessarily omitted. I shall briefly describe the species of information which the People's Encyclopædia in my opinion ought to include.

I.—Reading, writing, and ciphering.

In the existing state of society these are so constantly requisite in every business of life, that the humblest individual might almost with as much propriety appear abroad naked as without a knowledge of them. It is a reproach to any civilized community not to have established a general provision by which these elements of information might be acquired by every member of society. The time was when nearly all knowledge was orally communicated; a knowledge of religion, and even the contents of the Scriptures, could only be derived from the mouth of the priest, and new laws were divulged to the people in *viva voce* proclamations by the sheriff at the county courts. But printing has almost superseded speaking ; laws are communicated through acts of parliament, and religion through the medium of the liturgy. The single fact that public statutes are sent forth to the people in printed documents, and the well-known legal maxim that ignorance of laws affords no plea for their non-observance, appears to impose on the legislature the duty of placing within the reach of every one the means of learning to read. Writing and ciphering, though not so indispensable as reading, form also branches of popular instruction ; but it is unnecessary to dwell either on the pr_fit or pleasure to be derived from these acquirements.

2.—Domestic knowledge, including first, cottage or household economy, and second, the duties of a husband or parent under his own roof.

> Well to keep and make a fire
> Does no little skill require.

A book might be written on the theory of combustion. A poor man does not require this knowledge, but he requires good examples to teach him how to economize, and efficiently use fuel. Count Rumford did more for the world by his devotion to this single subject than Napoleon by all his slaughterings. The writer of this remembers taxing the science of either Dr. Birkbeck or Dr. Arnott to explain, on philosophical principles, why a poker laid across a low fire accelerates combustion. Neither of these learned gentlemen, I believe, gave a satisfactory solution of this problem, but that the effect is so any domestic will bear witness, or indeed it may be easily proved by experiment.

Baking and brewing are two important chemical processes in constant requisition. A well-known political writer, in his little book on " Cottage Economy," has treated both these subjects admirably: as also the fattening of pigs, and the keeping of bees and poultry. Londoners neither brew nor bake ; cooped up, perhaps, in a single room, in a narrow court, with hardly any furniture, their chief occupations are to dress, frequent the theatre and tea-gardens, and drink a poisonous compound which shall be nameless. In the country, especially the northern counties, the case is altered, where the oven and copper are almost inseparable adjuncts to every fire place. Cooking is an art of more general use than baking and brewing. For want of a knowledge of the best mode of dressing victuals, a large portion of the nutriment passes up the chimney, or is cast on the dunghill.

Not the least valuable branch of saving, however, is the *art of spending*. The poor are certainly the greatest prodigals. How lavishly their means are wasted ! They are mulcted three ways, in quantity, quality, and price : in the first, owing to the smallness of their purchases at once, by the turn of the scale or the pot ; in the last by a trumpery system of credit, fostered by those nuisances called small debtor courts, which are a real injury to buyers and sellers—fill the gaols, demoralize the poor, and

spread hate and revenge in every neighbourhood.
For the misfortune or the folly of being one week
behind in expenditure, and being necessitated to
resort to *one* shopkeeper during the week, and who
must be paid in whole or in part on Saturday night,
the poor pay, perhaps, thirty per cent. more than
the rich on all they consume. The retailer is not
to blame for this ; he must be paid for extra trouble
in weighing small quantities; it is also necessary
the extra profit laid on those who do pay should
make up his losses by those who do not—a system,
by the by, of taxing the just for the unjust, and
chiefly favourable to practitioners in insolvent
courts, and the dissolute and wasteful, who are
sheltered and encouraged in extravagance by the
facilities the credit system affords.

Upon economy in the poor Arthur Young has
made some valuable remarks, which I cannot help
transcribing :—

"This economy," says he, "is in all cases the more to be
urged, because the difference in comforts of the same families at
the same expense, well or ill-conducted, is greater, often than
that of different families at different expenses. There is more
difference, comparatively, in the mode of living from economy
than from income; the deficiency from income may possibly be
made up by increase of work or wages ; but the want of economy is irremediable, and the least income will undoubtedly do
more with it than the greatest without it. No master can, in
the first place, afford wages ; next no overseer can make allowances ; lastly, no magistrate can order relief enough, on any
calculation but that of their being severally well-managed. If
the poor do not prudently serve themselves none can effectively
assist them; if they are not their *own friends* none can effec-

tively befriend them : the idle in procuring, or the wasteful in using the means of subsistence, have neither that supply which is alone due, and can be alone afforded, to the honest, industrious, and prudent.   It highly, then, interests all conversant with the poor, who ought to be literally all, and it is hoped are most, to consult and co-operate with them in the practice of economy ; it is far more useful to teach them to spend less, or to save a little, than to give them much more."—*Annals of Agriculture*, vol. 25, p. 359—361.

Let it not be inferred from this that I recommend any saving that can be effected only by a stinted and degrading diet ; the economy I wish to inculcate consists in the avoidance of needless and ignorant waste : the aim of all, as before explained, ought to be the command of better food, better clothing, and better lodging; in short, a greater command over all the comforts and conveniences of living.

Let us proceed to the second or moral branch of domestic knowledge.   In this the chief lineaments of the character are cast.   Our religion, politics, morals, language, manners, and even gestures, are mostly derived from the parental type.   How careful, then, our fathers and mothers ought to be to set us good copies !   They ought to know they are sowing the seed of good or evil to unknown generations.   All their own children see, hear, feel, suffer, or enjoy, it will be the lot of future children to undergo and partake of.   Their words, precepts, and actions ; their examples as masters, citizens, parents, husbands, and wives, will be the law and precedent regulating the demeanour of future masters, citizens, husbands, parents, and wives. As heads of families each is the founder and governor of one of the little federative states of which the body politic is composed ; and it depends on their primary training and rule whether they shall be the authors of new sources of disorder and misery, or joy and benefit to the community.

. 3.—Art of preserving health.

The doctoring of a poor constitution abridges enjoyment like a heavy tax or low income. Health is money : to both sexes when married it is as good as a portion—it is better, for it is not only a fortune, but affords the best means of comfortably enjoying one. As a mere saving consideration, then, it is desirable to have the least possible need of the fraternity of Esculapius. But it may be shown the cultivation of health is intimately connected with the cultivation of morals. " A sound body, a sound mind," is proverbial. Superstitious fears, slavish notions, weak compliance, indolence, and negligence, as often arise from bodily debility as vicious principle. It is hardly necessary to say more on the importance of the art of preserving health as a branch of popular knowledge.

. It is not meant, however, that every one should be his own doctor ; that would be really making work for the physician. The object of the medical art is to *cure* diseases ; the object of popular medicine is their *prevention :* one operates by a knowledge of drugs, of which an unprofessional person ought never to presume he knows any thing ; the other chiefly by a knowledge of the effects of diet, air, and exercise. These last are, in truth, the physicians of Nature, and by due attention to them, ninety-nine diseases out of the hundred may be averted or cured. Medicine is mostly but the quack of these natural practitioners, and attempts, by shorter but artificial process, to do what they alone would accomplish. Diet is, perhaps, the most important of the three. Dr. Crichton places meagre fare at the head of a list of causes which weaken attention, and consequently debilitate the faculties of the mind. A profound writer remarks, that good diet is a necessary part of education. "Wretchedness," says he, "is incompatible with excellence: you never can make a wise and virtuous people out of a starving one." This is assuredly true. Hunger benumbs and parches the soul: it dries up all its nobler and more generous qualities, and renders it a dreary waste, soured by selfishness, discontent, hatred, and revenge.

By good diet, is not meant excessive or luxurious indulgence; these would not be good, but substantial, wholesome aliment, adapted to the age, constitution, and employment.

That the air is deteriorated by breathing, is generally known, but not universally; otherwise so many persons would not be careless of living, sleeping, and working in unventilated rooms, workshops, factories, and counting-houses. To tolerate about our person or habitation excretions of the animal economy, is justly considered injurious to health and repugnant to delicacy and cleanliness; it is not less so to inspire a contaminated atmosphere: for the *nutriment* of the air is quite as effectually extracted by inspiration as the nutriment of food is by digestion, and the residue in either case ought to be deemed equally offensive.

The old-fashioned practice of out-a-door recreation is the best recipe for oxidating the system, and taking air abundant in quantity and good in quality. Some years since, an attempt was made by Professor Clias to render gymnastic exercises a more general part of juvenile and adult education. Like all novelties on first introduction, they were carried to excess, or not judiciously adapted to their purpose; they were also checked by the mercantile revulsion of 1824-5, which nipped in the bud many other projects of utility. An allotment of land in each parish on the plan proposed by Mr. Slaney, for popular exercises, would be favourable to public health and morals. A revival of some of the old sports and pastimes would be an improvement in national manners; and the attractions of cards, dice, opium-eating, and dram-drinking, be benecially exchanged for the more wholesome recreation of former ages. " Worse practices," Stow remarks, " it is to be feared, have succeeded the more open pastimes of the elder time."

The *nursing of children* is an important branch of popular education, but it is a subject with which I shall not presume to meddle, especially as it has been recently well treated by female writers. Thank

God the cramming, bandaging, and half-suffocating system has disappeared, together with ghosts, hob-goblins and Jack-the-Giant-killing stories. Much however remains to be more generally diffused on this subject ; for thousands of helpless beings are regularly maimed, disfigured, and debilitated, not for want of care or affection, but want of knowledge.*

4.—Laws and moral philosophy.

It is not necessary every one should be a lawyer any more than a doctor, but a general acquaintance with our civil rights and institutions is as valuable as a general acquaintance with the maxims which govern health. A man should know how to walk

---

* Washing a new-born child with *cold* water or with spirits or strong soap, was one of the well-meant but ignorant bar-barisms formerly practised. It was a part of the hardening system which unfortunately forms too prominent a feature in the educational directions of Mr. Locke and John Wesley. The following is a summary of directions given for infant treatment, which appear judicious, and cannot be too much circulated :— Wash a new-born child with warm water and a soft cloth, using the gentlest friction ; while it is without teeth, it should live upon its mother's milk ; when it has four teeth, it may be weaned and fed on milk with a little bread ; as the number of its teeth increase, the solid part of its food should be in-creased ; and when it has all its teeth, it may be allowed animal food, and not before ; the quantity of its food should be attended to as much as the quality : children require no change of food to stimulate their appetites ; air and exercise cannot be secured to them too liberally ; cleanliness and frequent washing are essential to their comfort ; they should be clothed in flannel ; and their clothes should fit them so loosely as not to produce the slightest effect of pressure.

the streets with impunity, and though he may not be versed in the legal niceties, he should be master of the general rules which regulate the hiring of servants, contracts of wages, letting of houses, receiving and paying of money, and other transactions of every-day life. The object of law—though often strangely perverted—is *peace*, and meant as a highway and landmark, which prescribe individual rights, and thereby prevent obstructions and disputes. A popular knowledge of law is just enough to enable a person to keep out of it, which is exactly the legal acquirement Lord Bacon wished every man to possess.

As respects morals, men often want practice more than knowledge, and as our selfishness and passions are constantly warring against our duties, these are best enforced by the iteration of those simple maxims of truth and justice upon the observance of which individual and social welfare depend. The foundation of laws and sound morals might be advantageously explained, and the connexion between virtue and happiness would open an interesting field of popular eloquence and elucidation.

5.—Property and government.

These are considered delicate subjects; but as the time is passed—if it ever existed—when they could be withheld from popular inquiry, it is best their origin and objects should be thoroughly investigated and understood. More they are discussed, and less in my opinion will they be endangered. The utility and necessity of laws and government, are facts

which stare every man in the face. No family, no
club, no workshop, could do without them; how
much less a whole community! The rights of property are equally unassailable; without them property would cease to exist, and in lieu of rich
and poor, we should all be alike poor and without
help. The inequalities in men's possessions are the
result of inequalities in their lives and endowments;
for the indolent and profligate can never expect to
reap the rewards of prudence and industry!

6.—Political economy.

This is a science of general concernment, and
abating the sophistries and obscurities with which it
has been adulterated, all its great problems may be,
and I trust have been, in the Second Part of this
publication, made intelligible to the popular mind.
Every one, either in the capacity of landlord, merchant, manufacturer, or workman, is interested in
rent, profit or wages, and the connexion of these
and their reciprocal influence it is the business
of the economist to explain. The tendency of combinations and trade unions—the utility of machinery—the effect of monopolies—commercial restrictions, and fluctuations in the value of the currency—
the mutual interests of capital and labour—the consequences of speculation and overtrading—the alternations of prosperity and depression inseparable from
commercial and manufacturing pursuits, are all
matters of vital interest, the very peace and wellbeing of the community depending on a familiar and
satisfactory demonstration of the important truths

they involve. Most of all this national science—for so it may be justly termed in England—elucidates the important relation between subsistence and population. Till this great problem is universally understood, we cannot look forward to any lasting improvement in the condition of the people. It is true, ameliorations in government, and an increase of productive power by useful inventions, will be temporarily beneficial; but these advantages will be speedily overtaken and neutralized by a rapidly increasing community. Wages will not be permanently higher, provisions cheaper, nor the hours of working shorter; the only abiding result to the industrious being an increase of number; their necessities and dependant condition remaining unchanged. The great point to make palpable and self-evident to all, is the cause *why a man educated, industrious, able and willing to labour*, and who ought to be of inestimable worth in society, is a valueless drug; nay, more, is worse than nothing, a positive loss to his fellow-men! Economists say, and I think truly, that the primary cause of this unnatural state is a redundancy of labour resulting in its concentration in a particular spot: if this be so, it ought to be made universally clear: no one whether in private or public capacity, should hesitate constantly and openly to declare his conviction of it, and then the remedy would be as little questioned as the existence of the disorder. A practical and general knowledge of this truth is really

2 L

the stepping-stone of popular education ; for
every one must know and feel that the physical
wants must be appeased before the mind can be
cultivated.

7.—Superstitious fears, weak and causeless
apprehensions.

The "chimeras dire" which were wont to haunt
the chamber of sickness, the nursery, and the rustic
village, have been partly dispelled by the progress
of science; but the misery and anxiety still originating in these causes are immense, and chiefly
from the absence of more efficient popular instruction. "If ignorance be bliss," it is a bliss alloyed
with many inconveniences from which superior intelligence is exempted. Two of the greatest mis-
fortunes of former times were the absence of religious toleration, and an unacquaintance with the
causes of natural phenomena : from the former
flowed bloody wars, persecutions, massacres, burn-
ings, and torturings; while the latter, if possible,
was attended with still greater calamities—because
universally diffused, and filling the minds of individuals of all ranks and ages with indescribable
terrors and apprehensions.

If the spread of information had only dispelled
the single illusion of spectral appearances, it would
have conferred on mankind inestimable benefits.
The dread of these mysterious agents haunted men
at home and abroad—by night and by day—and the
fear they had of the burglar or assassin was insi-

nitely less than that of some ghastly apparition at the lonely hour of midnight.

GLOSTER. Oh, Catesby, I have had such horrid dreams!
CATESBY. Shadows, my lord! below the soldier's heeding.
GLOSTER. Now by my this day's hopes, *shadows*, to-night,
    Have struck more terror to the soul of Richard,
    Than can the substance of ten thousand soldiers,
    Arm'd all in proof.—*Act v. sc. 5.*

Such were the alarms of the iron-nerved Richard. Let us, then, rejoice that all the trumpery bug-a-boos of ghosts, witches, fairies, omens, and dreams, have gone to the " tomb of the Capulets;" let us give honour, too, to the illustrious names—to Bacon, Locke, Hume, and Newton—who have contributed to so blessed a consummation. Grown people do not now mistake an old woman, though ugly, for a sorceress; they can pass through a lonely church-yard, a ruined tower, over a wild heath, or even sleep in an old manor-house—the wind whistling shrill the while—without fear of supernatural visita-tions; and have become wise enough to trace private and public calamities to other causes than the crossing of table-knives, the upsetting of salt, the click of an insect, the overshadowing of an eclipse, or even the portentous advent of a comet!

I have thus shortly indicated the more essential branches of popular instruction without pretending, however, that other and higher departments of knowledge ought not to be cultivated. The pursuit of science and letters of all kinds is good, were it only for the intellectual training and pleasing occupation it affords, its tendency to liberalize the mind, and abstract it from gross and vulgar enjoyments. But the course of instruction I have sketched appears indispensable to all—necessary to individual happiness and the wellbeing of the community.

II.—INSTRUMENTS OF POPULAR EDUCATION.

The subject of this section is the powers to whom the business of popular education ought to be intrusted. At present this important duty is chiefly shared among parents, schoolmasters, clergymen, the state, and society. The respective functions of these are not accurately defined—they are occasionally conflicting; but as the powers of some are only derivative, they may be considered under the heads of parents and the state, and it is the kinds of knowledge that ought to be confided to each of these I shall consider.

The obligation imposed on the state to make provision for the general instruction of the people in reading, appears to arise first, from the circumstance that the laws which every member of the community is bound to obey, and for the transgression of which ignorance is no excuse, are all made known through the medium of printing. Secondly, the doctrines of the national worship, as set forth in the Book of Common Prayer, and the denial of which, or even the speaking any thing derogatory thereof, subjects to criminal punishment and civil disabilities, are contained in a printed volume, which would be in-accessible to the people unless previously instructed in reading. Beyond this it does not appear any direct obligation is imposed on the state by its own acts to interfere in the business of education. But if not obligatory it is certainly politic the state should make provision for popular instruction, as the best foundation of national police, order, and prosperity.

Government is directly interested in the happiness of the community; internal discontent, national poverty, and civil tumult, endanger its security, and impair the resources by which it is supported: what-ever tends to make the people moral, happy, and at mutual peace, tends to strengthen and perpetuate its power over them. But the several subjects enu-merated in the last section as branches of Popular Education, have obviously an influence on individual and social welfare. Mere reading, writing, and even ciphering, are not knowledge so much as the instruments of its acquisition. Besides the know-ledge which may be considered merely personal to individuals, all the questions which bear on forms of government, on principles of legislation, morals, trade, capital, and industry, are of constant and over-powering interest in a civilized, commercial, and ma-nufacturing community. Inquiry and discussion on these subjects it is in vain to stifle; if right opinions are not disseminated respecting them they will be assuredly superseded by wrong ones. But govern-ment has no interest in the predominance of error;

every enlightened man knows that if our public
institutions are not perfect, they are susceptible of
improvement, and that the more their principles are
understood the more highly they will be prized.   As
government depends for support neither on imposture, fraud, nor iniquity, no state purpose is answered
by popular ignorance ; on the contrary, the entire
and not the partial enlightenment of the people is
not only the best guarantee of its security, but of
the wellbeing of the various classes of society over
which it presides.

Granting that the wisest policy of government is
identified with popular education, it only remains to
suggest how it may most efficiently aid in the undertaking.

A parish school for instruction in reading, writing,
and ciphering, is certainly as needful a branch of
civic economy as a parish church.   It is astonishing
we should so long have had an endowed pastor for
the instruction of adults, and not an endowed
schoolmaster for the instruction of infants.   Severe
enactments are constantly being made for the
punishment of juvenile delinquency, but none for
its prevention.   Beyond the establishment of primary schools for reading, writing, and ciphering, it
is, perhaps, not desirable a parochial education
should extend ; the remaining branches of popular
knowledge might be communicated through the
medium of parish libraries, mechanic institutions, or
the other co-operative machinery I am about to
mention.

The judges and magistracy are the recognised oracles of the law, deriving their appointment from government, and in number amounting to about 6000, are spread in the chief parishes of the kingdom. It belongs to them to administer and explain the public statutes to the people, and it would certainly be no great deviation, if any, from their judicial and ministerial duties, if they were also to take occasion to enforce their necessity and utility. Here, then, is one powerful machinery of popular instruction entirely under the control of the state, and which it could any time put in motion.

Next to the judicial administrators are the clergy, who, by their office, are the pastors and teachers of the community. An ignorant people may be fanatical, not pious; they may be degraded and brutal in habits, not rational and elevated in character. Knowledge is the basis of social improvement. But physical comfort must precede mental instruction, and before the people can be made wise unto their own happiness, it must be made clearly manifest to them upon what their happiness depends. It is to be regretted, therefore, that the clergy have restricted themselves to the enunciation of spiritual dogmas, and not more sedulously inculcated the domestic and civic virtues which influence the well-being of society. This deficiency of ecclesiastical duty it is in the power of government to remedy, and in lieu of the established worship being chiefly occupied in the iteration of creeds and formularies, without direct reference to the existing state of

society, be made a powerful instrument of practical
and social regeneration.

Lastly, the *fiscal* regulations of state ought to be
framed with a view to popular instruction. Beside
raising a revenue, taxation may be so adjusted as to
become an instrument of police, education, virtue,
and order. It is the *partial*, not the *full* enlightenment of the people government has to apprehend ;
whatever duties and imposts, therefore, tend to impede the spread of knowledge and fetter inquiry and
discussion must be inimical to its interests, and can
only be justified when there are no other less objectionable sources from which the taxes indispensable
to the public service can be levied.

These appear the extent of the obligations imposed
on the state, and the means it possesses through the
adjustment of taxation, the agency of the clergy,
magistracy, and judicial authorities, of promoting
popular instruction.

The duties which devolve on parents next remain
to be noticed. These have been set forth in the
preceding section, under the heads of domestic education—maintenance—preservation of health—providing useful trades and occupations—superstitious
fears—prudential virtues—laws, property, and government : upon instruction and knowledge in these
the future happiness of children will depend, and
their fitness to maintain and discharge their civil
rights and obligations. To describe parental duties
is enough without enforcing them, since nature has
implanted in the breast of every parent a strong

desire to promote whatever tends to the advantage of his offspring.

The power possessed by individuals, in the character of *masters and employers* of workpeople, to advance popular instruction, has been before alluded to, and is only secondary in importance to that of parents. In all the questions which affect the rights of property and inequalities in its disposition—the conflicting claims of capital and industry—the circumstances which regulate and influence the rate of wages, the middle classes have a deep interest; even their security and prosperity are identified with the dissemination of right opinions respecting them; for knowledge will assuredly demonstrate that master and workman are bound by reciprocal ties—have no antagonist interests—and that oppression by one, or a discontented demeanour by the other, are alike hostile to their mutual and permanent welfare. By private conversations, by the circulation of short treatises, by lectures, discussions and correspondence in local newspapers, the power of communicating useful knowledge on these subjects is immense. If the opportunity be neglected, the consequences to society may be perilous in the extreme. The manufacturing portion of the community is rapidly increasing in number; the questions which agitate the industrious orders are daily becoming more numerous and complicated, and it is possible that if they be not speedily resolved into something like self-evident propositions—the hatred, animosity, and conflicts which grow out of them, may equal in bitterness those which formerly resulted from the divisions and intolerance of religious denominations.

III.—OBJECTIONS TO NATIONAL EDUCATION.

Two classes of objections have been made to the state assuming the superintendence of education, one *moral*, the other *pecuniary*. Under the first head it is alleged that all public establishments include in them the idea of a permanence tending to foster and perpetuate prejudices—that an alliance between government and education is as impolitic as an alliance between church and state—and that government, by imposing upon itself the task of popular instruction, charges itself with a duty which is better performed when left to individual zeal and discernment.

All these objections originate in one supposition, namely, that the government *itself is bad*, and of course whatever tends to increase or prolong its authority, ought to be deprecated. But supposing government enlightened and responsible—that its interests are inseparable from those of the community, why then it can have no motive for upholding hurtful establishments, or perpetuating pernicious errors ; its interests are identified with the interests of the people, and it has precisely the same interest in every change or progression tending to social improvement. With respect to the adequacy of individual efforts, experience demonstrates their ineffi-

ciency in the fact that in every community a mass
of hurtful ignorance remains unless it be reclaimed
by the energy of government, aided by funds which
a public provision can alone supply.

The *second*, or pecuniary objection, amounts to
this : that a compulsory school-rate for education
supersedes and destroys voluntary efforts for the
same purpose, and which, in England, at least, it
has been recently assumed, have been found (almost
if not quite) adequate to the task of popular instruction.

This objection is precisely of the same nature as
the one made to a compulsory poor-rate, namely, that
it supersedes charity, and the same answer will apply
to it.   First, voluntary donations are of too temporary and fluctuating amount to be safely relied
upon for so constant and important a necessity as
national education.   Secondly, the trouble with
which they are collected, added to the lavish and
injudicious manner in which for want of system
they are disbursed, causes them to impose a greater
burden on the community than if funds for the same
purpose had been raised by a general and uniform
assessment.   Thirdly, that for an object in which
all have an interest, all ought to contribute ; and
that it is unjust to cast the labour and expense
of popular instruction exclusively on the benevolent
to the exemption of the rest of society.   Lastly, it is
probable education would not be so salutary and
efficient, left to the superintendence of individuals
as under the state ; it would be less systematic, and

the instruction communicated would necessarily be influenced by the prejudices and temporary interests of the conductors and supporters.

The progress and success of the voluntary mode of education in England appear to have been rather hastily assumed. Lord Brougham stated (House of Lords, March 14, 1833) that he had entertained doubts of the adequacy of voluntary subscriptions for the maintenance of education, but experience had induced him to alter his opinion. This change of sentiment arose from the replies received to a circular addressed by his lordship in 1828, to 500 clergymen of the Church of England, and which showed that education had been rapidly extending during the preceding ten years. The results of these returns have been already stated (p. iii.) as published in the *Companion to the Almanac* for 1829. But it is important to remark that these results have been derived rather from *working the rule of three* than positive data communicated in the replies to the Lord Chancellor's circular. Only 487 returns were received, that is, replies have only been obtained from *one twenty-first* part of the entire number of parishes in England. To draw general conclusions on the state of education throughout the kingdom, from such a limited circle of inquiry is, to say the least of it, precipitate. In the smaller parishes (500 of which are altogether without schools), and large towns, Lord Brougham admits, the means of education are defective. The truth is, education is generally either defective or injudiciously conducted, and the absence of a sound system of instruction will account for many anomalies in our social condition. In this respect, and perhaps no other, our public institutions are greatly behind those of Holland, Prussia, Saxe Weimar, Bavaria, and other German states. It is a subject that demands and most likely will obtain the attention of a reformed parliament.

IV.—MORAL INFLUENCE OF EDUCATION.

Within the last ten or fifteen years, crime and education have greatly increased. But further than being contemporary, there is no direct proof that education has had any share in causing an increase of criminality. There is no proof that the addition of a single culprit to the calendar has been caused by his learning to read and write, by his being taught at an infant school, by his attending a Mechanics' Institution, or by buying penny magazines. Till some direct proof of this kind be adduced to connect crime with education, every one will hesitate before inferring that the extension of popular instruction has been a cause of the increase of delinquency.

It is an error in reasoning of such every-day occurrence to consider contemporary events related as cause and effect, that it scarcely needs illustrating by examples. Fifteen years since, the commercial difficulties of the country were mostly ascribed to the transition from war to peace; more recently, they have been ascribed to the withdrawal of the one-pound notes; and perhaps hereafter they will be ascribed (by Tories at least) to the disfranchisement of Gatton and Old Sarum. Mankind are naturally prone, according to their interests and prejudices, to assign the causes of phenomena; and whatever absorbing event happens—though it is only the advent of a comet—has usually affiliated upon it, in the popular mind, all the subsequent changes that intervene, however incongruous in their nature.

Although it should be ascertained that popular education has in some degree tended to augment the number of criminals, it would be far from conclusive evidence that it has not been a positive good to society. For one that has been led astray, ninety-nine may have been directed into better courses than they would have otherwise pursued. Causes to which I shall soon advert may have been in operation tending to multiply offences, and which the corrective power of education may have been unable to control. Crimes may have increased in spite of, not by, the co-operative agency of intelligence.

Great social changes are seldom effected unaccompanied with partial though perhaps transient alloy. The emancipation from vassalage we have seen was productive of such scenes of distress and vagabondage, as had not been before witnessed; but, because a portion of the serfs misused, or were unqualified for the exercise of freedom, forms an insufficient argument against the policy of abolishing personal servitude. Rich countries are said to afford examples of more extreme indigence than poor countries : it may be so, but it would be wrong thence to infer that poverty affords the same means of general comfort and enjoyment as opulence. Periods of great commercial activity and enterprise are usually more fruitful in bankruptcies than periods of stagnation ; but no one would deny that the former is not a more cheerful and hearty state of society than the latter. The introduction of machinery has, doubtless, been productive of partial evil, but this cannot be put in competition with its general and lasting advantages. The consolidation of farms has been a source of suffering to the ejected tenantry, but its evils have been counterbalanced by the more productive employment of agricultural capital. Perhaps the political changes in which we are now involved may give rise to transitory inconveniences, by the obtrusion of impracticable claims ; but these are ephemeral evils which will not outweigh the advantages to be derived from the establishment, for a lengthened term, of a wise and responsible administration of public affairs. In all we must balance the general good against the partial evil. That we are in the right track, in respect of popular education, no one can have the slightest misgiving. I have argued as though education may have been accompanied with partial evil, but this is a position I by no means concede. No proof

has been adduced of the corruptive influence of education at all.   Neither Messrs. Lucas and Guerry,
in France, nor any writer or parliamentary committee in England has established, either in single
or masses of individuals, that there is a connexion
between the progress of knowledge and a deterioration of the human character.   I think further that
it is quite impossible such connexion should subsist ;
but before endeavouring to show this, I shall, as
I am desirous of putting my readers in possession
of the facts as well as the principles of this question,
advert to the progress of crime in England, and its
probable causes.

The total committals for offences in London and
Middlesex, from 1811 to 1817, amounted to 13,415;
in an equal period from 1821 to 1827 to 19,883 :
being an increase of forty-eight per cent.   But the
population is computed to have increased 19 per
cent.; leaving 29 *per cent.* to be accounted for by
other causes than an increase of population.*   In
England and Wales (the metropolis excepted) the
contemporary increase of crime had been still greater,
the increase in the number of committals amounting
to 86 *per cent.*†   Since these returns, there has
been no abatement in the progressive increase of
committals. (See Appendix.)

The class of offences that have chiefly increased,
are those against property.   The darker and more

* Report on the Police of the Metropolis, Session 1828, p. 7.
† Ibid.   Appendix, C. p. 304.

atrocious class of crimes, those directed against the
person, it is alleged, have not increased so fast as
population ; and the parliamentary committee on
commitments affirms that "life and limb" were never
less exposed to violence.

The causes assigned for the increase of crime by
the police committee of the metropolis, in 1828,
were principally the increase in population—the
cheapness of spirituous liquors—the neglect of
children by their parents—the want of employment—absence of suitable provisions for juvenile
delinquents—defective prison discipline and police.
To these may be added other causes, assigned by
another parliamentary committee* as accounting
partly for an increase of crime, and partly for its
" greater exhibition to public view" without evidenc-
ing any virtual increase of depravity—namely, the
payment of prosecutors, their expenses in cases
of misdemeanor—the Malicious Trespass Act—decline in domestic superintendence—readiness with
which magistrates commit for offences—defective
and unsuitable punishments—improvement in the
art of crime faster than the art of detection, and
bringing before the tribunals petty offences which
were formerly either settled by summary chastisement inflicted by the sufferer on the delinquent, or
passed over without magisterial cognizance.

In addition to these causes of augmented delin-

* Report on Criminal Commitments and Convictions.—
Parl. Pap. 545, Session 1828.

2 M

quency, I ventured, in an anonymous publication,* to suggest the following :

1. The increase of national wealth and consequent increase of offences growing out of the increased transactions of trade and commerce.

2. The continuance of public peace had closed the outlet in the army and navy, to vicious and dissipated characters.

3. Commercial avidity and speculation, anterior to 1824-5, had been productive of a decline in mercantile principle and character.

4. Recent alterations in criminal punishments may have influenced the state of crime.

5. The demoralizing tendency of the Debtor Laws arising out of increased mercantile transactions.

6. Greater extremes of condition, and the poverty occasioned by the competition of capital and labour for employment.

All these causes may have contributed in different degrees to swell the criminal calendar. They may have been so energetic in their operation as to outweigh the moral influence of a more diffusive education. Or some other causes that have yet eluded detection, may have contributed to this lamentable issue ; but whatever these causes may have been, I think popular education is not one of them, and for the following reasons :

First, it is only since 1820, that an impulse has been given to popular instruction,—a period much

* *Treatise on the Police and Crimes of the Metropolis*, ch. i. p. 211.—Longman, 1829.

too recent to have been productive of any change in public morals. Secondly, admitting that effective education had been longer in progress, it has been of such a character that it cannot possibly have wrought an unfavourable alteration in the national mind. No new system of morals or religion has been propagated within the last ten or fifteen years to affect in popular estimation the established rules of right and wrong. Reading, writing, and ciphering cannot possibly have had any such tendency; they are little more than mechanical acquirements, and have no more influence on personal character than learning the trade of pinmaking or weaving. To influence conduct, a new principle of action must be introduced, or a change effected in the circumstances of individuals. If men were made more necessitous or licentious by reading, they might become less scrupulous in their conduct, but reading is no promotive of poverty nor depravity, especially the kind of reading which has been constantly growing in public estimation. Every observer knows that the improvement in dress, diet, manners, and domestic habits, has been immense. To judge of this, we should contrast the present with the past state of society,—not the present with some ideal or desirable state of perfection. Admitting such a national change to have been effected, it appears to me a trifling drawback that the criminal calendar has been augmented. This may have arisen from circumstances wholly unconnected with education; it may have arisen from some of the causes already enumerated : but whatever has been the cause, I deem it an unimportant fact, that the number of criminals has been doubled or trebled—has increased from ten to twenty, or from fifty to one hundred thousand—provided, contemporaneously with this increase, the moral and physical condition of the many millions who constitute the remaining portion of a vast community, has been decidedly ameliorated.   I look to the mass, not to returns of criminal commitments, and in that I find abundant scope for exultation at the diffusion of popular intelligence.*

The salutary change in the character of the people, I do not ascribe to the plans of education put forward within the last eight or ten years.   The seed had been sown long before.   These plans have aided a good work already in progress, but it does not appear to me that they are directed, nor perhaps in-

---

* It is only by general reasoning we can argue this question. Statistical returns of crime, are yet too incomplete to enable us to determine arithmetically the moral influence of education. The only fact that has been satisfactorily established by figures is, that crimes of personal violence diminish with the spread of knowledge.   In Russia, where education may be scarcely said to exist, it has been stated by the Lord Chancellor (House of Lords, March 14) that out of 5800 crimes committed within a certain period, 3500 were accompanied by violence ; whilst in Pennsylvania, where education is generally diffused, out of 7400 crimes, only 640 were accompanied by violence, being in the proportion of 1-12th of the whole number, instead of 3-5ths, as in the former case.   See further on the increase of crime in the *Appendix*.

tended, to effect any moral change, to act either as
an incentive or preventive of crime. Knowledge,
when it refers to human action, teaches to discern
good from evil, and obviously directs and induces
us from mere self-love, to seek the one and avoid
the other. This position cannot be gainsayed.
Knowledge is *light*, and it is a paradox unworthy
of reply that men can track their way through life
as well without as with its guidance. It is therefore
a valuable acquisition to every possessor. But in
much of the knowledge which is now sedulously
diffused as popular instruction, it is difficult to discern its practical application to the condition of
those for whose good it is benevolently intended.
Where it is not confined to the exposition of abstract
science, it is chiefly addressed to the imagination ;
leaving to others the risk and the drudgery of inculcating useful, and perhaps unpalatable truths.
Human misery results not more from physical want
than the absence of that intellectual *wisdom* which
disciplines the passions, destroys prejudice, and trains
the mind to habits of forethought and retrospection. It is not by " economic enlargements" only,
but moral culture, our chief calamities can be sur-
mounted. Can physical knowledge only supply this
element of social wellbeing ? Of teachers of science
we have abundance, of moral and political philosophy
very few : yet the former is little more than the *art
of gain;* the latter of happiness. An acquaintance
with mathematics, natural philosophy, law, and
jurisprudence,—these of themselves are chiefly

valuable as occupational or professional attainments, qualifying for the manufactory, counting-house, the bar, senate, and laboratory;—they give intellectual power, but have no tendency to render the possessor either more virtuous or vicious.   Let me submit an example in illustration.   The legal classes, medical practitioners, and mercantile men, are mostly tolerably endowed with the information enumerated; but can it be said we find among them purer and more disinterested conduct, the natural affections stronger, more humanity, patriotism, and self-denial; in a word, are they as individuals more happy, or as citizens more valuable than those whose knowledge hardly extends beyond the Liturgy, or the inheritance of a few traditionary maxims of life ?   Unless, therefore, popular education includes morality as well as science it cannot be said efficiently to operate either as an instrument or preventive of crime ; it is simply an *engine of power ;* and whether directed to the useful or hurtful, must depend on impulses derived from other sources. By morality, it is almost unnecessary to explain, is not meant that which precludes, but augments enjoyment; being in fact little more than prudence, teaching us to shun whatever is hurtful to ourselves and fellow-creatures.

, The error of many popular teachers consists in a vain attempt to render that knowledge universal, which, from its own nature, and the wants of society cannot and need not be more than particular.   They aim too high for the common mind : they overlook the iron necessities which fix the lot of those for whom they generously toil, and seek to realize what is desirable rather than that which is attainable, or perhaps practically useful.

It is only the *results* of knowledge, not the steps of investigation by which they have been obtained, that we can hope to render familiar to the general mind. Habits of forethought, order, and reflection ; precepts derived from experience, often repeated and strengthened by example, form the basis of popular instruction. A deeper philosophy may be necessary to some ; but to the bulk of the community it is incompatible with their social state ; nor would its attainment compensate them for the sacrifices necessary to its acquisition. The progress of science may be compared to the advancement of agriculture ; the further it is carried proportionately less becomes the produce, till at last it barely defrays the cost of production. The most useful truths are seldom those most difficult to be comprehended ; and knowledge is like the earth whose most valuable treasures lie near the surface, and those who ascend higher or dig lower, are often repaid with much toil and little profit.

This is not an elevated nor perhaps popular doctrine, but it is probably near the truth, and at least practical. My purpose is not to depreciate intellectual acquirements, but to separate the grain from the chaff of science. A taste for knowledge of all kinds rewards itself, and no one can be in error by its cultivation. But it would be to practise a mischievous delusion on the working classes to hold out

the hope that popular education is meant solely as
an instrument of ambition and personal aggrandize-
ment.   No such thing, I apprehend, is intended by
its advocates.   Society is such—it has always been
such—and, so far as human penetration can reach,
will long continue such—that a great portion of us
are doomed to move in the humbler walks of life.
But though knowledge is neither an unfailing
stepping-stone to riches nor power, nor perhaps
virtue; it is assuredly the most trustworthy help to
personal independence and happiness.   Can it for
instance be supposed that a person master of the
popular information I have indicated in a former
section, would not be more likely than another,
without such aid, to be successful in life?   Would
he not be more likely to be happy as an individual,
a better husband, father, workman, and companion?
Knowledge, I repeat, is the eye of the mind, and to
suppose any one can pass through life as well
without as with it, is to suppose the blind can wend
their way as well as those who can see.   Without
knowledge personal freedom is an affliction, and as
a child is better under the care of parents than left to
itself, so a man born in slavery would be more likely
to be guaranteed from want and misery by the forethought of his superior, than an uninstructed freeman
unprovided with the intellectual culture which ap-
prizes him of the circumstances influencing his social
condition.

APPENDIX.

I.—PROGRESS OF WAGES AND PRICES.

WHETHER the Working Classes are better or worse clothed, fed, and lodged, than formerly, is chiefly valuable as an historical question. The chief point of present interest is, whether their condition is susceptible of improvement, whether they are as well-off as they ought to be, or can be made. A comparative statement of wages, and the price of bread-corn appears the best mode of determining their progressive state. Bread is not only the chief necessary of life, but its price influences the price of meat, and most other articles of ordinary consumption. Mr. Barton, from authentic sources, has prepared a statement, exhibiting from 1495 to 1813, the progress of wages and the price of wheat; also the rate of wages measured in equivalent pints of wheat. The price of wheat is the average price of the five preceding years. I have brought Mr. Barton's table down to 1833.

It will be remarked that wages fell rapidly from 1495 to 1610, about the period of the introduction of the 3d of Elizabeth, "For the Relief of the Poor;" that from the introduction of the Poor-laws to 1750, they continued to rise; and that subsequently to 1770 they again began to decline. From this it might be inferred that the Poor-laws were favourable to a *high price of labour*; it might be so to a certain extent, but the more influential cause of the advance of wages is to be sought in the

progress of population.   Population, it has been already shown (p. 61), advanced very slowly for the first
150 years after the establishment of a compulsory
provision for the poor; during this time it is probable the capital of the country increased faster than
population; subsequently slower; hence the rise
of wages in the former, and their fall in the latter
period. The application of machinery, the Bank Restriction Act, the resumption of cash payments, and
corn laws, may have all influenced the condition
of the working classes in various degrees; but the
great permanent cause has doubtless been the relative progress of population and national wealth.

HUSBANDRY WAGES.

Year.	Wheat per quarter.		Wages per week.		Wages in pints of wheat.
	s.	d.	s.	d.	
1495	4	10	1	10¼	199
1593	15	9	2	6	82
1610	37	8	3	5	46
1651	69	1	6	10	48
1661	54	0	6	9	61
1682	45	3	5	11	66
1685	39	4	3	11	51
1725	34	5	5	4	79
1751	32	0	6	0	96
1770	47	8	7	4	79
1790	50	0	8	1	82
1796	64	10	8	11	70
1803	91	8	11	5	63
1811	96	8*	14	6	76
1819	84	8	12	0	.73
1824	57	2	10	-0	89
1829	62	1	11	0	91
1832	63	9	12	0	90

  * In continuing Mr. Barton's table, the average price of
wheat during each intervening period to 1832 inclusive, is

WAGES OF CARPENTERS, BRICKLAYERS, MASONS, PLUMBERS, AND OTHER DOMESTIC ARTIFICERS.

Year.	Wheat per quarter.		Wages per week.		Wages in pints of wheat.
	s.	d.	s.	d.	
1495	4	10	2	9	292
1593	15	9	3	9	123
1610	37	8	4	6	61
1651	69	1	7	6	55
1685	39	4	5	9	74
1725	34	5	6	0	89
1730	40	2	15	9	200
1740	36	1	16	0	227
1750	32	1	15	6	247
1760	41	2	15	6	193
1770	47	8	15	9	169
1780	43	0	16	0	190
1790	49	11	16	6	169
1795	58	8	17	3	150
1800	79	9	18	0	116
1805	82	8	28	3	175
1810	91	8	30	0	167
1813	114	0	33	6	150
1819	84	8	33*	0	199
1824	57	2	33	0	295
1829	62	1	33	0	276
1832	63	9	33	0	265

given. The wages of husbandry labourers for 1819—24—29, are taken from *Lord Milton's Address to the Landowners*. They were the wages given in Northamptonshire, and rather lower than those paid in Sussex. Last year, wages at Eastbourne were 2s. per day; at Brede, 2s. 3d. winter and summer; at Northiam and Ewhurst, the same.—[*Extracts from Reports of Poor-law Commission*, pp. 13, 30, 34, 36.]

* From the table of contract prices at Greenwich Hospital, it will be seen that the daily wages of carpenters, bricklayers, masons, and plumbers, have undergone little variation since 1805.

II.—EXPENSES OF AN AGRICULTURAL FAMILY.

No. 1. *Expenses of the Family of an Agricultural Labourer in 1762.—London Magazine for 1762.*

	Per Week.		Per Annum.		
	s.	d.	£	s.	d.
1. Bread, flour, oatmeal - -	2	6	6	10	0
2. Roots, greens, beans, pease, fruit	0	5	1	3	10
3. Firing 6d., candles 3d., soap 2½d.	0	11½	2	9	10
4. Milk 1½d., butter 1½d., cheese 3d.	0	8¼	2	0	1
5. Flesh 6d., rent 6d., pins, worsted, thread, &c., 1d. }	1	1	2	16	4
6. Clothes, repairs, bedding, shoes	1	0	2	12	0
7. Salt, beer, exotics, vinegar, spices	0	8¼	1	11	5
8. Midwives, churching, lying-in	-	-	0	12	6
			£20	0	0

Taxes on the above consumption:—On malt 4s. 2d.; salt 1s. 8d.; soap and candles 3s.; leather 2s.; sundries 2d.—Total 11s.
N.B.—Tax about 1-36th.

No. 2. *Expenses of the Family of an Agricultural Labourer, consisting of 5½ persons, being an average of the expense of 65 families of Labourers in different parts of England, collected by Sir F. Eden in 1796.*

	Per Week.		Per Annum.		
	s.	d.	£	s.	d.
Bread, flour, or oatmeal - - -	6	5	16	13	8
Yeast and salt - - -	0	2	0	8	8
Bacon or other meat - -	1	2	3	0	8
Tea, sugar, and butter - -	1	2¼	3	3	11
Soap - - - - -	0	3¾	0	16	3
Candles - - - -	0	4	0	17	4
Cheese - - - -	0	4½	0	18	5
Beer - - - -	0	3	0	13	0
Milk - - - -	0	3	0	13	0
Potatoes - - -	0	7	1	10	4
Thread and worsted - -	0	2½	0	10	10
Rent - - - - -	-	-	1	13	3
Fuel - - - - -	-	-	1	13	3
Clothes - - - -	-	-	3	10	11
Births, burials, and sickness -	-	-	0	10	10
			£36	14	4

No. 3. *Expenditure at the Grocer's shop, paying one week
under the other, of an Agricultural Family near Newbury,
consisting of a man, his wife, and six children.—Reports
of Poor-law Commission, p. 251, London, 1833.*

					s.	d.
7 gallons of bread	-	-	-		9	11
1 lb. of sugar	-	-	-		0	6
2 oz. of tea	-	-	-	-	0	8
Soap	-	-	-	-	0	4
Candles	-	-	-	-	0	4
Salt, pepper, mustard, vinegar, &c.		-			0	2
2 lbs. of bacon	-	-	-		1	4
					13	3

Exclusive of beer, coals, rent, clothes, and other necessaries.

No. 4. *Proper food for the Able-bodied labourer, with a
wife and four children, per week.—Plain Statement of
the Case of the Labourer, p. 23, London, 1831.*

					s.	d.
5 gallons of bread	-	-		-	7	6
3 lbs. of bacon, at 7d. per lb.	-		-		1	9
2 lbs. of butter, at 10d.	-		-		2	8
2 lbs. of cheese, at 6d.	-		-		1	0
Tea	-	-	-	-	0	9
1 lb. of sugar	-	-		-	0	7
Beer, 7 quarts, at 2d. per quart			-		1	2
1 bushel of coals	-	-		-	2	2
3 faggots	-	-	-	-	0	9
½ lb. of soap	-	-		-	0	4
½ lb. of candles	-	-		-	0	4
Total weekly expenses of the family	-				17	0

Exclusive of rent, clothes, and other necessaries.

III.—PROPORTION OF TAX PAID BY A LABOURER's FAMILY.

From the preceding statements, Nos. 1 to 4, it
appears the weekly expenses of the family of an
agricultural labourer in 1762, were 7s. 4½d.; in 1796,

11s. 3½d.; in 1832, exclusive of beer, coals, rent, and clothes, 13s. 3d.; in 1831 they were estimated, exclusive of rent and clothes, at 17s. weekly. The several cases do not admit of exact comparison, owing to the difference in their items; but supposing the expense in *food* of a labourer's family to be correctly estimated in No. 4, it shows how inadequate the wages now paid of 10s., 12s., or at most 15s. weekly, are to the comfortable—and certainly not more than comfortable—maintenance of a labourer, his wife, and four children.

The TAX paid by a *labourer* in 1762, No. 1, is estimated $\frac{1}{35}$th part of his expenses. In a former part of this publication (p. 220), I find I rather understated the pressure of taxation on the industrious classes. The duties on beer, salt, leather, candles, and coals, have been repealed: all the other articles of a labourer's consumption are subject to duties which enhance their prices. I shall specify the duties on each, in the order the articles stand in No. 4.

Bread, bacon, butter, and cheese.—The prices of all these articles are raised to the labourer by the duties levied on their importation for the *protection*, as it is said, of agriculture. The duty on wheat varies from 1l. 5s. a quarter to 1s., according as the price rises from 61s. to 70s. a quarter; on bacon the import duty is 1l. 8s. per cwt.; on butter, 20s. per cwt.; on cheese, 10s. 6d. per cwt. It is impossible to calculate exactly the enhancement of prices caused by these duties; were they repealed, there is no reason to think that the prices of provisions in this country would greatly exceed the prices in France. During a series of years the prices of corn and all the necessaries of life have been full one-third lower in France than in England; and with respect to *bread*, the fact at the present moment stands thus:

the price of the finest wheaten flour in London is
50s. per sack; the highest price of the finest wheaten
flour in Paris is 46 francs per 159 killogrammes,
equal to only 28s. 6d. the English sack of 280 lbs.,
being a difference of 41½ per cent. on the price of
flour;* and the difference is as great in most other
descriptions of food. It is not too much, then, to
say, that *one-third* of the weekly outgoings of a
labourer in bread, bacon, butter, and cheese, is
caused by agricultural taxes.

Tea.——The duty on tea is 96 per cwt., *ad valorem*,
and 100 per cent. on all teas sold above 2s. per lb.,
at the East India Company's sales. This is the government tax; the addition to the prices caused by
the company's monopoly is about as much more.
Bohea is the cheapest of all the teas brought from
China, and is that most generally used by the labouring classes. Its price at the company's sales
has lately fluctuated between 1s. 6d. and 1s. 7d.
per lb.; and were it not for the company's exclusive
privileges, it might be had at 8½d. or 9d., which is
the price at Hamburgh and New York. If a labourer use coffee in place of tea, he escapes the
monopoly, but not the tax. The duty on foreign
coffee is 1s. 3d. per lb.; on British plantation coffee,
6d. per lb. At present prices, the duty on the former
amounts to 100 per cent.; on the latter, which is
the sort used by the labouring people, it is 150 per
cent.! *Two-thirds*, therefore, of the labourer's expenses in the tea or coffee pot, may be traced to
political causes.

Sugar.——Duty on West India sugar 24s. per cwt.,
or 2$\frac{8}{11}$d. per pound; on East India, 32s. per cwt.,

---

* The difference is still greater between the prices of corn
in England and Dantzic, Hamburgh, and other places on the
continent, as may be seen by reference to Earl Fitzwilliam's
resolutions on the corn laws, moved this session, April 30th.

or $3\frac{1}{4}d$. per pound. The price of sugar, exclusive
of duty, may be taken at an average of the last few
years, at from 22s. to 35s.; being, in the former
case, *less* than the tax.

Beer.—The duty on malt is 20s. 8d. per quarter:
on hops, 2d. a pound. Three barrels and a half of
beer are ordinarily brewed out of a quarter of malt
and 12 pounds of hops: so that the direct duties
are $2\frac{1}{4}d$. on each gallon of beer. This, however, is
a small part of the enhancement of price occasioned
by the malt duty. Barley is now selling at 25s. a
quarter, and the average price of malt is 65s. a quarter, which is a difference of 19s. 4d., exclusive of
duty. The whole of this difference, it has been
affirmed, might be saved by the entire repeal of the
malt duty and the duty on foreign barley, bringing
the pot of beer to *one-third* its present price.*

Soap.—The direct duty charged on hard soap,

* It is a curious fact, that the consumption of malt in England and Wales has been *stationary* for nearly half a century,
though the population has more than doubled during that period.
(M'Culloch's *Commercial Dictionary*, p. 723.) The tables, however, show that the public brewers, since 1787, have contrived
to manufacture *one-third more strong beer out of the same quantity of malt!* So that both the quantity and quality of the national beverage have declined. The consumption of genuine
tea has also been steadily declining, compared with the population. The sales of the East India Company show that the
average consumption per head of *their* teas in 1801, was
1 lb. 13.6 oz.; in 1831, per head, 1 lb. 9.2 oz.; showing a decline of full 17 per cent. during the last thirty years. (*Ibid.*, p.
1028.) As the fashion of tea-drinking has certainly not declined, it may be concluded, even after allowing for the increased consumption of coffee, either that the decoction has
been made weaker, like beer, or that the shops have sold something else in place of the Chinese plant. The numerous convictions of persons having adulterated tea in possession favour
the latter conclusion.

Monopoly and high duties have operated unfavourably on
public morals. " Lovers of tea or coffee," it is truly remarked,

which is that commonly used, is 3d. per lb., while the price of soap rarely exceeds 6d. per lb.; so that the direct duty is fully 100 per cent. But, besides this duty, the substances of which soap is made, namely, tallow, barilla, and turpentine or rosin, are respectively charged with duties of 3s. 4d., 2s., and 4s. 4d. a cwt.; and taking these indirect taxes into account, it may be truly said the labouring man's soap is taxed from 120 to 130 per cent., *ad valorem!*

Coals are not subject to any public tax; in London a local duty of 13d. a chaldron, or about one farthing per cwt., is levied.

Let us now restate No. 4, showing, in addition, the proportion of the labouring man's weekly expenditure, occasioned either by direct tax or monopoly.

Proper food for an Able-bodied labourer, having a wife and four children, per week; with the proportion of the price of each article of provision occasioned by tax or monopoly.

	Price.			Tax and Monopoly.	
	s.	d.		s.	d.
8 gallons of bread -	7	6	-	2	6
3 lbs. of bacon, at 7d. per lb.	1	9	-	0	7
2 lbs. of butter, at 10d. -	1	8	-	0	6¼
2 lbs. of cheese, at 6d. -	1	0	-	0	3
Tea - - -	0	9	-	0	6
Sugar - -	0	7	-	0	3½
Beer, 7 quarts, at 2d. per quart	1	2	-	0	7
1 bushel of coals - -	1	2	-	0	0¼
3 faggots - -	0	9	-	0	0
½ lb. of soap - -	0	4	-	0	2½
½ lb. of candles - -	0	4	-	0	0
	17	0		5	5½

"are rarely drinkers:" and Raynal ascribes the sobriety of the Chinese to the use of these grateful beverages, which produce all the good, without the evil consequences, of more powerful stimulants.

2 N

So that, of every 17*s*. expended by a working man in provisions, 5*s*. 5½*d*., or nearly one-third part, is occasioned by taxation and monopoly. If we leave out the agricultural taxes, and the 100 per cent. addition to the price of tea, occasioned by the monopoly of the East India Company, we shall find that the government duties on tea, sugar, malt, and soap, amount to 16*d*., or $\frac{1}{4}$ part of the poor man's weekly expenditure. This, it will be seen by reference to No. 1, is nearly treble the amount of tax paid in 1762. Such a representation points out an *obvious* mode by which government may effectually improve the condition of the working classes, namely, by a revision of the corn-laws, by throwing open the China trade, and by repealing the duties which enhance the prices of the necessaries of life.

Tables of Prices.—To judge of the relative condition of the people at different periods, it is necessary to have statements of both wages and the prices of articles of ordinary consumption. The following authentic table, therefore, of contract prices and wages at the Royal Hospital, Greenwich, is very valuable. But even a public document like this does not afford complete information, unless it could also inform us of the quality of the articles. The coats of the pensioners are contracted for now at about the same price (22*s*.) as they were nearly 100 years since, but the quality of the blue cloth used is very inferior to the ancient pattern. In 1729, shoes were contracted for at 4*s*. per pair; stockings 1*s*. 9*d*.; hats 1*s*. 9*d*. each; a suit of clothes 2*l*. 12*s*., a complete suit of bedding 3*l*. 5*s*.; in 1828 the contract prices of these articles were respectively 4*s*.3*d*., 1*s*.9½*d*., 3*s*., 1*l*. 18*s*. 1*d*., 2*l*. 5*s*. 9*d*. The steadiness in the wages of domestic artificers cannot fail to be remarked.

IV.—CONTRACT PRICES OF PROVISIONS AND WAGES AT GREENWICH HOSPITAL.*

Year.	Flesh per cwt.		Butter per lb.	Beer per barrel		Coals per chaldron.		Carpenters per day.		Bricklayers per day.		Masons per day.		Plumbers per day.	
	s.	d.	d.	s.	d.	s.	d.	s.	d.	s.	d.	s.	d.	s.	d.
1729	25	8	4	3	9	23	6	2	6	2	6	2	6	3	0
1730	25	8	5	4	1	24	6	2	6	2	6	2	6	3	0
1735	16	11	3	3	2	25	0	2	6	2	6	2	8	3	0
1740	23	0	5	5	1	29	0	2	6	2	6	2	8	2	6
1745	22	2	3	5	8	30	0	2	6	2	6	3	0	2	6
1750	20	6	5	4	8	27	7	2	6	2	6	2	8	2	6
1755	27	9	5	5	7	28	7	2	6	2	6	2	8	2	6
1760	31	6	5	7	2	32	8	2	6	2	4	2	8	3	0
1765	27	2	5	5	10	32	4	2	6	2	4	2	8	3	0
1770	28	6	6	7	1	29	1	2	6	2	4	2	10	3	0
1775	33	8	6	7	3	30	11	2	6	2	4	2	10	3	0
1780	32	6	6	8	2	37	3	2	6	2	4	2	10	3	3
1785	37	6	6	8	7	34	2	2	6	2	4	2	10	3	3
1790	35	10	6	10	4	34	4	2	6	3	0	2	10	3	3
1795	47	10	8	20	4	39	9	2	10	3	0	2	10	3	3
1800	64	4	11	17	9	51	7	4	6	4	10	5	0	4	6
1805	60	4	11	16	3	51	8	4	6	4	8	5	0	4	6
1806	61	0	11	15	5	53	4	5	0	4	8	5	0	4	6
1807	63	0	12	16	5	54	0	5	0	5	0	5	0	4	6
1808	63	0	13	17	0	55	9	5	4	5	1	5	1	5	3
1809	66	6	13	17	10	60	9	5	8	5	2	5	3	5	9
1810	72	0	13	16	3	60	8	5	6	5	3	5	9	5	9
1811	64	0	14	20	9	61	6	5	6	5	5	5	9	5	9
1812	78	0	15	31	10	56	1	5	6	5	5	5	9	5	9
1813	65	0	15	17	3	56	7	5	6	5	5	5	9	5	9
1814	74	6	14	15	4	62	2	5	6	5	1	5	9	5	9
1815	60	0	14	15	6	55	6	5	2	5	1	5	2	5	5
1816	51	4	9	20	7	49	6	5	2	5	1	5	5	5	9
1817	51	4	8	19	11	46	7	5	3	5	1	5	3	5	9
1818	57	1	11	18	2	48	6	5	3	5	1	5	3	5	9
1819	64	3	11	13	10	46	8	5	3	5	1	5	3	5	9
1820	70	4	9	12	10	45	9	5	3	5	1	5	3	5	9
1821	58	10	8	11	5	46	6	5	1	5	0	5	1	5	7
1822	20	6	7	13	5	44	6	5	0	4	10	5	0	5	6
1823	42	7	7	14	10	46	7	5	0	4	10	5	0	5	6
1824	42	8	8	16	6	43	0	5	0	4	10	5	0	5	6
1825	59	6	10	17	5	43	2	5	9	4	10	5	6	5	6
1826	57	8	9	13	8	40	4	5	9	4	10	5	6	5	9
1827	55	4	8	13	1	41	6	5	8	4	10	5	6	5	9
1828	50	7	8			40	8								

* In this and some of the following Tables, abstracted from Parliamentary Papers, to save room, fractions have been omitted; it causes a trifling disagreement in the totals. For more copious details on prices, see that article in Mr. M'Culloch's *Commercial Dictionary*.

V.—POPULATION OF GREAT BRITAIN.

Comparative Population of the several Counties of England in the Years 1700, 1750, 1801, 1811, 1821, and 1831; arranged in order of increase and industrial character.

COUNTIES.	1700	1750	1801	1811	1821	18..
Lancaster	166,200	297,400	672,731	828,309	1,052,859	1,33..
York W. R.	236,700	361,500	563,953	653,315	799,459	97..
Warwick	96,600	119,000	208,190	228,735	274,392	33..
Stafford	117,200	160,000	239,153	295,173	341,040	41..
Nottingham	65,200	77,600	140,350	162,900	145,873	22..
Chester	107,000	131,600	191,751	227,031	270,098	31..
Durham	95,500	115,000	160,361	177,625	207,673	253..
Monmouth	39,700	40,600	45,582	62,127	71,833	9..
Worcester	85,200	128,000	139,333	160,546	184,424	2..
Salop	101,600	130,500	167,631	194,298	206,153	22..
Surrey	154,000	247,100	269,043	323,851	398,658	4..
Kent	153,800	190,000	307,624	373,095	426,016	47..
Sussex	91,100	107,400	159,311	190,083	233,019	27..
Cornwall	106,800	135,000	188,269	216,667	257,447	30..
Cumberland	62,400	80,400	117,230	131,744	156,124	17..
Southampt.	118,700	137,100	219,656	245,080	283,298	31..
Gloucester	155,200	207,500	250,809	285,514	335,843	38..
Derby	91,500	109,500	161,142	185,487	213,333	24..
Leicester	80,000	95,000	130,081	150,419	174,571	19..
Middlesex	625,500	911,500	818,129	953,275	1,144,531	1,35..
York, E. R.	96,200	85,500	139,433	167,353	190,449	20..
Somerset	195,000	224,500	273,750	303,180	355,314	40..
Hertford	70,500	86,500	97,577	111,654	129,714	14..
Devon	248,200	272,500	343,001	383,308	439,040	49..
Essex	159,200	167,500	226,437	252,473	289,424	31..
York, N. R.	98,600	117,290	155,506	165,506	184,351	19..
Bedford	48,500	53,900	63,393	70,213	83,716	9..
Suffolk	152,700	150,800	210,431	234,211	270,542	29..
Berks	74,700	92,700	109,215	118,277	131,977	14..
Oxford	79,000	92,400	109,620	119,191	136,971	15..
Westmorland	28,600	38,500	41,617	45,922	51,359	5..
Northumb.	118,000	141,700	157,101	172,161	198,965	22..
Cambridge	76,000	72,400	89,346	101,109	121,909	14..
Norfolk	210,200	215,500	273,371	291,999	344,368	39..
Buckinghm.	80,500	99,700	107,444	117,650	134,068	14..
Lincoln	180,000	166,200	208,557	237,891	285,054	31..
Dorset	90,000	96,400	115,319	124,693	144,499	15..
Wilts	153,000	168,400	185,107	193,828	222,157	24..
Huntingdon	34,700	42,500	37,568	42,208	48,771	5..
Northampt.	119,500	124,300	131,757	141,353	162,483	17..
Hereford	68,900	74,100	89,191	94,073	103,240	11..
Rutland	16,600	13,500	16,356	16,380	18,487	19..
Total Agricultural	2,029,800	2,177,500	2,670,337	12,922,146	3,368,418	3,7..
Ditto Manufacturing	1,113,900	15,82,000	2,528,773	2,990,039	3,591,204	4,406
Ditto Metropolitan	2,602,700	2,314,200	3,130,054	3,639,043	4,298,317	4,952..
Total England	5,146,400	6,073,700	8,351,161	9,551,528	11,261,139	13,04..
Ditto Wales	365,500	450,200	541,546	611,788	717,438	80..
Ditto Scotland		1,265,380	1,599,068	1,805,688	2,093,456	2,36..
Ditto Great Britain		7,789,280	10,491,778	11,969,004	14,072,333	16,25..

Left margin labels: Manufac. & Mining — Metropol. & Manuf. — Agricultural

VI.—ANALYSIS OF OCCUPATIONS IN GREAT BRITAIN.

Descriptions.	Number of Families.		Persons.
	1821.	1831.	1831.
1. Agricultural occupiers -	250,000	250,000	1,500,000
2. Agricultural labourers -	748,956	800,000	4,800,000
3. Mining labourers - -	110,000	120,000	600,006
4. Millers, bakers, butchers	160,000	180,000	900,000
5. Artificers, builders, &c.	200,000	230,000	650,000
6. Manufacturers - - -	340,000	400,000	2,400,000
7. Tailors, shoemakers, hatters - - - - - -	150,000	180,000	1,020,000
8. Shopkeepers - - - -	310,239	350,000	2,100,000
9. Seamen and soldiers - -	319,300	277,017	831,000
10. Clerical, legal, and medicinal classes - - -	80,000	90,000	450,000
11. Disabled paupers - -	100,000	110,000	110,000
12. Proprietors & annuitants	192,888	316,487	1,116,398
Totals - -	2,941,383	3,303,504	16,557,398

VII.—OCCUPATIONS IN SCOTLAND.

District.	Number of Families in 1821, chiefly employed in		
	Agriculture.	Trade, Manufactures or Handicrafts.	All others.
Agricultural district -	67,829	51,036	48,850
Manufacturing ditto -	25,915	126,301	67,171
Highland counties -	37,355	12,927	16,976
Total Families -	130,699	190,264	126,997

VIII.——INCREASE PER CENT. OF POPULATION.

ENGLAND.	1801 to 1811.	1811 to 1821.	1821 to 1831.	1700 to 1831.
Agricultural counties - -	9½	15¼	10¾	84
Manufacturing counties -	18¼	20¾	22¼	295
Metropolitan counties -	16¼	18½	15¼	147
Total { England - - -	14½	17¾	16	154
Total { Wales - - - -	15	17¾	12	117
Total { Scotland - - -	13	15	13	87
GREAT BRITAIN - -	14¼	17½	15¼	144

The four preceding tables, with some alterations
of arrangement, have been derived from Mr. Marshall's *Statistics of the British Empire.*

The most extraordinary fact disclosed by these tables, and which has been before alluded to (p. 258),
is the prodigious increase of the manufacturing
population of England; having, since 1700, increased
295 per cent., and in the decennary period, from
1821 to 1831, 22¼ per cent. The increase of population in the agricultural counties, has been chiefly
in the towns, the number of people in the rural districts not having increased in an equal ratio. The
same observation applies to Scotland. But surely
Mr. Marshall must be in error (part ii. p. 132) in
intimating, "that the *rural* population of England,
as in the agricultural counties of Scotland, appears,
not materially, *if at all*, to have increased since
1700." This is irreconcilable with his *Analysis of
Occupations*, inserted above, whence it appears that
the number of families of agricultural labourers, had
increased from 728,956, in 1821, to 800,000, in
1831.

IX.—POPULATION OF THE METROPOLIS.

DIVISIONS.	1801.	Increase per cent.	1811.	Increase per cent.	1821.	Increase per cent.	1831.
London, within the Walls } City London, without the Walls (including the Inns of Court) } City	75,171	—	55,484	1	56,174	3	57,695
Southwark . . . . Borough	81,688	—	63,425	6	69,260	—	67,878
Westminster . . . . City	67,448	7	72,119	19	85,905	7	91,301
Parishes within the Bills of Mortality	158,210	8	162,085	18	182,085	11	202,080
Parishes within the Bills . City	364,596	37	498,719	24	616,628	23	761,348
Adjacent Parishes, not within the Bills	117,802	32	155,714	38	215,642	36	293,557
Metropolis	864,845	17	1,009,546	21	1,225,694	20	1,474,069

In 1700 the population of the Metropolis was 674,350: at present it amounts to upwards of 1,500,000, including the usual allowance for seamen and strangers, an increase of 222 per cent., while the population of England has increased 254 per cent. The population of Edinburgh has increased from 82,560 in 1801, to 138,235 in 1831.—for further details on Population, pp. 260, 346.

X.—POPULATION OF IRELAND.

At the end of Elizabeth's reign the population of Ireland was estimated at not more than 700,000, and before the rebellion in 1641, at 1,466,000.[*] In

1702	-	-	at 1,320,008	1767	- - at 2,544,276
1718	-	-	2,169,048	1777	- - 2,690,565
1725	-	-	2,317,374	1785	- - 2,845,932
1754	-	-	2,372,634	1792	- - 4,008,226

These returns were all vague, some being founded on the data of private individuals, others on the hearth-money collectors' returns. In 1805, Newenham estimated the population at 5,395,456, and an incomplete census of 1812 gives it at 5,937,356. The most correct censuses of the Irish population and houses are as follows :

Provinces.	1821.		1831.		Increase.	
	Population.	Houses.	Population.	Houses.	Population.	Houses.
Leinster . .	1,757,492	278,398	1,961,109	296,369	203,617	17,971
Ulster . .	1,998,494	359,801	2,353,928	412,023	355,434	52,222
Munster .	1,935,612	306,993	2,163,694	341,438	228,082	34,443
Connaught .	1,110,229	197,408	1,360,783	237,919	250,554	40,511
Totals . .	6,801,827	1,142,600	7,839,514	1,287,749	1,037,687	145,147

Mr. Slaney, who is an attentive observer of these matters, affirms (House of Commons, May 7, 1833) that the population of Ireland is on the decline : the apparent increase is ascribed to several places being enumerated in the returns of 1831 which were omitted in the census of 1821.

[*] Martin's *Ireland as it Was, Is, and Ought to Be*, p. 39.

XI.—BAPTISMS, BURIALS, AND MARRIAGES.

Table of the Annual Proportion of Baptisms, Burials, and Marriages, to the Population of England, calculated upon an average of the totals of such Baptisms, Burials, and Marriages, in the Five Years preceding the several Enumerations of 1801, 1811, 1821, 1831.

COUNTY OF	1796—1800.			1806—1810.			1816—1820.			1826—1830.		
	Baptisms.	Burials.	Marriages.	Baptisms.	Burials.	Marriages.	Baptisms.	Burials.	Marriages.	Baptisms.	Burials.	Marriages.
Bedford . .	35	50	113	34	51	131	35	56	126	37	57	120
Berks . .	38	51	146	38	53	144	33	55	140	33	52	149
Bucks . .	37	58	129	33	51	129	35	55	139	36	55	144
Cambridge .	33	45	118	31	44	120	31	55	117	32	46	124
Chester .	39	51	130	39	51	132	35	52	127	43	57	142
Cornwall .	33	58	120	32	62	142	32	70	146	34	68	147
Cumberland .	38	53	145	35	53	152	34	55	152	36	56	166
Derby . .	38	52	138	34	61	139	36	61	145	36	56	134
Devon . .	36	49	109	33	52	113	34	60	132	35	60	134
Dorset . .	41	62	142	35	56	139	36	64	144	35	56	138
Durham .	38	43	116	34	50	133	34	54	134	35	54	148
Essex . .	35	44	123	34	48	130	36	60	146	37	54	154
Gloucester .	37	55	127	36	64	120	36	62	111	35	62	116
Hereford .	40	63	183	36	61	144	36	60	171	37	56	149
Hertford .	38	54	161	34	58	166	35	58	171	36	49	127
Huntingdon .	33	45	104	35	60	124	35	63	122	36	47	131
Kent . .	30	41	116	30	50	115	31	51	130	34	49	141
Lancaster .	34	47	114	31	51	115	37	55	116	38	57	117
Leicester .	35	49	130	38	50	134	36	59	127	38	56	127
Lincoln .	32	49	117	31	50	122	31	60	124	31	51	135
Middlesex .	30	37	96	40	46	94	41	51	101	40	45	102
Monmouth .	55	73	160	50	70	145	53	72	151	59	83	131
Norfolk . .	32	47	136	31	56	134	32	59	130	33	51	142
Northampton	41	50	130	38	55	132	37	57	130	37	63	135
Northum- berland }	47	57	138	43	55	141	41	65	149	40	63	141
Nottingham .	32	51	116	33	53	119	33	55	124	31	51	128
Oxford . .	38	52	139	34	56	141	33	57	145	32	62	130
Rutland . .	33	50	131	34	56	161	36	62	142	34	53	138
Salop . .	34	54	142	35	60	142	36	55	148	35	54	140
Somerset . .	39	55	130	36	55	129	35	61	140	36	60	147
Southampton	34	46	104	30	46	102	32	61	128	35	56	131
Stafford .	34	49	134	31	53	119	33	62	123	32	51	128
Suffolk .	34	56	129	33	55	132	34	66	134	37	60	137
Surrey . .	37	42	131	37	46	129	39	51	139	38	50	129
Sussex . .	31	55	126	30	53	129	33	60	142	33	58	146
Warwick .	35	52	116	35	45	119	36	48	118	36	60	119
Westmorland	35	50	142	32	55	137	33	52	149	33	57	152
Wilts . .	41	60	142	36	56	138	36	64	134	35	57	148
Worcester .	34	46	137	32	52	129	34	53	140	31	53	127
York, East Riding }	39	53	129	30	49	108	34	55	122	35	50	116
York, North Riding }	36	53	142	31	51	134	35	61	147	35	56	146
York, West Riding }	34	49	124	33	54	123	36	61	124	33	57	136
Total . .	36	48	128	34	51	123	35	57	127	37	54	2 9

The preceding Table, calculated by Mr. Rickman, may be easily made intelligible by an example : as, in the case of BEDFORD, in which it appears that there was one burial in each fifty of the population in 1800 (63,393, p. 548) ; one baptism in each thirty-five, and one marriage in each 113, of the population. So of the proportion of baptisms, burials, and marriages, to the population in the five years ending 1810, 1820, and 1830.

From the bottom line of the table it appears the number of *burials*, in the whole of England, has decreased from one in forty-eight of the population in 1800, to one in fifty-four of the population in 1830. This diminished rate of mortality accounts for the increase of population, notwithstanding the contemporary diminution in the number of births from one in thirty-six in 1800, to one in thirty-seven in 1830, and of marriages from one in 123 to 129.

These *facts* testify in the most conclusive manner to the increasing intelligence and improving condition of the people during the last thirty years.

The *next* Table will show a remarkable change in the nature of the disorders producing the greatest number of deaths in the metropolis during the last sixty years. About thirty years ago one-third more children died of convulsions than at present. Small-pox destroyed half as many again, and teething one-third more, than they do now. Hooping-cough, asthma, cancer and apoplexy, have increased, but leprosy, scurvy, cholic and rickets, have nearly or entirely disappeared. The decrease in fevers, the stationary number of suicides, and the increasing number of those dying of age and natural decay, corroborate our preceding observation of the improving state of society.

XII.—MORTALITY OF THE METROPOLIS.

Deaths, and the Causes of them, within the Bills of Mortality for Four regular Periods, from 1770 to 1830.

CAUSES OF DEATH.	1770.	1790.	1810.	1830.
Abortion, and Still-Born . .	715	805	574	951
Abscess	..	17	42	91
Age and Debility . . .	1230	1600	1532	2242
Ague	8	3	3	30
Apoplexy and Sudden Death .	225	192	234	404
Asthma	427	311	674	1158
Bedridden	9	13	1	1
Bile	..	..	4	17
Bleeding	9	7	36	36
Bloody Flux	1	1	..	..
Bursten and Rupture (now called Hernia	11	13	22	25
Cancer	44	53	77	104
Canker	4	2	1	..
Chicken Pox	2	2	..	..
Childbirth	279	150	183	281
Cholic, Gripes, Twisting of the Guts	62	6	6	..
Cold	3	3	16	..
Consumption	4594	4852	5427	4704
Convulsions	6144	4003	3460	2362
Cough and Hooping-Cough . .	218	391	419	552
Cramp—see Head . . .	..	..	3	..
Croup	..	..	97	126
Diabetes	4	1	1	8
Diarrhœa — see Vomiting and Looseness .				
Dropsy	839	767	771	919
Dropsy on the Brain—see Head	..	..	213	723
Dropsy on the Chest . .	..	..	7	120
Epilepsy .				
Evil—see Scrofula . .	6	6	5	6
Eruptive Diseases . . .	..	..	..	22
Erysipelas — see St. Anthony's Fire	..	..	..	42
Fatigue	..	..	1	..
Fever of all kinds . . .	3224	2185	1139	996
Fistula	8	5	5	..
Flux	15	4	10	10
French Disease—see Venereal	57	27	29	..
Gout	65	43	30	16
Gravel, Strangury, and Stone —see Stone	24	41	16	..
Grief	5	4	5	3
Headache	2	..	1	..
Head-Mould-shot, Horse-shoe Head, and Water in the Head —see Dropsy on the Brain	39	49	1	..
Hemorrhage—see Bleeding .				
Heart, Disease of, . .	..	..	..	79
Hooping-Cough—see Cough				
Hydrophobia—see Bit by Mad Dogs				
Imposthume	9	2	2	..
Inflammation	70	142	676	2196
Inoculation	..	..	1	..
Insanity—see Lunatic . .	..	..	..	270
Itch	1	..	..	..
Jaundice	162	33	31	42
Jaw-Locked	..	..	2	12

MORTALITY OF THE METROPOLIS (Continued).

CAUSES OF DEATH.	1770.	1790.	1810.
Leprosy	1	3	..
Lethargy	7	2	..
Liver Grown	3	21	21
Lunatic (see Insanity)	58	52	193
Measles	325	111	1031
Miscarriage	5	1	3
Mortification	197	183	181
Palsy	66	80	99
Paralytic (see Palsy)	..	..	..
Pleurisy	18	7	28
Quinsy (see Croup)	6	2	6
Rash	2	2	..
Rheumatism	7	2	6
Rickets	4	2	..
Rising of the Lights	2	..	..
Scrofula (see Evil)			
Scurvy	4	5	4
Small Pox	1996	1617	1198
Sores and Ulcers	13	7	9
Sore Throat	26	5	6
St. Anthony's Fire (see Erysipelas)	3	..	2
Spasms	..	..	22
Still-Born (see Abortion)	..	..	..
Stoppage in the Stomach	22	7	12
Stone	..	..	..
Stricture	..	..	..
Suddenly (see Apoplexy)	..	..	..
Surfeit	2	2	..
Swelling	2	..	1
Teeth	792	410	438
Thrush	66	45	55
Tumour	..	..	..
Tympany	3	..	..
Vomiting and Looseness (see Diarrhœa)	7	..	2
Venereal (see French Disease)	..	..	..
Worms	6	9	9
CASUALTIES.			
Bit by Mad Dogs (see Hydrophobia)	..	..	..
Burned	16	16	47
Choked	..	2	2
Drowned	102	119	124
Drinking to excess	3	5	7
Executed	26	14	6
Found Dead	5	6	20
Fractured or Bruised	..	9	8
Frighted	..	2	2
Frozen	..	..	..
Killed by Accidents not enumerated	72	66	72
Killed by Fighting	..	..	..
Murdered	8	3	4
Overlaid	..	1	1
Poisoned	..	4	2
Run over	..	..	..
Scalded	2	8	2
Smothered	..	1	..
Starved	5	4	1
Suffocated	3	2	8
Suicide	22	31	29

XIII.—TABLE OF CHRISTENINGS AND DEATHS

Within the Bills of Mortality, for Four Periods, at Intervals of Twenty Years, with the Returns for 1832.

	1770.	1790.	1810.	1830.	1832.
CHRISTENED.					
Males	8,751	9,766	10,198	13,329	13,504
Females	8,348	9,214	9,742	13,444	13,476
BURIED.					
Males	11,210	9,192	10,411	11,170	14,788
Females	11,224	8,846	9,483	10,535	14,336
DIED.					
Under 2 years of age	7,990	6,677	5,853	8,115	5,443
Between 2 and 5	2,127	1,948	2,430	1,837	2,678
10 .. 5	926	748	660	871	1,270
10 .. 20	678	646	694	618	1,113
20 .. 30	1,789	1,277	1,218	1,416	2,315
30 .. 40	2,178	1,733	1,768	1,759	2,749
40 .. 50	2,002	1,786	2,418	2,026	3,688
50 .. 60	1,683	1,548	1,448	2,031	3,041
60 .. 70	1,456	1,233	1,587	2,065	2,949
70 .. 90	1,026	618	1,262	1,788	2,191
80 .. 90	397	276	478	815	848
90 .. 100	56	51	70	139	106
Age of 101	..	..	..	2	..
102	1	1	..	1	..
103	1	1	..	..	2
105	..	1	1	..	..
108	1	1	..	..	1

In 1831 the burials were 25,337, being an increase of 3692 over the preceding year. In 1832 the burials were 28,606, being an increase of only 3269, So that the increase of mortality was less in the latter than the former year; yet in 1832 there died of cholera 3200, in 1831 only 48.

In Paris the cholera was much more destructive; the deaths there in 1832 were 45,675, the births 26,364; of the former, 19,000, nearly one half of the whole number, was occasioned by the cholera. The arrondissements, in which the mortality was greatest, are the most unhealthy quarters of Paris, where the streets are narrow, and the houses very lofty.

XIV.—MORTALITY IN MANUFACTURING TOWNS,

Showing in every 10,000 persons buried, the proportion dying under 20 and 40 years of age.—Parl. Rep. on Factories Regulation Bill, Sess. 1832.

	Deaths under 20 years old.	Deaths under 40 years old.	Lived to 40 years and upwards.
In Rutland, a healthy county	3756	5031	4969
Essex, a marsh county -	4279	5805	4105
The Metropolis - -	4580	6111	3889
Chester, old and closely built, but not manufacturing - - -	4538	6066	3934
Norwich, old and closely built, manufacturing, but few or no factories	4962	6049	3951
Carlisle, 1779—1787 - -	5319	6325	3674
Carlisle, 1818—1830; —— partly manufacturing, & partly spinning - -	5668	6927	3071
Bradford (York), worsted spinning - - -	5896	7061	2939
Macclesfield, silk spinning and weaving - -	5889	7300	2700
Wigan, cotton-spinning, and manufacturing -	5911	7117	2883
Preston, ditto ditto - -	6083	7462	2538
Bury, ditto ditto - -	6017	7319	2681
Stockport, ditto ditto -	6005	7367	2633
Bolton, ditto ditto - -	6113	7459	2541
Leeds, manufacturing, and woollen, flax, and silk-spinning - - -	6213	7441	2559
Holbeach, flax-spinning -	6133	7337	2663

So that a considerably smaller proportion of persons die in the metropolis under twenty than in the manufacturing towns of Yorkshire and Lancashire. At Norwich, where the domestic manufacture prevails, fewer die under forty than at Leeds, Holbeach, Bolton, and Preston) where the factory system prevails) under twenty.   It shows that in factory towns the duration of life is greatly abridged ; still it appears from the next table, that this greater destruction of life does not arise altogether from working in factories, as the bulk of deaths in Leeds and Holbeach are under the age of five years, before children can be employed in factories. One cause assigned (*Monthly Repository*, No. 75) of the greater mortality of children is the deteriorating effect which factories have on the atmosphere ; but the more influential causes, I apprehend, are the premature weaning, insufficient nourishment, and neglect of infants, where the mother and elder branches of families are at work in factories.   Whatever may be the cause of the mortality of infants under five years, there can be no doubt— indeed, it would be inconsistent with every sanatory principle—that the existing mode of overworking children above that age shortens life.   The comparative salubrity of Norwich must arise from other causes than her domestic manufacture ; the uncleanliness and noxious smells arising from home employments must be unfavourable to health.*

* The influence of favourable circumstances in prolonging life has been established by Mr. Morgan, who found, that of 152,000 persons of the " comfortable middle classes," registered in the assurance office of which he is actuary, during 20 years, only 1930 had died at the end of that period ; 262 deaths were caused by natural decay and old age ; 246 by apoplexy ; 153 by consumption ; 146 by general fever ; 137 by dropsy ; 116 by palsy ; and the rest by various diseases.   The ages of the persons who died were as follows :

Persons			
7	from 10	to	20
37	20		30
166	30		40
299	40		50
458	50		60
536	60		70
344	70		80
82	80	and upwards.	

XV.—COMPARATIVE DURATION OF LIFE IN EVERY 10,000 PERSONS IN MANUFACTURING AND AGRICULTURAL DISTRICTS.—*Factories' Parl. Rep. Sess. 1832.*

	Under 5 years	5–9	10–14	15–19	20–29	30–39	40–49	50–59	60–69	70–79	80–89	90–99 & up	100 & upwards
Rutland, healthy county	2565	321	260	310	712	561	557	702	1189	1498	954	112	3
Essex, marshy	3150	454	273	283	551	615	743	962	1010	630	77	3	
Metropolis	3905	399	162	211	763	92	901	655	766	302	34	2	
Chester, old and closely built, but not manufacturing	3571	392	227	311	721	737	760	723	602	362	345	33	8
Norwich, old, closely built, manufacture domestic	4219	311	170	229	556	572	610	576	1100	606	93	4	
Carlisle, 1779–1787, before manufactories	4108	348	184	239	522	481	560	610	826	523	153	22	
Carlisle, now factories, partly manufacturing and spinning	4735	430	275	252	666	690	546	677	510	452	80	1	
Bradford (York), factories, worsted and spinning	1647	462	300	342	635	539	521	562	652	321	61	3	
Macclesfield, silk factories	4162	455	461	752	654	552	562	534	305	5	0		
Wigan, cotton factories and spinning	4590	409	229	373	644	502	446	656	360	380	52	1	
Preston, factories, cotton spinning	4917	321	284	321	731	639	353	561	653	532	208	34	3
Bury (Lancashire), woollen factories, cotton spinning	4664	414	318	387	732	550	519	530	612	072	285	23	1
Stockport, factories, cotton spinning	4579	432	300	374	729	631	626	600	619	546	213	25	4
Bolton-le-Moor, factories, cotton spinning	4939	405	301	358	722	691	513	536	622	553	255	31	1
Leeds, factories, woollen, flax, silk	5246	410	229	282	638	500	559	599	593	512	225	29	2
Holbeach, factories, flax	5090	405	372	316	598	556	580	556	575	603	325	19	5

XVI.—PROGRESS OF POOR-RATES.

A Statement of the Sums expended for the *Relief of the Poor*, in each county of England, and the total expenditure in Wales from 1750, to the year ending 25th of March, 1832; also the total Parish Assessment and Annual Average Price of Wheat in each year.

COUNTIES.	1750.	1776.	1803.	1815.	1820.	1830.	1832.
	£	£	£	£	£	£	£
Middlesex .	81,030	174,274	349,200	505,601	625,665	675,285	668,160
Lancaster .	21,236	50,985	148,282	213,847	317,057	297,674	301,372
York, W. R. .	20,218	48,749	186,467	257,624	246,814	281,158	282,624
Devon . . .	34,953	61,627	124,022	183,616	249,968	222,381	225,209
Kent . . .	41,997	78,830	206,508	295,290	294,519	356,461	364,361
Surrey . .	26,598	48,519	133,874	201,646	277,271	265,499	282,284
Somerset .	25,596	49,181	121,798	150,258	191,887	174,425	191,587
Norfolk . .	30,464	63,171	160,733	199,192	272,932	299,211	318,412
Stafford . .	9,812	31,480	83,411	111,642	153,132	133,670	138,071
Gloucester .	23,687	52,873	149,045	135,680	182,791	165,192	172,561
Essex . . .	38,233	72,568	137,140	226,252	312,037	282,133	277,663
Southampton	20,521	48,598	124,019	163,150	229,566	212,380	230,685
Lincoln . .	14,790	31,267	95,575	128,360	172,971	179,204	177,670
Warwick . .	10,445	42,896	117,383	127,664	181,984	170,180	168,413
Suffolk . .	28,063	55,839	119,063	155,289	245,076	268,623	279,490
Chester . .	14,741	28,922	66,627	100,669	121,169	105,238	105,138
Cornwall . .	9,660	21,997	54,648	78,090	115,254	103,369	101,620
Sussex . .	24,343	53,499	179,852	230,866	286,066	256,142	284,568
Wiltshire . .	22,938	52,714	128,635	137,626	188,808	198,008	199,866
Derby . . .	7677	16,771	54,459	71,179	103,764	80,060	81,463
Durham . .	7143	14,057	51,966	78,726	101,756	81,209	86,680
Salop . . .	7925	21,549	66,747	90,839	111,617	83,898	89,166
Northumbrlnd	3796	14,085	52,416	69,236	82,030	74,283	78,667
York, E. R. .	4110	10,804	41,568	75,438	105,867	99,500	105,629
Nottingham .	4375	11,665	44,222	71,419	105,348	78,342	74,576
Worcester .	9134	26,156	71,235	85,540	107,260	80,014	87,863
York, N. R. .	8581	12,155	48,702	65,536	91,733	92,367	83,526
Leicester .	7549	23,561	79,911	95,200	159,676	130,026	116,340
Northampton	12,367	34,632	94,607	123,038	162,546	155,031	154,120
Cumberland .	2450	7402	27,603	40,916	59,064	46,081	47,845
Dorset . . .	12,236	24,045	64,771	75,678	104,825	90,949	92,566
Oxford . .	12,831	28,131	68,669	106,495	143,230	130,597	136,664
Bucks . . .	17,139	31,130	86,151	101,814	133,165	135,139	144,587
Berks . . .	15,971	35,989	81,994	100,297	123,290	111,653	121,217
Hertford . .	16,452	25,241	56,380	77,991	100,667	99,680	96,844
Cambridge .	9171	17,729	54,464	65,951	91,163	101,147	103,922
Hereford . .	5056	9921	46,471	67,063	81,108	59,711	62,468
Bedford . .	9276	16,310	36,804	50,370	73,465	84,541	77,226
Monmouth .	2808	5433	16,283	27,050	33,622	24,628	28,979
Westmorland	1802	2767	13,636	20,330	29,412	25,512	26,154
Huntingdon .	1306	7814	23,867	31,470	38,796	42,128	41,180
Rutland . .	86	2641	9376	10,843	12,426	9644	9606
Total England	679,462	1,489,228	3,999,521	5,202,931	7,020,366	6,553,443	6,731,131
Ditto Wales .	19,971	32,504	48,370	215,217	309,239	276,509	304,837
Ditto England and Wales .	699,433	1,521,732	3,977,891	5,418,148	7,329,594	6,829,952	7,82,8968
Total Parish assessment in ditto .	730,135	1,721,316	5,318,904	7,457,676	9,719,548	8,161,281	8,622,920
Average Price of Wheat .	27-11	45-4	66-2	79-6	69-5	64-3	59-1

XVII.—POOR-RATES ON LAND, HOUSES, FACTORIES, &c.

Ionies levied for Poor's Rate and County Rate in 1826; showing
the proportion levied on Land, on Dwelling-houses, on Mills and
Factories, and on Manorial Profits and Incidentals; also the number
of Unendowed Schools, and Members of Friendly Societies.

COUNTIES.	Land.	Dwelling Houses.	Mills, Factories, &c.	Manorial Profits, &c.	Total Levied.	Unendowed Day Schools, 1826.	Members of Friendly Societies, 1815.
	£	£	£	£	£		
Bedford .	77,929	6,298	508	183	84,969	44	3,647
Berks .	89,596	21,014	2,446	839	113,895	37	3,858
Bucks .	123,470	17,495	2,702	248	143,915	48	5,917
Cambrdge	85,612	14,427	1,049	143	101,231	87	4,574
Chester .	88,606	20,592	5,315	1,752	116,265	23	19,029
Cornwall	85,979	14,016	1,858	7,408	109,261	109	27,390
Cumberl.	40,765	12,378	714	1,129	54,966	83	9,807
Derby .	71,376	12,735	2,128	1,455	87,694		22,412
Devon .	180,873	47,698	3,925	3,396	236,092	173	45,007
Dorset .	74,811	17,170	750	914	93,645	59	5,952
Durham .	63,297	16,668	3,624	11,442	95,031	94	15,115
Essex .	243,112	42,761	6,829	1,369	294,071	78	31,423
Gloucester	100,117	49,017	4,962	1,456	155,552	65	21,567
Hereford .	58,623	6,736	86	35	65,480	31	2,854
Hertford .	74,927	23,110	27,56	512	101,305	49	10,477
Huntngdn	38,912	5,504	570	97	45,083	31	2,470
Kent . .	253,375	103,584	11,660	3,327	371,946	209	15,640
Lancaster	168,422	118,261	50,461	12,525	349,669	30	137,655
Leicester	93,882	17,634	782	310	112,608	77	15,425
Lincoln .	174,766	23,306	38,887	887	202,846	159	8,655
Middlesex	57,221	509,365	36,353	787	603,726		60,579
Monmth.	25,662	4,206	791	1,214	31,873		7,923
Norfolk .	240,526	49,085	8,097	3,924	301,632	186	13,557
Nrthamtn	131,544	12,372	536	1,022	145,574	110	10,750
Nrthmlnd.	50,834	15,233	8,774	2,981	77,822	61	12,193
Nottnghm	52,625	24,124	2,971	291	80,011	15	19,144
Oxford .	109,306	21,863	1,149	469	132,767	85	5,922
Rotland .	10,960	847	75	7	11,889	19	1,398
Salop . .	72,763	14,615	1,227	2,347	90,752	83	23,638
Somerset	141,247	30,306	2,380	3,042	176,975	94	23,883
Southamt.	165,602	46,174	3,374	666	215,816	99	11,013
Stafford .	85,670	34,963	6,655	7,129	134,417	54	41,213
Suffolk .	221,332	36,525	4,398	712	262,967	153	13,335
Surrey .	80,357	144,064	22,983	2,645	250,049	74	21,505
Sussex .	214,304	42,752	4,610	466	262,132	117	4,790
Warwick .	94,842	49,393	10,674	3,082	157,991	71	26,330
Westmrld.	24,186	2,831	496	103	27,616	98	1,276
Wilts . .	157,231	24,662	3,234	1,321	186,448	86	15,305
Worcester	62,888	15,892	3,111	2,092	83,983	67	13,458
York, E.R.	71,530	32,414	2,338	2,478	109,760	90	11,371
———— N.R.	83,523	8,205	1,208	669	93,605	192	8,885
———— W.R.	180,597	78,472	23,269	5,782	288,120	54	74,005
England .	4,523,288	1,788,865	255,775	93,559	6,661,157	3260	
Wales .	272,194	25,363	3,790	3,323	304,670		45,097
Total of England & Wales }	4,795,482	1,814,228	259,565	96,882	6,966,157		861,657

XVIII.—POOR-RATES FOR THE YEAR ENDED MARCH 1832.

COUNTIES.	Total sums levied.	Payments for other purposes than the Poor.	Sums expended for the Poor.	Total sums expended.	Increase per cent.	Diminution per cent.	Select Vestries.	Assistant Overseers.
ENGLAND.	£	£	£	£	£	£		
Bedford	92,711	13,525	77,236	90,762	—	5	0	40
Berks	144,117	20,709	121,217	141,926	5	—	23	47
Buckingham	172,007	27,097	141,587	172,285	5	—	43	62
Cambridge	120,112	16,111	103,924	120,065	5	—	14	50
Chester	151,610	45,250	105,158	148,209	2	—	110	119
Cornwall	120,809	18,515	101,629	118,144	—	1	37	41
Cumberland	58,708	9,202	47,846	57,108	4	—	90	86
Derby	110,810	30,048	81,405	112,042	3	—	56	73
Devon	256,386	25,623	225,299	250,975	1	—	81	99
Dorset	110,087	15,108	92,680	107,788	2	—	25	48
Durham	102,941	15,454	86,081	101,511	5	—	80	68
Essex	323,320	46,758	277,403	323,121	2	—	35	82
Gloucester	206,174	37,008	172,141	209,466	3	—	44	85
Hereford	72,587	9,747	64,108	73,205	1	—	30	53
Hertford	113,744	17,246	96,164	114,410	2	—	12	38
Huntingdon	50,114	7,809	41,156	48,965	2	—	10	19
Kent	323,508	73,049	364,101	347,491	5	—	44	186
Lancaster	411,292	120,392	301,372	421,770	3	—	191	252
Leicester	143,416	29,395	116,210	136,011	2	—	57	46
Lincoln	242,403	51,940	177,650	229,587	2	—	119	112
Middlesex	958,444	293,573	688,130	981,691	1	—	14	52
Monmouth	37,888	10,135	28,078	38,211	6	—	18	78
Norfolk	362,132	34,815	318,412	358,227	6	—	58	101
Northampton	136,051	22,152	154,120	176,272	2	—	55	67
Northumberland	94,745	17,470	78,087	95,554	5	—	48	51
Nottingham	100,621	17,092	74,456	101,408	2	—	39	63
Oxford	138,118	20,990	136,684	157,074	3	—	42	50
Rutland	12,921	472	9,063	12,780	4	—	30	13
Salop	108,742	18,840	80,162	109,008	2	—	43	79
Somerset	224,482	21,088	141,042	226,572	8	—	71	110
Southampton	205,100	35,828	240,085	204,513	7	—	42	77
Stafford	176,857	45,705	142,074	179,096	—	—	60	97
Suffolk	211,102	42,013	270,18	313,145	5	—	41	117
Surrey	204,184	95,461	284,284	373,448	7	—	42	39
Sussex	323,864	44,072	284,680	328,709	5	—	30	87
Warwick	204,564	42,175	168,411	210,588	4	—	37	53
Westmorland	20,758	3,407	26,154	38,467	—	2	55	32
Wilts	242,841	30,615	189,088	229,703	—	—	24	66
Worcester	110,954	23,240	87,055	109,444	4	—	43	69
York	708,128	135,840	475,788	699,331	10	—	343	262
Total of England	8,250,417	1,585,520	6,741,431	8,376,651	3	—	2234	3134
WALES								
Anglesey	21,401	3,436	17,641	21,078	9	—	19	15
Brecon	22,888	5,645	19,741	23,397	6	—	12	10
Cardigan	21,158	1,078	19,157	23,225	9	—	3	14
Carmarthen	42,803	6,720	35,283	42,000	5	—	27	9
Carnarvon	24,553	3,099	20,792	24,882	—	2	16	20
Denbigh	45,046	7,744	36,060	44,745	5	—	14	25
Flint	26,346	5,324	21,031	26,913	5	—	10	20
Glamorgan	52,073	9,140	42,803	52,311	11	—	21	41
Merioneth	17,666	2,167	15,191	17,358	2	—	4	16
Montgomery	44,701	7,542	37,499	44,032	7	—	12	21
Pembroke	29,767	4,494	25,088	29,554	2	—	14	18
Radnor	17,016	3,202	14,055	17,317	4	—	5	2
Total of Wales	367,004	60,972	305,837	366,909	6	—	157	211
Total of England and Wales	8,622,920	1,646,492	7,036,968	8,683,161	4	—	2391	3345

XIX.—SAVINGS' BANKS, FRIENDLY AND CHARITABLE SOCIETIES.

	Total of Deposi- tors.	Friend- ly So- cieties.	Charitable Societies.	Increase or dec. in Accounts since 1829.	Total In- vestment.	Increase or dec. in amount since 1810.	Average of each depositor.
Bedfordshire	1,765	38	22	17 i	£69,061	£1,046 i	£39
Berkshire .	7,138	67	49	142 i	200,639	3,186 i	34
Buckinghmsh.	1,857	26	14	8 i	60,911	544 d	30
Cambridgesh.	1,678	46	22	30 i	60,799	2,876 i	37
Cheshire .	7,647	104	2	44 i	321,846	10,941 i	39
Cornwall .	5,513	93	14	55 i	240,874	685 i	42
Cumberland	4,016	22	21	28 i	131,913	2,025 i	32
Derbyshire	5,513	123	21	253 d	220,182	7,428 d	37
Devonshire	26,564	378	138	701 i	965,643	10,602 d	33
Dorsetshire	5,626	58	35	270 i	250,370	1,422 d	42
Durham .	4,578	54	22	244 d	158,298	14,355 d	32
Essex .	8,157	163	90	164 i	301,545	2,482 i	34
Gloucester .	13,660	185	77	91 d	563,524	10,095 d	39
Hampshire	7,860	104	53	256 i	319,516	8,240 i	38
Herefordshire	3,892	14	15	53 d	130,712	4,014 d	32
Hertfordshire	3,177	80	90	102 d	166,726	6,740 d	45
Huntiogdonsb	747	30	26	19 i	26,396	96 i	31
Kent .	16,885	171	100	213 i	556,710	16,815 d	31
Lancashire .	26,147	374	150	1949 i	968,144	66,141 i	38
Leicestershire	3,366	58	27	22 d	100,001	1,698 i	28
Lincolnshire	7,017	74	46	51 i	225,630	236 i	30
London (City)	19,392	12	3	1151 i	455,498	5,768 i	23
Middlesex	47,506	102	100	2966 i	1,398,498	49,448 i	29
Monmouthsh.	1,232	32	10	14 i	33,879	1,511 d	27
Norfolk .	6,168	69	18	155 i	198,554	5,484 i	31
Northmptnsh.	4,843	44	34	50 i	177,577	2,100 i	34
Northumbrlnd	6,987	90	19	15 i	307,772	8,906 d	42
Nottinghamsh	7,725	256	15	275 i	242,752	2,893 d	29
Oxfordshire	5,201	46	36	200 i	157,606	129 d	28
Shropshire	9,234	111	26	56 i	391,964	5,036 d	38
Somersetshire	12,141	179	70	460 i	562,414	10,828 d	42
Staffordshire	7,337	172	83	105 i	264,173	3,603 i	32
Suffolk .	5,371	114	37	161 i	190,567	1,512 d	32
Surrey .	13,369	76	28	432 i	303,811	1,176 i	29
Sussex .	8,506	51	42	45 i	276,703	3,915 i	31
Warwickshire	6,266	50	85	623 i	164,580	12,801 i	28
Westmorland	674	8	0	34 i	24,041	963 i	35
Wiltshire .	6,612	76	45	158 d	266,076	6,150 d	27
Worcestersh.	6,953	74	45	162 i	265,907	2,630 i	37
Yorkshire .	30,161	296	99	966 i	1,129,654	1,570 d	25
	367,813	4117	1787	9695 i	12,069,255	81,684	34

The preceding number of Depositors are thus divided :

Depositors.	No.	Increase or Decrease since 1829.	Average Amount of each.
Under £20 each . .	187,770	7,062 i	£7
————— 50	102,621	2,502 i	29
————— 100	48,343	208 d	68
————— 150	17,214	260 i	[123
————— 200	7,627	488 i	166
Above 200 each . .	4,237	551 d	247
Friendly Societies . .	4,117	111 d	162
Charitable Societies . .	1,787	424 d	71

Up to Nov. 21st, 1831, the returns stood thus :

	Depositors.	Total Investment.	Average.
England . .	374,169	£12,916,028	£32
Wales . .	10,374	349,794	31
Ireland . .	37,898	1,045,825	26

XX.—POOR-LAWS.

Number of Cases decided by the Judges on the Poor-laws up to Nov. 1832.—*Parl. Pap. No. 20, Sess. 1832.*

Relating to the Appointment of Overseers	79
Poor's-Rate	257
Overseers' Accounts, &c.	100
Rating Parishes in aid	23
Maintenance of Relations	37
Relief and Ordering of the Poor	25
Bastards	138
Apprentices	124
As to Settlement by Birth	37
Parentage	58
Marriage	47
Renting a Tenement	135
Serving an Office	29
Hiring and Service	254
Apprenticeship	154
Estate	93
Persons Irremovable until Chargeable	19
Certificates	69
Removal of the Poor	156
On Appeal to Sessions	139
Statutes in Force	118

XXI.—PROGRESS OF CRIME.

Statement of the Number of Persons charged with Criminal Offences committed for Trial every fifth year from 1805, and the Proportion of the Committals in 1832, to the Population of each County in 1831.

COUNTIES.	1805	1810	1815	1820	1825	1830	1831	1832	Crime to Population.
York . .	245	248	355	651	844	1207	1278	1388	1 to 688
Middlesex .	1217	1424	2005	2773	2902	3390	3514	3739	 388
Lancaster .	371	563	959	1063	2132	2928	2387	3014	 893
Devon . .	96	147	264	347	437	494	399	481	 1022
Kent . .	210	223	327	520	577	649	649	773	 606
Surrey . .	199	242	294	525	591	786	733	943	 525
Somerset .	106	118	221	405	523	643	616	696	 539
Norfolk .	163	118	185	382	400	429	549	532	 733
Stafford .	91	134	154	413	278	588	641	608	 568
Gloucester	141	174	285	417	455	708	524	683	 430
Essex . .	144	168	191	360	408	403	607	683	 498
Southampton	147	109	217	315	357	424	507	454	 677
Lincoln .	58	69	136	210	198	206	307	299	 1083
Warwick .	160	169	277	594	482	601	665	765	 478
Suffolk . .	109	816	146	254	272	362	371	453	 654
Chester .	80	83	186	332	306	534	513	578	 585
Cornwall .	45	38	54	163	109	193	145	195	 1350
Sussex . .	105	66	104	215	273	360	314	283	 982
Wilts . .	75	78	109	235	314	418	508	346	 683
Derby . .	30	33	57	94	84	106	202	219	 1083
Durham .	27	35	49	73	104	205	177	158	 1691
Salop . .	29	60	90	162	138	226	224	261	 852
Northumberld	38	57	69	110	87	82	108	89	 2786
Nottingham	74	67	121	251	219	300	316	343	 656
Worcester .	51	66	130	204	148	241	342	316	 648
Leicester .	47	55	71	156	148	196	192	248	 796
Northampton	42	31	61	132	120	152	108	195	 919
Cumberland	19	22	28	55	57	74	74	75	 2202
Dorset . .	28	37	61	73	119	205	177	166	 959
Oxford . .	38	32	66	116	118	108	220	217	 699
Bucks . .	33	47	50	97	100	151	211	188	 773
Berks . .	62	55	77	142	154	170	201	193	 352
Hertford .	43	64	80	144	162	274	194	203	 680
Cambridge .	40	19	64	86	137	147	165	201	 710
Hereford .	31	47	54	112	68	145	166	147	 755
Bedford .	20	22	28	61	123	134	103	100	 953
Monmouth	20	17	24	30	55	126	129	110	 808
Westmorlnd	6	1	13	17	16	22	17	25	 1985
Huntingdon	15	4	17	28	31	36	85	34	 1562
Rutland .	4	2	11	9	7	5	11	10	 1938
Total England	4327	5067	7710	13,425	14,214	17,750	19,260	20,486	 828
Do. England and Wales	4605	5146	7818	13,710	14,437	18,107	19,647	20,829	 897
Males	3267	3733	6036	11,595	11,989	15,134	16,600	17,480	
Females .	1338	1413	1782	2115	2545	2973	3047	3349	
Executed .	68	67	57	107	50	46	52	54	

An attentive consideration of the table (No. 21), will remove the chief difficulties connected with the progress of crime in England. It will be found by comparing its results with the facts developed in some of the preceding tables, that the increase of criminality is unconnected with the increase of pauperism and education; and that it arises from the rapid increase in the wealth and population of the metropolis and manufacturing districts.

By comparing the proportion of crime to population in the manufacturing and agricultural counties, it will be seen that the *excess* of delinquency is in the former, as is at once evident from the subjoined comparison:

Manufacturing Counties.		*Agricultural Counties.*	
Lancaster . . .	501	Devon . . .	1028
York . . .	892	Essex . . .	466
Warwick . . .	478	Bedford . . .	953
Stafford . . .	588	Suffolk . . .	656
Nottingham . .	656	Berks . . .	753
Chester . . .	583	Northumberland .	2786
Monmouth . . .	892	Kent . . .	646
		Hampshire . .	677
Average . . .	665	Wiltshire . .	891
		Average . .	960

In the seven manufacturing counties, one criminal to 665 of the population; in nine agricultural counties only one criminal to 960 of the population. The increase of crime in a faster ratio than the population may then be ascribed, as one of its chief causes, to the altered relations of national industry in the growing ascendancy of manufacturing over agricultural employments.

The increase of the metropolis is another circumstance to which the increase of crime may be traced. There is greater delinquency in London than in any other part of the kingdom. In 1832 the proportion of committals to the population of the metropolis, was one to 394;* which it will be seen by reference to the preceding table, is a greater proportion to the population, than in any county, either agricultural or manufacturing.

Ought it then to be inferred that the standard of morals has been depreciated by the increase of the metropolis, and transition in national industry? Certainly not; and for this conclusive reason, that there has been no increase in *female delinquency*.† By reference to the foot of the table, it is apparent that the number of female offenders has increased in a much less ratio than the male offenders. Now had there been a *growing* depravity in the community, it must have been shared in by the women as well as the men, and the existence of it would have been demonstrated by a corresponding augmentation in the number of female committals. The reason that crimes have increased among the men is, that property and transactions connected with property have increased. In agricultural counties there is less crime, because there is less wealth, and fewer commercial transfers, trusts, and exchanges. There is also less fluctuation and vicissitude in the condition of individuals. The same observations apply to inhabitants in London.

In Wales the proportion of offenders to the population is only one in 2348. In the highlands of Scotland, or the Pampas, I dare say it is still less; and on the open sea a minimum. In respect of crimes against property it is said,‡ that " ignorant, degraded, uncommercial, and impoverished Spain, is *three*

---

* *Parl. Papers*, No. 155, Session 1833.

† This peculiarity in criminal commitments I pointed out on a former occasion, in a *Treatise on the Police and Crimes of the Metropolis*, p. 346.

‡ *Inquiry into the State of the Manufacturing Population*, p. 20.

times less vicious than France, and *seven times* less vicious than England." The reason of this is obvious enough. In Spain, crimes if committed at all must be crimes against the *person* (and there they predominate) not against property, since there comparatively is none.* It is hard to be a thief where there is nothing to steal. Hence the peculiarity in her criminal calendar. But ought any one to infer from this that the moral character of Spain is superior to that of France or England? Every one acquainted with the three countries knows the contrary. It would be just as erroneous, and for similar reasons, to infer that our national character has depreciated in consequence of the increase of metropolitan and manufacturing wealth and population. The truth is, that both virtues and crimes increase with riches, the former I conceive in a faster ratio than the latter : unfortunately we have only statistical returns of the evil, not the good deeds of wealthy and civilized communities.

Happily in this country, neither pauperism, nor wealth, nor education, has lessened *public happiness*, but the contrary. This is shown incontestably

* In 1826 the following was the proportion of personal and property crimes, in the *dark* and *light* countries of Europe:

Countries.	Personal Crimes.	Property Crimes.
Netherlands	1 in 28,904	1 in 7140
England	23,395	799
France	17,573	1804
Spain	3804	5937

From a parliamentary return for Ireland of committals in 1832 (*Parl. Pap.*, No. 80, Sess. 1833) may be deduced the following results : Population, 7,734,365 ; criminal committals, 13,719 : proportion one committal to 565 of the population ; indicating a very dark state of society, in a country so low in wealth and commerce as Ireland, and shows her defective moral and political government. In Scotland the committals in 1832 was one in 973 of the population.

by the diminished rate of mortality. Let us then proceed with a firm step in our course, increasing national riches and education, and holding fast to our poor-laws.

XXII.—WAGES OF MANUFACTURERS AND ARTIFICERS.

Cotton manufacture.—The classes employed in this manufacture, as carried on in a circle of thirty miles diameter round Manchester, are mostly paid by the piece, working about twelve hours in the twenty-four. The wages are paid weekly, not once a fortnight or once a month, as is the case in collieries and many other places. The following is a statement of the number and average wages of the workpeople in the employ of Messrs. Birley, Hornby, and Kirk, made out in January, 1832:

	Spinners.			Weavers.			Number employed.
	s.	d.		s.	d.		
Men	20	6		15	1¼		379
Women	11	3¼		9	7¼		563
Children	5	10		5	4¾		634

The transition from hand to power-loom weaving has caused much distress in Lancashire. This vicissitude affects the whole of the Salford and Blackburn hundreds, which comprise three-fifths of the population of the county, and is partially felt in the other hundreds. As frequently happens in the application of machinery, the proportion between adult and infant labour has been altered; the number of hand-looms in employment has diminished to less than one-third; while an additional number of women* and children of both sexes, from fifteen to

* The increasing extent to which women are employed in the manufacturing towns may tend to alter their relative position in civil society. A strike for wages is sometimes organized by female operatives. This year (*Leeds Mercury*, May 4) the cord-

seventeen years of age, find employment in the power-loom factories. The country places suffer more than the manufacturing towns, where the various demands for labour enable many weavers to choose other occupations; and the power-looms, by giving employment to their children, alleviate the evils they have occasioned. The country weavers, having no such resources, their earnings are more reduced. Thus, in the neighbourhood of Burnley, an average hand-loom weaver cannot earn above 4s. 6d. a week, although a Manchester or Preston weaver can earn 6s. or 7s. weekly.

About one-fifth of the workpeople in the cotton manufacture are men, one-third women, and the remainder children. In thirty-six mills at Stockport, 11,444 persons are employed whose wages amount to 6689l. weekly; of these 320 are betwixt nine and ten years of age, 384 betwixt ten and eleven, 710 betwixt eleven and twelve, 2923 betwixt twelve and eighteen, and 7101 upwards of eighteen years of age.

Woollen manufacture.—The woollen manufacturers in the neighbourhood of Leeds amount to about 20,000, working twelve hours per day, six days per week, and may be divided into three classes:

1st, Weavers earning weekly about 14s.;

2d, Spinners and slubbers, 21s.;

3d, Dressers, 21s.*

Women may gain about 6s. per week; children from eight to twelve years old, 3s. to 5s.; from

setters in the neighbourhood of Scholes and Hightown, chiefly women, held a meeting, to the number of 1500, at Peep Green, at which it was determined not to set any more cards at less than a halfpenny a thousand. Alarmists may view these indications of female independence as more menacing to established institutions than the " education of the lower orders."

* *Parliamentary Report on Manufacturers' Employment*, p. 90, sess. 1830.

twelve to sixteen years, 6s. to 8s. Forty years since,
the *average* wages of men, women, and children, in
the woollen manufacture, were from 5s. to 6s. each
per week ; they are now from 9s. to 10s. each per
week.*   In the former period, masons, carpenters, &c., had 1s. 3d. and 1s. 6d. a day ; they have
now 3s., 3s. 6d., and 4s. a day.

Carpet manufacturers, Kidderminster.—These,
too, may be placed in three general classes :

1st class earning 30s. per week ;
2d class about 23s. per week ;
3d class 20s. per week.

The American tariff has lessened the export of
carpets to that country one-half.   All the workmen
are in a society or trade union, giving a small allowance to those out of work drawn from those in employment.   The total reduction of wages in this
employment since the peace, was estimated in 1830
to amount to about one-third on the wages paid in
1815.

Hardware and Metals.—From accounts laid before a committee of the House of Commons on Manufacturers' Employment, it appears there are at
least eleven different branches of manufacture in
steel and metals carried on in Sheffield and its vicinity, comprising manufacturers of—1st, Table-knives ;
2d, penknives and pocket-knives ; 3d, scissors ; 4th,
razors ; 5th, files ; 6th, saws ; 7th, edge-tools ; 8th,
fenders and stove-grates; 9th, Britannia metal goods;
10th, silver and silver plating ; 11th, cut nails, &c.
Each of these trades exhibits a curious instance of
the division of labour, there being, in each, three,
four, or five different sets of workmen engaged in
the completion of each article : as for instance, for
knives—forgers, grinders, and finishers ; for files—
forgers, grinders, cutters, and hardeners ; for saws—

* *Leeds Mercury*, March 23, 1833.

smiths, grinders, handlemakers, and finishers. And each of these subdivisions is again divided into best, second, and third rate workmen, earning rates of wages varying as follows :

The best class about . . 25s. per week.
The second class . . . 20s. ————
The third class . . . 16s. ————

For one of the highest class, there are three of the second and eight of the third. In several of these trades, boys earn proportionally ; and women also get employment at fair wages. All these persons generally work by the piece. They comprise not less than 16,000 persons in the town of Sheffield alone. Formerly two-thirds of their manufactures were used at home ; now the foreign consumption is about one-half the whole.

The same details are applicable to BIRMINGHAM, where the workmen may be divided into three classes, earning respectively about 12s., 18s., and 24s. per week, working ten hours each day, six days per week, and generally by the piece. Women and children are employed in many trades.

The wages of locksmiths at WOLVERHAMPTON have been greatly depressed : in 1830, though working fourteen hours a day, they were unable to earn more than from 11s. to 14s., being a great reduction in their former wages. The screwmakers (about 1000 in number) and hingemakers have laboured under a similar depression. The wages of these workmen were steady during the war ; in 1816 a great depression commenced, which continued in 1817 ; from 1818 to 1822, a gradual improvement took place ; in 1823-4-5, wages advanced higher than ever ; in 1826 they again began to descend. Before the peace, one-third of the locks, screws, hinges, and edge-tools, were for exportation ; now they do not exceed one-sixth : the Germans and

Flemings are beginning to compete with us, and the American tariff operated injuriously on heavy goods. The japanners (about 500 in number) have not experienced these reverses; their earnings vary from 20s. to 30s. a week.

The great depression in the hardware manufacture will appear from the subjoined summary of prices.

A STATEMENT of the Comparative Prices of Hardware Articles in and near Birmingham for Four several Periods.

DESCRIPTION.	Prices in								
	1818.		1824.		1828.		1830.		
	s.	d.	s.	d.	s.	d.	s.	d.	
Anvils	25	0	20	0	16	0	13	0	per cwt.
Awls, polished Liverpool	2	6	2	0	1	6	1	2	per gross
Bed Screws, 6 inches long	18	0	15	0	6	0	5	0	per gross
Bolts for Doors. 6 inches	6	0	5	0	2	3	1	6	per dozen
Braces for Carpenters, with 12 bits	9	0	6	3	4	2	3	5	per set
Bits, tinned, for Bridles	5	0	5	0	3	3	2	6	per dozen
Buttons for Coats	4	6	4	0	3	0	2	2	per gross
Buttons, small, for Waistcoats, &c.	2	0	2	0	1	3	0	6	per gross
Curry Combs, six barred	3	9	2	6	1	6	0	11	per dozen
Candlesticks, six inches, brass	3	11	3	0	1	7	1	2	per pair
Commode Knobs, brass, 2 inches	4	0	3	6	1	6	1	2	per dozen
Frying-pans	25	0	21	0	18	0	16	0	per cwt.
Hinges, cast butts, 1 inch	0	10	0	7½	0	3½	0	2¾	per dozen
Shoe Hammers, No. 9	6	0	3	9	3	0	2	9	per dozen
Latches for Doors, bright thumb	2	3	2	2	1	0	0	9	per dozen
Locks for Doors, iron rim, 6 inches	38	0	32	0	15	0	13	6	per dozen
Locks for Guns, single roller	6	0	5	2	1	10	1	6	each
Plated Stirrups	4	6	3	9	1	6	1	1	per pair
Saddle Irons, and other Castings	22	6	20	0	14	0	11	6	per cwt.
Shovel and Tongs, fire-irons	1	0	1	0	0	9	0	6	per pair
Tinned Table Spoons	17	0	15	0	10	0	7	0	per gross
Trace Chains	28	0	25	0	19	6	16	6	per cwt.
Vices for Blacksmiths, &c.	30	0	28	0	22	0	19	6	per cwt.
Japanned Tea-Trays, 30 inches	4	6	3	0	2	0	1	5	each
Iron Wire, No. 6	16	0	13	0	9	0	7	0	per bundle
Brass Wire	1	10	1	4	1	0	0	9	per lb.

The exertions making by foreigners to improve their manufactures, preclude the hope of any general and permanent advance in the scale of wages in this country. Our mechanical superiority is declining. The latest machines introduced into the cotton trade are of foreign invention, and even in the remotest part of the continent machinery on the English plan is invariably employed. In lieu of an advance in wages, we must look forward to a reduction in the price of food by the repeal of our impolitic Corn-laws. Without cheap food, we cannot have low wages; still low wages are indispensable to successful competition in the markets of the continent.

To show our relation to the foreigner in this respect, I shall abridge from the *Westminster Review* (No. 36) a short statement of the Cotton Trade abroad; it will also afford useful points of comparison of the rate of wages, employment of children, and hours of working in this country and on the continent.

France.—In 1831, a population of 200,000 was employed in the cotton manufacture in this country. The average wages paid are 5s. 8d. a week. The hours of labour are generally twelve; and fourteen in Alsace. Power-looms have not made much way in France, but in Alsace their number is increasing fast, and they succeed well. In 1830, France exported cotton goods to the amount of 2,192,240*l.* of which 1,483,640*l.* were printed cottons.

Switzerland.—The population employed in the cotton manufacture, is at least 28,000, and children are admitted into the factories at ten years of age. The hours of labour average eighty per week, and are often fourteen a day. The average wages paid are 4s. 5d. No. 40 twist can be produced, every thing included, at 14½d. per lb. when the raw material costs 8½d. In England, with cotton at the same price, it costs 14d. As nearly as can be calculated, the average wages in an English *coarse* mill are 8s. 4d. The fine twills of the Swiss, and the better description of prints, have successfully competed with the English.

Prussia and the Rhenish Provinces.—Here the cotton manufacture is extending, though it has not reached any considerable extent. The number of persons employed on spinning alone is 9000. They work sometimes twelve, but oftener fifteen or sixteen hours a day. Power-looms have been introduced into the Rhenish provinces. Wages not ascertained.

Saxony.—In this country, chiefly in the neighbourhood of Elberfield, the cotton manufacture is just commencing. Children are admitted at six or seven years of age, and the hours of labour are twelve a day. The average wages paid, are about 3s. 6d. a week. They can compete successfully with English yarn as high as No. 50 for warp, and No. 80 for weft.

Austria.—The cotton manufacture is rapidly advancing in Hungary, Austria Proper, and the Tyrol. It is, however, of recent growth. Children enter the mills at eight years of age. In the Tyrol, the average wages are 3s. 9d., and they can produce No. 40 twist at 15¼d. per lb. when the raw material is 8⅝d.

India.—Spinning manufactories are only just commencing their existence; but the vicinity of the raw material and the excessive cheapness of labour afford great advantages. There is a mill containing the best machinery, and 20,000 spindles lately established about twelve miles from Calcutta. They work seven days in the week, and eleven hours a day in winter, and thirteen or fourteen in summer. A spinner gets 7s. a month; a piecer 3s. to 4s.

United States of America.—From a report to Congress in 1832, it appears the quantity of cotton yarn produced was 67,862,652 lbs. The number

of males employed, 18,539 ; of females, 38,927 ;
total, 57,466. The average wages of each person
employed was 14s. 11d. The average for all ages
in a cotton mill in England are about 10s. and when
many power-looms are employed, 12s.

XXIII.—DIET, DOMESTIC ECONOMY AND MORALS OF
THE MANUFACTURING POPULATION.

"The population," says Dr. Kay, "employed in
the cotton factories, rises at five o'clock in the
morning, works in the mills from six till eight
o'clock, and returns home for half an hour or forty
minutes to breakfast. This meal generally consists
of tea or coffee, with a little bread. Oatmeal por-
ridge is sometimes, but of late rarely used, and
chiefly by the men ; but the stimulus of tea is preferred, and especially by the women. The tea is
almost always of a *bad*, and sometimes of a *deleterious quality ;* the infusion is weak, and little or no
milk is added. The operatives return to the mills
and workshops until twelve o'clock, when an hour is
allowed for dinner. Amongst those who obtain the
lower rates of wages, this meal generally consists
of *boiled potatoes.* The mess of potatoes is put into
one large dish ; melted lard and butter are poured
upon them, and a few pieces of fried fat bacon are
sometimes mingled with them, and but *seldom a little
meat.* Those who obtain better wages, or families
whose aggregate income is larger, add a greater
proportion of animal food to this meal, at least three
times in the week ; but the quantity consumed by
the labouring population is not great. The family
sits round the table, and each rapidly appropriates
his portion on a plate, or they all plunge their
spoons into the dish, and with an animal eagerness

2 P

satisfy the cravings of their appetite. At the expiration of the hour, they are all again employed in
the workshops or mills, where they continue until
seven o'clock, or a later hour, when they generally
again indulge in the use of tea, often mingled with
spirits accompanied by a little bread. Oatmeal or
potatoes are however taken by some a second time
in the evening. The comparatively innutritious
qualities of these articles of diet are most evident.* "

It is not from actual distress many workpeople
use this unsatisfactory and noxious diet, but from
bad habits and management. A large proportion
of them have wages sufficient to supply them with
solid and wholesome food, were they well laid out,
instead of being squandered in vain luxuries or
enervating excess. To preserve them in health,
their diet ought to consist of animal food, wheaten
bread, and malt liquor, and not much liquor of other
kinds.† From the long hours of labour, and close
atmosphere in which they are confined, the operative
feels the necessity of some artificial stimulus. Coffee, tea, and beer of good quality are most suitable
for this purpose. Instead of relying on these in
moderate quantities, what do the manufacturing
labourers do? Many of those receiving the highest
wages are in the habit of spending a portion of their
leisure after working hours, especially on a Saturday
evening and during the Sunday, in besotting them-

* The Moral and Physical Condition of the Working Classes
employed in the *Cotton Manufacture* in Manchester. 2nd edit.
pp. 23-4. By James Phillip Kay, M. D., London, 1832.

† It is remarked in one of the parliamentary reports on
prisons, that persons in confinement, especially if it be solitary,
require better and more substantial fare than those at liberty.
The reason assigned is the depression and exhaustion of spirits
consequent on the want of objects to engage the attention, and
this applies to the monotonous occupations of manufacturers
and artisans.

selves with ale and beer; and, still oftener, with the more efficient stimulus of gin. It is customary for them in many of the towns to stop at the gin-shops, and take a dram as they go to their work in the morning, and another as they return at night; and where, as is frequently the case, the houses of the workpeople lie in a cluster round the factory, it is not uncommon for a wholesale vender* of spirits to leave two gallons (the smallest quantity which can be sold without a licence) at one of the houses, which is distributed in small quantities to the others, and payment is made to the merchant through the original receiver. The quantity of gin drunk in this way is enormous; and children, and even girls, are initiated into this fatal practice at a very tender age. Ardent spirits are not the only stimulus which this class of people indulge in. Many of them take large quantites of *opium* in one form or another; sometimes in pills, sometimes as laudanum, sometimes in what they call an *anodyne* draft, which is a narcotic of the same kind. They find this a cheaper stimulus than gin, and many of them prefer it.

These remarks apply chiefly to the improvident and dissolute class of workpeople. Others evince more sense and a better economy in their modes of life; but it cannot be concealed that there are numerous classes whose rate of wages is such that with the best management will not procure the comforts and conveniences of living. This remark is not confined to hand-loom weavers, whose depression has resulted from a well-known cause. At Garstang, labourers' wages average only 2s. a day in summer, and 1s. 6d. in winter.† Their diet must

* An Inquiry into the State of the Manufacturing Population, &c. p. 11. Ridgway, 1831.

† Extracts from the Reports of the Poor-law Commission, p. 371.

2 r 2

of necessity be mean and deficient in quantity; it consists, says Mr. Henderson, of "milk, potatoes, herrings, bacon, and oat-bread ; very little *wheaten* bread is used." This was the condition of labourers in the fourteenth century.[*] The competition of the Irish has acted most unfavourably on the state of the poorer classes. They have not only lowered wages, but the standard of living. In Manchester, the habitations of the Irish are described as most destitute. They can scarcely be said to be furnished. They contain one or two chairs, a mean table, the most scanty culinary apparatus, and one or two beds loathsome with filth. A whole family is often accommodated on a single bed, and sometimes a heap of filthy straw, and a covering of old sacking, hide them in one undistinguished heap debased by vice, penury, and want of economy. Frequently, two or

[*] The following extract contains some curious particulars and shows that wages are still lower in Scotland than Lancashire :—"At *Dumfries* hiring market on Wednesday, healthy unmarried men, who understood their business, commanded readily 6l. for the half-year, with board and lodging, and in some few cases the pounds were made guineas. Dairy-maids and others were hired at 50s. and 55s. according to character, capability, and experience ; but the former was most common. From 1824 to 1832 the variations in the rate of wages have been exceedingly trifling, namely—for day-labourers, 1s. 4d. in summer, and from 1s. 2d. to 1s. 1d. in winter. In 1829-30, the wages of a cottar were 25l.; in 1831, they mounted to 26l.; and in 1832, fell to 25l. A bonny lass may clothe herself in a summer Sunday's dress, from head to heel, for a pound note! Her winter work-garb will cost a little more, say from 25s. to 28s. and both suits, with care, will last considerably more than a twelvemonth. Making included, a ploughman may clothe himself decently on Sundays for less than 2l. 10s. ; his working garb (mole-skin) costs about 16s. ; and if to these we superadd a ploughing-coat and stout shoes (10s. each), his whole bill to the draper and tailor will not exceed 4l. 6s. Portions of his wardrobe will last more than a twelvemonth, and, allowing for extras, his clothing expenditure may be kept within the limits of 6l.——*Dumfries Courier, April 6th, 1833.*

more families are crowded into a small house containing only two rooms, one in which they sleep, in the other eat, and often more than one family live in a damp cellar containing one room, in whose pestilential atmosphere from twelve to sixteen persons are crowded. To these fertile sources of disease are sometimes added the keeping of pigs, and other animals with other nuisances of the most revolting character.

The state of some of the streets in Manchester, as described by Dr. Kay (p. 36), for want of drainage, space, and scavengers, is horrible. They remind one of the traditionary accounts of Edinburgh formerly, and the present state of Lisbon. It is to be hoped in the projected reform and establishment of municipal corporations, that they will be so constituted as to become effective instruments, not only of police, but of the general health and local improvement of towns.

Besides dissolute habits, bad diet, and local uncleanliness, another source of unhealthiness in the manufacturing districts is the *severe and unremitting labour of workpeople.* The employment of spinners and stretchers is among the most laborious that exist, and is exceeded perhaps by that of mowing alone, and few mowers think of continuing their labour for twelve hours without intermission. Add to this, that these men never rest for an instant during their hours of working, except while their *mules* are *doffing,* in which process they also assist; and it must be obvious to every one, that it is next to impossible for any human being, however hardy or robust, to sustain this exertion, for any length of time, without permanently injuring his constitution. A collier never works above eight, and a farm labourer seldom above ten hours a day; and

It is, therefore, wholly out of all just proportion, that a spinner should labour for twelve hours regularly, and frequently for more. The labour of the other classes of hands as *carders, rovers, piecers, and weavers*, consists not so much in their actual manual exertion, which is very moderate, as in the constant attention which they are required to keep up, and the intolerable fatigue of long standing without being permitted to lean or sit down.*

It is almost unnecessary to remark on the low state of MORALS in factories. One who has the best opportunities for observing, remarks, " that the licentiousness which prevails among the dense population of manufacturing towns is carried to a degree which is appalling to contemplate, which baffles all statistical inquiries, and which can be learned only from the testimony of observers. And in addition to overt acts of vice, there is a coarseness and grossness of feeling, and an habitual indecency which we would fain hope and believe are not the prevailing characteristics of our country."† The illicit intercourse and general licentiousness of the sexes, result from the circumstances in which they are placed. They are exempt from the restraints of other classes ; they have few or no pleasures beyond those arising from sensual indulgence, and have hardly any motive for refraining from this indulgence ; it involves no loss of character, for their companions are as reckless as themselves ; it brings no risk of losing their employment, for their employers do not take cognizance of these matters.

* An Inquiry into the State of the Manufacturing Population, p. 18.
† Inquiry into the State of the Manufacturing Population, p. 25.

XXIV.——POOR-LAW COMMISSION.

I was apprized of the chief facts disclosed by this commission, while preparing the chapter on the poor-laws, and purposely deferred a few remarks on their tendency to the Appendix.

The inquiries of the commissioners show that abuses are not confined to church and state, but that a sort of *Green Bag* or *Black Book* may be filled against paupers as readily as against offenders of higher degree. While, however, we seek to profit by the labours of the commissioners, it is important that we should not be hurried into hasty and exaggerated conclusions, which might originate measures as inconsistent with humanity as repugnant to sound policy and the general feeling of the community. Several considerations will serve to moderate the force of the impressions arising from the first perusal of the information communicated by the itinerant commissioners.

First, it must be borne in mind, that the number of persons annually relieved out of the poor-rate amounts to 1,250,000, averaging 120 to each parish; that the sum expended in their relief amounts to 6,500,000*l.*, averaging 5*l.* each; and that, as the number of parishes in England amounts to nearly 11,000, there is at least so many separate and independent bodies occupied in the administration of the poor-laws.

Now, considering the number of persons relieved, the magnitude of the fund disbursed, and the multiplicity of local jurisdictions, can it be matter of surprise that a great many irregularities have crept into the administration of the poor-laws? Had a number of barristers been selected to collect evidence of abuses in any other great department of the public

service, as, for example, the army, navy, customs,
excise, or courts of law, can any one doubt that they
would not have been able to fill one or half a dozen
volumes (perhaps as many as have been filled with
the abuses of public charities) with instances of neglect of duty, fraud, and mismanagement? but how
much easier the task, when the inquiry extended
over such a wide-spread field as every workhouse and
parish-board of the kingdom!

Secondly, the uniform spirit and complexion of
the statements are such as clearly indicate that *the*
chief object of the commissioners was to collect evidence of *defects*, not of *excellences*, in the administration of the poor-laws: the consequence is, that
their testimony is decidedly *ex parte*, intended apparently to corroborate a " foregone conclusion," previously formed, perhaps, by the originators of the
commission, of the vicious tendency of a compulsory
assessment for the relief of indigence. I was in
some measure impressed with this conclusion in
looking over the table of contents affixed to the
volume of *Extracts on the Administration of the
Poor-laws*, " published by authority," and sold at
a very low price, for the sake, no doubt, of effective
circulation; my object was to ascertain the past and
present *rate of wages* in different parts of the country: but there was no information under the head
of " Wages," though it might, perhaps, have thrown
considerable light on existing pauperism: there was,
however, copious details of evils under the heads of
" Allowance," " Bastardy," " Beer-shops," " Charities," " Magistrates," and " Workhouses." If this
representation of the *partial* character of the evidence be correct, it is desirable the example set in
the factory question should be followed; we ought
to have a counter inquiry, so that the public may
know *both sides*: having learned the mischiefs, we

ought to be made acquainted with the benefits of
the poor-laws, as exemplified in the mass of misery
relieved—the disorders, theft, and mendicity prevented.   Mr. Henderson's Report, from Lancashire,
is an exception to the rest ; it is judicious and impartial ; and he observes, that " the effects of the
poor-laws, regarded as a *national charity*, may
be seen to advantage at Manchester." (*Extracts*,
p. 364.)   The same observation will apply generally, I apprehend, to the large towns, where the
poor-laws are administered with more intelligence
and under greater responsibilities than in agricultural districts.

Thirdly, an impression appears to have gone
abroad in many parishes, that the object of the visitations of the commissioners was to ascertain whether
the discontents recently manifested among the labouring poor had not arisen from *ill treatment ;* and
accordingly, in self-vindication, the parish authorities exerted themselves in painting the vices and in-
gratitude of paupers, and in showing that they were
not only well, but, in some instances, sumptuously
treated.   Without some such misapprehension, I
cannot account for what appears rather exaggerated
descriptions at pp. 216, 296, and 393.

These observations, I trust, will not be miscon-
strued.   What I have said in another place on the
poor-laws, will show that I am fully sensible of their
maladministration.   It is, however, the judicature,
rather than the jurisprudence, of the laws which is
defective ; and the chief source of abuse has been
the incompetence or want of information in the
magistracy and parish authorities, by whom they
have been administered.   For this defect the Report
of the Central Board of Commissioners will doubtless prescribe an effective remedy.   Another evil
will, no doubt, be also met, arising out of the con-

flicting injunction of Scripture, "to increase and multiply," and the conclusions of political economy, which point to a directly opposite course. A satisfactory and popular solution of this difficulty by the right reverend commissioners would probably tend more than any other expedient to the end sought by the landed interest, namely, a diminution in the amount of the poor assessment. Further, if the landowners could be brought to acquiesce in a revision of the CORN-LAWS, by which fluctuations in the price of bread, destructive to agricultural and manufacturing industry, could be averted, another important step would be made towards the extinction of pauperism.

To insulated examples of poor-law abuse, collected from 11,000 parishes, and 1,200,000 cases of relief administered, it is consolatory to be able to oppose the general facts, that of late years, under a somewhat better system, pauperism has declined relatively to the increase of population; and that the character and condition of the working people of England are superior to those of any other country in Europe.

The whole history and theory of pauperism, as set forth in this publication, may be comprised in the following propositions :

The labouring classes were anciently in a state of bondage, and pauperism grew out of the transition from slave to free labour.

The legislature long tried to meet this evil by *voluntary charity*, but the inadequacy of this forced upon them the necessity of a compulsory assessment for the relief of indigence.

The 43d of Elizabeth, of 1601, was not, as commonly supposed, the commencement of the poor-laws, but chiefly a consolidation of the enactments resulting from the experience of the two preceding centuries.

The important distinction between the ages of Elizabeth and William IV. is, that in the former there was abundance of work, but unwillingness to labour; in the latter, there is no want of industry, but a scarcity of employment.

The evil of an overstocked market of labour, which now afflicts society, can only be permanently remedied by diffusing among the working classes a familiar knowledge of the circumstances that influence their condition.

That this knowledge can only be efficiently diffused by the agency of the governing and wealthier classes of society.

And that, lastly, this knowledge will never be diffused by the intervention of these classes, till they find, by the increasing pressure of a poor assessment or other circumstance, lessening their own enjoyments and security, that they have an interest in diffusing it.

XXV.—MAXIMS OF CONDUCT.

Having in the chapter on Popular Education (p. 434) adverted to the utility of short maxims and traditionary sayings, I shall here present a specimen of the sort I mean. They are taken from a little work of mine, published under the title of Fielding's *Select Proverbs of all Nations*. The best recommendation I can give them is, that I have *tried* them, and witnessed others try them, and in both cases can bear testimony to their beneficial results. Errors of conduct as frequently arise from momentary forgetfulness of good precepts as ignorance of moral duty; and hence the advantage of having constantly present to recollection, for the guidance of our actions, these little sententious rules which the experience of ages has consecrated.

A fool always comes short of his reckoning.
A wilful man should be very wise.
Be a friend to yourself and others will.
Do not say you cannot be worse.
He that will not be counselled cannot be helped.
He that would know what shall be, must consider what hath been.
He that would live in peace and rest, must hear, and see, and say the best.
He that will have no trouble in this world, must not be born in it.
He that is ill to himself will be good to nobody.
It is too much for one good man to want.
Lawyers' gowns are lined with the wilfulness of their clients.
No condition so low but may have hopes; none so high but may have fears.
The unreasonable is never durable.
One might as well be out of the world, as be loved by nobody in it.
One thief makes a hundred suffer: that is *suspicion*.
Put your finger in the fire and say it was your fortune.

A sarcasm on those who ascribe a want of success in life to ill-luck, in place of their own want of forethought, industry, and perseverance; which last are the qualities that mostly make men rich, prosperous, and happy.

Remember the reckoning.

A motto to be engraven on the bottom of porter-pots, punch-bowls, and drinking-glasses.

Three removes are as bad as a fire.
Two things a man should never be angry at: what he can help, and what he cannot.
We are never so happy or unfortunate as we think ourselves.
When you are all agreed on the time, quoth the vicar, I'll make it rain.
Who looks not before finds himself behind.

RELIGION, VIRTUE, AND LEARNING.

A wise man may look like a fool in fools' company.
Away goes the devil when he finds the door shut against him.
An irritable and passionate temper is a downright drunkard.

A man may as well expect to be at ease without wealth as happy without virtue.

After praying to God not to lead you into temptation, do not throw yourself into it.

Buffoonery and scurrility are the corruption of wit, as knavery is of wisdom.

Content is the philosopher's stone, that turns all it touches into gold.

Disputations often leave truth in the middle and party at both ends.

Drunkenness turns a man out of himself, and leaves a beast in his room.

Drunkenness is a pair of spectacles, to see the devil and all his works.

Dying is as natural as living.

Education polishes good natures and corrects bad ones.

Every vice fights against nature.

Experience keeps a dear school, but fools will learn in no other.

Faults of ignorance are excusable only where the ignorance itself is so.

Forget others' faults by remembering your own.

Hell is full of good meanings, but heaven is full of good works.

Honest men are soon bound, but you can never bind a knave.

How can you think yourself the wiser for pleasing fools ?

If every one would mend one, all would be mended.

Knavery may serve a turn, but honesty is the best at long run.

Many that are wits in jest are fools in earnest.

Men's years and their faults are always more than they are willing to own.

The credit that is got by a lie only lasts till the truth comes out.

Who pardons the bad injures the good.

You will never repent of being patient and sober.

GOVERNMENT, LAWS, AND PUBLIC AFFAIRS.

Antiquity cannot privilege an error, nor novelty prejudice a truth.

Beggars fear no rebellion.

Better a lean peace than a fat victory.

He that buys magistracy must sell justice.

Much disorder brings with it much order.

The more laws the more offenders.

The king may bestow offices, but cannot bestow wit to manage them.

The mob has many heads, but no brains.

War is the feast of death.

What a great deal of good great men might do!

Wise and good men framed the laws, but fools and the wicked put them upon it.

ECONOMY, MANNERS, AND RICHES.

A man without politeness has need of great merit in its place.

Alike every day makes a clout on Sunday.

According to your purse govern your mouth.

All is fine that is fit.

A servant is known by his master's absence.

All is soon ready in an orderly house.

Anger and haste hinder good counsel.

An idle brain is the devil's workshop.

A young man idle, an old man needy.

A little neglect may breed a great deal of mischief.

A pin a day is a groat a year.

A stitch in time saves nine.

An affected superiority spoils company.

A skilful mechanic makes a good pilgrim.

A wicked book is the worse because it cannot repent.

Burn not your house to frighten away the mice.

Better give a shilling, than lend and lose half a crown.

Better have one plough going than two cradles.

Better half a loaf than no bread.

Business is the salt of life.

Do not all that you can do; spend not all that you have; believe not all that you hear; and tell not all that you know.

Every one should sweep before his own door.

Every one thinks that he has more than his share of brains.

Forecast is better than work hard.

Go not for every pain to the physician, for every quarrel to the lawyer, nor for every thirst to the pot.

Have not the cloak to make when it begins to rain.

He who would catch fish must not mind getting wet.

He that lives upon hope has but a slender diet.

He is fool enough himself who will bray against another ass.

He who says what he likes, hears what he does not like.

He is not drunk for nothing who pays his reason for his reckoning.

He hath made good progress in a business who has thought well of it beforehand.

He that spares when he is young may spend when he is old.

He that stumbles twice over one stone, it is no wonder if he break his neck.

He that has a great nose thinks every body is speaking of it.

Idle folks have most labour.

Idle men are dead all their lives long.

Idleness is the greatest prodigality in the world.

If you will not hear reason she will surely rap your knuckles.

Industry is fortune's right hand ; frugality her left.

If youth knew what age would crave, it would both get and save.

If you be not ill, be not ill-like.

It is a pity that those who taught you to talk, did not also teach you to hold your tongue.

Let your letter stay for the post, not the post for your letter.

Liberality is not in giving largely, but in giving wisely.

Many talk like philosophers and live like fools.

Many buy nothing with their money but repentance.

Not to oversee workmen is to leave them your purse open.

Nature sets every thing for sale to labour.

One that is perfectly idle is perfectly weary.

One barber shaves not so many but another finds work.

Purposing without performing is mere fooling.

Spend and be free, but make no waste.

Setting down in writing is a lasting memory.

Take heed will surely speed.

The stone that lies not in your way need not offend you.

To believe a business impossible is the way to make it so.

We never know the worth of water till the well is dry.

Bachelors' wives and maids' children are always well taught.

Before you marry, be sure of a house wherein to tarry.

Many men have more trouble to digest meat than to get meat.

Temperance, employment, and a cheerful spirit, are the great preservers of health.

Bitter pills may have blessed effects.

THE END.

POSTSCRIPT.

In the Chronological Digest, p. 95, I omitted to mention that in 1797 the first hint appears to have been given for the establishment of Savings' Banks. The idea of these institutions seems to have been taken from a communication of the late Mr. Jeremy Bentham, inserted in Young's *Annals of Agriculture*, setting forth a scheme for the management of paupers, part of which consisted in the establishment of what Mr. Bentham denominated a " frugality bank." (*Sup. to Ency. Brit.*, vol. ii. p. 95.)

The number of *one-pound notes* in circulation, prior to the passing of Peel's Bill, has been understated at p. 157. The 1*l.* notes in circulation of the Bank of England in 1818, appears, from the Appendix to the Bank Report of 1832, to have amounted to about 7,481,000*l.* The contemporary issue of 1*l.* notes by country bankers has been estimated at 7,500,000*l.* So that the small note currency formed about *one-fourth* part of the total issues of bank paper by the country banks and Bank of England. This, however, does not affect the argument; whatever might be the amount of the small notes, as their places were supplied by an equivalent issue of gold, their withdrawal could have had little tendency to contract the general circulation, and thereby influence prices and mercantile transactions.

Page 54, for *suppressing* read *supplying*; p. 124, line 19, for *sketch* read *stretch*; p. 253, line 11, for *expensive* read *expansive*; and p. 413, bottom line but one, for *congerieri* read *congeries.*

INDEX.

2 q

WHITING, BEAUFORT HOUSE, STRAND.

A FINE IS INCURRED IF THIS BOOK IS
NOT RETURNED TO THE LIBRARY ON
OR BEFORE THE LAST DATE STAMPED
BELOW.

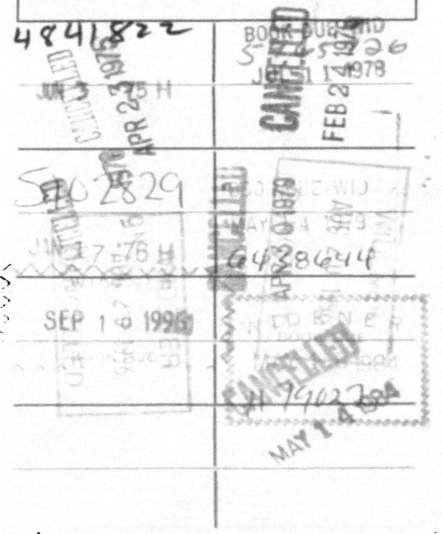

Check Out More Titles From HardPress Classics Series In this collection we are offering thousands of classic and hard to find books. This series spans a vast array of subjects — so you are bound to find something of interest to enjoy reading and learning about.

Subjects:
Architecture
Art
Biography & Autobiography
Body, Mind &Spirit
Children & Young Adult
Dramas
Education
Fiction
History
Language Arts & Disciplines
Law
Literary Collections
Music
Poetry
Psychology
Science
…and many more.

Visit us at www.hardpress.net

Im TheStory

personalised classic books

"Beautiful gift.. lovely finish. My Niece loves it, so precious!"

Helen R Brumfieldon

★★★★★

UNIQUE GIFT

FOR KIDS, PARTNERS AND FRIENDS

Timeless books such as:

Alice in Wonderland · The Jungle Book · The Wonderful Wizard of Oz
Peter and Wendy · Robin Hood · The Prince and The Pauper
The Railway Children · Treasure Island · A Christmas Carol

Romeo and Juliet · Dracula

Highly Customizable   Change Books Title   Replace Character Names with yours   Upload Photo for image page   Add Inscriptions

Visit

Im TheStory .com

and order yours today!

CPSIA information can be obtained
at www.ICGtesting.com
Printed in the USA
BVHW040242210819
556223BV00046B/1946/P